Germany

- - - - - - International Boundaries
- ★ National Capital
- • Major Cities
- ——— Other Road
- ——— Autobahn
- - - - - - Rivers

0   50   100 Kilometers
0   50   100 Miles

North Sea

Flensburg
Rodbyhavn Gedser
Puttgarden
Kiel
Rostock
Lubeck
Schwerin

Wittenburger
Wilhelmshaven
Emden
Bremerhaven
Hamburg

NETHERLANDS
Amsterdam
Groningen
Oldenburg Bremen
Hannover

GERMANY
Wittenberge
Potsdam **Berlin**
Frankfurt
POLAND

Enschede
Arnhem
Munster Bielefeld
Braunschweig Magdeburg
Cottbus
Zielona
Gora

Rotterdam
Eindhoven Duisburg
Essen Dortmund
Dessau
Halle Leipzig
Gorlitz
Jelenia
Gora

Antwerpen
Cologne
Dusseldorf
Kassel
Gottingen
Eisenach Erfurt
Jena
Dresden
Decin

Brussels
Maastricht
Aachen
Siegen
Bad
Hersfeld
Gera
Chemnitz
Zwickau
Usti nad Labem

BELGIUM
Liege
Koblenz
Hof
Hradec
Kralove

Charleroi
Frankfurt
Am Main
Wiesbaden
Bamberg
Cheb
Prague

Mainz
Wurzburg
Rhein-Main
Donau-Kanal
Pilzen
CZECH
REPUBLIC

Luxembourg
Saarbrucken
Mannheim
Heidelberg
Nurnberg
Regensberg
Ceske
Budejovice

Metz
Karlsruhe Heilbronn
Passau
Linz

Nancy
Strasbourg
Stuttgart
Danube
Ulm
Augsburg
Munchen

FRANCE
Freiburg
Konstanz
Garmisch-
Partenkirchen
Salzburg

AUSTRIA
Liezen

Mulhouse
Basel
Zurich
Innsbruck

Besancon
SWITZERLAND

Baltic Sea
Rugen
Sassnitz
Stralsund
Swinoujscie
Szczecin
Gorzow
Wielkopolski
Bornholm
(DENMARK)

A COMPENDIUM OF COMMONLY USED WORDS AND PHRASES IN FRENCH, GERMAN, ITALIAN, AND SPANISH

Unique features and highlights:

- Easy-to-follow *pronunciation keys* and complete phonetic transcriptions for all words and phrases in the book.

- Useful phrases for the *tourist*, grouped together by subject matter in a logical way so that the appropriate phrase is easy to locate when you need it.

- Thorough section on *food and drink*, with comprehensive food terms you will find on menus; these terms are often difficult or impossible to locate in dictionaries, but our section gives you a description of the preparation as well as a definition of what it is.

- *Emergency phrases* and terms you hope you won't need: legal complications, medical problems, theft or loss of valuables, replacement or repair of watches, cameras, and the like.

Enjoy your vacation and travel with confidence. You have a friend by your side.

THE TRAVELER'S
PHRASE BOOK

GAIL STEIN, M.A. • HENRY STRUTZ, M.A.
MARIO COSTANTINO, M.A. • HEYWOOD WALD, Ph.D.

Coordinating Editor (French and Italian)
HEYWOOD WALD, Ph.D.

Second Edition

All inquiries should be addressed to:
Barron's Educational Series, Inc.
250 Wireless Boulevard
Hauppauge, New York 11788
http://www.barronseduc.com

Library of Congress Catalog Card No. 00-131726

ISBN-13: 978-0-7641-1253-9
ISBN-10: 0-7641-1253-8

PRINTED IN CHINA

9 8

CONTENTS

FRENCH

France

- ⊙ National capital
- ● City

International border
Region border
Department border
Primary road
Railroad

Scale

0 25   75 km
0 25 50 75 mi

QUICK PRONUNCIATION GUIDE

CONSONANTS

In French, final consonants are usually silent, except for final C, R, F, and L (as in CaReFuL), which are usually pronounced.

FRENCH LETTER	ENGLISH SOUND	SYMBOL	EXAMPLE
b, d, f, k, l, m, n	same as English		
p, t, v, z	same as English		
c (before e, i, y)	SS (S at beginning of word)	S	cigare *see-gahr*
ç (before a, o, u)	SS (S at beginning of word)	S	garçon *gahr-ssohn*
c (before a, o, u)	K	K	comme *kohm*
g (before e, i, y)	S as in plea*s*ure	ZH	rouge *roozh*
ge (before a, o)	S as in plea*s*ure	ZH	mangeons *mahn-zhohn*
g (before a, o, u)	G	G	gant *gahn*
gn	nyuh as in o*ni*on	NY	oignon *oh-nyohn*
h	always silent		hôtel *oh-tehl*
j	S as in plea*s*ure	ZH	je *zhuh*
qu, final q	K	K	cinq *sank*
r	Say the R at the top back of the mouth as if you were gargling or spitting.	R	rue *rew*
ss	S	SS	poisson *pwah-ssohn*
s	beginning of word	S	six *sees*
	next to consonant	SS	disque *deessk*
s	between vowels	Z	poison *pwah-zohn*
th	T	T	thé *tay*

FRENCH LETTER	ENGLISH SOUND	SYMBOL	EXAMPLE
x	S in these words only	SS	six *seess*, dix *deess*, soixante *swah-ssahn̲t*
x	X	KSS	excellent *ehkss-eh-lahn̲*
x	X	GS	exemple *ehg-sahn̲-pluh*

NOTE: When combined with a word beginning with a vowel or *h*, *x* has a *z* sound. Beford a word beginning with a consonant, it is silent.

VOWELS

FRENCH LETTER	ENGLISH SOUND	SYMBOL	EXAMPLE
a, à, â	A as in yacht or A in after	AH	la *lah*
é, final er, final ez, et	A as in day	AY	musée *mew-zay*
e + 2 consonants e + final pronounced consonant e, ê, è	E as in ever	EH	sept *seht*
e	sometimes like E of early with no R sound	UH	le *luh*
i (î), y	EE as in meet	EE	île *eel*
i + vowel or ll	Y as in yes	EE	famille *fah-mee*
o + final pronounced consonant	O as in love	OH	homme *ohm*
o, o before se, o	O as in open	OH	au *oh*

FRENCH LETTER	ENGLISH SOUND	SYMBOL	EXAMPLE
last sound in word, au, eau ou	OO as in tooth	OO	où *oo*
oy, oi	WA as in watch	WAH	trois *trwah*
U	There is none. Round lips and say E and U at same time.	EW	du *dew*
U + vowel	WEE as in wee	WEE	huit *weet*

NASAL SOUNDS

Nasal sounds are produced through the mouth and the nose at the same time. Nasal sounds occur when N or M follows a vowel in the same syllable. There is NO nasal sound for VOWEL + NN, VOWEL + MM, VOWEL + N + VOWEL, VOWEL + M + VOWEL. NOTE: n means there is a nasalized pronunciation of the "N" sound. The tip of the tongue does not touch the roof of the mouth.

FRENCH LETTER	ENGLISH SOUND	SYMBOL	EXAMPLE
AN, AM, EN, EM	similar to on	AHN	France *Frahnss*
IN, IM, AIN, AIM	similar to an	AN	pain *pan*
IEN	similar to yan of Yankee	YAN	bien *byan*
ON, OM	similar to on of long.	OHN	bon *bohn*
UN, UM	similar to un of under.	UHN	un *uhn*

LIAISON and ELISION

Liaison and elision are two linguistic devices that add to the beauty and fluidity of the French language.

Liaison means linking. In French, the final consonant of a word is usually not pronounced. Sometimes, however, when the final consonant of one word is followed by a beginning vowel or H of the next word, liaison occurs.

EXAMPLE:

Nous arrivons.   *noo zah-ree-voh_n_*

With the following words in French, the final vowel is dropped if the next word starts with a vowel or H. The dropped vowel is replaced by an apostrophe. This is called elision.

EXAMPLE:

la auto = l'auto   *(loh-toh)*

le homme = l'homme   *(lohm)*

THE BASICS FOR GETTING BY

MOST FREQUENTLY USED EXPRESSIONS

Sir	**Monsieur**	*muh-ssyuh*
Madame	**Madame**	*mah-dahm*
Miss (Ms.)	**Mademoiselle**	*mahd-mwah-zehl*
I'm American.	**Je suis américain/ américaine (f.)**	*zhuh swee zah- may-ree-ka_n_/ ah-may-ree-kehn*
Do you speak English?	**Parlez-vous anglais?**	*pahr-lay voo ah_n_-gleh*
I speak a little French.	**Je parle un peu français.**	*zhuh pahrl uh_n_ puh frah_n_-seh*
Do you understand me?	**Vous me comprenez?**	*voo muh koh_n_-pruh-nay*
I understand.	**Je comprends.**	*zhuh koh_n_-prah_n_*

I don't understand.	**Je ne comprends pas.**	*zhuh nuh kohn-prahn-pah*
What did you say?	**Qu'est-ce que vous avez dit?**	*kehs-kuh voo zah-vay dee*
Please repeat.	**Répétez, s'il vous plaît.**	*ray-pay-tay seel voo pleh*
How do you say ___ in French?	**Comment dit-on ___ en français?**	*kohn-mahn dee-tohn ahn frahn-seh*
What does this/ that mean?	**Qu'est-ce que ça veut dire?**	*kehs-kuh sah vuh deer*
My name is ___.	**Je m'appelle ___.**	*zhuh mah-pehl*
What is your name?	**Comment vous appelez-vous?**	*kohn-mahn voo zah-play voo*
What is your name, address, phone number?	**Quelles sont vos coordonnées?**	*kehl sohn voh koh-ohr-doh-nay*
How are you?	**Comment allez-vous?**	*kohn-mahn tah-lay voo*
Very well, thanks.	**Très bien, merci.**	*treh byan mehr-see*
And you?	**Et vous?**	*ay voo*
How's everything?	**Ça va?**	*sah vah*
Everything's fine.	**Ça va.**	*sah vah*
I'm lost.	**Je me suis égaré(e).**	*zhuh muh swee zay-gah-ray*
I'm looking for ___.	**Je cherche ___.**	*zhuh shehrsh*

Where is ____?	**Où est ____?**	*oo eh*
■ the exit	**la sortie**	*lah sohr-tee*
■ the taxi stand	**l'arrêt de taxis**	*lah-reh duh tahk-ssee*
■ the bus stop	**l'arrêt de bus**	*lah-reh duh bewss*
■ the metro station	**l'arrêt de métro**	*lah-reh duh may-troh*
■ the train station	**la gare**	*lah gahr*
Where are ____?	**Où sont ____?**	*oo sohn*
■ the bathrooms	**les toilettes**	*lay twah-leht*
■ the telephones	**les téléphones**	*lay tay-lay-fohn*
■ the taxis	**les taxis**	*lay tahk-ssee*
It's ____.	**C'est ____.**	*seh*
■ to the left	**à gauche**	*ah gohsh*
■ to the right	**à droite**	*ah drwaht*
■ straight ahead	**tout droit**	*too drwah*
What's that?	**Qu'est-ce que c'est?**	*kehs-kuh seh*
I (don't) know.	**Je (ne) sais (pas).**	*zhuh (nuh) seh (pah)*
Do you have ____?	**Avez-vous ____?**	*ah-vay-voo*
I'd like ____.	**Je voudrais ____.**	*zhuh voo-dreh*
I need ____.	**Il me faut ____.**	*eel muh foh*
Please bring me ____.	**Apportez-moi, s'il vous plaît ____.**	*ah-pohr-tay mwah seel voo pleh*
Please give me ____.	**Donnez-moi, s'il vous plaît ____.**	*doh-nay mwah seel voo pleh*

Please show me _____.	**Montrez-moi, s'il vous plaît _____.**	*mohn-tray mwah seel voo pleh*
How much is it?	**C'est combien?**	*seh kohn-byan*
I'm hungry.	**J'ai faim.**	*zhay fan*
I'm thirsty.	**J'ai soif.**	*zhay swahf*
I'm tired.	**Je suis fatigué(e).**	*zhuh swee fah-tee-gay*
Good-bye.	**Au revoir.**	*oh ruh-vwahr*
See you later.	**À tout à l'heure.**	*ah toot ah luhr*
See you tomorrow.	**À demain.**	*ah duh-man*

QUESTIONS

Where is (are) _____?	**Où est (sont) ___?**	*oo eh (sohn)*
When?	**Quand?**	*kahn*
At what time?	**À quelle heure?**	*ah kehl uhr*
How much/many?	**Combien?**	*kohn-byan*
Who?	**Qui?**	*kee*
What?	**Que?/Quoi?**	*kuh/kwah*
Why?	**Pourquoi?**	*poor-kwah*
How?	**Comment?**	*kohn-mahn*

| Which? | **Quel/Quelle/ Quels/Quelles** | *kehl* |
| Which one(s)? | **Lequel/Laquelle/ Lesquel/Lesquelles** | *luh/lah/lay-kehl* |

PROBLEMS, PROBLEMS, PROBLEMS (EMERGENCIES)

Hurry up!	**Dépêchez-vous!**	*day-peh-shay-voo*
Look!	**Regardez!**	*ruh-gahr-day*
Watch out!	**Attention!**	*ah-tah<u>n</u>-syoh<u>n</u>*
Be careful!	**Soyez prudent(e)!**	*swah-yay prew-dah<u>n</u>(t)*
Calm down!	**Calmez-vous!**	*kahl-may voo*
Take it easy!	**Allez-y doucement!**	*ah-lay zee dooss-mah<u>n</u>*
Listen!	**Écoutez!**	*ay-koo-tay*
Wait!	**Attendez!**	*ah-tah<u>n</u>-day*
I have lost ____.	**J'ai perdu ____.**	*zhay pehr-dew*
Stop bothering me.	**Laissez-moi tranquille!**	*leh-say mwah trah<u>n</u>-keel*
Go away!	**Allez-vous-en!**	*ah-lay voo zah<u>n</u>*
Get out!	**Sortez!**	*sohr-tay*

I'm going to call the police!	**Je vais appeler la police!**	*zhuh veh zah-play lah poh-leess*
Help, police!	**Au secours, police.**	*oh skoor, poh-leess*
Someone has stolen ____.	**Quelqu'un a volé ____.**	*kehl-kuhn ah voh-lay*
■ my car	**ma voiture**	*mah vwah-tewr*
■ my passport	**mon passeport**	*mohn pahss-pohr*
■ my purse	**mon sac**	*mohn sahk*
■ my suitcase	**ma valise**	*mah vah-leez*
■ my wallet	**mon portefeuille**	*mohn pohr-tuh fuhy*
■ my watch	**ma montre**	*mah mohntr*
I want to go ____.	**Je voudrais aller ____.**	*zhuh voo-dreh zah-lay*
■ to the American Consulate	**au consulat américain**	*oh kohn-sew-lah ah-may-ree-kan*
■ to the American Embassy	**à l'ambassade américaine**	*ah lahn-bah-sahd ah-may-ree-kehn*
■ to the police station	**au commissariat de police**	*oh koh-mee-sah-ryah duh poh-leess*
I need help, quick!	**Vite. Aidez-moi!**	*veet eh-day mwah*
Can you help me, please?	**Pouvez-vous m'aider s'il vous plaît?**	*poo-vay voo meh-day seel voo pleh*
Does anyone here speak English?	**Il y a quelqu'un ici qui parle anglais?**	*eel yah kehl-kuhn ee-see kee pahrl ahn-gleh*
I need an interpreter.	**Il me faut un interprète.**	*eel muh foh tuhn an-tehr-preht*

NUMBERS

CARDINAL NUMBERS

0	**zéro**	*zay-roh*
1	**un**	*uhn*
2	**deux**	*duh*
3	**trois**	*trwah*
4	**quatre**	*kah-truh*
5	**cinq**	*sank*
6	**six**	*seess*
7	**sept**	*seht*
8	**huit**	*weet*
9	**neuf**	*nuhf*
10	**dix**	*deess*
11	**onze**	*ohnz*
12	**douze**	*dooz*
13	**treize**	*trehz*
14	**quatorze**	*kah-tohrz*
15	**quinze**	*kanz*
16	**seize**	*sehz*
17	**dix-sept**	*dee-seht*
18	**dix-huit**	*dee-zweet*
19	**dix-neuf**	*deez-nuhf*
20	**vingt**	*van*
21	**vingt et un**	*van-tay-uhn*

22	**vingt-deux**	*va<u>n</u>-duh*
23	**vingt-trois**	*va<u>n</u>-trwah*
24	**vingt-quatre**	*va<u>n</u>-kah-truh*
25	**vingt-cinq**	*va<u>n</u>-sa<u>n</u>k*
26	**vingt-six**	*va<u>n</u>-seess*
27	**vingt-sept**	*va<u>n</u>-seht*
28	**vingt-huit**	*va<u>n</u>-tweet*
29	**vingt-neuf**	*va<u>n</u>-nuhf*
30	**trente**	*trah<u>n</u>t*
31	**trente et un**	*trah<u>n</u>-tay-uh<u>n</u>*
32	**trente-deux**	*trah<u>n</u>t-duh*
40	**quarante**	*kah-rah<u>n</u>t*
41	**quarante et un**	*kah-rah<u>n</u>-tay-uh<u>n</u>*
42	**quarante-deux**	*kah-rah<u>n</u>t-duh*
50	**cinquante**	*sa<u>n</u>-kah<u>n</u>t*
51	**cinquante et un**	*sa<u>n</u>-kah<u>n</u>-tay-uh<u>n</u>*
52	**cinquante-deux**	*sa<u>n</u>-kah<u>n</u>t-duh*
60	**soixante**	*swah-ssah<u>n</u>t*
61	**soixante et un**	*swah-ssah<u>n</u>-tay-uh<u>n</u>*
62	**soixante-deux**	*swah-ssah<u>n</u>t-duh*
70	**soixante-dix**	*swah-ssah<u>n</u>t-deess*
71	**soixante et onze**	*swah-ssah<u>n</u>-tay-oh<u>n</u>z*
72	**soixante-douze**	*swah-ssah<u>n</u>t-dooz*
73	**soixante-treize**	*swah-ssah<u>n</u>t-trehz*
74	**soixante-quatorze**	*swah-ssah<u>n</u>t-kah-tohrz*

75	**soixante-quinze**	*swah-ssahnt-kanz*
76	**soixante-seize**	*swah-ssahnt-sehz*
77	**soixante-dix-sept**	*swah-ssahnt-dee-seht*
78	**soixante-dix-huit**	*swah-ssahnt-dee-zweet*
79	**soixante-dix-neuf**	*swah-ssahnt-deez-nuhf*
80	**quatre-vingts**	*kah-truh-van*
81	**quatre-vingt-un**	*kah-truh-van-uhn*
82	**quatre-vingt-deux**	*kah-truh-van-duh*
90	**quatre-vingt-dix**	*kah-truh-van-deess*
91	**quatre-vingt-onze**	*kah-truh-van-ohnz*
92	**quatre-vingt-douze**	*kah-truh-van-dooz*
100	**cent**	*sahn*
101	**cent un**	*sahn-uhn*
102	**cent deux**	*sahn-duh*
110	**cent dix**	*sahn-deess*
120	**cent vingt**	*sahn-van*
200	**deux cents**	*duh-sahn*
201	**deux cent un**	*duh-sahn-uhn*
330	**trois cent trente**	*trwah-sahn-trahnt*
1000	**mille**	*meel*
1001	**mille un**	*meel-uhn*
1100	**mille cent**	*meel-sahn*
	onze cents	*ohnz-sahn*

ORDINAL NUMBERS

first	**premier/première (1er)**	*pruh-myay/pruh-myehr*
second	**deuxième (2e)**	*duh-zyehm*
third	**troisième**	*trwah-zyehm*
fourth	**quatrième**	*kah-tree-yehm*
fifth	**cinquième**	*sa<u>n</u>-kyehm*
sixth	**sixième**	*see-zyehm*
seventh	**septième**	*seh-tyehm*
eighth	**huitième**	*wee-tyehm*
ninth	**neuvième**	*nuh-vyehm*
tenth	**dixième**	*dee-zyehm*

WHEN YOU ARRIVE

PASSPORT AND CUSTOMS

My name is _____.	**Je m'appelle _____.** *zhuh mah-pehl*
I'm American, Canadian, British, Australian.	**Je suis américain(e), canadien(ne), anglais(e), australien(ne).** *zhuh swee zah-may-ree-kah<u>n</u> (kehn), kah-nah-dya<u>n</u> (dyehn), ah<u>n</u>-gleh (glehz), ohs-trah-lya<u>n</u> (yehn)*
My address is _____.	**Mon adresse est _____.** *moh<u>n</u> nah-drehss eh*
I'm staying at _____.	**Je reste à _____.** *zhuh rehst ah*
Here is (are) _____.	**Voici _____.** *vwah-ssee*
■ my documents	**mes papiers** *may pah-pyay*
■ my passport	**mon passeport** *moh<u>n</u> pahss-pohr*

■ my identification card   **ma carte d'identité**   *mah kahrt dee-dah<u>n</u>-tee-tay*

I'm _____.   **Je suis _____.**   *zhuh swee*

■ on a business trip   **en voyage d'affaires**   *zah<u>n</u> vwah-yahzh dah-fehr*

■ on vacation   **en vacances**   *zah<u>n</u> vah-kah<u>nss</u>*

I'll be staying here _____.   **Je resterai ici _____.**   *zhuh rehss-tray ee-ssee*

■ a few days   **quelques jours**   *kehl-kuh zhoor*

■ a few weeks   **quelques semaines**   *kehl-kuh suh-mehn*

■ a week   **une semaine**   *ewn suh-mehn*

■ two weeks   **quinze jours**   *ka<u>n</u>z zhoor*

■ a month   **un mois**   *uh<u>n</u> mwah*

I'm traveling _____.   **Je voyage _____.**   *zhuh vwah-yahzh*

■ alone   **seul**   *suhl*

■ with my husband   **avec mon mari**   *ah-vehk moh<u>n</u> mah-ree*

■ with my wife   **avec ma femme**   *ah-vehk mah fahm*

■ with my family   **avec ma famille**   *ah-vehk mah fah-mee*

■ with my friends   **avec mes ami(e)s**   *ah-vehk may zah-mee*

Here are my bags.   **Voici mes bagages.**   *vwah-ssee may bah-gahzh*

I have nothing to declare.   **Je n'ai rien à déclarer.**   *zhuh nay rya<u>n</u> ah day-klah-ray*

I have only _____.   **J'ai seulement _____.**   *zhay suhl-mah<u>n</u>*

■ a carton of cigarettes   **une cartouche de cigarettes**   *ewn kahr-toosh duh see-gah-reht*

| a bottle of whisky | **une bouteille de whisky** *ewn boo-tehy duh wheess-kee* |

| They're gifts. | **Ce sont des cadeaux.** *suh sohn day kah-doh* |

| It's for my personal use. | **C'est pour usage personnel.** *seh poor ew-zazh pehr-soh-nehl* |

| Do I have to pay duty? | **Dois-je payer des droits de douane?** *dwahzh peh-yay day drwah duh dwahn* |

BAGGAGE AND PORTERS

| Where can I find a baggage cart? | **Où puis-je trouver un chariot à bagages?** *oo pweezh troo-vay uhn shah-ryoh ah bah-gahzh* |

| (I need a) porter. | **(Il me faut un) porteur.** *(eel muh foh tuhn) pohr-tuhr* |

| Please take our (my) bags. | **Prenez nos (mes) valises, s'il vous plaît.** *pruh-nay noh (may) vah-leez seel voo pleh* |

| that big one | **cette grande** *seht grahnd* |

| these two little ones | **ces deux petites** *say duh puh-teet* |

| Put them here (there). | **Mettez-les ici (là).** *meh-tay lay zee-ssee (lah)* |

| Be careful with that one! | **Faites attention avec celle-là!** *feht zah-tahn-syohn ah-vehk sehl lah* |

| I'll carry this one myself. | **Je porterai celle-ci moi-même.** *zhuh pohr-tray sehl see mwah mehm* |

| I'm missing a suitcase. | **Il me manque une valise.** *eel muh mahnk ewn vah-leez* |

Thank you (very much).	**Merci (beaucoup).**	*mehr-ssee (boh-koo)*
This is for you.	**C'est pour vous.**	*seh poor voo*

BANKING AND MONEY MATTERS

EXCHANGING MONEY

Where can I (change) _____?	**Où puis-je (changer) _____?**	*oo pweezh (shahn-zhay)*
◼ money	**de l'argent**	*duh lahr-zhahn*
◼ dollars	**des dollars**	*day doh-lahr*
◼ travelers' checks	**des chèques de voyage**	*day shehk duh vwah-yahzh*
◼ cash a personal check	**toucher un chèque personnel**	*too-shay uhn shehk pehr-soh-nehl*
Where is _____?	**Où se trouve _____?**	*oo suh troov*
◼ a bank	**une banque**	*ewn bahnk*
◼ a money exchange	**un bureau de change**	*uhn bew-roh duh shahnzh*
At what time do they open (close)?	**Ça ouvre (ferme) à quelle heure?**	*sah oo-vruh (fehrm) ah kehl uhr*
Where is the banking window?	**Où est le guichet?**	*oo eh luh gee-sheh*
Do you have an ATM machine?	**Avez-vous un distributeur (un guichet) automatique de billets?**	*ah-vay voo uhn dee-sstree-bew-tuhr (uhn gee-sheh) oh-toh-mah-teek duh bee-yeh*

How do you use it?	**On s'en sert comment?** *ohn sahn sehr koh-mahn*
What's the current exchange rate?	**Quel est le cours (du change) le plus récent?** *kehl eh luh koor (dew shahnzh) luh plew ray-sahn*
I'd like to cash this check.	**Je voudrais toucher ce chèque.** *zhuh voo-dreh too-shay suh shehk*
Where do I sign?	**Où dois-je signer?** *oo dwahzh see-nyay*
I'd like the money _____.	**Je voudrais l'argent _____.** *zhuh voo-dreh lahr-zhahn*
■ in (large) bills	**en (grosses) coupures** *ahn (grohss) koo-pewr*
■ in small change	**en petite monnaie** *ahn puh-teet moh-nay*
Do you accept credit cards?	**Acceptez-vous les cartes de crédit?** *ahk-ssehp-tay voo lay kahrt duh kray-dee*

AT THE HOTEL

CHECKING IN

I'd like a single (double) room for tonight _____.	**Je voudrais une chambre à un lit (à deux lits) pour ce soir _____.** *zhuh voo-dreh zewn shahn-bruh ah uhn lee (ah duh lee) poor suh swahr*
■ with a shower	**avec douche** *ah-vehk doosh*
■ with a bath	**avec salle de bains** *ah-vehk sahl duh ban*
■ with a balcony	**avec balcon** *ah-vehk bahl-kohn*

■ facing the ocean	**qui donne sur l'océan** *kee dohn sewr loh-ssay-ahn*
■ facing the street	**qui donne sur la rue** *kee dohn sewr lah rew*
■ facing the courtyard	**qui donne sur la cour** *kee dohn sewr lah koor*
Does it have _____?	**Il y a _____?** *eel yah*
■ air conditioning	**la climatisation** *lah klee-mah-tee-zah-ssyohn*
■ a hair dryer	**un sèche-cheveux** *uhn sehsh-shuh-vuh*
■ a television	**une télévision** *ewn tay-lay-vee-zyohn*
■ a safe	**un coffre-fort** *uhn kohfr-fohr*
■ a private bathroom	**une douche et des toilettes privées** *ewn doosh ay day twah-leht pree-vay*
■ a mini-bar	**un mini-bar** *uhn mee-nee bahr*
I (don't) have a reservation.	**J'ai (Je n'ai pas de) une réservation.** *zhay (zhuh nay pah duh) ewn ray-zehr-vah-syohn*
May I see the room?	**Puis-je voir la chambre?** *pweezh vwahr lah shahn-bruh*
I (don't) like it.	**Elle me plaît.** *ehl muh pleh* **Elle ne me plaît pas.** *ehl nuh muh pleh pah*
Do you have something _____?	**Avez-vous quelque chose _____?** *Ah-vay voo kehl-kuh shohz*
■ better	**de meilleur** *duh meh-yuhr*
■ larger	**de plus grand** *duh plew grahn*
■ smaller	**de plus petit** *duh plew puh-tee*

cheaper	**de meilleur marché** *duh meh-yuhr mahr-shay*
On what floor is it?	**C'est à quel étage?** *seht ah kehl ay-tahzh*
Is there an elevator?	**Il y a un ascenseur?** *eel yah uhn nah-sahn-suhr*
How much do you charge for _____?	**Quel est le tarif _____?** *kehl eh luh tah-reef*
the American plan	**pension complète** *pahn-ssyohn kohn-pleht*
bed and breakfast	**petit déjeuner compris** *puh-tee day-zhuh-nay kohn-pree*
breakfast and dinner	**en demi-pension** *ahn duh-mee pahn-ssyohn*
the room without meals	**pour la chambre sans repas** *poor lah shahn-bruh sahn ruh-pah*
Is everything included?	**Tout est compris?** *too teh kohn-pree*
I'll take this room.	**Je prends cette chambre.** *Zhuh prahn seht shahn-bruh*
What is my room number?	**Quel est le numéro de ma chambre?** *kehl eh luh new-may-roh duh mah shahn-bruh*
May I please have my key?	**Pourrais-je avoir la clef?** *poo-rehzh ah-vwahr lah klay*
Is there a reduction for children?	**Accordez-vous des réductions aux enfants?** *ah-kohr-day voo day ray-dewk-ssyohn oh zahn-fahn*
Could you put another bed in the room?	**Pourriez-vous mettre un autre lit dans la chambre?** *poo-ree-yay voo meh-truh uhn noh-truh lee dahn lah shahn-bruh*
Is there a charge? How much?	**Faut-il payer cela? Combien?** *foh teel peh-yay suh-lah? kohn-byan*

OTHER ACCOMMODATIONS

I'm looking for _____.	**Je cherche _____.**	*zhuh shehrsh*
▪ a boarding house	**une pension**	*ewn pahn-ssyohn*
▪ a private house	**une maison particulière**	*ewn meh-zohn pahr-tee-kew-lyehr*

I want to rent an apartment. **Je voudrais louer un appartement.** *zhuh voo-dreh loo-ay uhn nah-pahr-tuh-mahn*

I need a living room, bedroom, and kitchen. **Il me faut un salon, une chambre à coucher, et une cuisine.** *eel muh foh tuhn sah-lohn, ewn shahn-bruh ah koo-shay, ay ewn kwee-zeen*

Do you have a furnished room? **Avez-vous une chambre meublée? (garnie?)** *ah-vay voo zewn shahn-bruh muh-blay (gahr-nee)*

How much is the rent? **C'est combien le loyer?** *seh kohn-byan luh lwah-yay*

I'll be staying here for _____. **Je resterai ici _____.** *zhuh rehss-tray ee-ssee*

▪ one week	**une semaine**	*ewn suh-mehn*
▪ two weeks	**quinze jours**	*kahnz zhoor*
▪ one month	**un mois**	*uhn mwah*
▪ the whole summer	**tout l'été**	*too lay-tay*

I want a place that's centrally located near public transportation. **Je voudrais (avoir) une résidence située au centre ville près des transports publics.** *zhuh voo-dreh (zah-vwahr) ewn ray-zee-dahnss see-tew-ay oh sahn-truh veel preh deh trahnss-pohr pew-bleek*

Is there a youth hostel around here?	**Il y a une auberge de jeunesse par ici?** *eel yah ewn oh-behrzh duh zhuh-nehss preh dee-ssee*

ORDERING BREAKFAST

We'll have breakfast in the room.	**Nous prendrons le petit déjeuner dans la chambre.** *noo prahn-drohn luh puh-tee day-zhuh-nay dahn lah shahn-bruh*
Please send up _____.	**Faites monter _____, s'il vous plaît.** *feht mohn-tay _____ seel voo pleh*
We'd like _____.	**Nous voudrions _____.** *noo voo-dree-yohn*
▪ one (two) coffee(s)	**un (deux) café(s)** *uhn (duh) kah-fay*
▪ tea	**un thé** *uhn tay*
▪ hot chocolate	**un chocolat** *uhn shoh-koh-lah*
▪ a (some) croissant(s)	**un (des) croissant(s)** *uhn (day) krwah-ssahn*
▪ fruit	**des fruits** *day frwee*
▪ fruit juice	**du jus de fruit** *dew zhew duh frwee*
▪ scrambled (fried) (boiled) eggs	**des oeufs brouillés (au plat) (à la coque)** *day zuh broo-yay (oh plah) (ah lah kohk)*
▪ toast	**du pain grillé** *dew pan gree-yay*
▪ jam	**de la confiture** *duh lah kohn-fee-tewr*
▪ butter	**du beurre** *dew buhr*

HOTEL SERVICES

Where is (are) _____?	**Où est (sont) _____?** *oo eh (sohn)*
■ the dining room	**la salle à manger** *lah sahl ah mahn-zhay*
■ the bathroom	**les toilettes** *lay twah-leht*
■ the elevator	**l'ascenseur** *lah-ssahn-ssuhr*
■ the phone	**le téléphone** *luh tay-lay-fohn*
I need _____.	**Il me faut _____.** *eel muh foh*
■ a bellboy	**un chasseur** *tuhn shah-ssuhr*
■ a chambermaid	**une femme de chambre** *tewn fahm duh shahn-bruh*
Please give me _____.	**Veuillez me donner _____.** *vuh-yay muh doh-nay*
■ a towel	**une serviette** *ewn sehr-vyeht*
■ a bar of soap	**une savonnette** *ewn sah-voh-neht*
■ some hangers	**des cintres** *day san-truh*
■ a pillow	**un oreiller** *uhn noh-reh-yay*
■ a blanket	**une couverture** *ewn koo-vehr-tewr*
■ some ice	**de la glace** *duh lah glahss*
■ ice cubes	**des glaçons** *day glah-ssohn*
■ some ice water	**de l'eau glacée** *duh loh glah-ssay*
■ an ashtray	**un cendrier** *uhn sahn-dree-yay*
■ toilet paper	**un rouleau de papier hygiénique** *uhn roo-loh duh pah-pyay ee-zhyay-neek*
■ a bottle of mineral water	**une bouteille d'eau minérale** *ewn boo-tehy doh mee-nay-rahl*
■ an electric adaptor	**un transformateur** *uhn trahnss-fohr-mah-tuhr*

NOTE: Electric current is usually 220 volts. A European-style adaptor plug or an adaptable appliance is necessary for electric hair dryers or clocks. Large international hotels may have an adaptor plug at the reception desk, but smaller hotels or pensions are unlikely to be able to provide one.

Just a minute.	**Un moment.**	*uhn moh-mahn*
Come in.	**Entrez.**	*ahn-tray*
Put it on the table.	**Mettez ça sur la table.**	*meh-tay sah sewr lah tah-bluh*
Please wake me tomorrow at _____.	**Réveillez-moi demain matin à _____, s'il vous plaît.**	*ray-veh-yay mwah duh-man mah-tan ah _____ seel voo pleh*
There is no _____.	**Il n'y a pas _____.**	*eel nyah pah*

■ running water   **d'eau courante**   *doh koo-rahnt*

■ hot water   **d'eau chaude**   *doh shohd*

■ electricity   **d'électricité**   *day-lehk-tree-ssee-tay*

The _____ doesn't work.	**_____ ne fonctionne pas.**	*nuh fohnk-ssyohn pah*

■ air conditioner   **le climatiseur**   *luh klee-mah-tee-zuhr*

■ fan   **le ventilateur**   *luh vahn-tee-lah-tuhr*

■ faucet   **le robinet**   *luh roh-bee-neh*

■ lamp   **la lampe**   *lah lahnp*

■ radio   **la radio**   *lah rah-dyoh*

■ socket   **la prise de courant**   *lah preez duh koo-rahn*

■ switch   **le commutateur**   *luh koh-mew-tah-tuhr*

■ television   **la télévision**   *lah tay-lay-vee-zyohn*

Can you fix it?	**Pouvez-vous la réparer?** *poo-vay voo lah ray-pah-ray*
■ now	**maintenant** *mant-nahn*
■ as soon as possible	**aussitôt que possible** *oh-ssee-toh kuh poh-ssee-bluh*
The room is dirty.	**La chambre est sale.** *lah shahn-bruh eh sahl*
Are there any ____ for me?	**Il y a ____ pour moi?** *eel yah ____ poor mwah*
■ letters	**des lettres** *day leh-truh*
■ messages	**des messages** *day meh-ssahzh*
■ packages	**des colis** *day koh-lee*
■ postcards	**des cartes postales** *day kahrt pohss-tahl*
Can you make a phone call for me?	**Pouvez-vous faire un coup de téléphone pour moi?** *poo-vay voo fehr uhn koo duh tay-lay-fohn poor mwah*
I'd like to put this in the hotel safe.	**Je voudrais mettre ceci dans le coffre-fort de l'hôtel.** *zhuh voo-dreh meh-truh ssuh-ssee dahn luh koh-fruh-fohr duh loh-tehl*

CHECKING OUT

I'd like the bill, please.	**Je voudrais la note, s'il vous plaît.** *zhuh voo-dreh lah noht seel voo pleh*
I'm leaving today (tomorrow).	**Je pars aujourd'hui (demain).** *zhuh pahr oh-zhoor-dwee (duh-man)*
Please send someone up for the baggage.	**Faites monter quelqu'un pour les valises, s'il vous plaît.** *feht mohn-tay kehl-kuhn poor lay vah-leez seel voo pleh*

GETTING AROUND TOWN

THE SUBWAY (UNDERGROUND)

Is there a subway in this city?	**Y a-t-il un métro dans cette ville?** *ee ah teel uhn may-troh dahn seht veel*
Where is the nearest subway station?	**Où se trouve la station de métro la plus proche?** *oo suh troov lah stah-ssyohn duh may-troh lah plew prohsh*
How much is the fare?	**Quel est le prix du trajet?** *kehl eh luh pree dew trah-zheh*
Where can I buy a ticket?	**Où puis-je acheter un billet?** *oo pweezh ahsh-tay uhn bee-yeh*
Which line goes to _____?	**Quelle ligne va à _____?** *kehl lee-nyuh vah ah*
Does this train go to _____?	**Ce train va à _____?** *suh tran vah ah*
How many more stops are there?	**Il reste combien d'arrêts?** *eel rehsst kohn-byan dah-reh*
What's the next station?	**Quelle est la prochaine station?** *kehl eh lah proh-shehn stah-ssyohn*
Where should I get off to go to _____?	**Où dois-je descendre pour aller à _____?** *oo dwahzh day-sahn-druh poor ah-lay ah*
Do I have to change trains?	**Faut-il prendre une correspondance?** *foh teel prahn-druh ewn koh-rehss-pohn-dahnss*

Please tell me when we get there.	**S'il vous plaît, dites-moi quand nous y arrivons.** *seel voo pleh, deet mwah kahn noo zee ah-ree-vohn*

THE BUS (STREETCAR, TRAM)

Défense de parler au conducteur	Do not speak to the driver

Where is the bus stop? (bus terminal?)	**Où est l'arrêt de bus? (le terminus?)** *oo eh lah-reh duh bewss (luh tehr-mee-newss)*
How often do the buses run?	**Quelle est la fréquence des bus?** *kehl eh lah fray-kahnss day bewss*
I want to go to _____.	**Je voudrais aller à _____.** *zhuh voo-dreh zah-lay ah*
In which direction do I have to go?	**Dans quel sens dois-je aller?** *dahn kehl sahnss dwahzh ah-lay*
Which bus do I take to get to _____?	**Quel bus faut-il prendre pour aller à _____?** *kehl bewss foh teel prahn-druh poor ah-lay ah*
Is it far from here?	**C'est loin d'ici?** *seh lwan dee-ssee*
How many stops are there?	**Il y a combien d'arrêts?** *eel yah kohn-byan dah-reh*
Do I have to change?	**Faut-il changer de bus?** *foh teel shahn-zhay duh bewss*
Do you go to _____?	**Vous allez à _____?** *voo zah-lay ah*

Where do I get off?	**Où dois-je descendre?** *oo dwahzh day-sahn-druh*
Could you tell me when to get off?	**Pourriez-vous me dire quand je dois descendre?** *poo-ree-yay voo muh deer kahn zhuh dwah day-sahn-druh*

TAXIS

Is there a taxi stand around here?	**Il y a une station de taxis près d'ici?** *eel yah ewn stah-ssyohn duh tahk-ssee preh dee-ssee*
Where can I get a taxi?	**Où puis-je trouver un taxi?** *oo pweezh troo-vay uhn tahk-ssee*
Taxi! Are you available?	**Taxi! Etes-vous libre?** *tahk-ssee eht voo lee-bruh*
Take me (I want to go) _____.	**Conduisez-moi (Je voudrais aller)** _____. *kohn dwee-zay mwah (zhuh voo-dreh zah-lay)*
■ to the airport	**à l'aéroport** *ah lahy-roh-pohr*
■ to this address	**à cette adresse** *ah seht ah-drehss*
■ to the hotel _____	**à l'hôtel** *ah loh-tehl*
■ to the train station	**à la gare** *ah lah gahr*
■ to _____ Street	**à la rue** _____ *ah lah rew*
■ to _____ Avenue	**à l'avenue** _____ *ah lahv-new*
■ to _____ Boulevard	**au boulevard** _____ *oh bool-vahr*
Do you know where it is?	**Savez-vous où ça se trouve?** *sah-vay voo oo sah suh troov*
How much is it to _____?	**C'est combien pour aller à** _____? *seh kohn-byan poor ah-lay ah*

I'm in a hurry.	**Je suis pressé(e)!** *zhuh swee preh-ssay*
Don't go so fast.	**Ne conduisez pas si vite, s'il vous plaît.** *nuh kohn-dwee-zay pah see veet seel voo pleh*
Stop here at the corner.	**Arrêtez-vous ici, à l'angle.** *ah-reh-tay voo zee-ssee ah lahngl*
Stop at the next block.	**Arrêtez-vous à la prochaine rue.** *ah-reh-tay voo ah lah proh-shehn rew*
How much do I owe you?	**Je vous dois combien?** *zhuh voo dwah kohn-byan*
This is for you.	**Voilà pour vous.** *vwah-lah poor voo*

PLACES TO GO/SIGHTSEEING

Where is the Tourist Office?	**Où est le Syndicat d'Initiative?** *oo eh luh san-dee-kah dee-nee-ssyah-teev*
I need an (English speaking) guide.	**J'ai besoin d'un guide (qui parle anglais).** *zhay buh-zwan duhn geed (kee pahrl ahn-gleh)*
How much does he charge ____?	**C'est combien ____?** *seh kohn-byan*
■ per hour	**à l'heure** *ah luhr*
■ per day	**à la journée** *ah lah zhoor-nay*
There are two (four, six) of us.	**Nous sommes deux (quatre, six).** *noo sohm duh (kah-truh, seess)*

Where can I buy a guidebook? (a map?) (a street map?)	**Où puis-je acheter un guide touristique? (une carte?) (un plan de la ville?)** *oo pweezh ahsh-tay uhn geed too-reess-teek (ewn kahrt) (uhn plahn duh lah veel)*
What are the main attractions?	**Qu'est-ce qu'il y a de plus intéressant à voir?** *kehss keel yah duh plew zan-tay-reh-ssahn ah vwahr*
Are there trips through the city?	**Il y a des visites guidées à travers la ville?** *eel yah day vee-zeet gee-day ah trah-vehr lah veel*
Where do they leave from?	**D'où partent-elles?** *doo pahr tehl*
We want to see _____.	**Nous voudrions voir _____.** *noo vood-ree-yohn vwahr*

- the botanical garden **le jardin botanique** *luh zhahr-dan boh-tah-neek*
- the castle **le château** *luh shah-toh*
- the cathedral **la cathédrale** *lah kah-tay-drahl*
- the church **l'église** *lay-gleez*
- the concert hall **la salle de concert** *lah sahl duh kohn-ssehr*
- the downtown area **le centre de la ville** *luh sahn-truh duh la veel*
- the fountains **les fontaines** *lay fohn-tehn*
- the library **la bibliothèque** *lah bee-blee-oh-tehk*
- the main square **la place principale** *lah plahss pran-ssee-pahl*
- the market **le marché** *luh mahr-shay*
- the mosque **la mosquée** *lah mohss-kay*
- the museum (of fine arts) **le musée (des beaux arts)** *luh mew-zay (day boh zahr)*

■ a nightclub	**une boîte de nuit**	*ewn bwaht duh nwee*
■ the old part of town	**la vieille ville**	*lah vyehy veel*
■ the opera	**l'opéra**	*loh-pay-rah*
■ the palace	**le palais**	*luh pah-leh*
■ the park	**le parc**	*luh pahrk*
■ the stadium	**le stade**	*luh stahd*
■ the synagogue	**la synagogue**	*lah see-nah-gohg*
■ the university	**l'université**	*lew-nee-vehr-ssee-tay*
■ the zoo	**le zoo**	*luh zoh*

Is it open? **C'est ouvert?** *seh too-vehr*

Is it closed? **C'est fermé?** *seh fehr-may*

At what time does it open? **Ça ouvre à quelle heure?** *sah oo-vruh ah kehl uhr*

At what time does it close? **Ça ferme à quelle heure?** *sah fehrm ah kehl uhr*

What's the admission price? **Combien coûte un billet d'entrée?** *kohn-byan koot uhn-bee-yeh dahn-tray*

How much do children pay? **C'est combien pour les enfants?** *seh kohn-byan poor lay zahn-fahn*

Can they go in free? **Est-ce gratuit pour les enfants?** *ehss grah-twee poor lay zahn-fahn.*

Until what age? **Jusqu'à quel âge?** *zhewss-kah kehl ahzh*

Is it all right to take pictures? **Peut-on prendre des photos?** *puh tohn prahn-druh day foh-toh*

PLANNING A TRIP

AIR SERVICE

When is there a flight to _____?	**Il y a un vol pour _____ quand?** *eel yah uhn vohl poor _____ kahn*
I would like a round-trip (one-way) ticket in tourist class (first class).	**Je voudrais un aller et retour (un aller simple) en seconde classe (première classe).** *zhuh voo-dreh zuhn ah-lay ay ruh-toor (uhn nah-lay san-pluh) ahn suh-gohnd klahss (pruh-myehr klahss)*
A seat _____.	**Une place _____.** *ewn plahss*
■ in the smoking section	**dans la section fumeurs.** *dahn lah sehk-ssyohn few-muhr*
■ in the nonsmoking section	**dans la section non-fumeurs.** *dahn lah sehk-ssyohn nohn few-muhr*
■ next to the window	**à côté de la fenêtre** *ah koh-tay duh lah fuh-neh-truh*
■ on the aisle	**côté couloir** *koh-tay koo-lwahr*
What is the fare?	**Quel est le tarif?** *kehl eh luh tah-reef*
Are meals served?	**Sert-on des repas?** *sehr tohn day ruh-pah*
At what time does the plane leave?	**L'avion part à quelle heure?** *lah-vyohn pahr tah kehl uhr*
At what time do we arrive?	**À quelle heure arrivons-nous?** *ah kehl uhr ah-reev-ohn noo*
What is my flight number?	**Quel est le numéro de mon vol?** *kehl eh luh new-may-roh duh mohn vohl*

What gate do we leave from?	**De quelle porte partons-nous?** *duh kehl pohrt pahr-toh<u>n</u> noo*
I want to confirm (cancel) my reservation for flight _____.	**Je voudrais confirmer (annuler) ma réservation pour le vol numéro _____.** *zhuh voo-dreh koh<u>n</u>-feer-may (ah-new-lay) mah ray-zehr-vah-ssyoh<u>n</u> poor luh vohl new-may-roh*
I'd like to check my bags.	**Je voudrais enregistrer mes bagages.** *zhuh voo-dreh zah<u>n</u>-ruh-zheess-tray may bah-gahzh*
I have only carry-on baggage.	**J'ai seulement des bagages à main.** *zhay suhl-mah<u>n</u> day bah-gazh ah ma<u>n</u>*
Please pass my film (camera) through by hand.	**Passez mon film (appareil) à la main, s'il vous plaît.** *pah-ssay moh<u>n</u> film (ah-pah-rehy) ah lah ma<u>n</u> seel voo pleh*

SHIPBOARD TRAVEL

Where is the dock?	**Où est le dock?** *oo eh luh dohk*
When does the next boat leave for _____?	**Quand part le prochain bateau pour _____?** *kah<u>n</u> pahr luh proh-sha<u>n</u> bah-toh poor*
How long does the crossing take?	**La traversée dure combien de temps?** *lah trah-vehr-ssay dewr koh<u>n</u>-bya<u>n</u> duh tah<u>n</u>*
At what ports do we stop?	**Dans quels ports est-ce qu'on fait escale?** *dah<u>n</u> kehl pohr ehss koh<u>n</u> feh ehss-kahl*
How long is the stopover?	**L'escale dure combien de temps?** *lehss-kahl dewr koh<u>n</u>-bya<u>n</u> duh tah<u>n</u>*

When do we dock? | **Quand est-ce qu'on y arrive?**
kah_n tehss koh_n nee ah-reev

At what time do we have to be back on board? | **À quelle heure faut-il retourner au bateau?** *ah kehl uhr foh teel ruh-toor-nay oh bah-toh*

I'd like a _____ ticket. | **Je voudrais un billet _____.** *zhuh voo-dreh zuh_n bee-yeh*

■ first-class | **de première classe** *duh pruh-myehr klahss*

■ tourist-class | **de deuxième classe** *duh duh-zyehm klahss*

■ cabin | **de cabine** *duh kah-been*

Can you give me something for seasickness? | **Pouvez-vous me donner quelque chose contre le mal de mer?** *poo-vay voo muh doh-nay kehl-kuh shohz koh_n-truh luh mahl duh mehr*

TRAIN SERVICE

Where is the train station? (the ticket office) | **Où est la gare? (le guichet)** *oo eh lah gahr (luh gee-sheh)*

I'd like to see the schedule. | **Je voudrais voir l'horaire.** *zhuh voo-dreh vwahr loh-rehr*

A first-class (second-class) ticket to _____, please. | **Un billet de première classe (seconde classe) pour _____, s'il vous plaît.** *uh_n bee-yeh duh pruh-myehr klahss (suh-goh_nd klahss) poor _____ seel voo pleh*

■ a one-way (round-trip) ticket | **un aller simple (un aller et retour)** *uh_n nah-lay sa_n-pluh (uh_n nah-lay ay ruh-toor)*

I would like a (no) smoking compartment.	**Je voudrais un compartiment (non-) fumeurs.** *zhuh voo-dreh zuhn kohn-pahr-tee-mahn (nohn) few-muhr*
At what time does the train arrive (leave)?	**Le train arrive (part) à quelle heure?** *luh tran ah-reev (pahr) ah kehl uhr*
From what platform does it leave?	**Il part de quel quai (de quelle voie)?** *eel pahr duh kehl kay (duh kehl vwah)*
At what platform does it arrive?	**Il arrive à quel quai (à quelle voie)?** *eel ah-reev ah kehl kay (ah kehl vwah)*
Does this train stop at _____?	**Est-ce que ce train s'arrête à _____?** *ehss kuh suh tran sah-reht ah*
Is the train on time?	**Le train est à l'heure?** *luh tran eh tah luhr*
How long does it stop?	**Il s'arrête pendant combien de temps?** *eel sah-reht pan-dan kohn-byan duh tahn*
Is there time to get a bite?	**On a le temps de prendre quelque chose?** *ohn ah luh tahn duh prahn-druh kehl-kuh shohz*
Is there a dining car (sleeping car)?	**Il y a un wagon restaurant (un wagon-lit)?** *eel yah uhn vah-gohn rehss-toh-rahn (uhn vah-gohn lee)*
Is it _____?	**Est-ce _____?** *ehss*
■ a through train	**un rapide** *uhn rah-peed*
■ a local	**un omnibus** *uhn nohm-nee-bewss*
■ an express	**un express** *uhn nehkss-prehss*
Do I have to change trains?	**Dois-je changer de train?** *dwahzh shahn-zhay duh tran*

Is this seat taken?	**Est-ce que cette place est occupée?** *ehss kuh seht plahss eh toh-kew-pay*
Where are we now?	**Où sommes-nous maintenant?** *oo sohm noo mant-nahn*

DRIVING A CAR

SIGNS

Accotement non stabilisé	Soft shoulder
Allumez vos phares	Put on headlights
Arrêt interdit	No stopping
Attention	Caution
Céder le passage	Yield
Chaussée déformée	Poor roadway
Chute de pierres	Falling rocks
Circulation interdite	No thoroughfare
Descente (Pente) dangereuse	Steep slope (hill)
Déviation	Detour
Douane	Customs
École	School
Entrée interdite	No entrance
Fin d'interdiction de ____	End of ____ zone
Interdiction de doubler	No Passing
Interdiction de stationner	No Parking

Guarded railroad crossing

Yield

Stop

Right of way

Dangerous intersection ahead

Gasoline (petrol) ahead

Parking

No vehicles allowed

Dangerous curve

Pedestrian crossing

Oncoming traffic has right of way

No bicycles allowed

No parking allowed

No entry

No left turn

No U-turn

No passing

Border crossing

Traffic signal ahead

Speed limit

Traffic circle (roundabout) ahead

Minimum speed limit

All traffic turns left

End of no passing zone

One-way street

Detour

Danger ahead

Entrance to expressway

Expressway ends

Interdit aux piétons	No Pedestrians
Piste réservée aux transports publics	Lane for Public Transportation
Ralentir (Ralentissez)	Slow
Réservé aux piétons	Pedestrians only
Sens interdit	Wrong way
Sens unique	One Way
Serrez à gauche (à droite)	Keep left (right)
Sortie d'autoroute	Freeway (throughway) Exit
Sortie de véhicules	Vehicle Exit
Stationnement autorisé	Parking Permitted
Stationnement interdit	No Parking
Tenez la droite (gauche)	Keep to the right (left)
Verglas	Icy Road
Virage dangereux	Dangerous Curve
Voie de dégagement	Private Entrance
Zone Bleue	Blue Zone (parking)

CAR RENTALS

Where can I rent _____?	**Où puis-je louer _____.**	*oo pweezh loo-ay*
■ a car	**une voiture**	*ewn vwah-tewr*
■ a motorcycle	**une motocyclette**	*ewn moh-toh-see-kleht*
■ a bicycle	**une bicyclette**	*ewn bee-ssee-kleht*
■ a scooter	**un scooter**	*uh<u>n</u> skoo-tehr*

■ a moped	**une mobylette**	*ewn moh-bee-leht*

I want _____.	**Je voudrais _____.**	*zhuh voo-dreh*
■ a small car	**une petite voiture**	*zewn puh-teet vwah-tewr*
■ a large car	**une grande voiture**	*zewn grahnd vwah-tewr*
■ a sports car	**une voiture de sport**	*zewn vwah-tewr duh spohr*

I prefer automatic transmission.	**Je préfère la transmission automatique.** *zhuh pray-fehr lah trahnz-mee-ssyohn oh-toh-mah-teek*

How much does it cost _____?	**Quel est le tarif _____?**	*kehl eh luh tah-reef*
■ per day	**à la journée**	*ah lah zhoor-nay*
■ per week	**à la semaine**	*ah lah suh-mehn*
■ per kilometer	**au kilomètre**	*oh kee-loh-meh-truh*

How much is the insurance?	**Quel est le montant de l'assurance?** *kehl eh luh mohn-tahn duh lah-ssew-rahnss*
Is the gas included?	**Est-ce que l'essence est comprise?** *ehss kuh leh-ssahnss eh kohn-preez*
What kind of gas does it take?	**Quelle essence emploie-t-elle?** *kehl eh-ssahnss ahn-plwah-tehl*
Do you accept credit cards?	**Acceptez vous des cartes de crédit?** *ahk-ssehp-tay voo day kahrt duh kray-dee*
Which ones?	**Lesquelles?** *lay-kehl*
Here's my driver's license.	**Voici mon permis de conduire.** *vwah-ssee mohn pehr-mee duh kohn-dweer*

Do I have to leave a deposit?	**Dois-je verser des arrhes?** *dwahzh vehr-ssay day zahr*
I want to rent the car here and leave it in _____ (name of city).	**Je veux louer la voiture ici et la laisser à _____.** *zhuh vuh loo-ay lah vwah-tewr ee-ssee ay lah leh-ssay ah*
Is there a drop-off charge?	**Faut-il payer plus en cas de non-retour ici?** *foh-teel peh-yay plews ahn kah duh nohn-ruh-toor ee-ssee*

ON THE ROAD

Excuse me.	**Excusez-moi.** *ehkss-kew-zay mwah* **Pardon** *pahr-dohn*
Can you tell me _____?	**Pouvez-vous me dire _____?** *poo-vay voo muh deer*
How do I get to _____?	**Comment va-t-on à _____?** *koh-mahn vah-tohn ah*
I think we're lost.	**Nous sommes sur la mauvaise route.** *noo sohm sewr lah moh-vehz root*
Is this the road (way) to _____?	**Est-ce la route de _____?** *ehss lah root duh*
Do I go straight?	**Est-ce que je vais tout droit?** *ehss kuh zhuh veh too drwah*
Do I turn to the right (to the left)?	**Est-ce que je tourne à droite (à gauche)?** *ehss kuh zhuh toorn ah drwaht (ah gohsh)*
Where does this road go?	**Où mène cette route?** *oo mehn seht root*

How far is it from here to the next town?	**À quelle distance sommes-nous de la prochaine ville?** *ah kehl deess-tahnss sohm noo duh lah proh-shan veel*
How far away is _____?	**À quelle distance est _____?** *ah kehl deess-tahnss eh*
Is the next town far?	**La prochaine ville, est-elle loin?** *lah proh-shan veel eh-tehl lwan*
What's the next town called?	**Comment s'appelle la prochaine ville?** *koh-mahn sah-pehl lah proh-shan veel*
Do you have a road map?	**Avez-vous une carte routière?** *ah-vay voo zewn kahrt roo-tyehr*
Can you show it to me on the map?	**Pourriez-vous me l'indiquer sur la carte?** *poo-ree-yay voo muh lan-dee-kay sewr lah kahrt*
Is the road in good condition?	**Est-ce que la route est en bon état?** *ehss kuh lah root eh tahn bohn nay-tah*
Is this the most direct way?	**Est-ce le chemin le plus direct?** *ehss luh shuh-man luh plew dee-rehkt*
Is it a toll road?	**Est-ce une autoroute à péage?** *ehss ewn oh-toh-root ah pay-ahzh*

AT THE SERVICE STATION

Where is a gas station?	**Où se trouve une station-service?** *oo suh troov ewn stah-ssyohn sehr-veess*

Fill'er up with _____ please.	**Faites-le plein, s'il vous plaît _____.**	*feht-luh plan seel-voo pleh*
◼ diesel	**du gas-oil**	*dew gahz-wahl*
◼ regular	**de l'ordinaire**	*duh lohr-dee-nehr*
◼ super	**du super**	*dew sew-pehr*

Give me _____ liters please.	**Donnez m'en _____ litres, s'il vous plaît.**	*doh-nay mahn _____ lee-truh seel voo pleh*

Please check _____.	**Veuillez vérifier _____.**	*vuh-yay vay-ree-fyay*
◼ the battery	**la batterie**	*lah bah-tree*
◼ the brakes	**les freins**	*lay fran*
◼ the carburetor	**le carburateur**	*luh kahr-bew-rah-tuhr*
◼ the oil	**le niveau de l'huile**	*luh nee-voh duh lweel*
◼ the spark plugs	**les bougies (f.)**	*lay boo-zhee*
◼ the tires	**les pneus**	*lay pnuh*
◼ the water	**le niveau de l'eau**	*luh nee-voh duh loh*

I think there's something wrong with _____.	**Je crois que _____ ne fonctionne pas.**	*zhuh krwah kuh _____ nuh fohnk-ssyohn pas*
◼ the brakes	**les freins**	*lay fran*
◼ the directional signal	**le clignotant**	*luh klee-nyoh-tahn*
◼ the electrical system	**l'installation électrique**	*lan-stah-lah-ssyohn ay-lchk-treek*
◼ the exhaust	**l'échappement (m.)**	*lay-shahp-mahn*
◼ the fan	**le ventilateur**	*luh vahn-tee-lah-tuhr*
◼ the fan belt	**la courroie de ventilateur**	*lah koor-wah duh vahn-tee-lah-tuhr*

the fuel pump	**la pompe à essence**	*lah pohnp ah eh-ssahnss*
the gears	**l'engrenage (m.)**	*lahn-gruh-nahzh*
the gearshift	**le changement de vitesses**	*luh shahnzh-mahn duh vee-tehss*
the headlight	**le phare**	*luh fahr*
the hood	**le capot**	*luh kah-poh*
the horn	**le klaxon**	*luh klahk-ssohn*
the ignition	**l'allumage (m.)**	*lah-lew-mahzh*
the radio	**la radio**	*lah rah-dyoh*
the starter	**le démarreur**	*luh day-mah-ruhr*
the taillight	**le feu arrière**	*luh fuh ah-ryehr*
the transmission	**la transmission**	*lah trahnz-mee-ssyohn*
the trunk	**le coffre**	*luh koh-fruh*
the water pump	**la pompe à eau**	*lah pohnp ah oh*
the windshield wipers	**les essuie-glaces**	*lay zeh-sswee glahss*

What's the matter?	**Qu'est-ce qui ne va pas?**	*kehss kee nuh vah pah*
Is it possible to (Can you) fix it today?	**Pouvez-vous la réparer aujourd'hui?**	*poo-vay voo lah ray-pah-ray oh-zhoor-dwee*
How long will it take?	**Combien de temps faudra-t-il?**	*kohn-byan duh tahn foh-drah-teel*
Is everything O.K. now?	**Tout est arrangé (réparé) maintenant?**	*too teh tah-rahn-zhay (ray-pah-ray) mant-nahn*
How much do I owe you?	**Combien vous dois-je?**	*kohn-byan voo dwahzh*

ENTERTAINMENT AND DIVERSIONS

MOVIES

What are they showing today?	**Qu'est-ce qu'on joue aujourd'hui?** *kehss kohn zhoo oh-zhoor-dwee*
It's _____.	**C'est _____.** *seh*
■ a mystery	**un mystère** *tuhn mee-sstehr*
■ a comedy	**une comédie** *tewn koh-may-dee*
■ a drama	**un drame** *tuhn drahm*
■ a musical	**une comédie musicale** *tewn koh-may-dee mew-zee-kahl*
■ a romance	**une histoire d'amour** *tewn eess-twahr dah-moor*
■ a Western	**un western** *tuhn wehss-tehrn*
■ a war film	**un film de guerre** *tuhn feelm duh gehr*
■ a science fiction film	**un film de science fiction** *tuhn feelm duh see-yahnss feek-ssyohn*
Is it in English?	**Est-ce en anglais?** *ehss ahn nahn-gleh*
Are there English subtitles?	**Il y a des sous-titres en anglais?** *eel yah day soo-tee-truh ahn nahn-gleh*
Where is the box office (time schedule)?	**Où est le bureau de location (l'horaire)?** *oo eh luh bew-roh duh loh-kah-ssyohn (loh-rehr)*
What time does the (first) show begin?	**À quelle heure commence le (premier) spectacle?** *ah kehl uhr koh-mahnss luh (pruh-myay) spehk-tah-kluh*

What time does the (last) show end?	**À quelle heure se termine le (dernier) spectacle?** *ah kehl uhr suh tehr-meen luh (dehr-nyay) spehk-tah-kluh*

THEATER

I need tickets for tonight.	**Il me faut des billets pour ce soir.** *eel muh foh day bee-yeh poor suh swahr*
Two _____ seats.	**Deux places _____.** *duh plahss*
■ orchestra	**à l'orchestre** *ah lohr-kehss-truh*
■ balcony	**au balcon** *oh bahl-kohn*
■ first balcony	**au premier balcon** *oh pruh-myay bahl-kohn*
■ mezzanine	**au parterre** *oh pahr-tehr*

OPERA-BALLET-CONCERTS

We would like to go to _____.	**Nous voudrions aller à _____.** *noo voo-dree-yohn zah-lay ah*
■ a ballet	**un ballet** *uhn bah-leh*
■ a concert	**un concert** *uhn kohn-ssehr*
■ an opera	**un opéra** *uhn noh-pay-rah*
Is there a _____ nearby?	**Il y a par ici _____?** *eel yah pahr ee-ssee*
■ concert hall	**une salle de concert** *ewn sahl duh kohn-ssehr*
■ opera house	**un opéra** *uhn noh-pay-rah*

What are they playing?	**Qu'est-ce qu'on joue?**	*kehss kohn zhoo*

Who is the conductor?	**Qui est le chef d'orchestre?** *kee eh luh shehf dohr-kehss-truh*	

I prefer _____.   **Je préfère _____.**   *zhuh pray-fehr*

■ classical music   **la musique classique**   *lah mew-zeek klah-sseek*

■ modern music   **la musique moderne**   *lah mew-zeek moh-dehrn*

■ folk dances   **les danses folkloriques**   *lay dahnss fohl-kloh-reek*

Are there any seats for tonight's performance?   **Il y a des places pour ce soir?**   *eel yah day plahss poor suh swahr*

When does the season end?   **Quand se termine la saison théâtrale?**   *kahn suh tehr-meen lah seh-zohn tay-ah-trahl*

Should I get the tickets in advance?   **Faut-il acheter les billets d'avance?**   *foh teel ahsh-tay lay bee-yeh dah-vahnss*

Do I have to dress formally?   **La tenue de soirée est de rigueur?**   *lah tuh-new duh swah-ray eh duh ree-guhr*

How much are the front row seats?   **Combien coûtent les places au premier rang?**   *kohn-byan koot lay plahss oh pruh-myay rahn*

What are the least expensive seats?   **Quelles sont les places les moins chères?**   *kehl sohn lay plahss lay mwan shehr*

How much are the tickets?	**Combien coûtent les billets?** *kohn-byan koot lay bee-yeh*
May I have a program?	**Un programme, s'il vous plaît.** *uhn proh-grahm seel voo pleh*
What opera are they putting on?	**Quel opéra jouent-ils?** *kehl oh-pay-rah zhoo teel*

NIGHTCLUBS

Let's go to a nightclub!	**Allons dans une boîte de nuit!** *ah-lohn dahn zewn bwaht duh nwee*
Is a reservation necessary?	**Faut-il réserver?** *foh teel ray-zehr-vay*
I feel like dancing.	**J'ai envie de danser.** *zhay ahn-vee duh dahn-ssay*
Is there a discotheque here?	**Il y a une discothèque par ici?** *eel yah ewn deess-koh-tehk pahr ee-ssee*
I'd like a table near the dance floor.	**Je voudrais avoir une table près de la piste (de danse).** *zhuh voo-dreh zah-vwahr ewn tah-bluh preh duh lah peesst (duh dahnss)*
Is there a minimum (cover charge)?	**Il y a un prix d'entrée?** *eel yah uhn pree dahn-tray*
Where is the checkroom?	**Où est le vestiaire?** *oo eh luh vehss-tyehr*
At what time does the show begin?	**À quelle heure commence le spectacle?** *ah kehl uhr koh-mahnss luh spehk-tah-kluh*

SPECTATOR SPORTS

SOCCER

I'd like to see a soccer match.
Je voudrais voir un match de football. *zhuh voo-dreh vwahr uhn mahtch duh foot-bohl*

Where's the stadium?
Où est le stade? *oo eh luh stahd*

At what time does the match begin?
Le match commence à quelle heure? *luh mahtch koh-mahnss ah kehl uhr*

When are they going to kick off?
Quand vont-ils donner le coup d'envoi? *kahn vohn teel doh-nay luh koo dahn-vwah*

What teams are playing?
Quelles équipes jouent? *kehl zay-keep zhoo*

What is the score?
Quel est le score? *kehl eh luh skohr*

JAI ALAI

I'd like to see a jai alai match.
Je voudrais voir un match de pelote. *zhuh voo-dreh vwahr uhn mahtch duh puh-loht*

Where can I get tickets?
Où puis-je me procurer des billets? *oo pweezh muh proh-kew-ray day bee-yeh*

Where is the jai alai court?
Où est le fronton? *oo eh luh frohn-tohn*

Where do I place my bet?
Où fait-on les paris? *oo feh-tohn lay pah-ree*

Where is the window?
Où est le guichet? *oo eh luh gee-sheh*

ACTIVE SPORTS

TENNIS

Do you play tennis?	**Jouez-vous au tennis?** *zhoo-ay voo oh teh-neess*
I'd like to play tennis.	**Je voudrais jouer au tennis.** *zhuh voo-dreh-zhoo-ay oh teh-neess*
I (don't) play very well.	**Je (ne) joue (pas) bien.** *zhuh (nuh) zhoo (pah) bya<u>n</u>*
Do you know where there is a (good) court?	**Savez-vous où se trouve un bon court de tennis?** *sah-vay voo oo suh troov uh<u>n</u> boh<u>n</u> koohr duh teh-neess*
Can I rent racquets and balls?	**Puis-je louer des raquettes et des balles?** *pweezh loo-ay day rah-keht ay day bahl*
How much do they charge per hour (per day)?	**Quel est le tarif à l'heure/à la journée?** *kehl eh luh tah-reef ah luhr/ah lah zhoor-nay*

BEACH/POOL

I'd like to go to the beach (to the pool).	**J'ai envie d'aller a la plage (à la piscine).** *zhay ah<u>n</u>-vee dah-lay ah lah plahzh (ah lah pee-sseen)*
Is there a beach nearby?	**Il y a une plage tout près?** *eel yah ewn plahzh too preh*
How do you get there?	**On y va comment?** *oh<u>n</u> nee vah koh-mah<u>n</u>*

Which bus will take us to the beach?	**Quel bus faut-il prendre pour aller à la plage?** *kehl bewss foh teel prahn-druh poor ah-lay ah lah plahzh*
Is there a pool in the hotel?	**Il y a une piscine à l'hôtel?** *eel yah ewn pee-sseen ah loh-tehl*
Is it an indoor (outdoor) pool?	**Est-ce une piscine couverte (en plein air)?** *ehss ewn pee-sseen koo-vehrt (ahn pleh nehr)*
I (don't) know how to swim well.	**Je (ne) sais (pas) bien nager.** *zhuh (nuh) seh (pah) byan nah-zhay*
Is it safe to swim here?	**Peut-on nager ici sans danger?** *puh-tohn nah-zhay ee-ssee sahn dahn-zhay*
Are the waves big?	**Il y a de grandes vagues?** *eel yah duh grahnd vahg*
Are there sharks?	**Il y a des requins?** *eel yah day ruh-kan*
Is there any danger for children?	**Il y a du danger pour les enfants?** *eel yah dew dahn-zhay poor lay zahn-fahn*
Is there a lifeguard?	**Il y a un maître-nageur?** *eel yah uhn meh-truh nah-zhuhr*
Where can I get ____?	**Où puis-je obtenir ____?** *oo pweezh ohp-tuh-neer*
■ an air mattress	**un matelas pneumatique** *uhn maht-lah pnuh-mah-teek*
■ a bathing suit	**un maillot de bain** *uhn mah-yoh duh ban*
■ a beach ball	**un ballon de plage** *uhn bah-lohn duh plahzh*

■ a beach chair — **une chaise longue pour la plage** *ewn shehz lohng poor lah plahzh*

■ a beach towel — **une serviette de plage** *ewn sehr-vyeht duh plahzh*

■ a chaise lounge — **une chaise longue** *ewn shehz lohng*

■ sunglasses — **des lunettes de soleil** *day lew-neht duh soh-leh*

■ suntan lotion — **la lotion pour bronzer** *lah loh-ssyohn poor brohn-zay*

■ a surfboard — **une planche de surf** *ewn plahnsh duh sewrf*

■ water skis — **des skis nautiques** *day skee noh-teek*

ON THE SLOPES

Which ski area do you recommend? — **Quelle station de ski recommandez-vous?** *kehl stah-ssyohn duh skee ruh-koh-mahn-day voo*

I am a novice (intermediate, expert) skier. — **Je suis un(e) débutant(e) (un skieur moyen; un expert).** *zhuh swee zuhn (zewn) day bew-tahn(t) (zuhn skee-uhr mwah-yan/uhn ehks-pehr)*

What kind of lifts are there? — **Il y a quel type de téléski?** *eel yah kehl teep duh tay-lay-sskee*

How much does the lift cost? — **Combien coûte le trajet?** *kohn-byan koot luh trah-zheh*

Do they give lessons? — **On donne des leçons?** *ohn dohn day luh-ssohn*

Is there any cross-country skiing? — **On fait du ski de fond?** *ohn feh dew skee duh fohn*

Is there enough snow this time of year?	**Il y a assez de neige en ce moment?** *eel yah ah-ssay duh nehzh ah<u>n</u> suh moh-mah<u>n</u>*
How do I get there?	**On va comment à cet endroit-là?** *oh<u>n</u> vah koh-mah<u>n</u> ah seht ah<u>n</u>-drwah lah*
Can I rent _____ there?	**Peut-on y louer _____?** *puh-toh<u>n</u> nee loo-ay*
■ equipment	**un équipement de ski** *uh<u>n</u> nay-keep-mah<u>n</u> duh skee*
■ poles	**des bâtons** *day bah-toh<u>n</u>*
■ skis	**des skis** *day skee*
■ ski bindings	**des fixations de ski** *day feek-ssah-syoh<u>n</u> duh skee*
■ ski boots	**des chaussures de ski** *day shoh-ssewr duh skee*

ON THE LINKS

Is there a golf course here?	**Il y a un terrain de golf par ici?** *eel yah uh<u>n</u> teh-ra<u>n</u> duh gohlf pahr ee-ssee*
Can one rent clubs?	**Peut-on louer des clubs?** *puh toh<u>n</u> loo-ay day kluhb*

CAMPING

Is there a camping site near here?	**Il y a un terrain de camping par ici?** *eel yah uh<u>n</u> teh-ra<u>n</u> duh kah<u>n</u>-peeng pahr ee-ssee*
Can you show me how to get there?	**Pouvez-vous m'indiquer comment y aller?** *poo-vay voo ma<u>n</u>-dee-kay koh-mah<u>n</u> tee ah-lay*

Where is it on the map?	**Où se trouve-t-il sur la carte?** *oo suh troov teel sewr lah kahrt*
Where can we park our trailer?	**Où pouvons-nous garer notre caravane?** *oo poo-vohn noo gah-ray noh-truh kah-rah-vahn*
Where can we spend the night?	**Où pouvons-nous passer la nuit?** *oo poo-vohn noo pah-ssay lah nwee*
Can we camp for the night?	**Pouvons-nous camper cette nuit?** *poo-vohn noo kahn-pay seht nwee*
Is there _____?	**Il y a _____?** *eel yah*
■ drinking water	**de l'eau potable** *duh loh poh-tah-bluh*
■ running water	**de l'eau courante** *duh loh koo-rahnt*
■ gas	**du gaz** *dew gahz*
■ electricity	**de l'électricité** *duh lay-lehk-tree-ssee-tay*
■ a children's playground	**un terrain de jeu pour enfants** *uhn teh-ran duh zhuh poor ahn-fahn*
■ a grocery store	**une épicerie** *ewn ay-peess-ree*
■ toilets	**des toilettes** *day twah-leht*
■ showers	**des douches** *day doosh*
■ washrooms	**des lavabos** *day lah-vah-boh*
■ tents	**des tentes** *day tahnt*
■ cooking facilities	**des installations pour faire la cuisine** *day zan-stah-lah-ssyohn poor fehr lah kwee-zeen*
How much do they charge per person? (per trailer)?	**Quel est le tarif par personne (pour une caravane)?** *kehl eh luh tah-reef pahr pehr-ssohn (poor ewn kah-ran-vahn)*

We intend staying
_____ days/weeks.

Nous comptons rester _____
jours/semaines. *noo kohn-tohn
rehss-tay _____ zhoor/suh-mehn*

IN THE COUNTRYSIDE

I'd like to drive
through the
countryside.

**Je voudrais conduire dans la
campagne.** *zhuh voo-dreh kohn-
dweer dahn lah kahn-pah-nyuh*

Where can I rent
a car for the day?

**Où puis-je louer une voiture à la
journée?** *oo pweezh loo-ay ewn
vwah-tewr ah lah zhoor-nay*

Are there tours to
the country?

**Il y a des excursions à la
campagne?** *eel yah day zehkss-
kewr-zyohn ah lah kahn-pah-nyuh*

When do they leave?

Quand sont les départs? *kahn
ssohn lay day-pahr*

From where do they
leave?

D'où partent-elles? *doo pahrt-ehl*

Where does this
_____ lead to?

Où mène _____? *oo mehn*

■ path

ce sentier *suh sahn-tyay*

■ road

ce chemin *suh shuh-man*

■ highway

cette grande route *seht grahnd
root*

How far away is
_____?

À quelle distance est _____?
ah kehl deess-tahnss eh

■ the city

la ville *lah veel*

■ the inn

l'auberge (f.) *loh-behrzh*

How long does it take to ____?	**Combien de temps faut-il pour aller à ____?** *kohn-byan duh tahn foh teel poor ah-lay ah*
I'm lost.	**J'ai perdu mon chemin.** *zhay pehr-dew mohn shuh-man*
Can you show me the way to ____?	**Pouvez-vous m'indiquer le chemin pour ____?** *poo-vay voo man-dee-kay luh shuh-man poor*

FOOD AND DRINK

Auberge, Relais, Hostellerie	a country inn.
Bistro	a small neighborhood restaurant in town, similar to a pub or tavern and usually very informal.
Brasserie	a large café that serves quick meals throughout the day or evening; most meals involve only the entrée, such as a steak or chop.
Cabaret	a nightclub where you may also eat a meal.
Café	a neighborhood spot to socialize, either indoors or out, where you can linger over coffee or a glass of wine or beer and perhaps have a little snack. Cafés also serve breakfast (usually a **croissant** and **café au lait**) and later in the day serve soft drinks and ice cream.
Casse-croûte	a restaurant specializing in sandwiches.

Crêperie	a small stand specializing in the preparation of crêpes—thin pancakes dusted with sugar or covered with jam and rolled up.
Fast-food	a small place to eat an American-style snack, mostly hamburgers and French fries; most are in Paris along the Champs-Elysée, and many are American chains such as McDonald's and Burger King.
Restaurant	an establishment that can range from a small, family-owned inn, where mom seats you, and dad cooks the meal, and the children serve you, to a formal, three-star palace where you receive the most elegant service and most beautifully garnished foods.
Self	a cafeteria, popular with students and usually located near a university.
Troquet	a wine shop where you can also have a snack.

EATING OUT

Do you know a good restaurant?	**Connaissez-vous un bon restaurant?** *koh-neh-ssay voo uhn bohn rehss-toh-rahn*
It is very expensive?	**C'est très cher?** *seh treh shehr*
Do you know a restaurant that serves regional dishes?	**Connaissez-vous un restaurant de de cuisine régionale?** *koh-neh-ssay voo uhn rehss-toh-rahn duh kwee-zeen ray-zhyoh-nahl*

I'd like to make a reservation _____.

Je voudrais retenir une table
_____. *zhuh voo-dreh ruh-tuh-neer*
ewn tah-bluh

- for tonight

   pour ce soir *poor suh swahr*

- for tomorrow evening

   pour demain soir *poor duh-man*
   swahr

- for two (four) persons

   pour deux (quatre) personnes
   poor duh (kah-truh) pehr-ssohn

- at 8 (8:30 P.M.)

   à vingt heures (vingt heures
   trente) *ah van-tuhr (van-tuhr*
   trahnt)

Waiter!

Monsieur! (Garçon!) *muh-ssyuh*
(gahr-son)

Miss!

Mademoiselle! *mahd-mwah-zehl*

A table for two in the corner (near the window).

Une table pour deux dans un coin
(près de la fenêtre). *ewn tah-bluh*
poor duh dahn zuhn kwan (preh duh
lah fuh-neh-truh)

We'd like to have lunch (dinner) now.

Nous voudrions déjeuner (dîner)
maintenant. *noo voo-dree-yohn*
day-zhuh-nay (dee-nay) mant-nahn

The menu, please.

La carte (Le menu), s'il vous plaît.
lah kahrt (luh muh-new) seel voo pleh

I'd like the price-fixed menu.

Je voudrais le menu prix-fixe.
zhuh voo-dreh luh muh-new pree
feekss

What's today's special?

Quel est le plat du jour? *kehl eh*
luh plah dew zhoor

What's the house specialty?

Quelle est la spécialité de la
maison? *kehl eh lah spay-ssyah-*
lee-tay duh lah meh-zohn

What do you recommend?	**Qu'est-ce que vous me recommandez?** *kehss kuh voo muh ruh-koh-mah<u>n</u>-day*
Do you serve children's portions?	**Servez-vous des demi-portions pour les enfants?** *sehr-vay voo day duh-mee pohr-ssyoh<u>n</u> poor lay zah<u>n</u>-fah<u>n</u>*
Do you have a house wine?	**Avez-vous du vin ordinaire?** *ah-vay voo dew va<u>n</u> ohr-dee-nehr*
Is it dry (mellow, sweet)?	**Est-ce sec (moelleux, doux)?** *ehss sehk (mwah-luh, doo)*
Please bring us _____.	**Apportez-nous s'il vous plaît _____.** *ah-pohr-tay noo seel voo pleh*
■ rolls	**des petits pains** *day puh-tee pa<u>n</u>*
■ bread	**du pain** *dew pa<u>n</u>*
■ butter	**du beurre** *dew buhr*
Waiter, we need _____.	**Monsieur (Garçon), apportez-nous _____, s'il vous plaît.** *muh-ssyuh (gahr-son) ah-pohr-tay noo _____ seel voo pleh*
■ a bowl	**un bol** *uh<u>n</u> bohl*
■ a carafe	**un carafe** *uh<u>n</u> kah-rahf*
■ a cup	**une tasse** *ewn tahss*
■ a dinner plate	**une assiette** *ewn-nah-syeht*
■ a fork	**une fourchette** *ewn foor-sheht*
■ a glass	**un verre** *uh<u>n</u> vehr*
■ a knife	**un couteau** *uh<u>n</u> koo-to*
■ a menu	**un menu, une carte** *uh<u>n</u> muh-new, ewn kahrt*
■ a napkin	**une serviette** *ewn sehr-vyeht*
■ a place setting	**un couvert** *uh<u>n</u> koo-vehr*

■ a saucer	**une soucoupe**	*ewn soo-koop*
■ a soup dish	**une assiette à soupe**	*ewn-nah-syeht ah soop*
■ a tablecloth	**une nappe**	*ewn nahp*
■ a teaspoon	**une cuiller**	*ewn kwee-yehr*
■ a toothpick	**un cure-dent**	*uhn kewr-dahn*
■ a wineglass	**un verre à vin**	*uhn vehr ah van*

APPETIZERS (STARTERS)

● **Artichauts à la vinaigrette:** Artichokes in a vinaigrette dressing.

● **Crudités variées:** Assorted vegetables—sliced tomatoes, shredded carrots, sliced cooked beets—in a vinaigrette dressing.

● **Escargots à la bourguignonne:** Snails cooked and served in the shell, seasoned with a garlic, shallot, and parsley butter.

● **Foie gras:** Fresh, often uncooked liver of a force-fed goose; sliced and served with toasted French bread slices.

● **Pâté:** Any of a number of meat loaves, made from puréed liver and usually also with meat—pork, veal, or chicken. **Pâté de foie gras** is made with goose liver; **pâté de campagne** is "of the country" and is a coarser mixed meat pâté; **pâté en croute** is a liver pâté encased in pastry.

● **Quiche lorraine:** An egg custard tart, sometimes with bacon strips or bits; some versions now also made with Gruyère cheese.

● **Quenelles:** Light dumplings, usually made from **brochet** (pike) but also from shellfish; served in a white sauce.

● **Rillettes:** A pork mixture that has been potted, then served as a spread, usually with French bread.

● **Terrine:** A type of pâté, usually served from a deep pot rather than sliced as pâté would be. Terrines can be made from pork, poultry, game, or fish.

SOUPS

● **Bisque d'écrevisses:** A creamy soup made with crawfish; other bisques are made with lobster, shrimp, or oysters.

● **Bouillabaisse:** A seafood stew, made with a variety of fish and shellfish depending on the region, seasoned with saffron and fennel or pernod.

● **Consommé:** A clear broth, made usually from chicken or beef and flavored with herbs; **en gelée** is consommé that has been jelled and sliced; **madrilène** is with tomatoes; **printanier** has a variety of vegetables.

● **Crème:** A creamy soup, made from any of a number of vegetables and usually enriched with egg yolks. **D'Argenteuil** is cream of asparagus soup; **de volaille** is a creamy chicken soup.

● **Petite marmite:** A rich consommé served with meat and vegetables.

● **Potage:** A coarser soup, usually made with a purée of vegetables; some varieties of potage are **parmentier** (leeks and potatoes), **au cresson** (watercress), and **julienne** (shredded vegetables).

● **Soupe à l'oignon:** Famous French onion soup, served over French bread and covered with cheese.

● **Velouté:** A creamy soup, most common of which are **de volaille** (cream of chicken) and **de tomate** (tomato).

EGG DISHES

● **Oeufs bercy:** Eggs baked with sausages in a tomato sauce.

● **Oeufs en cocotte:** Eggs gently baked in individual cups until softly cooked, sometimes with cream, then eaten with a spoon.

● **Oeufs en gelée:** Poached eggs that are set into jelled consommé and served chilled as a salad.

● **Omelette:** A French omelette is puffy and contains a variety of fillings—**aux fines herbes** is with a mixture of parsley, chives, and tarragon.

● **Piperade:** Scrambled eggs mixed with tomatoes, onions, and sweet peppers.

● **Soufflé:** Soufflés can be made with almost any ingredients—vegetables, chicken livers, cheese, ham, and so on; they are always light and puffy.

FISH COURSE

les anchois	*lay zahn-shwah*	anchovies
les anguilles	*lay zahn-gee*	eel
le bar	*luh bahr*	bass (hake)
la barbue	*lah bahr-bew*	brill
la baudroie	*lah boh-drwah*	anglerfish, monkfish
le brochet	*luh broh-sheh*	pike
le cabillaud	*luh kah-bee-yoh*	cod
le calmar	*luh kahl-mahr*	squid
la carpe	*lah kahrp*	carp
le carrelet	*luh kahr-leh*	flounder
le congre	*luh kohn-gruh*	conger eel
les crevettes	*lay kruh-veht*	shrimp
la daurade	*lah doh-rahd*	porgy

les écrevisses	*lay zay-kruh-veess*	crawfish
les escargots	*lay zehss-kahr-goh*	snails
les harengs (fumés)	*lay ah-rah<u>n</u> (few-may)*	herring (smoked)
le homard	*luh oh-mahr*	lobster
les huîtres	*lay zwee-truh*	oysters
la lamproie	*lah lah<u>n</u>-prwah*	lamprey
la langouste	*lah lah<u>n</u>-goosst*	spiny lobster
les langoustines	*lay lah<u>n</u>-goo-ssteen*	large shrimp
la lotte	*lah loht*	monkfish
le loup de mer	*luh loo duh mehr*	sea bass
le maquereau	*luh mah-kroh*	mackerel
le merlan	*luh mehr-lah<u>n</u>*	whiting
la morue	*lah moh-rew*	cod
les moules	*lay mool*	mussels
les palourdes	*lay pah-loord*	clams
la perche	*lah pehrsh*	perch
les poulpes	*lay poolp*	octopus
la rascasse	*lah rahss-kahss*	scorpionfish
les sardines	*lay sahr-deen*	sardines
le saumon	*luh soh-moh<u>n</u>*	salmon
les scampi	*lay skah<u>n</u>-pee*	large shrimp
le thon	*luh toh<u>n</u>*	tuna
la truite	*lah trweet*	trout
le turbot	*luh tewr-boh*	European turbot

POULTRY AND GAME

la caille	*lah kahy*	quail
le cerf	*luh sehr*	venison
le canard, caneton	*luh kah-nahr, kahn-tohn*	duckling
le chapon	*luh shah-pohn*	capon
le chevreuil	*luh shuh-vruhy*	venison
le cochon de lait	*luh koh-shohn duh leh*	suckling pig
la dinde	*lah dand*	turkey
le faisan	*luh feh-zahn*	pheasant
le lapin	*luh lah-pan*	rabbit
le lièvre	*luh lyeh-vruh*	hare
l'oie (f.)	*lwah*	goose
le perdreau, la perdrix	*luh pehr-droh, lah pehr-dree*	partridge
le pigeon, le pigeonneau	*luh pee-zhohn, luh pee-zhoh-noh*	squab
la pintade, le pintadeau	*lah pan-tahd, luh pan-tah-doh*	guinea fowl
la poule	*lah pool*	stewing fowl
le poulet, poussin, la volaille	*luh poo-leh, poo-ssan, lah voh-lahy*	chicken

MEATS

l'agneau (m.)	*lah-nyoh*	lamb
le boeuf	*luh buhf*	beef

la chèvre	*lah sheh-vruh*	goat
le jambon	*luh zhah<u>n</u>-boh<u>n</u>*	ham
le mouton	*luh moo-toh<u>n</u>*	mutton
le porc	*luh pohr*	pork
le veau	*luh voh*	veal
les andouilles	*lay zah<u>n</u>-dooy*	pork sausages
le bifteck	*luh beef-tehk*	steak
le boudin	*luh boo-da<u>n</u>*	blood sausage
le carré d'agneau	*luh kah-ray dah-nyoh*	rack of lamb
le cervelas	*luh sehr-vuh-lah*	garlicky pork sausage
la cervelle	*lah sehr-vehl*	brains
la charcuterie	*lah shahr-kew-tree*	assorted sausages, pâtés, and terrines
le chateaubriand	*luh shah-toh-bree-ah<u>n</u>*	porterhouse steak
la côte de boeuf	*lah koht duh buhf*	ribs of beef
les côtelettes	*lay koht-leht*	cutlets
les côtes de porc, de veau	*lay koht duh pohr, duh voh*	chops, pork or veal
les crépinettes	*lay kray-pee-neht*	small sausages
l'entrecôte (f.)	*lah<u>n</u>-truh-koht*	sirloin steak
l'escalope (f.)	*lehss-kah-lohp*	cutlet
le filet de boeuf	*luh fee-leh duh buhf*	fillet of beef
le foie	*luh fwah*	liver

le gigot d'agneau	*luh zhee-goh dah-nyoh*	leg of lamb
la langue	*lah lah<u>ng</u>*	tongue
le lard	*luh lahr*	bacon
les médaillons de veau	*lay may-dah-yoh<u>n</u> duh voh*	medallions of veal
les noisettes	*lay nwah-zeht*	small fillets
les pieds de porc	*lay pyay duh pohr*	pig's feet
le ris de veau	*luh ree duh voh*	veal sweetbreads
les rognons d'ag-neau	*lay roh-nyoh<u>n</u> dah-nyoh*	lamb kidneys
le rosbif	*luh rohss-beef*	roast beef
les saucisses	*lay soh-sseess*	sausages
la selle d'agneau	*lah sehl dah-nyoh*	saddle of lamb
le steak	*luh stehk*	steak
le tournedos	*luh toor-nuh-doh*	small fillets of beef
les tripes	*lay treep*	tripe

I like it _____.	**Je le (la) prefère _____.**	*zhuh luh (lah) pray-fehr*
■ baked	**cuit au four**	*kwee(t) o foor*
■ boiled	**bouilli**	*boo-yee*
■ braised (stewed)	**braisé(e)**	*breh-zay*
■ breaded	**au gratin, gratiné**	*o grah-ta<u>n</u>, grah-tee-nay*
■ broiled	**rôti**	*ro-tee*
■ browned	**gratiné**	*grah-tee-nay*

■ chopped	**hâché**	*ah-shay*
■ fried	**frit(e)**	*free(t)*
■ grilled	**grillé**	*gree-yay*
■ in its natural juices	**au jus**	*o zhew*
■ mashed, pureed	**en purée**	*ahn pew-ray*
■ poached	**poché**	*poh-shay*
■ roasted	**rôti**	*ro-tee*
■ with sauce	**en sauce**	*ahn sos*
■ sautéed	**sauté**	*so-tay*
■ steamed	**à la vapeur**	*ah lah vah-puhr*
■ stewed	**en cocotte**	*ahn koh-koht*
■ well-done	**très cuit**	*treh kwee*
■ medium well	**bien cuit**	*byan kwee*
■ medium	**à point**	*ah pwan*
■ medium rare	**mi-saignant**	*mee seh-nyahn*
■ rare	**saignant**	*seh-nyahn*
■ very rare	**bleu**	*bluh*
I prefer my eggs _____.	**Je préfère mes oeufs _____.**	*zhuh pray-fehr may zuh*
■ fried	**au plat**	*o plah*
■ hard-boiled	**durs**	*dewr*
■ medium-boiled	**mollets**	*moh-leh*
■ poached	**pochés**	*poh-shay*
■ scrambled	**brouillés**	*broo-yay*
■ soft-boiled	**à la coque**	*ah lah kohk*

PROBLEMS

It's cold.	**C'est froid(e).**	*seh frwah(d)*
It's too rare.	**Ce n'est pas assez cuit(e).**	*suh neh pah zah-say kwee(t)*

It's overcooked.	**C'est trop cuit(e).**	*seh tro kwee(t)*
It's tough.	**C'est dur(e).**	*seh dewr*
It's burned.	**C'est brûlé(e).**	*seh brew-lay*
It's too salty.	**C'est trop salé(e).**	*seh tro sah-lay*
It's too sweet.	**C'est trop sucré(e).**	*seh tro sew-kray*
It's too spicy.	**C'est trop épicé(e).**	*seh tro ay-pee-say*
It doesn't smell good.	**Ça ne sent pas bon.**	*sah nuh sahn pah bohn*

VEGETABLES

l'artichaut (m.)	*lahr-tee-shoh*	artichoke
les asperges	*lay zahss-pehrzh*	asparagus
l'aubergine (f.)	*loh-behr-zheen*	eggplant
la betterave	*lah beh-trahv*	beet
les carottes	*lay kah-roht*	carrots
le céleri	*luh sayl-ree*	celery
le mäis	*luh mah-yeess*	corn
le céleri rave	*luh sayl-ree rahv*	knob celery
les champignons	*lay shahn-pee-nyohn*	mushrooms
le chou	*luh shoo*	cabbage (green)
le chou-fleur	*luh shoo-fluhr*	cauliflower
la courgette	*lah koor-zheht*	zucchini
le cresson	*luh kreh-ssohn*	watercress
les épinards	*lay zay-pee-nahr*	spinach
les flageolets	*lay flah-zhoh-leh*	green shell beans
les haricots verts	*lay ah-ree-koh vehr*	green beans
les oignons	*lay zoh-nyohn*	onions
l'oseille (f.)	*loh-zehy*	sorrel

le piment	*luh pee-mahn*	green pepper
les pois	*lay pwah*	peas
le poireau	*luh pwah-roh*	leek
les pommes de terre	*lay pohm duh tehr*	potatoes
la tomate	*lah toh-maht*	tomato

SEASONINGS

I'd like ____.	**Je voudrais ____.**	*zhuh voo-dreh*
■ artificial sweetener	**du sucre artificiel**	*dew sew-kruh ahr-tee-fee-syehl*
■ butter	**du beurre**	*dew buhr*
■ horseradish	**du raifort**	*dew reh-fohr*
■ ketchup	**du ketchup**	*dew keht-chuhp*
■ margarine	**de la margarine**	*duh lah mahr-gah-reen*
■ mayonnaise	**de la mayonnaise**	*duh lah mah-yoh-nehz*
■ mustard	**de la moutarde**	*duh lah moo-tahrd*
■ olive oil	**de l'huile d'olive**	*duh lweel doh-leev*
■ pepper (black)	**du poivre (noir)**	*dew pwah-vruh (nwahr)*
■ pepper (red)	**du poivre (rouge)**	*dew pwah-vruh (roozh)*
■ salt	**du sel**	*dew sehl*
■ sugar	**du sucre**	*dew sew-kruh*
■ vinegar	**du vinaigre**	*dew vee-neh-gruh*
■ Worcestershire sauce	**de la sauce anglaise**	*du lah sohss ahn-glehz*

CHEESE COURSE

What is that cheese?	**Quel est ce fromage?**	*kehl eh suh froh-mahzh*
Is it _____?	**Est-il _____?**	*eh-teel*
■ mild	**maigre**	*meh-gruh*
■ sharp	**piquant**	*pee-kahn*
■ hard	**fermenté**	*fehr-mahn-tay*
■ soft	**à pâte molle**	*ah paht mohl*

Among the more popular cheeses are the following.

● **Banon:** Made from sheep's or goat's milk, a soft cheese with a natural rind; a mild cheese with a nutty flavor.

● **Bleu d'auvergne:** Made from cow's milk, this soft cheese has an internal mold and when cut, the veins are visible. Has a very sharp flavor.

● **Boursin:** A soft cow's milk cheese, with a mild flavor, sometimes enhanced with herbs.

● **Brie:** A variety of cheeses made from cow's milk and with a bloomy rind. Varieties range in flavor from mild to very pronounced, some with a fruity flavor.

● **Camembert:** Less delicate than brie, but also a cow's milk cheese with a thin white rind. Should be eaten firm.

● **Cantal:** A cow's milk cheese that varies with length of aging. Some varieties are softer and milder, while more aged ones are hard and with a more pronounced flavor.

● **Chèvre:** Any of an almost infinite variety of goat's milk cheeses, which vary from very soft to quite firm, and from mild and creamy to tart and crumbly. There will always be a few chèvres on the cheese tray.

● **Colombière:** This cow's milk cheese is soft and supple, with a mild flavor.

- **Munster:** A cow's milk cheese that is soft and spicy, with a tangy flavor. In Alsace, where the cheese comes from, it is eaten young.

- **Pont-l'evêque:** A cow's milk cheese that is very smooth and supple, with a pronounced flavor.

- **Port-salut:** The brand name for the Saint-Paulin from the monastery of Port-du-Salut.

- **Reblochon:** A soft cow's milk cheese with a mild and creamy flavor.

- **Roquefort:** A sheep's milk cheese that is soft and pungent. The cheese is cured in caves, an ancient process with rigid standards for production. Texture is very buttery.

- **Saint-Paulin:** Made from cow's milk, this is a velvety smooth cheese with a mild flavor.

- **Tomme de savoie:** A mild cow's milk cheese with a nutty flavor.

FRUITS AND NUTS

l'abricot	*lah-bree-koh*	apricot
l'ananas	*lah-nah-nah*	pineapple
la banane	*lah bah-nahn*	banana
les cassis	*lay kah-sseess*	black currants
la cerise	*lah suh-reez*	cherry
le citron	*luh see-trohn*	lemon
la datte	*lah daht*	date
la figue	*lah feeg*	fig
les fraises	*lay frehz*	strawberries
les fraises des bois	*lay frehz day bwah*	wild strawberries
les framboises	*lay frahn-bwahz*	raspberries
les groseilles	*lay groh-sehy*	red currants

la limette	*lah lee-meht*	lime
la mandarine	*lah mah<u>n</u>-dah-reen*	tangerine
le melon	*luh muh-loh<u>n</u>*	melon
les mûres	*lay mewr*	mulberries
les myrtilles	*lay meer-tee*	blueberries
l'orange	*loh-rah<u>n</u>zh*	orange
la noix de coco	*lah nwah duh koh-koh*	coconut
le pamplemousse	*luh pah<u>n</u>-pluh-mooss*	grapefruit
la pêche	*lah pehsh*	peach
la poire	*lah pwahr*	pear
la pomme	*lah pohm*	apple
la prune	*lah prewn*	plum
le pruneau	*luh prew-noh*	prune
le raisin	*luh reh-za<u>n</u>*	grape
le raisin sec	*luh reh-za<u>n</u> sehk*	raisin
l'amande (f.)	*lah-mah<u>n</u>d*	almond
le marron	*luh mah-roh<u>n</u>*	chestnut
la noisette	*lah nwah-zeht*	hazelnut
les noix	*lay nwah*	nuts

DESSERTS—SWEETS

- **Bavaroise:** A bavarian cream; mont-blanc is a bavarian cream made with chestnuts.
- **Beignets:** Fritters, often made from fruit such as apple.
- **Bombe:** An ice cream construction, often with different flavors and sometimes also with sherbet.

- **Charlotte:** An assemblage of sponge fingers and pudding; usually the sponge cake is used to line the dish and the pudding is in the center.

- **Crème caramel:** An egg custard served with a caramel sauce.

- **Crêpes:** Dessert crêpes, the most famous of which are **Crêpes Suzette**, made with orange flavoring and served flaming with Grand Marnier.

- **Gâteau:** An elaborate layer cake, made with thin layers of sponge cake and pastry cream, and decorated.

- **Mousse au chocolat:** An airy pudding made with chocolate, cream, eggs, and brandy, garnished with whipped cream.

- **Macédoine de fruits:** A fresh fruit salad.

- **Oeufs à la neige:** Soft meringue ovals served floating on a custard sauce.

- **Omelette norvégienne:** Baked Alaska.

- **Pâtisserie:** Pastry selection of any variety, including éclairs, millefeuilles, savarin, Saint-Honoré (creampuff cake).

- **Poires Belle-Hélène:** Poached pears, served with vanilla ice cream and chocolate sauce.

- **Profiteroles:** Cream puffs, served with chocolate sauce.

- **Soufflé:** There are an endless variety of sweet soufflés, the most famous one being the Grand Marnier soufflé.

- **Tarte:** An open-faced fruit pie, often made with apples or plums.

In addition, ice cream is a French favorite, as is sherbet and *granité* (fruit ice).

ice cream	**une glace**	*ewn glahss*
■ chocolate	**au chocolat**	*oh shoh-koh-lah*

■ vanilla	**à la vanille**	*ah lah vah-nee*
■ strawberry	**à la fraise**	*ah lah frehz*
sundae	**une coupe**	*ewn koop*
sherbet	**un sorbet**	*uh<u>n</u> sohr-beh*
fruit ice	**un granité**	*uh<u>n</u> grah-nee-tay*

SPECIAL CIRCUMSTANCES

I am on a diet.	**Je suis au régime.** *zhuh swee zo ray-zheem*
I'm a vegetarian.	**Je suis végétarien(ne).** *zhuh swee vay-zhay-tah-rya<u>n</u> (ryen)*
I can't eat anything made with _____.	**Je ne peux rien manger de cuisiné au (à la) _____.** *zhuh nuh puh rya<u>n</u> mah<u>n</u>-zhay duh kwee-zee-nay o (ah lah)*
I can't have _____.	**Je ne tolère _____.** *zhuh nuh toh-lehr*
■ any dairy products	**aucun produit laitier** *o-kuh<u>n</u> proh-dwee leh-tyay*
■ any alcohol	**aucun produit alcoolique** *o-kuh<u>n</u> proh-dwee ahl-koh-leek*
■ any saturated fats	**aucune matière grasse animale** *o-kewn mah-tyehr grahs ah-nee-mahl*
■ any seafood	**aucun fruit de mer** *o-kuh<u>n</u> frweed mehr*
I'm looking for a dish _____.	**Je cherche un plat _____.** *zhuh shehrsh uh<u>n</u> plah*
■ high in fiber	**riche en fibre** *reesh ah<u>n</u> feebr*
■ low in cholesterol	**léger en cholestérol** *lay-zhay ah<u>n</u> koh-lehs-tay-rohl*

■ low in fat   **léger en matières grasses**   *lay-zhay ah<u>n</u> mah-tyehr grahs*

■ low in sodium   **léger en sodium**   *lay-zhay ah<u>n</u> sohd-yuhm*

■ nondairy   **non-laitier**   *noh<u>n</u>-leh-tyay*

■ salt-free   **sans sel**   *sah<u>n</u> sehl*

■ sugar-free   **sans sucre**   *sah<u>n</u> sewkr*

■ without artificial coloring   **sans colorant**   *sah<u>n</u> koh-loh-rah<u>n</u>*

■ without preservatives   **sans conservateurs**   *sah<u>n</u> koh<u>n</u>-sehr-vah-tuhr*

BEVERAGES

Waiter, please bring me _____.   **Monsieur (Garçon), apportez-moi** _____.   *muh-ssyuh (gahr-son) ah-pohr-tay mwah*

coffee   **du café**   *dew kah-fay*

■ (decaffeinated)   **décaféiné**   *day-kah-fay-ee-nay*

■ with milk (morning only)   **du café au lait**   *dew kah-fay oh leh*

■ espresso   **du café-express**   *dew kah-fay ehkss-prehss*

■ with cream   **du café-crème**   *dew kah-fay krehm*

■ black coffee   **du café noir**   *dew kah-fay nwahr*

■ decaffeinated coffee   **du café decaféiné**   *dew kah-fay day-kah-fay-ee-nay*

■ iced coffee   **du café glacé**   *dew kah-fay glah-ssay*

cider (alcoholic)   **du cidre**   *dew see-druh*

juice   **du jus de fruits**   *dew zhew duh frwee*

lemonade   **de la citronnade**   *duh lah see-troh-nahd*

milk	**du lait**	*dew leh*
■ cold	**froid**	*frwah*
■ hot	**chaud**	*shoh*
■ milk shake	**un frappé**	*uhn frah-pay*
orangeade	**une orangeade**	*ewn oh-rahn-zhahd*
punch	**un punch**	*uhn puhnsh*
soda	**un soda**	*uhn soh-dah*
tea	**un thé**	*uhn tay*
■ with milk	**au lait**	*oh leh*
■ with lemon	**au citron**	*oh see-trohn*
■ with sugar	**sucré**	*sew-kray*
■ iced	**glacé**	*glah-ssay*
water	**de l'eau (f.)**	*duh loh*
■ cold	**de l'eau fraîche**	*duh loh frehsh*
■ ice	**de l'eau glacée**	*duh loh glah-ssay*
■ mineral	**de l'eau minérale**	*duh loh mee-nay-rahl*
■ with carbonation	**gazeuse**	*gah-zuhz*
■ without carbonation	**plate**	*plaht*

SETTLING UP

The check, please.	**L'addition, s'il vous plaît.**	*lah-dee-ssyohn seel voo pleh*
Separate checks.	**Des additions séparées.**	*day zah-dee-ssoyhn say-pah-ray*
Is the service (tip) included?	**Le service est compris?**	*luh sehr-veess eh kohn-pree*
I didn't order this.	**Je n'ai pas commandé ceci.**	*zhuh nay pah koh-mahn-day suh-ssee*
I think there's a a mistake.	**Je crois qu'il y a une erreur.**	*zhuh krwah keel yah ewn ehr-ruhr*

This is for you. **Ceci est pour vous.** *suh-ssee eh poor voo*

APÉRITIFS AND WINES

APÉRITIFS

Most French people prefer to drink an apéritif before a meal rather than a cocktail. An apéritif is an appetite stimulant, and can be a variety of drinks, ranging from a simple vermouth or vermouth mixed with a liqueur (such as cassis), to a distilled drink such as Cynar, made from artichoke hearts. Among the most popular are:

Byrrh **Dubonnet** **Saint-Raphaël**	wine- and brandy-based, flavored with herbs and bitters
Pernod **Ricard**	anise-based, licorice-flavored
Vermouth	fortified wine made from red or white grapes
Cynar	bitter tasting, distilled from artichoke hearts

WINE

The high quality of the soil and the moderate climate have given French vineyards their historically unique position among wine-producing countries. Wine served with meals follows a progression from the light white wines to richer, heartier reds. (One wouldn't drink a Mâcon after a Pommard, or a Bordeaux after a Burgundy.)

White wines and rosés are served very cold (52°F). Beaujolais, although red, should be lightly chilled. Bordeaux is served at room temperature (62°F), Burgundy just above room temperature. Sweet wines should be chilled, and Champagne iced. The chart below will help you select a wine to suit your tastes and your food.

wine	**le vin**	*luh van*
■ red wine	**le vin rouge**	*luh van roozh*
■ rosé	**le vin rosé**	*luh van roh-zay*
■ sparkling wine	**le vin mousseux**	*luh van moo-ssuh*
■ sherry	**un sherry**	*uhn sheh-ree*
■ white wine	**le vin blanc**	*luh van blahn*

MEETING PEOPLE

SMALL TALK

Where are you from?	**D'où êtes-vous?** *doo eht voo*
Do you live here?	**Habitez-vous ici?** *ah-bee-tay voo zee-ssee*
What is your name, address, and phone number?	**Quelles sont vos coordonnées?** *kehl sohn voh koh-ohr-doh-nay*
I am _____.	**Je suis _____.** *zhuh swee*
■ from the United States	**des États-Unis** *day zay-tah zew-nee*
■ from England	**d'Angleterre** *dahn-gluh-tehr*
■ from Canada	**du Canada** *dew kah-nah-dah*
■ from Australia	**d' Australie** *dohss-trah-lee*
I like France (Paris) very much.	**J'aime beaucoup la France (Paris).** *zhehm boh-koo lah frahnss (pah-ree)*
How long will you be staying?	**Combien de temps resterez-vous ici?** *kohn-byan duh than rehss-tray voo zee-ssee*
I'll stay for a few days (a week).	**Je resterai quelques jours (une semaine).** *zhuh rehss-tray kehl-kuh zhoor (ewn suh-mehn)*

Where are you staying?	**Où restez-vous?**	*oo rehss-tay voo*
What do you think of _____?	**Que pensez-vous de _____?**	*kuh pahn-ssay voo duh*
I (don't) like it very much.	**Je (ne) l'aime (pas) beaucoup.**	*zhuh (nuh) lehm (pah) boh-koo*
I think it's very _____.	**Je pense qu'il (qu'elle) est _____.**	*zhuh pahnss keel (kehl) eh*
■ beautiful	**beau (belle)**	*boh (behl)*
■ interesting	**intéressant(e)**	*an-tay-reh-ssahn(t)*
■ magnificent	**magnifique**	*mah-nyee-feek*
■ wonderful	**formidable**	*fohr-mee-dah-bluh*

GREETINGS AND INTRODUCTIONS

May I introduce _____?	**Je peux vous présenter _____?**	*zhuh puh voo pray-zahn-tay*
■ my family	**ma famille**	*mah fah-meey*
■ my brother	**mon frère**	*mohn frehr*
■ my father	**mon père**	*mohn pehr*
■ my friend	**mon ami(e)**	*mohn nah-mee*
■ my boyfriend	**mon petit ami**	*mohn puh-tee tah-mee*
■ my girlfriend	**ma petite amie**	*mah puh-teet tah-mee*
■ my husband	**mon mari**	*mohn mah-ree*
■ my mother	**ma mère**	*mah mehr*
■ my sister	**ma soeur**	*mah suhr*
■ my sweetheart	**mon(ma) fiancé(e)**	*mohn (mah) fee-yahn-ssay*
■ my wife	**ma femme**	*mah fahm*

Glad to meet you.	**Enchanté(e).**	*ahn-shahn-tay*
The pleasure is mine.	**Moi de même.**	*mwah duh mehm*
Allow me to introduce myself.	**Permettez-moi de me présenter.** *pehr-meh-tay mwah duh muh pray-zahn-tay*	
My name is _____.	**Je m'appelle _____.**	*zhuh mah-pehl*
I am a (an) _____	**Je suis _____.**	*zhuh swee*

DATING AND SOCIALIZING

Would you like to dance?	**Vous voulez danser?** *voo voo-lay dahn-ssay*
Yes, all right. With pleasure.	**Oui, d'accord. Avec plaisir.** *wee dah-kohr ah-vehk pleh-zeer*
Would you like a cigarette (a drink)?	**Voudriez-vous une cigarette (une boisson)?** *voo-dree-yay voo zewn see-gah-reht (ewn bwah-ssohn)*
Do you have a light?	**Avez-vous du feu?** *ah-vay voo dew fuh*
Do you mind if I smoke?	**Ça vous dérange si je fume?** *sah voo day-rahnzh see zhuh fewm*
May I take you home?	**Puis-je vous raccompagner chez vous?** *pweezh voo rah-kohn-pah-nyah shay voo*
May I call you?	**Puis-je vous téléphoner?** *pweezh voo tay-lay-foh-nay*

What is your telephone number?	**Quel est votre numéro de téléphone?** *kehl eh voh-truh new-may-roh duh tay-lay fohn*
Here's my telephone number (address).	**Voici mon numéro de téléphone (mon adresse).** *vwah-ssee mohn new-may-roh duh tay-lay fohn (mohn nah-drehss)*
You must visit us.	**Vous devez nous rendre visite.** *voo duh-vay noo rahn-druh vee-zeet*
Are you free tomorrow?	**Etes-vous libre demain?** *eht voo lee-bruh duh-man*
Are you free this evening?	**Etes-vous libre ce soir?** *eht voo lee-bruh suh swahr*
Would you like to go out together?	**Voudriez-vous sortir ensemble?** *voo-dree-yay voo sohr-teer ahn-sahn-bluh*
I'll wait for you in front of the hotel.	**Je vous attendrai devant l'hôtel.** *zhuh voo zah-tahn-dray duh-vahn loh-tehl*
I'll pick you up at your house (hotel).	**Je viendrai vous prendre chez vous (à votre hôtel).** *zhuh vyan-dray voo prahn-druh shay voo (ah voh-truh oh-tehl)*

SAYING GOOD-BYE

Nice to have met you.	**(Je suis) enchanté(e) d'avoir fait votre connaissance.** *(zhuh sweez) ahn-shahn-tay dah-vwahr feh voh-truh koh-neh-ssahnss*
The pleasure is mine.	**Le plaisir est partagé.** *luh pleh-zeer eh pahr-tah-zhay*

Regards to _____. **Mon meilleur souvenir à _____.**
mohn meh-yuhr soo-vuh-neer ah

SHOPPING

GOING SHOPPING

I'd like to go shopping today. **Je voudrais aller faire des courses aujourd'hui.** *zhuh voo-dreh zah-lay fehr day koorss oh-zhoor-dwee*

Where is _____? **Où se trouve _____?** *oo suh troov*

■ a bakery **une boulangerie** *ewn boo-lahnzh-ree*

■ a bookstore **une librairie** *ewn lee-breh-ree*

■ a butcher **une boucherie** *ewn boosh-ree*

■ a camera shop **un magasin d'appareils-photo** *uhn mah-gah-zan dah-pah-rehy foh-toh*

■ a candy store **une confiserie** *ewn kohn-feess-ree*

■ a clothing store **un magasin de vêtements** *uhn mah-gah-zan duh veht-mahn*

  for children's clothes **pour enfants** *poor ahn-fahn*

  for men **pour hommes** *poor ohm*
  for women **pour femmes** *poor fahm*

■ a delicatessen **une charcuterie** *ewn shahr-kew-tree*

■ a department store **un grand magasin** *uhn grahn mah-gah-zan*

■ a drugstore **une pharmacie** *ewn fahr-mah-ssee*

■ a florist **un fleuriste** *uhn fluh-reesst*

■ a gift (souvenir) shop	**un magasin de souvenirs** *uhn mah-gah-zan duh soov-neer*
■ a grocery store	**une épicerie** *ewn ay-peess-ree*
■ a hardware store	**une quincaillerie** *ewn kahn-kahy-ree*
■ a jewelry store	**une bijouterie** *ewn bee-zhoo-tree*
■ a liquor store	**un magasin de vins et spiritueux** *uhn mah-gah-zan duh van ay spee-ree-tew-uh*
■ a newsstand	**un kiosque à journaux** *uhn kee-ohsk ah zhoor-noh*
■ an optician	**un opticien** *uhn nohp-tee-ssyan*
■ a record store	**un magasin de disques** *uhn mah gah-zan duh deessk*
■ a shoemaker	**un cordonnier** *uhn kohr-doh-nyay*
■ a shoe store	**un magasin de chaussures** *uhn mah-gah-zan duh shoh-ssewr*
■ a supermarket	**un supermarché** *uhn sew-pehr-mahr-shay*
■ a tobacco shop	**un bureau de tabac** *uhn bew-roh duh tah-bah*
■ a toy store	**un magasin de jouets** *uhn mah-gah-zan duh zhoo-eh*
■ a watchmaker	**un horloger** *uhn nohr-lohzh-yay*
■ a wine merchant	**un négociant en vins** *uhn nay-gohss-yahn ahn van*

BOOKS

Where is the best (biggest) bookstore here?	**Où se trouve la meilleure (la plus grande) librairie par ici?** *oo suh troov lah meh-yuhr (lah plew grahnd) lee-breh-ree pahr ee-ssee*

I'm looking for a copy of _____.	**Je cherche un exemplaire de _____.** *zhuh shehrsh uhn nehg-zahn-plehr duh*
The author of the book is _____.	**L'auteur du livre est _____.** *loh-tuhr dew lee-vruh eh*
I don't know the title (author).	**Je ne sais pas le titre (le nom de l'auteur).** *zhuh nuh seh pah luh tee-truh (le nohn duh loh-tuhr)*
I'm just looking.	**Je regarde tout simplement.** *zhuh ruh-gahrd too san-pluh-mahn*
Do you have books (novels) in English?	**Avez-vous des livres (des romans) en anglais?** *ah-vay voo day lee-vruh (day roh-mahn) ahn ahn-gleh*
I would like _____.	**Je voudrais _____.** *zhuh voo-dreh*
■ a guidebook	**un guide touristique** *uhn geed too-reess-teek*
■ a map of the city	**un plan de la ville** *uhn plahn duh lah veel*
■ a pocket dictionary	**un dictionnaire de poche** *uhn deek-ssyoh-nehr duh pohsh*
■ a French-English dictionary	**un dictionnaire français-anglais** *uhn deek-ssyoh-nehr frahn-sseh ahn-gleh*

CLOTHING

Where is the _____ department?	**Où est le rayon des _____.** *oo eh luh reh-yohn day*
Would you please show me _____?	**Veuillez me montrer?** *vuh-yay muh mohn-tray*
■ a bathing suit	**un maillot de bain** *uhn mah-yoh duh ban*

■ a belt	**une ceinture**	*ewn san-tewr*
■ a blouse	**un chemisier**	*uhn shuh-mee-zyay*
■ boots	**des bottes (f.)**	*day boht*
■ a bra	**un soutien-gorge**	*uhn soo-tyan gohrzh*
■ a dress	**une robe**	*ewn rohb*
■ an evening gown	**une robe du soir**	*ewn rohb duh swahr*
■ gloves	**des gants (m.)**	*day gahn*
■ handkerchiefs	**des mouchoirs**	*day moo-shwahr*
■ a hat	**un chapeau**	*uhn shah-poh*
■ a jacket	**un veston**	*uhn vehss-tohn*
■ jeans	**un jean**	*uhn zheen*
■ a jogging suit	**un survêt, un jogging**	*uhn sewr-veh uhn zhoh-geeng*
■ an overcoat	**un manteau/pardessus**	*uhn mahn-toh/pahr-duh-ssew*
■ pajamas	**un pyjama**	*uhn pee-zhah-mah*
■ panties (women)	**un slip**	*uhn sleep*
■ pants	**un pantalon**	*uhn pahn-tah-lohn*
■ pantyhose	**des collants**	*day koh-lahn*
■ a raincoat	**un imperméable**	*uhn nan-pehr-may-ah-bluh*
■ a robe	**une robe de chambre**	*ewn rohb duh shahn-bruh*
■ sandals	**des sandales (f.)**	*day sahn-dahl*
■ a scarf	**une écharpe**	*ewn ay-shahrp*
■ a shirt	**une chemise**	*ewn shuh-meez*
■ shoes	**des chaussures (f.)**	*day shoh-ssewr*
■ shorts (briefs)	**un caleçon**	*ewn kahl-ssohn*
■ a skirt	**une jupe**	*ewn zhewp*
■ a slip	**un jupon**	*uhn zhew-pohn*
■ slippers	**des pantoufles (f.)**	*day pahn-too-fluh*

■ sneakers	**des baskets (f.)**	*day bahs-keht*
	des tennis (f.)	*day teh-nees*
■ socks	**des chaussettes**	*day shoh-sseht*
■ stockings	**des bas**	*day bah*
■ a suit	**un complet** (for men)/**un tailleur** (for women)	*uhn kohn-pleh/uhn tah-yuhr*
■ a sweater	**un chandail**	*uhn shahn-dahy*
	un pull	*uhn pewl*
■ a T-shirt	**un tee-shirt**	*uhn tee-shehrt*
■ a tie	**une cravate**	*ewn krah-vaht*
■ an umbrella	**un parapluie**	*unn pah-rah-plwee*
■ an undershirt (T-shirt)	**un sous-vêtement**	*uhn soo veht-mahn*
■ a vest	**un gilet**	*uhn zhee-leh*
■ a wallet	**un portefeuille**	*uhn pohr-tuh-fuhy*
I'd like short (long) sleeves.	**Je voudrais les manches courtes (longues).**	*zhuh voo-dreh lay mahnsh koort (lohng)*
■ sleeveless	**sans manches**	*sahn mahnsh*
Do you have anything _____?	**Avez-vous quelque chose _____?**	*ah-vay voo kehl-kuh shohz*
■ else	**d'autre**	*doh-truh*
■ larger	**de plus grand**	*duh plew grahn*
■ smaller	**de plus petit**	*duh plew puh-tee*
■ longer	**de plus long**	*duh plew lohn*
■ shorter	**de plus court**	*duh plew koor*
■ more (less) expensive	**de plus (moins) cher**	*duh plew (mwan) shehr*
■ of better quality	**de meilleure qualité**	*duh meh-yuhr kah-lee-tay*
■ cheaper	**de moins cher**	*duh mwan shehr*

I don't like the color.	**Je n'aime pas la couleur.**	*zhuh nehm pah lah koo-luhr*

Do you have it in _____?
L'avez-vous en _____? *lah-vay voo zahn*

- beige   **beige**   *behzh*
- black   **noir**   *nwahr*
- blue   **bleu**   *bluh*
- brown   **brun/marron**   *bruhn/mah-rohn*
- gray   **gris**   *gree*
- green   **vert**   *vehr*
- navy blue   **bleu marine**   *bluh mah-reen*
- orange   **orange**   *oh-rahnzh*
- pink   **rose**   *rohze*
- purple   **mauve**   *mohv*
- red   **rouge**   *roozh*
- white   **blanc**   *blahn*
- yellow   **jaune**   *zhohn*

I prefer a lighter (darker) color.
Je préfère une couleur plus claire (foncée). *zhuh pray-fehr ewn koo-luhr plew klehr (fohn-ssay)*

ELECTRIC APPLIANCES

Electric current in the U.S. is 110V AC, whereas in France it is 220V AC. Unless your electric shaver or alarm clock is able to handle both currents, you will need to purchase an adaptor. When making a purchase, please be aware that *some* French products are engineered to work with either system whereas others will require an adaptor. When making a purchase, be careful to check the warranty to ensure that the product is covered internationally.

FOOD AND HOUSEHOLD ITEMS

I'd like _____.

Je voudrais _____. *zhuh voo-dreh*

Could you give me _____.

Pourriez-vous me donner _____.
poo-ree-yay voo muh doh-nay

■ a bar of soap

une savonnette *ewn sah-voh-neht*

■ a bottle of juice

une bouteille de jus de fruits
ewn boo-tehy duh zhew duh frwee

■ a box of cereal

une boîte de céréales *ewn bwaht duh say-ray-ahl*

■ a can of tomato sauce

une boîte de sauce-tomate *ewn bwaht duh sohss toh-maht*

■ a dozen eggs

une douzaine d'oeufs *ewn doo-zehn duh*

■ a jar of coffee

un bocal de café *uhn boh-kal duh kah-fay*

■ a kilo (2.2 lbs.) of potatoes

un kilo de pommes de terre
uhn kee-loh duh pohm duh tehr

■ a half-kilo of butter

un demi-kilo de beurre *uhn duh-mee kee-loh duh buhr*

■ 200 grams (about $\frac{1}{2}$ pound) of cookies

deux cents grammes de biscuits
duh sahn grahm duh beess-kwee

■ a hundred grams of bologna

cent grammes de mortadelle
sahn grahm duh mohr-tah-dehl

■ a half-kilo (1.1 lbs.) of cherries

un demi-kilo de cerises *uhn duh-mee kee-loh duh suh-reez*

■ a liter (quart) of milk

un litre de lait *uhn lee-truh duh leh*

■ a package of candies

un paquet de bonbons *uhn pah-keh duh bohn-bohn*

■ $\frac{1}{4}$ pound of cheese	**cent grammes de fromage** *sahn grahm duh froh-mahzh*
■ a quart of milk	**un litre de lait** *uhn lee-truh duh leh*
■ a roll of toilet paper	**un rouleau de papier hygiénique** *uhn roo-loh duh pah-pyay ee-zhyay-neek*
■ a kilo of oranges	**un kilo d'oranges** *uhn kee-loh doh-rahnzh*

JEWELRY

I'd like to see ____.	**Je voudrais voir ____.** *zhuh voo-dreh vwahr*
■ a bracelet	**un bracelet** *uhn brahss-leh*
■ a brooch, a pin	**une broche** *ewn brohsh*
■ a chain	**une chaînette** *ewn sheh-neht*
■ a charm	**un porte-bonheur** *uhn pohrt boh-nuhr*
■ some earrings	**des boucles d'oreille** *day boo-kluh doh-rehy*
■ a necklace	**un collier** *uhn koh-lyay*
■ a ring	**une bague** *ewn bahg*
an engagement ring	**une bague de fiançailles** *ewn bahg duh fee-ahn-ssahy*
a wedding ring	**une alliance** *ewn ah-lee-ahnss*
■ a watch (digital)	**une montre (digitale)** *ewn mohn-truh (dee-zhee-tahl)*
Is this ____?	**Est-ce ____?** *ehss*
■ gold	**en or** *ahn nohr*
■ platinum	**en platine** *ahn plah-teen*
■ silver	**en argent** *ahn nahr-zhahn*

■ stainless steel	**en acier inoxydable** *ahn nah-ssyay ee-nohk-ssee-dah-bluh*
■ solid gold	**en or massif** *ahn nohr mah-sseef*
■ gold-plated?	**en plaqué or?** *ahn plah-kay ohr*
How many carats is it?	**Combien de carats y a-t-il?** *kohn byan duh kah-rah ee ah teel*
What is that stone?	**Quelle est cette pierre?** *kehl eh seht pyehr*
I would like _____.	**Je voudrais _____.** *zhuh voo-dreh*
■ an amethyst	**une améthyste** *zewn ah-may-teesst*
■ an aquamarine	**une aigue-marine** *zewn ehg mah-reen*
■ a diamond	**un diamant** *zuhn dee-ah-mahn*
■ an emerald	**une émeraude** *zewn aym-rohd*
■ ivory	**un ivoire** *zuhn nee-vwahr*
■ jade	**un jade** *zuhn zhahd*
■ onyx	**un onyx** *zuhn oh-neeks*
■ pearls	**des perles** *day pehrl*
■ a ruby	**un rubis** *zuhn rew-bee*
■ a sapphire	**un saphir** *zuhn sah-feer*
■ a topaz	**une topaze** *zewn toh-pahz*
■ turquoise	**une turquoise** *zewn tewr-kwahz*
How much is it?	**Cela coûte combien?** *suh-lah koot kohn-byan*
I'll take it.	**Je le (la) prends.** *zhuh luh (lah) prahn*

AUDIOVISUAL EQUIPMENT

Is there a record shop around here?	**Il y a un magasin de disques par ici?** *eel yah uhn mah-gah-zan duh deessk pahr ee-ssee*
Do you sell _____?	**Vendez-vous _____?** *vahn-day voo*
■ cassettes	**des cassettes** *day kah-seht*
■ CDs	**des CDs** *day say-day*
■ records	**des disques** *day deessk*
Do you have the songs of _____?	**Avez-vous les chansons de _____?** *ah-vay voo lay shahn-sohn duh*
Do you have the latest hits of _____?	**Avez-vous les derniers succès de _____?** *ah-vay-voo lay dehr-nyah sewk-sseh duh*
Is it recorded digitally?	**Est-ce un enregistrement digital?** *ehs uhn ahn-reh-zheess-truh-mahn dee-zhee-tahl*
Where is the _____ section?	**Où est le rayon de _____?** *oo eh luh reh-yohn duh*
■ blues	**blues** *blewz*
■ classical music	**la musique classique** *lah mew-zeek klah-sseek*
■ folk music	**la musique folklorique** *lah mew-zeek fohl-kloh-reek*
■ jazz	**du jazz** *dew zhahz*
■ French music	**la musique française** *lah mew-zeek frahn-ssehz*
■ opera	**l'opéra (m.)** *loh-pay-rah*
■ pop music	**la musique pop** *lah mew-zeek pohp*
■ rock music	**la musique rock** *lah mew-zeek ruhk*

NEWSSTAND

Do you carry newspapers (magazines) in English?	**Avez-vous des journaux (magazines) en anglais?** *ah-vay voo day zhoor-noh (mah-gah-zeen) ahn nahn-gleh*
How much is it?	**C'est combien?** *seh kohn-byan*
I'd like _____.	**Je voudrais _____.** *zhuh voo-dreh*
■ a daily	**un quotidien** *zuhn koh-tee-dyan*
■ a weekly	**un hebdomadaire** *zuhn ehb-doh-mah-dehr*
■ a monthly	**un mensuel** *zuhn mahn-ssew-ehl*
I'd like to buy some postcards.	**Je voudrais acheter des cartes postales.** *zhuh voo-dreh zahsh-tay day kahrt pohss-tahl*
Do you have stamps?	**Avez-vous des timbres?** *ah-vay voo day tan-bruh*

PHOTOGRAPHIC SUPPLIES

Where is there a camera shop?	**Il y a un magasin de photos où?** *eel yah uhn mah-gah-zan duh foh-toh oo*
Do you develop film here?	**Développez-vous les films ici?** *day-vloh-pay voo lay feelm ee-ssee*
How much does it cost for one roll?	**Ça coûte combien le développement d'une pellicule?** *sah koot kohn-byan luh day-vlohp-mahn dewn peh-lee-kewl*

I have two rolls.	**J'ai deux pellicules.**	*zhay duh peh-lee-kewl*

I want _____.	**Je voudrais _____.** *zhuh voo-dreh*

■ a print of each with a glossy finish
une épreuve de chacune sur papier brillant *zewn ay-pruhv duh shah-kewn sewr pah-pyay bree-yahn*

with a matte finish
sur papier mat *sewr pah-pyay maht*

■ an enlargement
un agrandissement *zuhn nah-grahn-deess-mahn*

I want a roll of 24 (36) exposures of color (black and white) film.
Je voudrais une pellicule de vingt-quatre (trente-six) en couleur (noir et blanc). *zhuh voo-dreh zewn peh-lee-kewl duh van-kah-truh (trahn-seess) ahn koo-luhr (nwahr ay blahn)*

■ for slides
pour diapositives *poor dee-ah-poh-zee-teev*

■ a film pack, number . . .
une cartouche, numéro . . . *ewn kahr-toosh, new-may-roh*

When can I pick up the pictures?
Quand puis-je venir chercher les photos? *kahn pweezh vuh-neer shehr-shay lay foh-toh*

Do you sell cameras?
Vendez-vous des appareils? *vahn-day voo day zah-pah-rehy*

I want an expensive (inexpensive) (disposable) camera.
Je cherche un appareil cher (pas très cher) (jetable) *zhuh shehrsh uhn nah-pah-rehy shehr (pah treh shehr) (zheh-tah-bluh)*

GIFT SHOP

I'd like _____.	**Je voudrais _____.** *zhuh voo-dreh*
■ a pretty gift	**un joli cadeau** *zuhn zhoh-lee kah-doh*
■ a small gift	**un petit cadeau** *zuhn puh-tee kah-doh*
■ a souvenir	**un souvenir** *zuhn soov-neer*
It's for _____.	**C'est pour _____.** *seh poor*
Could you suggest something?	**Pourriez-vous me suggérer quelque chose?** *poo-ree-yay voo muh sewg-zhay-ray kehl-kuh shohz*
Would you show me your selection of _____?	**Voudriez-vous me montrer votre choix de _____?** *voo-dree-yay voo muh mohn-tray voh-truh shwah duh*
■ blown glass	**verre soufflé** *vehr soo-flay*
■ carved objects	**objets sculptés** *ohb-zheh skewl-tay*
■ cut crystal	**cristal taillé** *kreess-tahl tah-yay*
■ dolls	**poupées** *poo-pay*
■ earthenware (pottery)	**poterie** *poh-tree*
■ fans	**éventails** *ay-vahn-tahy*
■ jewelry	**bijouterie** *bee-zhoo-tree*
■ lace	**dentelles** *dahn-tehl*
■ leather goods	**objets en cuir** *ohb-zheh ahn kweer*
■ liqueurs	**liqueurs** *lee-kuhr*
■ musical instruments	**instruments de musique** *an-strew-mahn duh mew-zeek*
■ perfumes	**parfums** *pahr-fuhn*

- pictures **tableaux** *tah-bloh*
- posters **affiches** *ah-feesh*
- religious articles **articles religieux** *ahr-tee-kluh ruh-lee-zhuh*

I don't want to spend more than ____ francs.
Je ne voudrais pas dépenser plus de ____ francs. *zhuh nuh voo-dreh pah day-pahn-ssay plew duh ____ frahn*

STATIONERY

I want to buy ____.
Je voudrais acheter ____. *zhuh voo-dreh zahsh-tay*

- a ball-point pen **un stylo à bille** *uhn stee-loh ah bee*
- a deck of cards **un paquet de cartes** *uhn pah-keh duh kahrt*
- envelopes **des enveloppes** *day zahn-vlohp*
- an eraser **une gomme** *ewn gohm*
- glue **de la colle** *duh lah kohl*
- a notebook **un cahier** *uhn kah-yay*
- paper **du papier** *dew pah-pyay*
- pencils **des crayons** *day kreh-yohn*
- a pencil sharpener **un taille-crayon** *uhn tahy kreh-yohn*
- a ruler **une règle** *ewn reh-gluh*
- Scotch tape **une bande adhésive (du scotch)** *ewn bahnd ahd-ay-zeev (dew skohtsh)*
- some string **de la ficelle** *duh lah fee-ssehl*
- stationery **du papier à lettres** *dew pah-pyay ah leh-truh*

■ wrapping paper	**du papier d'emballage**	*dew pah-pyay dahn-bah-lahzh*
■ a writing pad	**un bloc**	*uhn blohk*

TOBACCO SHOP

A pack (carton) of cigarettes, please.	**Un paquet (une cartouche) de cigarettes, s'il vous plaît.** *uhn pah-keh (ewn kahr-toosh) duh see-gah-reht seel voo pleh*
■ filtered	**avec filtre** *ah-vehk feel-truh*
■ unfiltered	**sans filtre** *sahn feel-truh*
■ menthol	**mentholées** *mahn-toh-lay*
■ king-size	**long format** *lohn fohr-mah*
Are these cigarettes (very) strong (mild)?	**Ces cigarettes sont elles (très) fortes (douces)?** *say see-gah-reht sohn tehl (treh) fohrt (dooss)*
Do you have American cigarettes?	**Avez-vous des cigarettes américaines?** *ah-vay voo day see-gah-reht ah-may-ree-kehn*
What brands?	**Quelles marques?** *kehl mahrk*
Please give me a pack of matches also.	**Donnez-moi aussi une boîte d'allumettes, s'il vous plaît.** *doh-nay mwah oh-ssee ewn bwaht dah-lew-meht seel voo pleh*

TOILETRIES

Do you have _____?	**Avez-vous _____?**	*ah-vay voo*
■ a brush	**une brosse**	*ewn brohss*

■ cleansing cream	**une crème démaquillante**	*ewn krehm day-mah-kee-yahnt*
■ a comb	**un peigne**	*uhn peh-nyuh*
■ condoms	**des préservatifs**	*day pray-zehr-vah-teef*
■ (disposable) diapers	**des couches (disponibles)**	*day koosh (deess-poh-nee-bluh)*
■ emery boards	**des limes à ongles**	*day leem ah ohn-gluh*
■ eyeliner	**du traceur à paupières**	*dew trah-ssuhr ah poh-pyehr*
■ eyebrow pencil	**un crayon pour les yeux**	*uhn kreh-yohn poor lay zyuh*
■ eye shadow	**du fard à paupières**	*dew fahr ah poh-pyehr*
■ gel	**du gel coiffant**	*dew zhehl kwah-fahn*
■ hairspray	**de la laque**	*duh lah lahk*
■ lipstick	**du rouge à lèvres**	*dew roozh ah leh-vruh*
■ makeup	**du maquillage**	*dew mah-kee-yahzh*
■ mascara	**du mascara**	*dew mahss-kah-rah*
■ a mirror	**un miroir**	*uhn meer-wahr*
■ mousse	**de la mousse coiffante**	*duh lah mooss kwah-fahnt*
■ mouthwash	**de l'eau dentifrice**	*deh-loh dahn-tee-freess*
■ nail clippers	**un coupe-ongles**	*uhn koop ohn-gluh*
■ a nail file	**une lime à ongles**	*ewn leem ah ohn-gluh*

■ nail polish	**du vernis à ongles**	*dew vehr-nee ah ohn-gluh*
■ nail polish remover	**du dissolvant**	*dew dee-ssohl-vahn*
■ a prophylactic	**un préservatif**	*uhn pray-sehr-vah-teef*
■ a razor	**un rasoir**	*uhn rah-zwahr*
■ razor blades	**une lame de rasoir**	*ewn lahm duh rah-zwahr*
■ rouge	**du fard**	*dew fahr*
■ sanitary napkins	**des serviettes hygiéniques**	*day sehr-vyeht ee-zhyay-neek*
■ (cuticle) scissors	**des ciseaux**	*day see-zoh*
■ shampoo	**du shampooing**	*dew shahn-pwan*
■ shaving lotion	**la lotion à raser**	*lah loh-ssyohn ah rah-zay*
■ soap	**du savon**	*dew sah-vohn*
■ a sponge	**une éponge**	*ewn ay-pohnzh*
■ talcum powder	**du talc**	*dew tahlk*
■ tampons	**des tampons périodiques**	*day tahn-pohn pay-ree-oh-deek*
■ tissues	**des mouchoirs en papier**	*day moo-shwahr ahn pah-pyay*
■ toilet paper	**du papier hygiénique**	*dew pah-pyay ee-zhyay-neek*
■ a toothbrush	**une brosse à dents**	*ewn brohss ah dahnt*
■ toothpaste	**de la pâte dentifrice**	*duh lah paht dahn-tee-freess*
■ tweezers	**une pince à épiler**	*ewn panss ah ay-pee-lay*

PERSONAL CARE AND SERVICES

AT THE BARBER/BEAUTY SALON

Where is there a good _____?	**Où y a-t-il un bon _____?** *oo ee ah teel uhn bohn*
■ barber shop	**coiffeur?** *kwah-fuhr*
■ beauty salon	**salon de beauté** *sah-lohn duh boh-tay*
I'd like an appointment for (day) at (hour).	**Je voudrais prendre rendez-vous pour _____ à _____.** *zhuh voo-dreh prahndr rahn-day-voo poor _____ ah*
Do I have to wait long?	**Faut-il attendre long temps?** *foh teel ah-tahn-druh lohn-tahn*
I would like _____.	**Je voudrais _____.** *zhuh voo-dreh*
■ a color rinse	**un shampooing colorant** *uhn shahn-pwan koh-loh-rahn*
■ a facial massage	**un massage facial** *uhn mah-ssahzh fah-ssyahl*
■ a haircut	**une coupe de cheveux** *ewn koop duh shuh-vuh*
blunt	**en carré** *ahn kah-ray*
layered	**dégradée** *day-grah-day*
■ highlights	**des reflets** *day ruh-fleh*
■ a manicure	**une manucure** *ewn mah-new-kewr*
■ a pedicure	**une pédicurie** *ewn pay-dee-kew-ree*
■ a permanent	**une permanente** *ewn pehr-mah-nahnt*
■ a shampoo	**un shampooing** *uhn shahn-pwan*

■ a shave	**me faire raser**	*muh fehr rah-zay*
■ a tint	**des reflets**	*day ruh-fleh*
■ a touch-up	**une retouche**	*ewn ruh-toosh*
■ a trim	**une coupe**	*ewn koop*
■ a wash and set	**un shampooing et une mise en plis**	*uhn shahn-pwan ay ewn meez ahn plee*
■ a waxing	**une épilation**	*ewn ay-pee-lah-syohn*

I want it (very) short (long).	**Je les veux (très) courts (longs).**	*zhuh lay vuh (treh) koor (lohn)*
You can cut a little _____.	**Vous pouvez dégager un peu _____.**	*voo poo-vay day-gah-zhay uhn puh*
■ in back	**derrière**	*deh-ryehr*
■ in front	**devant**	*duh-vahn*
■ off the top	**dessus**	*duh-ssew*
■ on the sides	**aux côtés**	*oh koh-tay*
I part my hair _____.	**Je fais la raie _____.**	*zhuh feh lah ray*
■ on the left	**à gauche**	*ah gohsh*
■ on the right	**à droite**	*ah drwaht*
■ in the middle	**au milieu**	*oh meel-yuh*
I comb my hair straight back.	**Je me peigne en arrière.**	*zhuh muh peh-nyuh ahn nah-ryehr*
Cut a little bit more here.	**Coupez un peu plus ici.**	*koo-pay uhn puh plew ee-ssee*
That's enough.	**Ça suffit.**	*sah sew-fee*
It's fine that way.	**C'est parfait comme ça.**	*seh pahr-feh kohm sah*

I (don't) want _____.	**Je (ne) veux (pas de) _____.**	*zhuh (nuh) vuh (pah duh)*
■ hairspray	**la laque**	*lah lahk*
■ shampoo	**un shampooing**	*uhn shan-pwan*
■ lotion	**une lotion**	*ewn loh-ssyohn*

Trim my _____. **Rafraîchissez-moi _____.** *rah-freh-sshee-ssay mwah*

■ beard **la barbe** *lah bahrb*

■ moustache **la moustache** *lah mooss-tahsh*

■ sideburns **les favoris** *lay fah-voh-ree*

I'd like to look at myself in the mirror. **Je voudrais me regarder dans le miroir.** *zhuh voo-dreh muh ruh-gahr-day dahn luh meer-wahr*

How much do I owe you? **Je vous dois combien?** *zhuh voo dwah kohn-byan*

I'd like to see a color chart. **Je voudrais voir une échelle de teintes.** *zhuh voo-dreh vwahr ewn ay-shehl duh tant*

I want _____. **Je voudrais _____.** *zhuh voo-dreh*

■ auburn **auburn** *oh-buhrn*

■ black **noir** *nwahr*

■ (light) blond **blond (clair)** *blohn (klehr)*

■ brunette **brun** *bruhn*

■ a darker color **une teinte plus foncée** *ewn tant plew fohn-ssay*

■ a lighter color **une teinte plus claire** *ewn tant plew klehr*

■ the same color **la même couleur** *lah mehm koo-luhr*

LAUNDRY AND DRY CLEANING

Where is the nearest _____?	**Où est la _____ la plus proche?** *oo eh lah _____ lah plew prohsh*
■ laundry	**blanchisserie** *blahn-sheess-ree*
■ laundromat	**laverie automatique** *lah-vree oh-toh-mah-teek*
■ dry cleaner's	**teinturerie** *tahn-tew-ruh-ree*
I have a lot of clothes to be _____.	**J'ai beaucoup de vêtements à faire _____.** *zhay boh-koo duh veht-mahn ah fehr*
■ dry-cleaned	**nettoyer à sec** *neh-twah-yay ah sehk*
■ washed	**laver** *lah-vay*
■ mended	**réparer** *ray-pah-ray*
■ ironed	**repasser** *ruh-pah-ssay*
This isn't my laundry.	**Ce n'est pas ma lessive.** *suh neh pah mah lay-sseev*

SHOE REPAIRS

Put on (half) soles and rubber heels.	**Mettez les (demi-) semelles et les talons en caoutchouc.** *meh-tay lay (duh-mee) suh-mehl ay lay tah-lohn ahn kah-oo-tshoo*
I'd like to have my shoes shined (too).	**Je voudrais un cirage (aussi).** *zhuh voo-dreh zuhn see-rahzh (oh-ssee)*

WATCH REPAIRS

I need _____.	**Il me faut _____.**	*eel muh foh*
■ a battery	**une pile**	*tewn peel*
■ a crystal, glass	**un verre**	*tuhn vehr*
■ an hour hand	**une petite aiguille**	*tewn puh-teet ay-gwee*
■ a minute hand	**une aiguille des minutes**	*tewn ay-gwee day mee-newt*
■ a screw	**une vis**	*tewn veess*
■ a second hand	**une aiguille des secondes**	*tewn ay-gwee day suh-gohnd*
■ a watchband	**un bracelet de montre**	*tuhn brahs-leh duh mohn-truh*
Can you look at it?	**Pouvez-vous l'examiner?**	*poo-vay voo lehg-zah-mee-nay*
Can you clean it?	**Pouvez-vous la nettoyer?**	*poo-vay voo lah neh-twah-yay*
I dropped it.	**Je l'ai laissé tomber.**	*zhuh lay leh-ssay tohn-bay*
It's fast (slow).	**Cette montre avance (retarde).**	*seht mohn-truh ah-vahnss (ruh-tahrd)*
It's stopped.	**Elle s'est arrêtée.**	*ehl seh tah-reh-tay*

CAMERA REPAIRS

My camera doesn't work well.	**Mon appareil ne fonctionne pas bien.**	*mohn nah-pah-rehy nuh fohnk-ssyohn pah byan*
It fell (into the water).	**Il est tombé (dans l'eau).**	*eel eh tohn-bay (dahn loh)*

MEDICAL CARE

AT THE PHARMACY

Where is the nearest (all-night) pharmacy?	**Où se trouve la pharmacie de garde (de nuit) la plus proche?** *oo suh troov lah fahr-mah-ssee duh gahrd (duh nwee) lah plew prohsh*
At what time does the pharmacy open (close)?	**À quelle heure ouvre (ferme) la pharmacie?** *ah kehl uhr oo-vruh (fehrm) lah fahr-mah-ssee*
I need something for _____.	**Il me faut quelque chose pour _____.** *eel muh foh kehl-kuh shohz poor*
◼ a cold	**un rhume** *uhn rewm*
◼ constipation	**la constipation** *lah kohn-sstee-pah-ssyohn*
◼ a cough	**une toux** *ewn too*
◼ diarrhea	**la diarrhée** *lah dee-ah-ray*
◼ a fever	**une fièvre** *ewn fyeh-vruh*
◼ hay fever	**le rhume des foins** *luh rewm day fwan*
◼ a headache	**un mal de tête** *uhn mahl duh teht*
◼ insomnia	**l'insomnie** *lan-sohm-nee*
◼ the flu	**la grippe** *lah greep*
◼ nausea	**la nausée** *lah noh-zay*
◼ sunburn	**les coups de soleil** *lay koo duh soh-lehy*
◼ a toothache	**un mal de dents** *uhn mahl duh dahn*

an upset stomach	**les indigestions**	*lay zan-dee-zhehss-tyohn*
Is a prescription needed for the medicine?	**Faut-il avoir une ordonnance pour ce médicament?**	*foh-teel ah-vwahr ewn ohr-doh-nahnss poor suh may-dee-kah-mahn*
Can you fill this prescription for me now?	**Pourriez-vous me préparer cette ordonnance maintenant?**	*poo-ree-yay voo muh pray-pah-ray seht ohr-doh-nahnss mant-nahn*
It's an emergency.	**C'est urgent.**	*seh tewr-zhahn*
Can I wait for it?	**Puis-je l'attendre?**	*pweezh lah-tahn-druh*
How long will it take?	**Ça prendra combien de temps?**	*sah prahn-drah kohn-byan duh tahn*
When can I come for it?	**Quand puis-je venir la chercher?**	*kahn pweezh vuh-neer lah shehr-shay*
I would like _____.	**Je voudrais _____.**	*zhuh voo-dreh*
alcohol	**de l'alcool**	*duh lahl-kohl*
an antacid	**un anti-acide**	*zuhn nahn-tee ah-sseed*
an antiseptic	**un antiseptique**	*zuhn nahn-tee-ssehp-teek*
aspirins	**des aspirines**	*day zahss-pee-reen*
bandages	**des bandes**	*day bahnd*
Band-Aids	**des bandages**	*day bahn-dazh*
(absorbent) cotton	**du coton**	*dew koh-tohn*

■ cough drops	**des pastilles contre la toux** *day pahss-tee kohn-truh lah too*
■ cough syrup	**du sirop contre la toux** *dew see-roh kohn-truh lah too*
■ eardrops	**des gouttes pour les oreilles** *day goot poor lay zoh-rehy*
■ eyedrops	**des gouttes pour les yeux** *day goot poor lay zyuh*
■ iodine	**de la teinture d'iode** *duh lah tan-tewr dyohd*
■ a (mild) laxative	**un laxatif (léger)** *zuhn lahk-ssah-teef (lay-zhay)*
■ milk of magnesia	**le lait de magnésie** *luh leh duh mah-nyay-zee*
■ suppositories	**les suppositoires** *lay sew-poh-zee-twahr*
■ a thermometer	**un thermomètre** *uhn tehr-moh-meh-truh*
■ tranquilizers	**des tranquillisants** *day trahn-kee-lee-zahn*
■ vitamins	**des vitamines** *day vee-tah-meen*

DOCTORS

I don't feel well. I feel sick.	**Je ne me sens pas bien.** *zhuh nuh muh sahn pah byan*
I need a doctor.	**Il me faut un médecin.** *eel muh foh tuhn mayd-ssan*
Do you know a doctor who speaks English?	**Connaissez-vous un médecin qui parle anglais?** *koh-neh-ssay voo uhn mayd-ssan kee pahrl ahn-gleh*
Where is his office?	**Où se trouve son cabinet?** *oo suh troov sohn kah-bee-neh*

I have _____.	**J'ai _____.** *zhay*
an abscess	**un abcès** *uhn nahb-sseh*
a broken bone	**une fracture** *ewn frahk-tewr*
a bruise	**une contusion** *ewn kohn-tew-zyohn*
a burn	**une brûlure** *ewn brew-lewr*
the chills	**des frissons** *day free-ssohn*
a cold	**un rhume** *uhn rewm*
a chest cold	**une bronchite** *ewn brohn-sheet*
a head cold	**un rhume de cerveau** *uhn rewm duh sehr-voh*
cramps	**des crampes** *day krahnp*
a cut	**une coupure** *ewn koo-pewr*
diarrhea	**la diarrhée** *lah dee-ah-ray*
a fever	**de la fièvre** *duh lah fyeh-vruh*
a fracture	**une fracture** *ewn frahk-tewr*
a headache	**mal à la tête** *mahl ah lah teht*
an infection	**une infection** *ewn an-fehk-ssyohn*
a lump	**une grosseur** *ewn groh-ssuhr*
something in my eye	**quelque chose dans l'oeil** *kehl-kuh shohz dahn luhy*
a sore throat	**mal à la gorge** *mahl ah lah gohrzh*
a stomachache	**mal à l'estomac** *mahl ah lehss-toh-mah*
swelling	**une enflure** *ewn ahn-flewr*
a wound	**une blessure** *ewn bleh-ssewr*

I am constipated.	**Je suis constipé(e).** *zhuh swee kòhn-sstee-pay*
It hurts me here.	**J'ai mal ici.** *zhay mahl ee-ssee*
My whole body hurts.	**Tout mon corps me fait mal.** *too mohn kohr muh feh mahl*

My _____ hurts since (yesterday, two days ago, last week).	**J'ai mal _____ depuis (hier, deux jours, la semaine passée).** *zhay mahl duh-pwee (yehr duh zhoor lah suh-mehn pah-ssay)*
▪ ankle	**à la cheville** *ah lah shuh-vee*
▪ arm	**au bras** *oh brah*
▪ back	**au dos** *oh doh*
▪ chest	**à la poitrine** *ah lah pwah-treen*
▪ ear	**à l'oreille** *ah loh-rehy*
▪ elbow	**au coude** *oh kood*
▪ eyes	**aux yeux** *oh zyuh*
▪ face	**à la figure** *ah lah fee-gewr*
▪ finger	**au doigt** *oh dwah*
▪ foot	**au pied** *oh pyay*
▪ glands	**aux ganglions** *oh gah_n_-glee-yoh_n_*
▪ hand	**à la main** *ah lah ma_n_*
▪ head	**à la tête** *ah lah teht*
▪ hip	**à la hanche** *ah lah ah_n_sh*
▪ knee	**au genou** *oh zhuh-noo*
▪ leg	**à la jambe** *ah lah zhah_n_b*
▪ lip	**à la lèvre** *ah lah leh-vruh*
▪ mouth	**à la bouche** *ah lah boosh*
▪ neck	**au cou** *oh koo*
▪ nose	**au nez** *oh nay*
▪ shoulder	**à l'épaule** *ah lay-pohl*
▪ throat	**à la gorge** *ah lah gohrzh*
▪ thumb	**au pouce** *oh pooss*
▪ toe	**à l'orteil** *ah lohr-tehy*
▪ tooth	**aux dents** *oh dah_n_*
▪ wrist	**au poignet** *oh pwah-nyeh*
There is (no) _____ in my family.	**Il y a (Il n'y a pas) _____ dans ma famille.** *eel yah (eel nyah pah) _____ dah_n_ mah fah-mee*

- asthma **l'asthme (m.)** *lahs-muh*
- diabetes **la diabète** *lah dee-yah-beht*
- heart disease **la maladie cardiaque** *lah mah-lah-dee kahr-dyahk*

I'm (not) allergic to antibiotics.
Je (ne) suis (pas) allergique aux antibiotiques. *zhuh (nuh) swee (pah) zah-lehr-zheek oh zahn-tee-bee-oh-teek*

I have a pain in my chest.
J'ai une douleur à la poitrine. *zhay ewn doo-luhr ah lah pwah-treen*

I had a heart attack _____ year(s) ago.
J'ai eu une crise cardiaque il y a ___ ans. *zhay ew ewn kreez kahr-dyahk eel yah ___ ahn*

I'm taking this medicine.
Je prends ce médicament. *zhuh prahn suh may-dee-kah-mahn*

I'm pregnant.
Je suis enceinte. *zhuh zwee zahn-sant*

I feel faint.
Je vais m'évanouir. *zhuh veh may-vah-nweer*

I'm dizzy.
J'ai des vertiges. *zhay day vehr-teezh*

I feel weak.
Je me sens faible. *zhuh muh sahn feh-bluh*

I want to sit down for a while.
Je voudrais m'asseoir un moment. *zhuh voo-dreh mah-sswahr uhn moh-mahn*

I feel all right now.
Je vais bien maintenant. *zhuh veh byan mant-nahn*

I feel better.
Je vais mieux. *zhuh veh myuh*

I feel worse.	**Je me sens moins bien.** *zhuh muh sahn mwan byan*
Do I have _____?	**Est-ce que j'ai _____?** *ehss kuh zhay*
■ appendicitis	**l'appendicite** *lah-pahn-dee-sseet*
■ the flu	**la grippe** *lah greep*
■ tonsilitis	**une amygdalite** *ewn nah-meeg-dah-leet*
Is it serious (contagious)?	**C'est grave (contagieux)?** *seh grahv (kohn-tah-zhyuh)*
Do I have to go to the hospital?	**Dois-je aller à l'hôpital?** *dwahzh ah-lay ah loh-pee-tahl*
When can I continue my trip?	**Quand pourrai-je pour-suivre mon voyage?** *kahn poo-rayzh poor-swee-vruh mohn vwah-yahzh*

SPECIAL NEEDS

Where can I get _____?	**Où puis-je obtenir _____?** *oo pweezh ohb-tuh-neer*
■ a cane	**une canne** *ewn kahn*
■ crutches	**des béquilles (f.)** *day bay-kee*
■ a hearing aid	**un audiophone** *uhn noh-dyoh-fohn*
■ a walker	**un déambulateur** *uhn day-ahn-bew-lah-tuhr*
■ a wheelchair	**un fauteuil roulant** *uhn foh-tuhy roo-lahn*
What services are available for the handicapped?	**Quels services sont disponibles aux handicapés?** *kehl sehr-veess sohn deess-poh-nee-bluh oh zahn-dee-kah-pay*

IN THE HOSPITAL (ACCIDENTS)

Help!	**Au secours!** *oh suh-koor*
Help me, please.	**Aidez-moi, s'il vous plaît.** *eh-day mwah seel voo pleh*
Get a doctor, quick!	**Vite, appelez un médecin!** *veet ah-play uhn mayd-ssan*
Call an ambulance!	**Faites venir une ambulance!** *feht vuh-neer ewn ahn-bew-lahnss*
Take me (him, her) to the hospital.	**Emmenez-moi (le, la) à l'hôpital.** *ahn-muh-nay mwah (luh, lah) ah loh-pee-tahl*
I need first aid.	**J'ai besoin de premiers soins.** *zhay buh-zwan duh pruh-myay swan*
I fell.	**Je suis tombé(e).** *zhuh swee tohn-bay*
I burned myself.	**Je me suis brûlé(e).** *zhuh muh swee brew-lay*
I cut myself.	**Je me suis coupé(e).** *zhuh muh swee koo-pay*
I'm bleeding.	**Je saigne.** *zhuh seh-nyuh*
He's lost a lot of blood.	**Il a perdu beaucoup de sang.** *eel ah pehr-dew boh-koo duh sahn*
My leg is swollen.	**Ma jambe est enflée.** *mah zhahnb eh tahn-flay*

AT THE DENTIST

I have to go to the dentist.	**Il me faut aller chez le dentiste.** *eel muh foh tah-lay shay luh dahn-teesst*
Can you recommend a dentist?	**Pouvez-vous me recommander un dentiste?** *poo-vay voo muh ruh-koh-mahn-day uhn dahn-teesst*
I have a bad toothache.	**J'ai un mal de dents à tout casser. (J'ai une rage de dents.)** *zhay uhn mahl duh dahn ah too kah-ssay (zhay ewn rahzh duh dahn)*
What is your fee?	**Combien je vous dois?** *kohn-byan zhuh voo dwah*
I've lost a filling.	**J'ai perdu un plombage.** *zhay pehr-dew uhn plohn-bahzh*
I've broken a tooth.	**Je me suis cassé une dent.** *zhuh muh swee kah-ssay ewn dahn*
My gums hurt me.	**Les gencives me font mal.** *lay zhahn-sseev muh fohn mahl*
Is there an infection?	**Il y a une infection?** *eel yah ewn an-fehk-ssyohn*
Will you have to pull the tooth?	**Faut-il arracher la dent?** *foh teel ah-rah-shay lah dahn*
Can you fill it?	**Pouvez-vous l'obturer?** *poo-vay voo lohb-tew-ray*
Can you fix _____?	**Pouvez-vous réparer?** *poo-vay voo ray-pah-ray*
■ this bridge	**ce bridge** *suh breedzh*

■ this crown   **cette couronne**   *seht koo-rohn*

■ this denture   **ce dentier**   *suh dah<u>n</u>-tyay*

When should I come back?   **Quand faut-il revenir?**   *kah<u>n</u> foh-teel ruh-vuh-neer*

COMMUNICATIONS

POST OFFICE

I want to mail a letter.   **Je voudrais mettre cette lettre à la poste.** *zhuh voo-dreh meh-truh seht leh-truh ah lah pohsst*

Where's the post office?   **Où se trouve le bureau de poste?** *oo suh troov luh bew-roh duh pohsst*

Where's a mailbox?   **Où se trouve une boîte aux lettres?** *oo suh troov ewn bwaht oh leh-truh*

What is the postage on _____ to the United States?   **Quel est l'affranchissement _____ pour les États-Unis?** *kehl eh lah-frah<u>n</u>-sheess-mah<u>n</u> poor lay zay-tah zew-nee*

■ a letter   **d'une lettre**   *dewn leh-truh*

■ an air mail letter   **pour une lettre envoyée par avion** *poor ewn leh-truh ah<u>n</u>-vwah-yay pahr ah-vyoh<u>n</u>*

■ an insured letter   **pour une lettre recommandée** *poor ewn leh-truh ruh-koh-mah<u>n</u>-day*

■ a registered letter   **pour une lettre recommandée** *poor ewn leh-truh ruh-koh-mah<u>n</u>-day*

■ a special delivery letter   **pour une lettre par exprès**   *poor ewn leh-truh pahr ehkss-preh*

■ a package   **d'un colis**   *duh<u>n</u> koh-lee*

■ a postcard	**d'une carte postale** *dewn kahrt pohss-tahl*
When will it arrive?	**Quand arrivera-t-il (t-elle)?** *kah<u>n</u> tah-ree-vrah teel (tehl)*
Where is the _____ window?	**Où est le guichet _____?** *oo eh luh gee-sheh*
■ general delivery	**pour la poste restante** *poor lah pohsst rehss-tah<u>n</u>t*
■ money order	**pour les mandats-poste** *poor lay mah<u>n</u>-dah pohsst*
■ stamp	**pour les timbres-poste** *poor lay ta<u>n</u>-bruh pohsst*
Are there any letters for me?	**Il y a des lettres pour moi?** *eel yah day leh-truh poor mwah*
My name is _____.	**Je m'appelle _____.** *zhuh mah-pehl*
I'd like _____.	**Je voudrais _____.** *zhuh voo-dreh*
■ 10 postcards	**dix cartes postales** *dee kahrt pohss-tahl*
■ 5 (air mail) stamps	**cinq timbres (courrier aérien)** *sa<u>n</u>k tah<u>n</u>-bruh (koo-ryay ah-ay-rya<u>n</u>)*

TELEGRAMS

I'd like to send a telegram (night letter) to _____.	**Je voudrais envoyer un télégramme (une lettre-télégramme) à _____.** *zhuh voo-dreh zah<u>n</u>-vwah-yay uh<u>n</u> tay-lay-grahm (ewn leh-truh tay-lay-grahm) ah*
How much is it per word?	**Quel est le tarif par mot?** *kehl eh luh tah-reef pahr moh*

Where are the forms?	**Où sont les formulaires (imprimés)?** *oo sohn lay fohr-mew-lehr (an-pree-may)*
I want to send it collect.	**Je voudrais l'envoyer en P.C.V.** *zhuh voo-dreh lahn-vwah-yay ahn pay say vay*
When will it arrive?	**Il arrivera quand?** *eel ah-ree-vrah kahn*

TELEPHONES

Where is _____?	**Où y a-t-il _____?** *oo ee ah-teel*
■ a public telephone	**un téléphone public** *uhn tay-lay-fohn pew-bleek*
■ a telephone booth	**une cabine téléphonique** *ewn kah-been tay-lay-foh-neek*
■ a telephone directory	**un annuaire téléphonique** *uhn nah-new-ehr tay-lay-foh-neek*
May I use your phone?	**Puis-je me servir de votre téléphone?** *pweezh muh sehr-veer duh voh-truh tay-lay-fohn*
I want to make a _____.	**Je voudrais téléphoner _____.** *zhuh voo-dreh tay-lay-foh-nay*
■ local call	**en ville** *ahn veel*
■ long-distance call	**à l'extérieur** *ah lehkss-tay-ryuhr*
■ person-to-person call	**avec préavis** *ah-vehk pray-ah-vee*
How do I get the _____?	**Que fait-on pour _____?** *kuh feh-tohn poor*

■ operator **parler à la téléphoniste?** *pahr-lay ah lah tay-lay-foh-neesst*

■ area code **obtenir le code régional** *ohp-tuh-neer luh kohd ray-zhyohn-nahl*

My number is _____. **Mon numéro est _____.** *mohn new-may-roh eh*

I'd like to speak to _____. **Je voudrais parler à _____.** *zhuh voo-dreh pahr-lay ah*

Is Mr. _____ in? **Monsieur _____, est là?** *muh-ssyuh _____ eh lah*

This is _____. **Ici _____.** *ee-ssee*

Hello. **Allô.** *ah-loh*

Who is calling? **Qui est à l'appareil?** *kee eh tah lah-pah-rehy*

I can't hear. **Je ne peux pas vous entendre.** *zhuh nuh puh pah voo zahn-tahn-druh*

Speak louder. **Parlez plus fort.** *pahr-lay plew fohr*

Don't hang up. **Ne quittez pas.** *nuh kee-tay pah*

Do you have an answering machine? **Avez-vous un répondeur automatique?** *ah-vay voo uhn ray-pohn-duhr oh-toh-mah-teek*

I want to leave a message. **Je voudrais laisser un message.** *zhuh voo-dreh leh-ssay uhn meh-ssahzh*

FAXES

Do you have a fax machine?	**Avez-vous un fax?** *ah-vay voo uhn fahkss*
What is your fax number?	**Quel est le numéro de votre fax?** *kehl eh luh new-may-roh duh vohtr fahkss*
I'd like to send a fax.	**Je voudrais envoyer un fax.** *zhuh voo-dreh zahn-vwah-yay uhn fahkss*
May I fax this, please?	**Puis-je faxer ceci, s'il vous plaît?** *pweezh fahk-ssay suh-see seel voo pleh*
May I fax this letter (document) to you?	**Puis-je vous faxer cette lettre (ce document)?** *pweezh voo fahk-ssay seht lehtr (suh doh-kew-mahn)*
Fax it to me.	**Faxez-le (la) –moi.** *fahk-ssay-luh (lah) mwah.*
I didn't get your fax.	**Je n'ai pas reçu votre fax.** *zhuh nay pah ruh-sew vohtr fahkss.*
Did you receive my fax?	**Avez-vous reçu mon fax?** *ah-vay voo ruh-sew mohn fahkss*
Your fax is illegible.	**Votre fax n'est pas lisible.** *vohtr fahkss neh pah lee-zee-bluh*
Please send it again.	**Veuillez le (la) faxer de nouveau.** *vuh-yay luh (lah) fahk-ssay duh noo-voh*

COMPUTERS

What kind of computer do you have?	**Quel système (type, genre) d'ordinateur avez-vous?** *kehl seess-tehm (teep, zhahn-ruh) dohr-dee-nah-tuhr ah-vay voo*

What operating system are you using?	**Quel système opérant employez-vous?** *kehl sees-tehm oh-pay-rah<u>n</u> ah<u>n</u>-plwah-yay-voo*
What word processing program are you using?	**Quel système de traitement de texte employez-vous?** *kehl sees-tehm duh treht-mah<u>n</u> duh tehksst ah<u>n</u>-plwah-yay-voo*
What spreadsheet program are you using?	**Quel tableur employez-vous?** *kehl tah-bluhr ah<u>n</u>-plwah-yay-voo*
What peripherals do you have?	**Quels périphériques avez-vous?** *kehl pay-ree-fay-reek ah-vay voo*
Are our systems compatible?	**Nos systèmes, sont-ils compatibles?** *noh sees-tehm soh<u>n</u> teel koh<u>n</u>-pah-tee-bluh*
Do you have _____?	**Avez-vous _____?** *ah-vay voo*
Do you use _____?	**Employez-vous _____?** *ah<u>n</u>-plwah-yay-voo*
What is your e-mail address?	**Quelle est votre adresse e-mail?** *kehl eh voh-truh ah-drehss ee-mehl*

GENERAL INFORMATION

TELLING TIME

What time is it?	**Quelle heure est-il?** *kehl uhr eh teel*

It is _____.	**Il est _____.** *eel eh*
■ noon	**midi** *mee-dee*
■ 8:00	**huit heures** *weet-uhr*
■ 1:05	**une heure cinq** *ewn-uhr sank*
■ 2:10	**deux heures dix** *duh-zuhr deess*
■ 3:15	**trois heures et quart** *trwah-zuhr ay kahr*
■ 4:20	**quatre heures vingt** *kahtruh-uhr van*
■ 5:25	**cinq heures vingt-cinq** *sank-uhr van-sank*
■ 6:30	**six heures et demie** *seez-uhr ay duh-mee*

EXPRESSIONS OF TIME

At what time?	**À quelle heure _____?** *ah kehl-uhr*
When?	**Quand?** *kahn*
at _____ o'clock	**à _____ heures** *ah _____ uhr*
at exactly noon	**à midi précis** *ah mee-dee pray-ssee*
at exactly 5 o'clock	**à cinq heures précises** *ah sank uhr pray-sseez*
in an hour	**dans une heure** *dahn zewn-uhr*
in 2 hours	**dans deux heures** *dahn duhz-uhr*
between 8 and 9 o'clock	**entre huit et neuf heures** *ahn-truh weet ay nuhv-uhr*
until 5 o'clock	**jusqu'à cinq heures** *zhewss-kah sank uhr*

since what time _____?	**depuis quelle heure _____?**	*duh-pwee kehl uhr*
since 7 o'clock	**depuis sept heures**	*duh-pwee seht uhr*
per hour	**par heure**	*pahr uhr*
three hours ago	**il y a trois heures**	*eel yah trwah-zuhr*
early	**tôt** *toh* **de bonne heure**	*duh bohn-uhr*
late	**tard**	*tahr*
late (in arriving)	**en retard**	*ahn ruh-tahr*
on, in time	**à l'heure**	*ah luhr*
noon	**midi**	*mee-dee*
midnight	**minuit**	*mee-nwee*
in the morning	**le matin**	*luh mah-tan*
in the afternoon	**l'après-midi**	*lah-preh mee-dee*
in the evening	**le soir**	*luh swahr*
at night	**la nuit**	*lah nwee*
second	**une seconde**	*ewn suh-gohnd*
minute	**une minute**	*ewn mee-newt*
hour	**une heure**	*ewn uhr*

a quarter of an hour	**un quart d'heure**	*uhn kahr duhr*
a half hour	**une demi-heure**	*ewn duh-mee uhr*

Official time is based on the 24-hour clock. You will find schedules for planes, trains, radio and television programs, movies, sports events, and the like expressed in terms of a point within the 24-hour sequence. The time may be written as follows:

Noon	12 h 00	12.00
1:15 A.M.	01 h 15	1.15
1:15 P.M.	13 h 15	13.15
Midnight	00 h 00	00.00

DAYS OF THE WEEK

What day is today?	**Quel jour est-ce aujourd' hui?** *kehl zhoor ess oh-zhoor-dwee* **Quel jour sommes-nous aujourd'hui?** *kehl zhoor sohm noo oh-zhoor-dwee*
Today is ____.	**C'est aujourd'hui ____.** *seh toh-zhoor-dwee* **Nous sommes ____.** *noo sohm*
Monday	**lundi** *luhn-dee*
Tuesday	**mardi** *mahr-dee*
Wednesday	**mercredi** *mehr-kruh-dee*
Thursday	**jeudi** *zhuh-dee*
Friday	**vendredi** *vahn-druh-dee*
Saturday	**samedi** *sahm-dee*
Sunday	**dimanche** *dee-mahnsh*

NOTE: In French, the names of the days and the months and seasons are written in small letters.

last Monday	**lundi dernier**	*luhn-dee dehr-nyay*
the eve	**la veille**	*lah vehy*
the day before yesterday	**avant-hier**	*ah-vahn-tyehr*
yesterday	**hier**	*yehr*
today	**aujourd'hui**	*oh-zhoor-dwee*
tomorrow	**demain**	*duh-man*
the day after tomorrow	**après-demain**	*ah-preh-duh-man*
the next day	**le lendemain**	*luh lahn-duh-man*
next Monday	**lundi prochain**	*luhn-dee proh-shan*
the day	**le jour**	*luh zhoor*
2 days ago	**il y a deux jours**	*eel-yah duh zhoor*
in 2 days	**dans deux jours**	*dahn duh zhoor*
every day	**tous les jours**	*too lay zhoor*
day off	**(le) jour de congé**	*(luh) zhoor duh kohn-zhay*
holiday	**(le) jour de fête**	*(luh) zhoor duh feht*
birthday	**l'anniversaire**	*lah-nee-vehr-ssehr*
per day	**par jour**	*pahr zhoor*
during the day	**pendant la journée**	*pahn-dahn lah zhoor-nay*

from this day on	**dès aujourd'hui** *deh zoh-zhoor-dwee*
the week	**la semaine** *lah suh-mehn*
a weekday	**un jour de semaine** *uhn zhoor duh suh-mehn*
the weekend	**le week-end** *luh week-ehnd*
last week	**la semaine passée** *lah suh-mehn pah-ssay*
this week	**cette semaine** *seht suh-mehn*
next week	**la semaine prochaine** *lah suh-mehn proh-shehn*
a week from today	**dans une semaine** *dahn-zewn suh-mehn*
2 weeks from tomorrow	**de demain en quinze** *duh duh-man ahn kanz*
during the week	**pendant la semaine** *pahn-dahn lah suh-mehn*

MONTHS OF THE YEAR

January	**janvier** *zhan-vee-yay*
February	**février** *fay-vree-yay*
March	**mars** *mahrss*
April	**avril** *ah-vreel*
May	**mai** *meh*
June	**juin** *zhwan*

July	**juillet**	*zhwee-yeh*
August	**août**	*oo* or *oot*
September	**septembre**	*sehp-tahn-bruh*
October	**octobre**	*ohk-toh-bruh*
November	**novembre**	*noh-vah<u>n</u>-bruh*
December	**décembre**	*day-ssahn-bruh*
the month	**le mois**	*luh mwah*
2 months ago	**il y a deux mois**	*eel yah duh mwah*
last month	**le mois dernier**	*luh mwah dehr-nyay*
this month	**ce mois**	*suh mwah*
next month	**le mois prochain**	*luh mwah proh-sha<u>n</u>*
during the month of	**pendant le mois de**	*pah<u>n</u>-dah<u>n</u> luh mwah duh*
since the month of	**depuis le mois de**	*duh-pwee luh mwah duh*
for the month of	**pour le mois de**	*poor luh mwah duh*
every month	**tous les mois**	*too lay mwah*
per month	**par mois**	*pahr mwah*
What is today's date?	**Quelle est la date d'aujourd'hui?** *kehl ay lah daht doh-zhoor-dwee*	

Today is _____.	**C'est aujourd'hui ___.** *seht oh-zhoor-dwee*
Monday, May 1	**lundi, le premier mai** *luhn-dee luh pruh-myay meh*
Tuesday, June 2	**mardi, le deux juin** *mahr-dee luh duh zhwan*

NOTE: Use the ordinal number only for the first of the month.

the year	**l'an/l'année** *lahn/lah-nay*
per year	**par an** *pahr ahn*
all year	**toute l'année** *toot lah-nay*
every year	**chaque année** *shahk ah-nay*
during the year	**pendant l'année** *pahn-dahn lah-nay*

THE FOUR SEASONS

spring	**le printemps** *luh pran-tahn*
summer	**l'été** *lay-tay*
autumn	**l'automne** *loh-tohn*
winter	**l'hiver** *lee-vehr*
in the spring	**au printemps** *oh pran-tahn*
in the summer	**en été** *ahn-nay tay*
in the autumn	**en automne** *ahn-noh-tohn*
in the winter	**en hiver** *ahn nee-vehr*

WEATHER

What is the weather like?	**Quel temps fait-il?**	*kehl tahn feh-teel*
It is beautiful.	**Il fait beau.**	*eel feh boh*
It is hot.	**Il fait chaud.**	*eel feh shoh*
It is sunny.	**Il fait du soleil.**	*eel feh dew soh-lehy*
It is bad.	**Il fait mauvais.**	*eel feh moh-veh*
It is cold.	**Il fait froid.**	*eel feh frwah*
It is cool.	**Il fait frais.**	*eel feh freh*
It is windy.	**Il fait du vent.**	*eel feh dew vah<u>n</u>*
It is foggy.	**Il fait du brouillard.**	*eel feh dew broo-yahr*
It is humid.	**Il fait humide.**	*eel feh ew-meed*
It is snowing.	**Il neige.**	*eel nehzh*
It is raining.	**Il pleut.**	*eel pluh*

DIRECTIONS

the north	**le nord**	*luh nohr*
the south	**le sud**	*luh sewd*
the east	**l'est**	*lehsst*
the west	**l'ouest**	*lwehsst*

IMPORTANT SIGNS

À louer	*ah loo-ay*	For rent, hire
Ascenseur	*ah-sah<u>n</u>-ssuhr*	Elevator
Attention	*ah-tah<u>n</u>-ssyoh<u>n</u>*	Careful
À vendre	*ah vah<u>n</u>-druh*	For sale
Dames	*dahm*	Ladies
Danger	*dah<u>n</u>-zhay*	Danger
Danger de mort	*dah<u>n</u>-zhay duh mohr*	Danger of death
Défense de _____	*day-fah<u>n</u>ss duh*	Do not _____
Défense d'entrer	*day-fah<u>n</u>ss dah<u>n</u>-tray*	Do not enter
Défense de cracher	*day-fah<u>n</u>ss duh krah-shay*	No spitting
Défense de fumer	*day-fah<u>n</u>ss duh few-may*	No smoking
Défense de marcher sur l'herbe	*day-fah<u>n</u>ss duh mahr-shay sewr lehrb*	Keep off the grass
Eau non potable	*oh noh<u>n</u> poh-tah-bluh*	Don't drink the water
École	*ay-kohl*	School
Entrée	*ah<u>n</u>-tray*	Entrance
Entrée interdite	*ah<u>n</u>-tray a<u>n</u>-tehr-deet*	No Entrance
Entrée libre	*ah<u>n</u>-tray lee-bruh*	Free Admission
Fermé	*fehr-may*	Closed

Fumeurs	*few-muhr*	Smokers
Hommes	*ohm*	Men
Hôpital	*oh-pee-tahl*	Hospital
Horaire	*oh-rehr*	Schedule
Libre	*lee-bruh*	Free/Unoccupied
Messieurs	*meh-ssyuh*	Gentlemen
Ne pas toucher	*nuh pah too-shay*	Don't touch
Nonfumeurs	*nohn few-muhr*	Nonsmokers
Occupé	*oh-kew-pay*	Occupied
Ouvert	*oo-vehr*	Open
Passage souterrain	*pah-ssahzh soo-teh-ran*	Underground Passage
Poussez	*poo-ssay*	Push
Privé	*pree-vay*	Private
Quai/Voie	*kay/vwah*	Track, Platform
Renseignements	*rahn-sseh-nyuh-mahn*	Information
Réservé	*ray-zehr-vay*	Reserved
Salle d'attente	*sahl dah-tahnt*	Waiting room
Soldes	*sohld*	Sales
Sonnez	*soh-nay*	Ring
Sortie	*sohr-tee*	Exit
Sortie de secours	*sohr-tee duh-suh-koor*	Emergency exit

Stationnement inderdit	*stah-ssyohn-mahn an-tehr-dee*	No parking
Tirez	*tee-ray*	Pull
Toilettes	*twah-leht*	Toilets

COMMON ABBREVIATIONS

ACF	**Automobile Club de France**	Automobile Club of France
apr. J.-C.	**après Jésus-Christ**	A.D.
av. J.-C.	**avant Jésus-Christ**	B.C.
bd.	**boulevard**	boulevard
c.-à-d.	**c'est-à-dire**	that is to say, i.e.
CEE	**Communauté économique européenne (Marché commun)**	European Economic Community (Common Market)
CGT	**Compagnie générale transatlantique**	French Line
Cie.	**compagnie**	Company
EU	**États-Unis**	United States (U.S.)
h.	**heure(s)**	hour, o'clock
M.	**Monsieur**	Mr.
Mlle	**Mademoiselle**	Miss
MM	**Messieurs**	Gentlemen
Mme	**Madame**	Mrs.
ONU	**Organisation des Nations Unies**	United Nations (U.N.)
p.	**page**	page
p. ex.	**par example**	for example
P et T.	**Postes et Télécommunications**	Post Office and Telecommunications

RATP	**Régie Autonome des Transports Parisiens**	Paris Transport Authority
RD	**Route Départementale**	local road
RN	**Route Nationale**	national road
SA	**Société anonyme**	Ltd., Inc.
SI	**Syndicat d'initiative**	Tourist Information Office
SNCF	**Société Nationale des Chemins de fer Français**	French National Railways
s.v.p.	**s'il vous plaît**	please

GERMAN

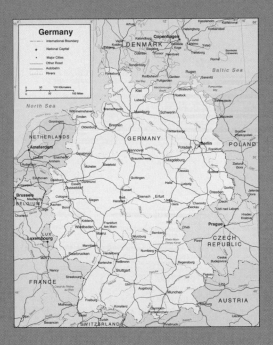

QUICK PRONUNCIATION GUIDE

VOWELS

Vowels may be long or short. A vowel is long when:

1. doubled (B<u>ee</u>thoven, B<u>oo</u>t, W<u>aa</u>ge)
2. followed by an <u>h</u> (Br<u>a</u>hms, <u>O</u>hm, F<u>e</u>hler)
3. followed by a single consonant (Sch<u>u</u>bert, M<u>o</u>zart, T<u>o</u>n)

When followed by two or more consonants, a vowel is usually short, as in B<u>a</u>ch.

VOWELS	SOUND IN ENGLISH	EXAMPLE
a	aa (**long:** f<u>a</u>r)	**haben** (*HAA-ben*)
	ah (**short:** h<u>o</u>t)	**hatte** (*HAH-teh*)
ä	ay (**long:** w<u>ay</u>)	**Bäder** (*BAY-duh*)
	eh (**short:** m<u>e</u>t)	**Gepäck** (*geh-PEHK*)
e	ay (**long:** h<u>ay</u>)	**leben** (*LAY-ben*)
	eh (**short:** <u>e</u>nd)	**helfen** (*HEHL-fen*)
	e (**unstressed syllables** ending in -<u>n</u>, -<u>l</u>, and -<u>t</u>, like -<u>en</u> in hidden)	**lieben** (*LEE-ben*)
	uh (**unstressed syllables** ending in –<u>er</u>: moth<u>er</u>)	**Ritter** (*RIT-uh*)
i	ee (**long:** fl<u>ee</u>t)	**Ihnen** (*EE-nen*)
	i (**short:** w<u>i</u>t)	**wissen** (*VI-ssen*)
ie	ee (always **long:** mart<u>ini</u>)	**Liebe** (*LEE-beh*)
o	oh (**long:** r<u>o</u>se)	**Rose** (*ROH-zeh*)
	o (**short:** l<u>o</u>ve)	**komm** (*k<u>o</u>m*)
ö	er (like h<u>er</u>, but sounded with the lips forward and rounded)	**hören** (*HER-en*)
u	oo (**long:** bl<u>oo</u>m)	**Schuh** (*sh<u>oo</u>*)
	u (**short:** b<u>u</u>ll)	**Bulle** (*BUL-eh*)
ü	ew (like dr<u>ea</u>m, but with lips forward and rounded)	**Brüder** (*BREW-duh*)
y	ew (like the German <u>ü</u>)	**lyrisch** (*LEW-rish*)

DIPHTHONGS

LETTERS	SOUND IN ENGLISH	EXAMPLE
ai, ay ei, ey	eye (e<u>ye</u>)	schr<u>ei</u>ben (SHR<u>EYE</u>-ben)
au	ow (br<u>ow</u>n)	br<u>au</u>n (br<u>ow</u>n)
äu, eu	oy (j<u>oy</u>)	tr<u>eu</u> (tr<u>oy</u>)

CONSONANTS

LETTERS	SOUND IN ENGLISH	EXAMPLE
f, h, k, l, m, n, p, t, x	usually pronounced as in English	
b	p (between vowel and consonant or at end of word: ma<u>p</u>)	Lei<u>b</u> (ley<u>e</u>p)
	b (elsewhere as in English)	<u>b</u>in (<u>b</u>in)
c	ts (before <u>e</u>, <u>i</u>, <u>ö</u>, and <u>ä</u>: wi<u>ts</u>)	<u>C</u>äsar (<u>TS</u>AY-zahr)
	k (elsewhere: <u>c</u>old)	<u>C</u>oburg (<u>K</u>OH-boork)
ch	kh (strongly aspirated (breathy) sound: "Hawaiian <u>h</u>ula-<u>h</u>ula," or "<u>H</u>ugh")	dur<u>ch</u> (door<u>kh</u>)
chs	k (sometimes: <u>k</u>ind)	La<u>chs</u> (lah<u>ks</u>)
d	t (between vowel and consonant and at end of word: ca<u>t</u>)	Hun<u>d</u> (hun<u>t</u>)
	d (otherwise: <u>d</u>ollar)	<u>D</u>ank (<u>d</u>ank)
g	g (**hard**: <u>g</u>ods)	<u>G</u>eist (<u>g</u>eyest)
	k (at end of word: backpa<u>ck</u>)	Ta<u>g</u> (taa<u>k</u>)
	kh (words ending in <u>ig</u>: <u>h</u>appy or w<u>h</u>isky)	wind<u>ig</u> (VIN-di<u>kh</u>)
j	y (<u>y</u>ear)	<u>J</u>ahr (<u>y</u>aar)
qu	kv (<u>k</u>, followed by <u>v</u> as in <u>v</u>eal)	<u>Qu</u>ell (<u>kv</u>ehl)

LETTERS	SOUND IN ENGLISH	EXAMPLE
r	r (preferably rolled in the throat, as in French, or trilled with the tip of the tongue, as in Spanish or Irish or Scottish brogues)	**Reise** (*REYE-zeh*)
s	z (preceding vowels or between them: <u>z</u>ap)	**See** (*<u>z</u>ay*)
	sh (at beginning of syllable, before <u>p</u> and <u>t</u>: <u>sh</u>ell)	**spielen** (*<u>SH</u>PEE-len*)
	s, ss (elsewhere: <u>s</u>ing)	**Wa<u>s</u> i<u>st</u> da<u>s</u>?** (*vah<u>s</u> ist dah<u>s</u>*)
ß, ss	s, ss (always: <u>s</u>ell)	**weiß** (*veye<u>s</u>*)
		wi<u>ss</u>en (*VI-<u>ss</u>en*)
sch	sh (<u>sh</u>ow)	**<u>sch</u>lau** (*<u>sh</u>low*)
tsch	ch (<u>ch</u>eer)	**Kit<u>sch</u>** (*ki<u>ch</u>*)
tz	ts (wi<u>ts</u>)	**Ka<u>tz</u>e** (*KAH-<u>ts</u>eh*)
v	f (<u>f</u>ather)	**<u>V</u>ater** (*<u>F</u>AA-tuh*)
	v (words of non-Germanic origin: violin)	**<u>V</u>ioline** (*<u>v</u>ee-o-LEE-neh*)
w	v (<u>v</u>est)	**<u>W</u>asser** (*<u>V</u>ah-suh*)
z	ts (gri<u>ts</u>)	**<u>Z</u>eit** (*<u>ts</u>eyet*)

THE BASICS FOR GETTING BY

MOST FREQUENTLY USED EXPRESSIONS

Yes.	**Ja.**	*yaa*
No.	**Nein.**	*neyen*
Maybe.	**Vielleicht.**	*fee-LEYEKHT*
Never again!	**Nie wieder!**	*nee VEED-uh*

Please.	**Bitte.**	*BIT-eh*
Thank you.	**Danke.**	*DAHNK-eh*
You're (very) welcome.	**Bitte (sehr).**	*BIT-eh (zayr)*
Don't mention it.	**Gern geschehen.**	*gehrn ge-SHAY-en*
Excuse me.	**Verziehung!**	*fehr-TSEYE-ung*
I'm sorry.	**Es tut mir leid.**	*ehs toot meer leyet*
Just a second.	**Augenblick mal!**	*OW-gen-blik maal*
That is (not) ___.	**Das ist (nicht) ___.**	*dahs ist (nikht)*
■ right	**richtig**	*RIKHT-ikh*
■ important	**wichtig**	*VIKHT-ikh*
■ good	**gut**	*goot*
■ true	**wahr**	*vaar*
■ beautiful	**schön**	*shern*
■ necessary	**nötig**	*NERT-ikh*
It doesn't matter.	**Das macht nichts.**	*dahs mahkht nikhts*
(The) gentleman, Mr.	**(Der) Herr.**	*(dehr) hehrr*
(The) lady, Mrs.	**(Die) Frau.**	*(dee) frow*
(The) girl, Miss.	**(Das) Fräulein.**	*(dahs) FROY-leyen*
Good morning.	**Guten Morgen.**	*GOOT-en MORG-en*
Good afternoon.	**Guten Tag.**	*GOOT-en taak*

Good evening.	**Guten Abend.**	*GOOT-en AAB-ent*
Good night.	**Gute Nacht.**	*GOOT-eh nahkht*
Good-bye.	**Auf Wiedersehen!**	*owf VEED-uh-zayen*
See you soon.	**Bis bald.**	*bis bahlt*
See you later.	**Bis später.**	*bis SHPAYT-uh*
I speak little German.	**Ich spreche wenig Deutsch.**	*ikh SHPREHKH-eh VAYN-ikh doytch*
Do you speak English?	**Sprechen Sie Englisch?**	*SHPREHKH-eh zee EHNG-lish*
Please speak more slowly.	**Bitte sprechen Sie langsamer!**	*BIT-eh SHPREKH-en zee LAHNG-zaam-uh*
Please repeat.	**Wiederholen Sie bitte!**	*VEED-uh-hoh-len zee BIT-eh*
Do you understand?	**Verstehen Sie?**	*fehr-SHTAY-en zee*
I (don't) understand.	**Ich verstehe (nicht).**	*ikh fehr-SHTAY-eh (nikht)*
What does that mean?	**Was bedeutet das?**	*vahss be-DOYT-et dahs*
Do you know ____?	**Wissen Sie ____?**	*VISS-en zee*
I don't know.	**Ich weiß nicht.**	*ikh veyess nikht*
What is that?	**Was ist das?**	*vahs ist dahs*

I am an American. (-*in* for women)	**Ich bin Amerikaner (Amerikanerin).**	*ikh bin aa-meh-ri-KAAN-uh (aa-meh-ri-KAAN-uh-rin)*
I am English.	**Ich bin Engländer (Engländerin).**	*ikh bin EHNG-lehnd-uh (EHNG-lehnd-uh-rin)*
I am Canadian.	**Ich bin Kanadier (Kanadierin).**	*ikh bin kah-NAA-diuh (kah-NAA-diuh-rin)*
I am Australian.	**Ich bin Australier (Australierin).**	*ikh bin ow-STRAA-liuh (ow-STRAA-liuh-rin)*
My name is ____.	**Ich heiße ____.**	*ikh HEYESS-eh*
What's your name?	**Wie heißen Sie?**	*vee HEYESS-en zee*
How are you? (How do you do?)	**Wie geht es Ihnen?**	*vee gayt ehs EEN-en*
Fine, thank you. And you?	**Gut, danke. Und Ihnen?**	*goot DAHNK-eh unt EEN-en*
How much does that cost?	**Wieviel kostet das?**	*VEE-feel KOST-et dahs*
I'm ____.	**Ich bin ____.**	*ikh bin*
■ hungry	**hungrig**	*HUNG-rikh*
■ thirsty	**durstig**	*DOORST-ikh*
■ tired	**müde**	*MEWD-eh*
■ sick	**krank**	*krahnk*

Please bring me ___.	**Bitte bringen Sie mir ___.**	*BIT-eh BRING-en zee meer*
■ a glass of water (beer, hard liquor)	**ein Glas Wasser (Bier, Schnaps)**	*eyen glaass VAHSS-uh (beer, shnahps)*

QUESTIONS

Why?	**Warum?**	*vah-RUM*
When?	**Wann?**	*vahn*
Where?	**Wo?**	*voh*
What?	**Was?**	*vahs*
How?	**Wie?**	*vee*
Who?	**Wer?**	*vayr*

PROBLEMS, PROBLEMS, PROBLEMS (EMERGENCIES)

I'm looking for ___.	**Ich suche ___.**	*ikh ZOOKH-eh*
■ my hotel	**mein Hotel**	*meyen ho-TEL*
■ my friends	**meine Freunde**	*MEYEN-eh FROYND-eh*
■ my suitcase	**meinen Koffer**	*MEYEN-en KOF-uh*
■ the railroad station	**den Bahnhof**	*dayn BAAN-hohf*
■ my husband	**meinen Mann**	*MEYEN-en mahn*
■ my wife	**meine Frau**	*MEYEN-eh frow*
■ my child	**mein Kind**	*meyen kint*
■ my bus	**meinen Bus**	*MEYEN-en bus*

I'm lost. (on foot)	**Ich habe mich verlaufen.**	*ikh HAAB-en mikh fehr-LOWF-en*
I'm lost. (driving)	**Ich habe mich verfahren.**	*ikh HAAB-eh mikh fehr-FAAR-en*
Can you help me please?	**Können Sie mir bitte helfen?**	*KERN-en zee meer BIT-eh HELF-en*
Does anyone here speak English?	**Spricht hier jemand Englisch?**	*shprikht heer YAY-mahnt EHNG-lish*
Where is the American (British, Canadian, Australian) Consulate?	**Wo ist das amerikanische (britische, kanadische, australische) Konsulat?**	*voh ist dahs aa-meh-ri-KAAN-ish-eh (BRIT-ish-eh, kah-NAA-dish-eh, ow-STRAA-lish-eh) kon-zoo-LAAT*
Which way do I go?	**In welche Richtung soll ich gehen?**	*in VELKH-eh RIKHT-ung zol ikh GAY-en*
▦ to the left	**links**	*links*
▦ to the right	**rechts**	*rehkhts*
▦ straight ahead	**geradeaus**	*ge-RAAD-eh-OWS*
____ is stolen.	____ **ist gestohlen.**	*ist ge-SHTOHL-en*
▦ My car	**mein Wagen**	*meyen VAAG-en*
▦ My briefcase	**meine Aktentasche**	*MEYEN-eh AHKT-en-tahsh-eh*
▦ My jewels	**mein Schmuck**	*meyen shmuk*
▦ My money	**mein Geld**	*meyen gelt*
▦ My purse	**meine Handtasche**	*MEYEN-eh HAHNT-tahsh-eh*
▦ My suitcase	**mein Koffer**	*meyen KOF-uh*
▦ My ticket	**meine Fahrkarte**	*MEYEN-eh FAAR-kahrt-eh*

■ My wallet	**meine Geldbörse**	*MEYEN-eh*
		GELT-berz-eh
■ My watch	**meine Uhr**	*MEYEN-eh oor*
Call the police!	**Rufen Sie die Polizei!**	*ROOF-en zee dee pol-its-EYE*

NUMBERS

CARDINAL NUMBERS

0	**null**	*nul*
1	**eins**	*eyenss*
2	**zwei, zwo** (over the telephone)	*tsveye, tsvoh*
3	**drei**	*dreye*
4	**vier**	*feer*
5	**fünf**	*fewnf*
6	**sechs**	*zehks*
7	**sieben**	*ZEEB-en*
8	**acht**	*ahkht*
9	**neun**	*noyn*
10	**zehn**	*tsayn*
11	**elf**	*elf*
12	**zwölf**	*tsverlf*
13	**dreizehn**	*DREYE-tsayn*
14	**vierzehn**	*FEER-tsayn*
15	**fünfzehn**	*FEWNF-tsayn*
16	**sechzehn**	*ZEHKH-tsayn*

17	**siebzehn**	*ZEEP-tsayn*
18	**achtzehn**	*AHKHT-tsayn*
19	**neunzehn**	*NOYN-tsayn*
20	**zwanzig**	*TSVAHN-tsikh*
21	**einundzwanzig**	*EYEN-unt-tsvahn-tsikh*
22	**zweiundzwanzig**	*TSVEYE-unt-tsvahn-tsikh*
23	**dreiundzwanzig**	*DREYE-unt-tsvahn-tsikh*
24	**vierundzwanzig**	*FEER-unt-tsvahn-tsikh*
25	**fünfundzwanzig**	*FEWNF-unt-tsvahn-tsikh*
26	**sechsundzwanzig**	*ZEHKS-unt-tsvahn-tsikh*
27	**siebenundzwanzig**	*ZEEB-en-unt-tsvahn-tsikh*
28	**achtundzwanzig**	*AHKHT-unt-tsvahn-tsikh*
29	**neunundzwanzig**	*NOYN-unt-tsvahn-tsikh*
30	**dreißig**	*DREYESS-ikh*
31	**einunddreißig**	*EYEN-unt-dreyess-ikh*
40	**vierzig**	*FEER-tsikh*
41	**einundvierzig**	*EYEN-unt-feer-tsikh*
50	**fünfzig**	*FEWNF-tsikh*
60	**sechzig**	*ZEHKH-tsikh*

70	**siebzig**	*ZEEP-tsikh*
80	**achtzig**	*AHKH-tsikh*
90	**neunzig**	*NOYN-tsikh*
100	**(ein)hundert**	*(eyen)HUN-dehrt*
101	**hunderteins**	*HUN-dehrt-eyenss*
102	**hundertzwei**	*HUN-dehrt-tsveye*
200	**zweihundert**	*TSVEYE-hun-dehrt*
300	**dreihundert**	*DREYE-hun-dehrt*
400	**vierhundert**	*FEER-hun-dehrt*
500	**fünfhundert**	*FEWNF-hun-derht*
600	**sechshundert**	*ZEHKS-hun-derht*
700	**siebenhundert**	*ZEEB-en-hun-derht*
800	**achthundert**	*AHKHT-hun-derht*
900	**neunhundert**	*NOYN-hun-derht*
1000	**(ein)tausend**	*(eyen)TOW-zehnt*
2000	**zweitausend**	*TSVEYE-tow-zehnt*
1,000,000	**eine Million**	*EYEN-eh mil-YOHN*
1,000,000,000	**eine Milliarde**	*EYEN-eh mil-YAHRD-eh*

ORDINAL NUMBERS

first	**erst-**	*ayrst*
second	**zweit-**	*tsveyet*
third	**dritt-**	*drit*
fourth	**viert-**	*feert*
fifth	**fünft-**	*fewnft*

sixth	**sechst-**	*zehkst*
seventh	**siebt-**	*zeept*
eighth	**acht-**	*ahkht*
ninth	**neunt-**	*noynt*
tenth	**zehnt-**	*tsaynt*

WHEN YOU ARRIVE

PASSPORT AND CUSTOMS

Here is my passport.	**Hier ist mein Pass.** *heer ist meyen pahss*
Would you please stamp my passport?	**Würden Sie mir bitte meinen Pass stempeln?** *VEWRD-en zee meer BIT-eh MEYEN-ehn pahss SHTEMP-eln*
I will not be working in Europe.	**In Europa werde ich nicht arbeiten.** *In OY-roh-paa VEHRD-eh ikh nikht AHR-beye-ten*
I'm traveling on vacation.	**Ich mache eine Ferienreise.** *ikh MAHKH-eh EYEN-eh FAIR-yen-reye-zeh*
I'm on a business trip.	**Ich bin auf Geschäftsreise hier.** *ikh bin owf geh-SHEHFTS reye-zeh heer*
I'm visiting my relatives.	**Ich besuche meine Verwandten.** *ikh be-ZOOKH-eh MEYEN-eh fehr-VAHNT-en*
I'm just passing through.	**Ich bin nur auf der Durchreise.** *ikh bin noor owf dehr DOORKH-reye-zeh*

I'll be staying ____.	**Ich bleibe ____.** *ikh BLEYEB-eh*
▨ a few days	**einige Tage** *EYEN-ig-eh TAAG-eh*
▨ a few weeks	**einige Wochen** *EYEN-ig-eh VOKH-ehn*
▨ sixty days	**sechzig Tage** *ZEKH-tsikh TAAG-eh*
▨ a month	**einen Monat** *EYEN-en MOHN-aat*

I'm traveling ____.	**Ich reise ____.** *ikh REYE-zeh*
▨ alone	**allein** *ah-LEYEN*
▨ with my family	**mit meiner Familie** *mit MEYEN-uh fah-MEEL-yeh*
▨ with my wife	**mit meiner Frau** *mit MEYEN-uh frow*
▨ with my husband	**mit meinem Mann** *mit MEYEN-em mahn*

I have nothing to declare.	**Ich habe nichts zu verzollen.** *ikh HAAB-eh nikhts tsoo fehr-TSOL-en*
Here is my luggage.	**Hier ist mein Gepäck.** *heer ist meyen geh-PEHK*
Do I have to pay duty on this?	**Ist dies zollpflichtig?** *ist dees TSOL-pflikh-tikh*
These are gifts.	**Das sind Geschenke.** *dahs zint ge-SHENK-eh*
This is for my personal use.	**Das ist für meinen persönlichen Gebrauch.** *dahs ist fewr MEYEN-en pehr-ZERN-likh-en ge-BROWKH*

BAGGAGE AND PORTERS

| I'm looking for the luggage carts. | **Ich suche die Kofferkulis.** *ikh ZOOKH-eh dee KOF-uh-koo-lees* |

I need a porter.	**Ich brauche einen Gepäckträger.** *ikh BROWKH-eh EYEN-en geh-PEHK-trayg-uh*
That's my (our) luggage.	**Das ist mein (unser) Gepäck.** *dahs ist meyen (UNZ-uh) geh-PEHK*
Accompany us to the taxi (the bus, the railroad entrance).	**Begleiten Sie uns zum Taxi (Bus, Eisenbahneingang).** *beh-GLEYET-en zee uns tsoom TAHKS-ee (bus, EYEZ-en-baan-eyen-gahng)*
Be careful with that one!	**Vorsicht damit!** *FOR-zikht dah-MIT*
A suitcase is missing.	**Ein Koffer fehlt.** *eyen KOF-uh faylt*
Where is the lost and found?	**Wo ist das Fundbüro?** *voh ist dahs FUNT-bew-roh*
I'll carry this one myself.	**Diesen trag ich selber.** *DEEZ-en traag ikh ZELB-uh*
How much do I owe you?	**Wieviel macht das?** *VEE-feel mahkht dahs*

BANKING AND MONEY MATTERS

EXCHANGING MONEY

I want to change ____.	**Ich möchte ____ wechseln.** *ikh MERKH-teh ____ VEHK-seln*
■ money	**Geld** *gehlt*
■ dollars (pounds)	**Dollar (Pfund)** *DO-lahr (pfunt)*
■ travelers' checks	**Reiseschecks** *REYEZ-eh-shehks*

What is the exchange rate for dollars (euros)?	**Wie ist der Wechselkurs für Dollar (Euro)?** *vee ist dehr VEHK-sel-koors fewr DO-lahr (OY-roh)*
What commission do you charge?	**Welche Gebühr erheben Sie?** *VEHL-kheh geh-BEWR ehr-HAY-ben zee?*
Give me large (small) bills.	**Geben Sie mir große (kleine) Scheine.** *GAYB-en zee meer GROHSS-eh (KLEYEN-eh) SHEYEN-eh*
I also need some change.	**Ich brauche auch etwas Kleingeld.** *ikh BROWKH-eh owkh ET-vahs KLEYEN-gelt*
I think you made a mistake.	**Ich glaube, Sie haben sich ver- rechnet.** *ikh GLOWB-eh zee HAAB-en zikh fehr-REKH-net*
I want to cash a per- sonal check.	**Ich möchte einen Barscheck ein- lösen.** *ikh MERKHT-eh EYEN-eh BAAR-shehk EYEN-ler-zen*

AT THE HOTEL

RESERVATIONS AND RECEPTION

I'd like a single (double) room for tonight.	**Ich möchte ein Einzelzimmer (Doppelzimmer) für heute nacht.** *ikh MERKHT-eh eyen EYEN-tsel- tsim-uh (DOP-el-tsim-uh) fewr HOYT-eh nahkht*
I want a room with a private bath.	**Ich möchte ein Zimmer mit Privatbad.** *ikh MERKHT-eh eyen TSIM-uh mit pri-VAAT-baat*
I want a room with ____.	**Ich möchte ein Zimmer mit ____.** *ikh MERKHT-eh eyen TSIM-uh mit*

- air conditioning **Klimaanlage** *KLEEM-ah-ahn-laa-geh*

- a balcony **Balkon** *bahl-KOHN*

- a bathtub **einer Badewanne** *EYEN-uh BAAD-eh-vahn-eh*

- television **Fernsehen** *FEHRN-zayen*

- cable TV **Kabelfernsehen** *KAAB-el-fehrn-zayen*

- a nice view **schöner Aussicht** *SHERN-uh OWS-zikht*

- private toilet **eigenem WC** *EYEG-enem VAY-tsay*

- radio **Radio** *RAAD-ee-oh*

- shower **Dusche** *DOOSH-eh*

- a telephone in the room **Telefonanschluss** *TAYL-e-fohn-ahn-shluss*

- twin beds **zwei Betten** *tsveye BEHT-en*

- a view of the sea **Blick aufs Meer** *blik owfs mayr*

May I see the room? **Darf ich mir das Zimmer ansehen?** *dahrf ikh meer dahs TSIM-uh AHN-zay-en*

I (don't) like it. **Es gefällt mir (nicht).** *ehs ge-FEHLT meer (nikht)*

I'll take it. **Ich nehm's.** *ikh naymss*

I will not take it. **Ich nehm's nicht.** *ikh naymss (nikht)*

Do you have another room? **Haben Sie ein anderes Zimmer?** *HAAB-en zee eyen AHND-eh-res TSIM-uh*

I (don't) have a reservation. **Ich habe (nicht) reservieren lassen.** *ikh HAAB-eh (nikht) reh-zehr-VEER-en LASS-en*

May I leave this in your safe?	**Darf ich dies in Ihrem Tresor lassen?** *dahrf ikh dees in EE-rem treh-ZOHR LASS-en*
Would you have something ____.	**Hätten Sie etwas ____.** *HEHT-en zee ET-vahs*
■ in front	**vorne** *FORN-eh*
■ in back	**hinten** *HINT-en*
■ lower down	**weiter unten** *VEYET-uh UNT-en*
■ higher up	**weiter oben** *VEYET-uh OHB-en*
I want something ____.	**Ich will etwas ____.** *ikh vill ET-vahs*
■ quieter	**Ruhigeres** *ROOH-i-geh-res*
■ bigger	**Größeres** *GRERSS-eh-res*
■ cheaper	**Billigeres** *BILL-i-geh-res*
■ better	**Besseres** *BESS-eh-res*
■ more elegant	**Eleganteres** *eh-lay-GAHNT-eh-res*
■ more modest	**Bescheideneres** *beh-SHEYED-e-neh-res*
How much does it cost?	**Wieviel kostet es?** *VEE-feel KOST-et ehs*
Is breakfast (service, everything) included?	**Ist das Frühstück (Bedienung, alles) mit einbegriffen?** *ist dahs FREW-shtewk (beh-DEEN-ung, AH-les) mit EYEN-beh-gri-fen*

HOTEL SERVICES

I need ____.	**Ich brauche ____.** *ikh BROWKH-eh*
We need ____.	**Wir brauchen ____.** *veer BROWKH-en*
■ an ashtray	**einen Aschenbecher** *EYEN-en AHSH-en-bekh-uh*

■ a blanket	**eine Decke** *EYEN-eh DEHK-eh*
■ matches	**Streichhölzer** *SHTREYEKH-herl-tsuh*
■ envelopes	**Briefumschläge** *BREEF-um-shlay-geh*
■ writing paper	**Schreibpapier** *SHREYEP-paa-peer*
■ postcards	**Postkarten** *POST-kaar-ten*
■ soap	**Seife** *ZEYEF-eh*
■ toilet paper	**Toilettenpapier** *toy-LET-en-paa-peer*
■ towels	**Tücher** *TEWKH-uh*
■ an extra bed	**ein zusätzliches Bett** *eyen TSOO-zehts-li-khes beht*
■ an extra pillow	**ein extra Kopfkissen** *eyen EHKS-traa KOPF-kiss-en*
■ a wastepaper basket	**einen Papierkorb** *EYEN-en paa-PEER-korp*
■ ice cubes	**Eiswürfel** *EYESS-vewr-fel*
■ more hangers	**mehr Kleiderbügel** *mayr KLEYED-uh-bew-gel*
What's the voltage here?	**Welche Stromspannung haben Sie hier?** *VEHLKH-eh SHTROHM-shpahn-ung HAAB-en zee heer*
Where is ____?	**Wo ist ____?** *voh ist*
■ the elevator	**der Aufzug** *dehr OWF-tsook*
■ the bathroom	**das Bad** *dahs baat*
■ the shower	**die Dusche** *dee DOOSH-eh*
■ the breakfast room	**das Frühstückszimmer** *dahs FREW-shtewks-tsim-uh*
■ the dining room	**der Speisesaal** *dehr SHPEYEZ-eh-zaal*
■ the checkroom	**die Garderobe** *dee gahrd-eh-ROHB-eh*

■ the pool	**das Schwimmbad** *dahs SHVIM-baat*
■ the children's playroom	**der Aufenthaltsraum für Kinder** *dehr OWF-ent-hahlts-rowm fewr KIND-uh*
■ the telephone (book)	**das Telefon (buch)** *dahs TAY-leh-fohn (bookh)*
What's my room number?	**Welche Zimmernummer habe ich?** *VELKH-eh TSIM-uh-num-uh HAAB-eh ikh*
Shall I register now or later?	**Soll ich mich jetzt oder später eintragen?** *zol ikh mikh yehtst OHD-uh SHPAYT-uh EYEN-traa-gen*
I'll leave the key here.	**Ich lasse den Schlüssel hier.** *ikh LAHSS-eh dayn SHLEWSS-el heer*
Please wake me tomorrow at ___ o'clock.	**Bitte wecken sie mich morgen um ___ Uhr.** *BIT-eh VEHK-en zee mikh MORG-en um ___ oor*
Please don't forget.	**Bitte vergessen Sie es nicht.** *BIT-eh fehr-GESS-en zee ehs nikht*
I don't wish to be disturbed.	**Ich will nicht gestört werden.** *ikh vil nikht geh-SHTERT VAYRD-en*
Where is ___?	**Wo ist ___?** *voh ist*
■ the bellboy	**der Hotelpage** *dehr ho-TEL-paa-zheh*
■ the elevator operator	**der Liftjunge** *dehr LIFT-yun-geh*
■ the porter	**der Hausdiener** *dehr HOWS-dee-nuh*
■ the chambermaid	**das Zimmermädchen** *dahs TSIM-uh-mayd-khen*

■ the manager **der Geschäftsführer** *dehr geh-SHEHFTS-few-ruh*

■ the switchboard operator **die Telefonistin** *dee tay-leh-foh-NIST-in*

There is ____. **Es gibt ____.** *ehs gipt*

■ no hot water **kein heißes Wasser** *keyen HEYESS-es VAHSS-uh*

■ no heat **keine Heizung** *KEYEN-eh HEYETS-ung*

The room is cold. **Das Zimmer ist kalt.** *dahs TSIM-uh ist kahlt*

The room is dirty. **Das Zimmer ist schmutzig.** *dahs TSIM-uh ist SHMUTS-ikh*

The window (door, blind) is stuck. **Das Fenster (die Tür, die Jalousie) klemmt.** *dahs FENST-uh (dee tewr, dee zhah-loo-ZEE) klemt*

The ____ is defective. **____ ist defekt.** *ist deh-FEHKT*

■ air conditioning **die Klimaanlage** *dee KLEE-mah-ahn-laa-geh*

■ fan **der Ventilator** *dehr ven-tee-LAAT-or*

■ ventilator **der Lüfter** *dehr LEWFT-uh*

■ radio **das Radio** *dahs RAAD-ee-oh*

■ television set **der Fernseher** *dehr FEHRN-zay-uh*

■ lamp **die Lampe** *dee LAHMP-eh*

■ plug **die Steckdose** *dee SHTEK-doh-zeh*

■ switch **der Schalter** *dehr SHAHLT-uh*

■ toilet **die Toilette** *dee toy-LET-eh*

The bathtub (the shower, the wash basin) is clogged.	**Die Badewanne (die Dusche, das Waschbecken) ist verstopft.** *dee BAAD-eh-vahn-eh (dee DOOSH-eh, dahs VAHSH-behk-en) ist fehr-SHTOPFT*

BREAKFAST AND ROOM SERVICE

Is breakfast included in the price of the room?	**Ist der Zimmerpreis mit Frühstück?** *ist dehr TSIM-uh-preyes mit FREW-shtewk*
I want a soft-boiled egg.	**Ich möchte ein weichgekochtes Ei.** *ikh MERKHT-eh eyen VEYEKH-geh-kokh-tes eye*
■ a medium-boiled egg	**ein wachsweichgekochtes Ei** *eyen VAHKS-veyekh-geh-kokh-tes eye*
■ a hard-boiled egg	**ein hartgekochtes Ei** *eyen HAHRT-geh-kokh-tes eye*
I'd like ____.	**Ich möchte gerne ____.** *ikh MERKH-teh GEHRN-eh*
■ coffee	**Kaffee** *KAHF-fay*
■ tea	**Tee** *tay*
■ chocolate	**Schokolade** *shoko-LAAD-eh*
■ milk	**Milch** *milkh*
■ orange juice	**Apfelsinensaft** *AHP-fehl-zeen-en-zahft*
■ yogurt	**Joghurt** *YOH-goort*
■ an omelette	**eine Omelette** *EYEN-eh omeh-LET-eh*
■ fried eggs	**Spiegeleier** *SHPEEG-ehl-eye-uh*
■ scrambled eggs	**Rühreier** *REWR-eye-uh*
■ eggs and bacon (ham)	**Eier mit Speck (Schinken)** *EYE-uh mit shpek (SHINK-en)*

I'd like more ____.	**Ich möchte mehr ____.** *ikh MERKHT-eh mayr*
■ butter	**Butter** *BUT-uh*
■ jam	**Marmelade** *mahr-meh-LAAD-eh*
■ sugar	**Zucker** *TSUK-uh*
■ cream	**Sahne** *ZAAN-eh*
■ bread	**Brot** *broht*
■ rolls	**Brötchen** *BRERT-khen*
■ honey	**Honig** *HOHN-ikh*
■ lemon	**Zitrone** *tsi-TROHN-eh*
Do you have room service?	**Gibt es Zimmerbedienung?** *gipt ehs TSIM-uh-be-dien-ung*
How much does it cost with full room and board?	**Wieviel kostet es mit voller Verpflegung?** *VEE-feel KOST-et ehs mit FOL-uh fehr-PFLAYG-ung*
How much is half-board?	**Was ist der Preis für Halbpension?** *vahs ist dehr preyes fewr HAHLP-pehn-zee-ohn*
How long must I stay before I can get a reduction in price?	**Wie lange muss ich bleiben, bevor ich eine Preisermäßigung bekommen kann?** *vee LAHNG-eh muss ikh BLEYEB-en beh-FOR ikh EYEN-eh PREYESS-ehr-mayss-ig-ung beh-KOM-en kahn*
Come in.	**Herein!** *heh-REYEN*
Put it ____.	**Stellen Sie es ____.** *SHTEL-en zee ehs*
■ over there	**da drüben** *daa DREWB-en*
■ on the table	**aüf den Tisch** *owf dayn tish*
Just a minute.	**Augenblick nur.** *OWG-en-blik noor*

OTHER ACCOMMODATIONS

Is there a youth hostel (a castle hotel, an inn) here?	**Gibt es eine Jugendherberge (ein Schlosshotel, ein Gasthaus) hier?** *gipt ehs EYEN-eh YOOG-ent-hehr-behr-geh (eyen SHLOSS-ho-tel, eyen GAHST-hows) heer*
I'm looking for a room in a boarding-house.	**Ich suche ein Zimmer in einer Pension.** *ikh ZOOKH-eh eyen TSIM-uh in EYEN-uh penz-YOHN*
Where is the local tourist office?	**Wo ist das Fremdenverkehrs-büro?** *voh ist dahs FREMD-en-fehr-kayrs-bew-roh*
Are there reduced off-season rates?	**Gibt es eine Preisermäßigung außerhalb der Hauptsaison?** *gipt ehs EYEN-eh PREYESS-er-mayss-ig-ung OWSS-ehr-hahlp dehr HOWPT-zay-zon*
I'm looking for a hotel with ____.	**Ich suche ein Hotel mit ____ .** *ikh ZOOKH-eh eyen ho-TEL mit*
■ garage	**Garage** *gah-RAA-zheh*
■ parking	**eigenem Parkplatz** *EYE-ge-nem PAHRK-plahts*
■ indoor pool	**Hallenbad** *HAHL-en-baat*
I'll be staying for ____ .	**Ich bleibe ____.** *ikh BLEYEB-eh*
■ two weeks	**zwei Wochen** *tsveye VOKH-en*
■ one month	**einen Monat** *EYEN-en MOH-naat*
■ the whole season	**die ganze Saison** *dee GAHNTS-eh ZAY-zon*
I want something ____ .	**Ich möchte etwas** *ikh MERKHT-eh ET-vahs*

■ downtown	**im Zentrum** *im TSENT-room*
■ in the old part of town	**in der Altstadt** *in dehr AHLT-shtaht*
■ with modern conveniences	**mit modernem Komfort** *mit mod-EHRN-em kom-FOHR*

DEPARTURE

We're checking out tomorrow.	**Wir reisen morgen ab.** *veer REYEZ-en MORG-en ahp*
Are there any letters (messages) for me?	**Gibt es Briefe (Nachrichten) für mich?** *gipt ehs BREEF-eh (NAHKH-rikht-en) fewr mikh*
Please prepare my bill.	**Bitte bereiten Sie meine Rechnung vor.** *BIT-eh beh-REYET-en zee MEYEN-eh REKH-nung for*

GETTING AROUND TOWN

SUBWAYS, BUSES, AND STREETCARS

Where can I buy a ticket?	**Wo kann ich eine Fahrkarte kaufen?** *voh kahn ikh EYEN-eh FAAR-kahr-teh KOWF-en*
When does the next bus leave?	**Wann fährt der nächste Bus?** *vahn fayrt dehr NAYKST-eh bus*
Where is the bus stop?	**Wo ist die Bushaltestelle?** *voh ist dee BUS-hahl-teh-shteh-leh SHTRAASS-en-baan*

Where is the nearest subway station?	**Wo ist die nächste U-Bahn Station (Untergrundbahn)?** *voh ist dee NAYKH-steh oo-baan shtah-TSYOHN (UNT-uh-grunt-baan)*
How much is the fare?	**Wie viel kostet die Fahrt?** *VEE-feel KOST-et dee faart*
Which is the line that goes to ___?	**Welche Linie fährt nach ___?** *VEHLKH-eh LEEN-yeh fehrt nahkh*
Does this train go to ___?	**Fährt dieser Zug nach ___?** *fehrt DEEZ-uh tsook nahkh*
What's the next stop?	**Was ist die nächste Haltestelle?** *vahs ist dee NEHKHST-eh HAHLT-eh-shtel-eh*
Where should I get off?	**Wo muss ich aussteigen?** *voh muss ikh OWS-shteyeg-en*
Do I have to change trains?	**Muß ich umsteigen?** *muss ikh UM-shteyeg-en*
Please tell me when we get there.	**Bitte sagen Sie mir, wann wir dort ankommen.** *BIT-eh ZAAG-en zee meer vahn veer dort AHN-kom-en*

TAXIS

Please call a taxi for me.	**Rufen Sie bitte eine Taxe für mich.** *ROOF-en zee BIT-eh EYEN-eh TAHKS-eh fewr mikh*
How much is the ride to Wandsbek?	**Wie viel kostet die Fahrt nach Wandsbek?** *VEE-feel KOST-et dee faart nakh WAHNTS-behk?*

Please wait for me.	**Warten Sie auf mich bitte.** *VAART-en zee owf mikh BIT-eh*
Let me off at the next corner.	**Lassen Sie mich an der nächsten Ecke aussteigen!** *LASS-en zee mikh ahn dehr NAYKST-en EK-eh OWS-shteye-gen*

SIGHTSEEING

I'm looking for the Tourist Office.	**Ich suche das Fremden-verkehrsbüro.** *ikh ZOOKH-eh dahs FREHM-den-fehr-kayrs-bew-roh*
Is there a guided tour of the city? (bus tour)	**Gibt es eine Stadtrundfahrt?** *gipt ehs EYEN-eh SHTAHT-runt-faart*
Is there an English-speaking tour?	**Gibt es eine englischsprachige Führung?** *gipt ehs EYEN-eh ENG-lish-shpraa-khi-geh FEWR-ung*
I need a guidebook.	**Ich brauche einen Reiseführer.** *ikh BROWKH-eh EYEN-en REYEZ-eh-few-ruh*
What are the chief sights?	**Was sind die Hauptsehenswürdig-keiten?** *vahs zint dee HOWPT-zay-ens-vewr-dikh-keye-ten DINGT geh-ZAY-en HAAB-en*
Is (are) the ____ very far from here?	**Ist (sind) ____ sehr weit von hier?** *ist (zint) ____ zayr veyet fon heer*
■ abbey	**die Abtei** *dee ahp-TEYE*
■ amusement park	**der Vergnügungspark** *dehr fehr-GNEWG-ungks-paark*

■ artists' quarter	**das Künstlerviertel** *dahs KEWNST-lehr-feer-tel*
■ botanical garden	**der Botanische Garten** *dehr bo-TAAN-ish-eh GAART-en*
■ castle	**das Schloss/die Burg, Festung** *dahs shloss/dee boork FEST-ung*
■ cathedral	**der Dom/die Kathedrale** *dehr dohm/dee kaa-tayd-RAAL-eh*
■ cemetery	**der Friedhof** *dehr FREET-hohf*
■ city center	**die Stadtmitte/das Zentrum** *dee SHTAHT-mit-eh/dahs TSENT-rum*
■ city hall	**das Rathaus** *dahs RAAT-hows*
■ church	**die Kirche** *dee KEERKH-eh*
■ commercial district	**das Geschäftsviertel** *dahs geh-SHEHFTS-feer-tel*
■ concert hall	**die Konzerthalle** *dee kon-TSAYRT-hah-leh*
■ docks	**die Hafenanlagen** *dee HAA-fen-ahn-laa-gen*
■ fountain	**der Springbrunnen** *dehr SHPRING-bru-nen*
■ gardens	**die Gärten/Grünanlagen** *dee GEHRT-en/GREWN-ahn-laa-gen*
■ library	**die Bibliothek** *dee bib-lee-oh-TAYK*
■ market	**der Markt** *dehr maarkt*
■ monastery	**das Kloster** *dahs KLOHST-uh*
■ monument	**das Denkmal** *dahs DEHNK-maal*
■ museum	**das Museum** *dahs moo-ZAY-um*
■ a nightclub	**ein Nachtlokal** *eyen NAHKHT-lo-kaal*
■ old part of town	**die Altstadt** *dee AHLT-shtaht*
■ open-air museum	**das Freilichtmuseum** *dahs FREYE-likht-moo-zay-um*

■ opera	**das Opernhaus** *dahs OH-pehrn-howss*
■ palace	**das Schloss/Palais/der Palast** *dahs shloss/pah-LAY/dehr pah-LAHST*
■ ramparts	**die Stadtmauer** *dee STAHT-mow-uh*
■ river	**der Fluss** *dehr fluss*
■ ruins	**die Ruinen** *dee roo-EEN-en*
■ stadium	**das Stadion** *dahs SHTAAD-ee-ohn*
■ theater	**das Theater** *dahs tay-AAT-uh*
■ tower	**der Turm** *dehr toorm*
■ university	**die Universität** *dee u-nee-vayr-zi-TAYT*
Is it all right to go in now?	**Darf man jetzt rein?** *dahrf mahn yetst reyen*
What time does it open (close)?	**Um wieviel Uhr wird geöffnet (geschlossen)?** *um VEE-feel oor veert geh-ERF-net (geh-SHLOSS-en)*
Must children (students) pay full price?	**Müssen Kinder (Studenten) den vollen Preis bezahlen?** *MEWSS-en KIND-uh (shtu-DENT-en) dayn FOL-en preyess beh-TSAAL-en*
I want three tickets.	**Ich möchte drei Eintrittskarten.** *ikh MERKH-teh dreye EYEN-trits-kaar-ten*
Two adults and one child at half price.	**Zwei Erwachsene und ein Kind zum halben Preis.** *tsveye ehr-VAHKS-en-eh unt eyen kint tsoom HAHLB-en preyess*
Is taking photographs allowed?	**Darf man fotografieren?** *dahr mahn foh-toh-grah-FEER-en*

PLANNING A TRIP

AT THE AIRPORT AND ON THE PLANE

Can I fly to Stuttgart directly from here?	**Kann ich von hier direkt nach Stuttgart fliegen?** *kahn ikh fon heer dee-REHKT naakh SHTUT-gahrt FLEEG-en*
Or do I have to change planes?	**Oder muss ich umsteigen?** *OHD-uh muss ikh UM-shteye-gen*
How much is a one-way trip (a round-trip)?	**Was kostet ein einfacher Flug (ein Rückflug)?** *vahs KOST-et eyen EYEN-fahkh-uh flook (eyen REWK-flook)*
When do I have to check in?	**Wann muss ich mich melden?** *vahn muss ikh mikh MEHLD-en*
At what time does it leave?	**Um wieviel Uhr ist der Abflug?** *um VEE-feel oor ist dehr AHP-flook*
I want a seat next to the window in the (non)smoking section.	**Ich möchte einen Fensterplatz (Nicht)Raucher haben.** *ikh MERKH-teh EYEN-en FEHNST-uh-plahts (nikht)ROWKH-uh HAAB-en*
When do we land?	**Wann landen wir?** *vahn LAHND-en veer*
Is there a meal served on flight number ____?	**Gibt es eine Mahlzeit auf Flug Nummer ____?** *gipt ehs EYEN-eh MAAL-tseyet owf flook NUM-uh*
I have only carry-on baggage.	**Ich habe nur Handgepäck.** *ikh HAAB-eh noor HAHNT-geh-pehk*

Please pass my film (camera) through by hand. | **Bitte reichen Sie mir meinen Film (meine Kamera).** *BIT-eh REYEKH-en zee meer MEYEN-en film (MEYEN-eh KAA-meh-raa)*

SHIPBOARD TRAVEL

Can I go by steamer from Düsseldorf to Cologne? | **Kann ich mit dem Rheindampfer von Düsseldorf nach Köln fahren?** *kahn ikh mit dem REYEN-dahmp-fuh fon DEWSS-el-dorf nahkh kerln FAAR-en*

When does the last ferry (the next boat) leave? | **Wann geht die letzte Fähre (das nächste Boot)?** *vahn gayt dee LEHTST-eh FAIR-eh (dahs NAYKST-eh boht)*

Is there also a hydrofoil (hovercraft)? | **Gibt es auch ein Luftkissenboot?** *gipt ehs owkh eyen LUFT-kissen-boht*

How long does the crossing to Helgoland take? | **Wie lange dauert die Überfahrt nach Helgoland?** *vee LAHNG-eh DOW-ehrt dee EWB-uh-faart nahkh HEHL-goh-lahnt*

I'd like a cabin ____. | **Ich möchte eine Kabine ____.** *ikh MERKHT-eh EYEN-eh kah-BEEN-eh*

■ in the luxury class | **in der Luxusklasse** *in dehr LUKS-us-klahss-eh*

■ in the first (second) class | **in der ersten (zweiten) Klasse** *in dehr EHRST-en (TSVEYET-en) KLAHSS-eh*

When do we have to board the ship again? | **Wann müssen wir wieder das Schiff besteigen?** *vahn MEWSS-en veer VEED-uh dahs shif be-STEYEG-en*

Do you have something for seasickness?	**Haben Sie etwas gegen Seekrankheit?** *HAAB-en zee ET-vahs GAYG-en ZAY-krahnk-heyet*

TRAINS

Please call me a taxi.	**Bitte besorgen Sie mir ein Taxi.** *BIT-eh beh-ZORG-en zee meer eyen TAHK-see*
Please help me with my luggage.	**Bitte helfen Sie mir mit meinem Gepäck.** *BIT-eh HELF-en zee meer mit MEYEN-em ge-PEHK*
Is there a baggage check office?	**Gibt es eine Gepäckaufbewahrung?** *gipt ehs EYEN-eh geh-PEHK-owf-be-vaar-ung*
Where are the luggage lockers?	**Wo sind die Schließfächer?** *voh zint dee SHLEESS-fekh-uh*
Where is the ticket office?	**Wo ist der Fahrkartenschalter?** *voh ist dehr FAAR-kahr-ten-shahl-tuh*
A one-way (a round-trip) ticket to Heidelberg.	**Eine einfache Fahrkarte (eine Rückfahrkarte) nach Heidelberg.** *EYEN-eh EYEN-fahkh-eh FAAR-kahr-teh (EYEN-eh REWK-faar-kahr-teh) nahkh HEYED-el-behrk*
Can children travel at half-price?	**Können Kinder zum halben Preis fahren?** *KERN-en KIND-uh tsoom HAHLB-en preyess FAAR-en*
What is the fare to Vienna?	**Was kostet die Fahrt nach Wien?** *vahs KOST-et dee faart nahkh veen*

Does the train stop in Linz?	**Hält der Zug in Linz?** *hehlt dehr tsook in lints*
On what platform does the train from Hamburg arrive?	**Auf welchem Bahnsteig kommt der Zug aus Hamburg an?** *owf WELKH-em BAAN-shteyek komt dehr tsook ows HAHM-boork ahn*
When does the next train for Zürich leave?	**Wann fährt der nächste Zug nach Zürich?** *vahn fehrt dehr NAYKST-eh tsook nahkh TSEW-rikh*
Is this car a smoker or nonsmoker?	**Ist dieser Wagen Raucher oder Nichtraucher?** *ist DEEZ-uh VAAG-en ROWKH-uh OHD-uh nikht ROWKH-uh*
Is this seat taken?	**Ist hier noch frei?** *ist heer nokh freye*
Do you have a timetable?	**Haben Sie einen Fahrplan?** *HAAB-en zee EYEN-en FAAR-plaan*
Is there a dining car?	**Gibt es einen Speisewagen?** *gipt ehs EIN-en SHPEYE-zeh-vaa-gen*
Is it up front or to the rear?	**Ist er vorne oder hinten?** *ist ehr FORN-eh OHD-uh HINT-en*
Is the train carrying a sleeping car?	**Führt der Zug einen Schlafwagen?** *fewrt dehr tsook EYEN-en SHLAAF-vaa-gen*
All aboard!	**Einsteigen!** *EYEN-shteye-gen*
Where should I get off?	**Wo soll ich aussteigen?** *voh zol ikh OWS-shteye-gen*
Must I change trains?	**Muss ich umsteigen?** *muss ikh UM-steye-gen*

Can I take the express from Osnabrück to Bassum?	**Kann ich mit dem Fernschnellzug von Osnabrück nach Bassum fahren?** *kahn ikh mit daym FEHRN-shnel-tsook fon oss-nah-BREWK nakh BAHSS-um FAAR-en*
Or must I change to a local train?	**Oder muss ich in einen Personenzug umsteigen?** *OHD-uh muss ikh in EYEN-en pehr-ZOHN-en-tsook UM-steye-gen*

DRIVING A CAR

ROAD SIGNS

AUF 8 KM	For 8 Kilometers
AUSFAHRT FREI HALTEN	Keep Driveway Clear
BLAUE ZONE	Blue Parking Zone (requires special parking disk)
DURCHGANGS-VERKEHR	Through Traffic
EINBAHN-STRASSE	One-way Street
EINFAHRT FREI HALTEN	Do Not Block Entrance
EINORDNEN	Get in Lane
ENDE DES PARK-VERBOTS	End of No Parking Zone
____ (NICHT) ERLAUBT	____ (not) Allowed

FROSTSCHÄDEN	Frost Damage
FUSSGÄNGER-ZONE	Pedestrian Zone
GEFÄHRLICHES GEFÄLLE	Dangerous Descent
GEFÄHRLICHE STEIGUNG	Dangerous (steep) Hill
HALT, POLIZEI	Stop, Police
HUPEN VERBO-TEN	No Honking
KEIN DURCHGANG FÜR FUSSGÄNGER	Closed to Pedestrians
KURZPARKZONE	Limited Parking Zone
LANGSAM FAHREN	Drive Slowly
LAWINENGEFAHR	Danger of Avalanche
LINKS FAHREN	Keep Left
LKW	Alternate Truck Route
NUR FÜR ANLIEGER	Residents Only
PARKEN VERBOTEN	No Parking
RECHTS FAHREN	Keep Right
SCHLECHTE FAHRBAHN	Bad Road Surface
SCHULE	School
SPURRILLEN	Grooves in Road

Guarded railroad crossing

Yield

Stop

Right of way

Dangerous intersection ahead

Gasoline (petrol) ahead

Parking

No vehicles allowed

Dangerous curve

Pedestrian crossing

Oncoming traffic has right of way

No bicycles allowed

No parking allowed

No entry

No left turn

No U-turn

No passing

Border crossing

Traffic signal ahead

Speed limit

Traffic circle (roundabout) ahead

Minimum speed limit

All traffic turns left

End of no passing zone

One-way street

Detour

Danger ahead

Entrance to expressway

Expressway ends

STEINSCHLAG	Falling Rocks
STRASSENAR-BEITEN AUF 5 KILOMETER	Road Work for 5 Kilometers
UMLEITUNG	Detour
VERKEHRSSTAU AUF 15 KILOMETER	Traffic Backups (jams) for the Next 15 Kilometers
____ VERBOTEN	____ Not Allowed
VORSICHT	Caution

CAR RENTALS

I need ____.	**Ich brauche ____.** *ikh BROWKH-eh*
■ a car	**einen Wagen** *EYEN-en VAAG-en*
■ a motorcycle	**ein Motorrad** *eyen moh-TOHR-raat*
■ a bicycle	**ein Fahrrad** *eyen FAAR-raat*
Is there a car rental office nearby?	**Gibt es eine Autovertmietung in der Nähe?** *gipt ehs EYEN-eh OW-toh-fehr-meet-ung in dehr NAY-eh*
Can they send somebody to pick me up at my hotel?	**Kann mich jemand im Hotel abholen?** *kahn mikh YAY-mahnt im ho-TEL AHP-hohl-en*
I need a big (small) car.	**Ich brauche einen grossen (kleinen) Wagen.** *ikh BROWKH-eh EYEN-en GROHSS-en (KLEYEN-en) VAAG-en*
How much does it cost per ____?	**Wieviel kostet es pro ____?** *VEE-feel KOST-et ehs proh*

- day
- week
- month
- kilometer

Tag *taak*
Woche *VOKH-eh*
Monat *MOH-naat*
Kilometer *kee-loh-MAYT-uh*

How much is the insurance?
Was kostet die Versicherung?
vahs KOST-et dee fehr-ZIKH-ehr-ung

Do I have to pay for gas?
Muss ich das Benzin bezahlen?
muss ikh dahs behn-TSEEN beh-TSAAL-en

Do I have to leave a deposit?
Muss ich etwas hinterlegen? *muss ikh EHT-vahs hin-tehr-LAYG-en*

Even with this credit card?
Selbst mit dieser Kreditkarte?
zehlpst mit DEEZ-uh kray-DIT-kaart-eh

I want to rent the car here and leave it in Munich.
Ich will das Auto hier mieten und es in München wieder abgeben.
ikh vil dahs OW-toh heer MEET-en unt ehs in MEWN-khen VEED-uh AHP-gayb-en

Is there an additional charge for that?
Entstehen mir dadurch zuätzliche Kosten? *ehnt-SHTAY-en meer daa-DURKH TSOO-zehts-likh-eh KOST-en*

What kind of gasoline does it use?
Mit welchem Benzin fährt der Wagen? *mit VEHLKH-em behn-TSEEN fayrt dehr VAAG-en*

Here is my driver's license.
Hier haben Sie meinen Führerschein. *heer HAAB-en zee MEYEN-en FEWR-ehr-sheyen*

ON THE ROAD

Pardon me.	**Entschuldigen Sie, bitte.** *ehnt-SHULD-ig-en zee BIT-eh*
Is this the road to ____?	**Ist dies die Straße nach ____?** *ist dees dee SHTRAASS-eh nahkh*
Where does this road lead?	**Wohin führt diese Straße?** *VOH-hin fewrt DEEZ-eh SHTRAASS-eh*
How do we get to ____?	**Wie kommen wir nach ____?** *Vee KOM-en veer nahkh*
Is this road shorter (longer)?	**Ist diese Straße kürzer (länger)?** *ist DEEZ-eh SHTRAASS-eh KEWRTS-ehr (LEHNG-ehr)*
Is it still very far to ____?	**Ist es noch sehr weit nach ____?** *ist ehs nokh zayr veyet nahkh*
What's the next town called?	**Wie heißt der nächste Ort?** *vee heyesst dehr NAYKST-eh ort*
Do you have a road map?	**Haben Sie eine Autokarte?** *HAAB-en zee EYEN-eh OW-toh-kaart-eh*
Can you show it to me on the map?	**Können Sie ihn mir auf der Karte zeigen?** *KERN-en zee een meer owf dehr KAART-eh TSEYEG-en*
Shall I drive straight ahead?	**Soll ich geradeaus fahren?** *zol ikh geh-RAAD-eh-owss FAAR-en*
Where must I turn?	**Wo muss ich abbiegen?** *voh muss ikh AHP-beeg-en*
Left?	**Links?** *links*
Right?	**Rechts?** *rehkhts*

AT THE SERVICE STATION

I'm looking for a gas station.	**Ich suche eine Tankstelle.** *ikh ZOOKH-eh EYEN-eh TAHNK-shtehl-eh*
Where is the nearest gas station (with service)?	**Wo ist die nächste Tankstelle (mit Bedienung)?** *voh ist dee NAYKST-eh TAHNK-shtehl-eh (mit beh-DEEN-ung)*
Fill 'er up, please.	**Voll, bitte.** *fol BIT-eh*
Give me twenty-five liters.	**Geben Sie mir fünfundzwanzig Liter.** *GAYB-en zee meer FEWNF-unt-tsvahn-tsikh LEET-uh*

- regular   **Normal** *nor-MAAL*
- super   **Super** *ZOOP-uh*

Please check the oil and water.	**Bitte kontrollieren Sie Ölstand und Wasser.** *BIT-eh kon-tro-LEER-en zee ERL-shtahnt unt VAHSS-uh*
Please check ____.	**Prüfen Sie bitte ____.** *PREWF-en zee BIT-eh*

- the battery   **die Batterie** *dee bah-teh-REE*
- the brakes   **die Bremsen** *dee BREHM-zen*
- the carburetor   **den Vergaser** *dayn fehr-GAAZ-uh*
- the spark plugs   **die Zündkerzen** *dee TSEWNT-kehrts-en*
- the ignition system   **die Zündung** *dee TSEWND-ung*
- the lights   **die Beleuchtung** *dee beh-LOYKHT-ung*
- the tires   **die Reifen** *dee REYEF-en*
- the spare tire   **den Ersatzreifen** *dayn ehr-ZATS-reyef-en*
- the tire pressure   **den Reifendruck** *dayn REYEF-en-druk*

Can you change the tire (the oil) now?	**Können Sie den Reifen (das Öl) jetzt wechseln?** *KERN-en zee dayn REYEF-en (dahs erl) yetst VEHK-sehln*

ACCIDENTS AND REPAIRS

My car has broken down.	**Mein Wagen hat eine Panne.** *meyen VAAG-en haht EYEN-eh PAHN-eh*
It overheats.	**Er ist überhitzt.** *ehr ist EWB-uh-hitst*
I have a flat tire.	**Der Reifen ist kaputt.** *dehr REYEF-en ist kah-PUT*
The car is stuck.	**Der Wagen ist verklemmt.** *dehr VAAG-en ist fehr-KLEHMT*
Is there a garage (for repairs) near here?	**Gibt es eine Reparaturwerkstatt in der Nähe?** *gipt ehs EYEN-eh reh-paa-rah-TOOR-vehrk-shtaht in dehr NAY-eh*
Can you help me?	**Können Sie mir helfen?** *KERN-en zee meer HELF-en*
I have no tools.	**Ich habe keine Werkzeuge.** *ikh HAAB-eh KEYEN-eh VEHRK-tsoyg-eh*
I can't change the tire.	**Ich kann den Reifen nicht wechsein.** *ikh kahn dayn REYEF-en nikht VEHKS-ein*
I need a mechanic (a tow truck).	**Ich brauche einen Mechaniker (Abschleppwagen).** *ikh BROWKH-eh EYEN-en meh-KHAA-nik-uh (AHP-shlehp-vaag-en)*

Can you lend me ____?	**Können Sie mir ____ leihen?** *KERN-en zee meer ____ LEYE-en*
■ a flashlight	**eine Taschenlampe** *EYEN-eh TAHSH-en-lahmp-eh*
■ a hammer	**einen Hammer** *EYEN-en HAHM-uh*
■ a jack	**einen Wagenheber** *EYEN-en VAAG-en-hayb-uh*
■ a monkey wrench	**einen Schraubenschlüssel** *EYEN-en SHROWB-en-shlewssel*
■ pliers	**eine Zange** *EYEN-eh TSAHNG-eh*
■ a screwdriver	**einen Schraubenzieher** *EYEN-en SHROWB-en-tsee-uh*
Can you fix the car?	**Können Sie den Wagen reparieren?** *KERN-en zee dayn VAAG-en ray-paa-REER-en*
Do you have the part?	**Haben Sie das Ersatzteil?** *HAAB-en zee dahs ehr-ZAHTS-teyel*
I need ____.	**Ich brauche ____.** *ikh BROWKH-eh*
■ a bulb	**eine Birne** *EYEN-eh BIRN-eh*
■ a filter	**einen Filter** *EYEN-en FILT-uh*
■ a fuse	**eine Sicherung** *EYEN-eh ZIKH-ehr-ung*
Can you repair it temporarily?	**Können Sie es provisorisch reparieren?** *KERN-en zee ehs provi-ZOHR-ish ray-paa-REER-en*
How long will it take?	**Wie lange dauert's?** *vee LAHNG-eh DOW-ehrts*
Couldn't it possibly be done today?	**Geht's vielleicht doch heute noch?** *gayts fee-LEYEKHT dokh HOYT-eh nokh*

Is everything OK now?	**Ist jetzt alles in Ordnung?** *ist yetst AH-lehs in ORT-nung*
How much do I owe you?	**Was schulde ich Ihnen?** *vahs SHULD-eh ikh EEN-en*

ENTERTAINMENT AND DIVERSIONS

MOVIES, THEATER, CONCERTS, OPERA, BALLET

Let's go ____.	**Gehen wir ____.** *GAY-en veer*
◼ to the movies	**ins Kino** *ins KEEN-oh*
◼ to the museum	**ins Museum** *ins moo-ZAY-um*
◼ to the theater	**ins Theater** *ins tay-AAT-uh*
◼ to the opera	**in die Oper** *in dee OHP-uh*
What sort of a movie is it?	**Was für ein Film ist es?** *vahs fewr eyen film ist ehs*
It's ____.	**Est ist ____.** *ehs ist*
◼ a mystery	**ein Krimi** *eyen KREEM-ee*
◼ a comedy	**eine Komödie** *EYEN-eh ko-MERD-yeh*
◼ a drama	**ein Drama** *eyen DRAAM-ah*
◼ a musical	**ein Musical** *eyen MYOOZ-ikal*
◼ a romance	**eine Liebesgeschichte** *EYEN-eh LEEB-es-ge-SCHIKHT-eh*
◼ a war film	**ein Kriegsfilm** *eyen KREEKS-film*
◼ a science fiction film	**ein Science-fictionfilm** *eyen SEYE ens-FICKSH-en-film*

■ a romantic movie	**ein romantischer Film** *eyen roh-MAHNT-isch-uh film*
■ a horror film	**ein Horror film** *eyen HOR-or-film*
Is it in English?	**Ist es in Englisch?** *ist ehs in EHNG-lish*
Are there English subtitles?	**Hat er englische Untertitel?** *haht ehr EHNG-lish-eh UNT-uh-TEET-el*
Where is the time schedule?	**Wo ist der Zeitplan?** *voh ist dehr TSEIT-plaan*
What time does the (first) show begin?	**Wann beginnt die (erste) Vorstellung?** *vahn beh-GINT dee (EHRST-eh) FOR-shtel-ung*
What time does the (last) show end?	**Wann endet die (letzte) Vorstellung?** *vahn EHND-eht dee (LETST-eh) FOR-shtel-ung*

BUYING A TICKET

Can you get tickets for me?	**Können Sie Karten für mich besorgen?** *KERN-en zee KAART-en fewr mikh beh-ZORG-en*
I need two seats in the ____.	**Ich brauche zwei Sitze/Plätze im ____.** *ikh BROWKH-eh tsveye SITZ-eh/PLETS-eh im*
■ orchestra	**Orchester** *or-KHES-tuh*
■ balcony	**orbesten Rang** *OH-behrst-en rahng*
■ first balcony	**ersten Rang** *EHRST-en rahng*
■ mezzanine	**Mezzanin** *mehts-ah-NEEN*
I prefer ____.	**Ich höre am liebsten ____.** *ikh HEWR-eh am LEEP-sten*

■ classical music	**klassische musik** *KLAHS-ish-eh mooz-EEK*
■ popular music	**Popmusik** *POP-mooz-EEK*
■ soft rock	**Softrock** *SOFT-rock*
■ heavy metal	**Heavymetal** *heavy metal*
■ opera	**Oper** *OHP-uh*
■ ballet	**Ballett** *bah-LETT*
■ folk dancing	**Volkstänze** *FOLKS-tehnts-eh*

NIGHTCLUBS

I'd like to go to an interesting nightclub tonight.	**Ich möchte gerne in ein interessantes Nachtlokal heute abend gehen.** *ikh MERKHT-eh GEHRN-eh in eyen in-teh-ress-AHNT-es NAKHT-loh-kaal HOYT-eh AAB-ent GAY-en*
■ a beer or wine tavern with happy music.	**Eine Bier- oder Weinstube mit fröhlicher Musik.** *EYEN-eh beer OHD-uh VEYEN-shtoob-eh mit FRER-likh-ehr moo-ZEEK*
■ a discotheque with young people.	**Eine Diskothek mit jungen Leuten.** *EYEN-eh dis-koh-TAYK mit YUNG-en LOYT-en*
■ a lavish nightclub with a floor show.	**ein Nachtlokal von Format mit Attraktionen.** *eyen NAHKHT-lo-kaal fon for-MAAT mit aht-rahk-tsee-OHN-en*
Is a reservation necessary?	**Muss man reservieren lassen?** *muss mahn reh-zehr-VEER-en LASS-en*
Is evening dress required?	**Wird Abendgarderobe verlangt?** *veert AAB-ent-gaar-deh-roh-beh fehr-LAHNKT*

| I'd like a good table. | **Ich möchte einen guten Tisch.** *ikh MERKHT-eh EYEN-en GOOT-en tish* |
| Is there a minimum? | **Gibt es eine Mindestgebühr?** *gipt ehs EYEN-eh MIND-ehst-geh-BEWR* |

SPORTS

I'd like to ___.	**Ich möchte ___.** *ikh MERKHT-eh*
■ do aerobics	**Aerobic betreiben** *ah-eh-ROHB-ik beh-TREYEB-en*
■ play baseball	**Baseball spielen** *BAYSS-bahl SHPEEL-en*
■ play basketball	**Baksetball spielen** *BAHS-keht-bahl SHPEEL-en*
■ go bicycling	**Rad fahren** *raat FAAR-en*
■ go boating	**Boot fahren** *boht FAAR-en*
■ do bodybuilding	**Bodybuilding betreiben** *BO-dee-bil-ding beh-TREYEB-en*
■ go canoeing	**Paddelboot fahren** *PAHD-el-boht faar-en*
■ go diving	**Wasser sprigen** *VAHSS-uh shpring-en*
■ fish	**angeln** *AHNG-eln*
■ play golf	**Golf spielen** *golf SHPEEL-en*
■ play hockey	**Hockey spielen** *HOK-eh SHPEEL-en*
■ go horseback riding	**reiten** *REYET-en*
■ go hunting	**auf die Jagd gehen** *owf dee jahkt GAY-en*

■ ice-skate	**Schlittschuh laufen** *SHLIT-shoo LOWF-en*
■ go mountain climbing	**bergsteigen** *BEHRK-shteyeg-en*
■ parasail	**parasegeln** *pah-rah ZAYG-eln*
■ go roller skating	**Rollschuh laufen** *ROL-shoo LOWF-en*
■ go sailing	**Segelsport fahren** *ZAYG-el-shport FAAR-en*
■ scuba dive	**Sporttauchen betreiben** *SHPORT-towkh-en beh-TREYEB-en*
■ ski	**Ski laufen** *skee LOWF-en*
■ surf	**surfen** *SERF-en*
■ swim	**schwimmen** *SHVIM-en*
■ play tennis	**Tennis spielen** *TEN-iss SHPEEL-en*
■ play volleyball	**Volleyball spielen** *VOL-ee-bahl SHPEEL-en*

PLAYING FIELDS

Shall we go ____.	**Gehen wir ____.** *GAY-en veer*
■ to the beach	**an den Strand** *ahn dayn shtrahnt*
■ to the court	**auf den Platz** *owf dayn plahts*
■ to the field	**aufs Feld** *owfs felt*
■ to the golf course	**auf den Golfplatz** *owf dayn GOLF-plahts*
■ to the gymnasium	**in die Turnhalle** *in dee TOORN-hahl-eh*
■ to the mountains	**in die Berge** *in dee BEHRG-eh*
■ to the ocean	**an den Ozean** *ahn dayn ots-ay-AHN*
■ to the park	**in den Park** *in dayn pahrk*
■ to the path	**an den Pfad** *ahn dayn pfaat*

■ to the pool   **zum Schwimmbad**   *tsoom SHVIM-baht*

■ to the (roller-skating) rink   **zur Rollschuhbahn**   *tsoor ROL-shoo-baan*

■ to the (ice-skating) rink   **zur Schlittschuhbahn**   *tsoor SHLIT-shoo-baan*

■ to the sea   **an die See**   *ahn dee zay*

■ to the stadium   **zum Stadion**   *tsoom SHTAAD-ee-ohn*

■ to the track   **zur Rennbahn**   *tsoor REN-baan*

SWIMMING

Where can I find a swimming pool?   **Wo kann ich ein Schwimmbad finden?**   *voh kahn ikh eyen SHVIM-baat FIND-en*

What's the water temperature?   **Welche Temperatur hat das Wasser?**   *VELKH-eh lem-pay-raa-TOOR haht dahs VAHSS-uh*

How do I get there?   **Wie komme ich dort hin?**   *vee KOM-eh ikh dort hin*

When is low tide (high tide)?   **Wann ist Ebbe (Flut)?**   *vahn ist EHB-eh (floot)*

Is there a lake in the area?   **Gibt es einen See in der Gegend?**   *gipt ehs EYEN-en zay in dehr GAY-gent*

What's the admission charge?   **Was kostet der Eintritt?**   *vahs KOST-et dehr EYEN-trit*

Is it safe to swim there?   **Kann man dort ohne Gefahr schwimmen?**   *kahn mahn dort OHN-eh geh-FAAR SHVIM-en*

Is there a lifeguard?   **Gibt es einen Rettungsdienst?**   *gipt ehs EYEN-en REHT-unks-deenst*

Can you swim in the river (pond)?	**Kann man im Fluss (Teich) schwimmen?** *kahn mahn im fluss (teyekh) SHVIM-en*
Is the water clean?	**Ist das Wasser rein?** *ist dahs VAHSS-uh reyen*
Where can I get ____?	**Wo kann ich ____ bekommen?** *voh kahn ikh ____ beh-KOM-en*

- an air mattress **eine Luftmatratze** *EYEN-eh luft-maht-rahts-eh*

- a bathing suit **einen Badeanzug** *EYEN-en BAAD-eh-ahn-tsook*

- a chaise lounge **einen Liegestuhl** *EYEN-en LEEG-eh-shtool*

- diving equipment **eine Tauchausrüstung** *EYEN-eh TOWKH-owss-rewst-ung*

- sunglasses **eine Sonnenbrille** *EYEN-eh ZON-en-bril-eh*

- suntan lotion **Sonnencreme** *ZON-en-kraym*

WINTER SPORTS

Are the very high passes still open to traffic?	**Sind die ganz hohen Pässe noch dem Verkehr offen?** *zint dee gahnts HOH-en PEHSS-eh nokh daym fehr-KAYR OFF-en*
Can you take the train there?	**Kann man mit dem Zug dort hinfahren?** *kahn mahn mit daym tsook dort HIN-faar-en*
Is there a cable car or cogwheel railway?	**Gibt es eine Seilschwebe oder Bergbahn?** *gipt ehs EYEN-eh ZEYEL-shvayb-eh OHD-uh BAIRK-baan*
Are there ski lifts?	**Gibt es dort Schilifts?** *gipt ehs dort SHEE-lifts*

■ chair lifts or T-bars	**Sessel- oder Schlepplifts** *ZEHSS-el OHD-uh SHLEP-lifts*
I need skiing lessons.	**Ich brauche Schiunterricht.** *ikh BROWKH-eh SHEE-un-tehr-rikht*
■ skating lessons	**Unterricht im Schlittschuhlaufen** *UNT-ehr-rikht im SHLIT-shoo-lowf-en*
Is there an ice-skating rink?	**Gibt es eine Eisbahn?** *gipt ehs EYEN-eh EYESS-baan*
Is it possible to rent _____?	**Ist es möglich _____ zu mieten?** *ist ehs MERG-likh _____ tsoo MEET-en*
■ skiing equipment	**eine Schiausrüstung** *EYEN-eh SHEE-owss-rewst-ung*
■ a sled	**einen Schlitten** *EYEN-en SHLIT-en*
■ poles	**Schistöcke** *SHEE-shterk-eh*
■ boots	**Stiefel** *SHTEEF-el*

CAMPING

We're looking for a camping site around here.	**Wir suchen einen Campingplatz in der Nähe.** *veer ZUKH-en EYEN-en KEHMP-ing-plahts in dehr NAY-eh*
How far is it?	**Wie weit ist er?** *vee veyet ist ehr*
I hope it isn't too crowded.	**Hoffentlich ist er nicht zu voll.** *HOF-ent-likh ist ehr nikht tsoo fol*
Might it be possible to camp on your property?	**Dürften wir vielleicht auf Ihrem Grundstück zelten?** *DEWRFT-en veer feel-LEYEKHT owf EER-em GRUND-shtwek TSELT-en*

Where can we spend the night?	**Wo können wir übernachten?** *voh KERN-en veer EWB-uh-nakht-en*
Where can we park our trailer?	**Wo können wir unseren Wohnwagen abstellen?** *voh KERN-en veer UN-zehr-en VOHN-vaag-en AHP-shtel-en*
How do we get to this camping place?	**Wie kommen wir zu diesem Campingplatz?** *vee KOM-en veer tsoo DEEZ-em KEHMP-ing-plahts*
Is there ____ there?	**Gibt es ____ dort?** *gipt ehs ____ dort*
■ drinking water	**Trinkwasser** *TRINK-vaass-uh*
■ running water	**fließendes Wasser** *FLEESS-end-es VAASS-uh*
■ a children's play-ground	**einen Spielplatz für Kinder** *EYEN-en SHPEEL-plahts fewr KIND-uh*
Are there ____?	**Gibt es ____?** *gipt es*
■ showers	**Duschen** *DOO-shen*
■ baths	**Bäder** *BAY-duh*
■ toilets	**Toiletten** *toy-LET-en*
■ tents	**Zelte** *TSELT-eh*
What does it cost per ____?	**Was kostet es pro ____?** *vahs KOST-et es proh*
■ person	**Person** *pehr-ZOHN*
■ car	**Wagen** *VAAG-en*
■ trailer	**Wohnwagen** *VOHN-vaag-en*
We'd like to stay ____ days (weeks).	**Wir möchten ____ Tage (Wochen) bleiben.** *veer MERKHT-en ____ TAAG-eh (VOKH-en) BLEYEB-en eer-gahng MAHKH-en*

FOOD AND DRINK

DRINKING AND DINING

Is there a good, not too expensive, German restaurant around here?	**Gibt es ein gutes, nicht zu teures deutsches Restaurant in der Nähe?** *gipt ehs eyen GOOT-es nikht tsoo TOYR-es DOY-ches res-tow-RAHNT in dehr NAY-eh*
Can you recommend an inexpensive restaurant _____?	**Können Sie mir ein preiswertes Restaurant empfehlen _____?** *KERN-en zee meer eyen PREYES-vehrt-es res-tow-RAHNT emp-FAYL-en*
■ with German specialties	**mit deutschen Spezialitäten** *mit DOY-chen shpehts-yah-li-TAYT-en*
■ with local specialties	**mit hiesigen Spezialitäten** *mit HEEZ-ig-en shpehts-yah-li-TAYT-en*
Do you have a table for me (us)?	**Haben Sie einen Tisch für mich (uns)?** *HAAB-en zee EYEN-en tish fewr mikh (uns)?*
Where are the toilets?	**Wo sind die Toiletten?** *voh zint dee toy-LET-en*
Where can I wash my hands?	**Wo kann ich mir die Hände waschen?** *voh kahn ikh meer dee HEHND-eh VAHSH-en*
Would we have to wait long?	**Müssten wir lange warten?** *MEWSST-en veer LAHNG-eh VAART-en*
I need (we need) another _____.	**Ich brauche (wir brauchen) noch _____.** *ikh BROWKH-eh (veer BROWKH-en) nokh*

- spoon   **einen Löffel** *EYEN-en LERF-el*
- fork   **eine Gabel** *EYEN-eh GAAB-el*
- knife   **ein Messer** *eyen MESS-uh*
- glass   **ein Glas** *eyen glaas*
- plate   **einen Teller** *EYEN-en TEL-uh*
- chair   **einen Stuhl** *EYEN-en shtool*
- ashtray   **einen Aschenbecher** *EYEN-en AHSH-en-bekh-uh*
- napkin   **eine Serviette** *EYEN-eh zehr-VYEHT-eh*

APPETIZERS

Aal in Gelee *aal in zheh-LAY*	eel in aspic (ballotine of eel)
Appetithäppchen *ah-peh-TEET-hehp-khyen*	canapés
Artischockenherzen in Öl *ahr-ti-SHOK-en-herts-en in erl*	hearts of artichokes in oil
Bismarckhering *BIS-mahrk-hayr-ing*	marinated herring with onions
Bückling *BEWK-ling*	kipper, bloater
Fleischpastete *FLEYESH-pahs-tayt-eh*	meat pie, meat loaf
Froschschenkel *FROSH-shehnk-el*	frogs' legs
Gänseleberpastete *GEHN-zeh-lay-buh-pahs-tayt-eh*	goose liver pâté
Gänseleber im eigenen Fett *GEHN-zeh-lay-buh im EYEG-en-en fet*	goose liver (cold) in its own fat

Geräucherte Gänsebrust *geh-ROYKH-ert-eh GEHN-zeh-brust*	smoked breast of goose
Geftüllte Champignons *geh-FEWLT-eh shahm-pin-YONGS*	stuffed mushrooms
Hoppel-Poppel *HOP-pel-POP-pel*	scrambled eggs with fried potatoes and ham
Hummer *HUM-uh*	lobster
Käsehäppchen *KAY-zeh-hehp-khyen*	bits of cheese
Katenschinken *KAAT-en-shink-en*	lightly smoked Westphalian ham
Kaviar mit Zwiebeln und Zitrone *KAA-viah mit TSVEEB-eln unt tsit-ROHN-eh*	caviar with onions and lemon
Königinpastete *KERN-eeg-in-pahs-tayt-eh*	mushrooms and bits of chicken and tongue in a puff-pastry shell
Krabben *KRAHB-en*	tiny shrimps
Krebs *krayps*	crawfish, crayfish, crab
Lachs *lahks*	salmon
Languste *lahn-GUS-teh*	spiny lobster
Makrele *mah-KRAY-leh*	mackerel

Matjeshering *MAH-tyehs-hayr-ing* "maiden herring" (a young, white, salted herring usually served with new potatoes)

Meefischli *MAY-fish-lee* small baked fish from the Main River (a Würzburg specialty)

Ochsenmaulsalat *OKS-en-mowl-zah-laat* ox-maw salad

Russische Eier *RUSS-ish-eh EYE-uh* Russian eggs (hard-boiled eggs with mayonnaise)

Rehpastete *RAY-pahs-tayt-eh* venison pâté

Sardellen *zahr-DEL-en* anchovies

Schinken *SHINK-en* ham

Schnecken *SHNEHK-en* snails

Soleier *ZOHL-eye-uh* eggs boiled in brine

Spargelspitzen *SHPAHRG-el-shpits-en* asparagus tips

Strammer Max *STRAHM-uh mahks* well-seasoned diced pork served with eggs and onions

Verschiedene kleine Vorspeisen *fer-SHEED-en-eh KLEYE-neh for-SHPEYEZ-en* various little appetizers (hors d'oeuvres)

| Wurstsalat | *VOORST-zah-laat* | cold cuts chopped and served with onions and oil |

BEER

| Beer, please. | **Ein Bier, bitte.** *eyen beer BIT-eh* |

You can have either:

| a bottle of beer | **eine Flasche Bier** *EYEN-eh FLAH-sheh beer* |

or

| draught beer | **Bier (frisch) vom Faß** *beer (frish) fom fahss* |

You may prefer dark (**dunkles,** *DUNK-les*) or light (**helles,** *HELL-es*) beer.

As to quantities, you can have:

a glass	**ein Glas** *eyen glaas*
half a liter (about a pint)	**einen halben Liter** *EYEN-en HAHLB-en LEET-uh*
a mug (liter)	**eine Maß** *EYEN-eh maas*

You may be familiar with some types of beer. Others may be new to you.

| Altbier | *AHLT-beer* | A bitter beer high in hops (**Hopfen**), said by some to be a tranquilizer. |
| Alsterwasser | *AHL-stuh-vahss-uh* | A light beer with a dash of lemonade. |

Bockbier	*BOK-beer*	Beers with a high alcohol and malt content.
Doppelbock	*DOPP-ehl-boh*	
Märzenbier	*MEHRTS-en-beer*	
Malzbier	*MAHLTS-beer*	A rather sweet, dark beer low in alcohol but not in calories.
Pilsener	*PILZ-en-uh*	A light beer originally brewed in Bohemia.
Schlenkerle	*SHLEHNK-ehr-leh*	A beer made of smoked hops, with a lightly smoked flavor, a specialty of Stuttgart.
Starkbier	*SHTAHRK-beer*	Strong, calorific beer.
Weißbier	*VEYESS-beer*	A pale ale brewed from wheat.

WINES

Do you have a wine list?	**Haben Sie eine Weinkarte?** *HAAB-en zee EYEN-eh VEYEN-kaart-eh*

If there is no wine list, ask:

What kinds of wine do you have?	**Was für Weine haben Sie?** *vahs fewr VEYEN-eh HAAB-en zee*
A bottle of white wine (red wine).	**Eine Flasche Weißwein (Rotwein).** *EYEN-eh FLAHSH-eh VEYESS-veyen (ROHT-veyen)*
Another ____.	**Noch ____.** *nokh*
■ glass	**ein Glas** *eyen glass*
■ bottle	**eine Flasche** *EYEN-eh FLAHSH-eh*

- half-pint glass   **ein Viertel** *eyen FEERT-el*
- quarter-pint glass   **ein Achtel** *eyen AHKHT-el*
- liter   **einen Liter** *EYEN-en LEET-uh*
- carafe   **eine Karaffe** *EYEN-eh kahr-AHF-eh*
- half bottle   **eine halbe Flasche** *EYEN-eh HAHLB-eh FLAHSH-eh*

NONALCOHOLIC BEVERAGES

hot chocolate

heiße Schokolade *HEYESS-eh SHO-ko-laad-eh*

(black, red) currant juice

(schwarzer, roter) Johannisbeersaft *(SHVAHRTS-uh ROHT-uh) yo-HAHN-is-bayr-zahft*

mineral water

Mineralwasser *min-eh-RAAL-vahs-uh*

orangeade

Orangeade *or-ahn-ZHAAD-eh*

soda water (artificially carbonated)

Selterswasser *ZEHLT-uhs-vahs-uh*

soda water

Sprudelwasser *SHPROOD-el-vahs-uh*

spring water

Quellwasser *KVEL-vahs-uh*

apple juice

Apfelsaft *AHPF-el-zahft*

SOUPS AND STEWS

What is the soup of the day?

Was ist die Tagessuppe? *vahs ist dee TAA-gehs-zup-eh*

What soups do you have today?

Was für Suppen gibt es heute? *vas fewr ZUP-en geept ehs HOYT-eh*

Aalsuppe *AAL-zup-eh*   eel soup

Backerbsensuppe *BAHK-ehrps-en-zup-eh* — broth with crisp, round noodles

Bauernsuppe *BOW-ern-zup-eh* — cabbage and sausage soup

Bohnensuppe *BOHN-en-zup-eh* — bean soup (usually with bacon)

Erbsensuppe *EHRP-sen-zup-eh* — pea soup

Fischsuppe *FISH-zup-eh* — fish soup

Fischbeuschelsuppe *FISH-boy-shel-zup-eh* — fish-roe soup with vegetables

Fridattensuppe *free-DAHT-en-zup-eh* — broth with pancake strips

Frühlingssuppe *FREW-lings-zup-eh* — spring vegetable soup

Grießnockerlsuppe *GREES-nok-ehrl-zup-eh* — semolina-dumpling soup

Gerstenbrühe *GEHRST-en-brew-eh* — barley broth

Gulaschsuppe *GOOL-ahsh-zup-eh* — stewed beef in a spicy soup

Hühnerreissuppe *HEWN-er-reyes-zup-eh* — chicken-rice soup

Hummersuppe *HUM-uh-zup-eh* — lobster soup

Kalte Obstsuppe, Kaltschale *KAHLT-eh OHPST-zup-eh, KAHLT-shahl-eh* — cold fruit soup, usually containing cream, beer, or wine

Kartoffelsuppe *kahr-TOF-el-zup-eh* — potato soup

Kartoffellauchsuppe *kahr-TOF-el-LOWKH-zup-eh*

potato-leek soup

Knödelsuppe *KNERD-el-zup-eh*

dumpling soup

Königinsuppe *KERN-ig-in-zup-eh*

contains beef, sour cream, and almonds

Kraftbrühe mit Ei *KRAFT-brew-eh mit eye*

beef consommé with raw egg

■ **mit Topfteigerbsen** *mit TOPF-teyek-ehrps-en*

with fried peas

■ **mit Markknochen Einlage** *mit MAHRK-knokh-en EYEN-laag-eh*

with bone marrow filling

Leberknödelsuppe *LAY-behr-knerd-el-zup-eh*

liver dumpling soup

Linsensuppe *LINZ-en-zup-eh*

lentil soup

Mehlsuppe Basler Art *MAYL-zup-eh BAAZL-uh aart*

cheese soup with flour, Basle style

Nudelsuppe *NOO-del-zup-eh*

noodle soup

Ochsenschwanzsuppe *OK-sen-shvahnts-zup-eh*

oxtail soup

Pichelsteiner Eintopf *PIKH-el-shteyen-uh EYEN-topf*

meat and vegetable stew

Schildkrötensuppe *SHILT-krert-en-zup-eh*

turtle soup

Schweinsragoutsuppe *SHVEYENS-rah-goo-zup-eh*

pork-ragout soup

Semmelsuppe *ZEH-mel-zup-eh*

dumpling soup

Serbische Bohnensuppe *ZERB-ish-eh BOHN-en-zup-eh*		spicy bean soup
Spargelsuppe *SHPAHR-gel-zup-eh*		asparagus soup
Tomatensuppe *toh-MAAT-en-zup-eh*		tomato soup
Zwiebelsuppe *TSVEE-bel-zup-eh*		onion soup

MEATS

medium, please	**mittel, bitte** *MIT-ehl BIT-eh*	
rare (bloody)	**blutig** *BLOOT-ikh*	
underdone	**englisch** *EHNG-lish*	

You can have your meat prepared in the following ways:

baked	**gebacken** *geh-BAH-ken*
boiled or cooked	**gekocht** *geh-KOKHT*
stewed or braised	**geschmort** *geh-SHMOHRT*
roasted	**geröstet** *geh-RERST-et*
fried	**gebraten** *geh-BRAAT-en*
steamed, stewed	**gedämpft** *geh-DEHMPFT*
stuffed	**gefüllt** *geh-FEWLT*
chopped	**gehackt** *geh-HAHKT*
breaded	**paniert** *pah-NEERT*
garnished	**garniert** *gahr-NEERT*

Very popular

Bauernomelett *BOW-ehrn-om-let*		bacon and onion omelette

Bauernschmaus *BOW-ehrn-shmowss*	sauerkraut with smoked pork, sausages, dumplings, and potatoes
Bauernwurst *BOW-ehrn-voorst*	pork sausage with mustard seeds and peppercorns
Berliner Buletten *behr-LEEN-uh bul-EHT-en*	fried meatballs, Berlin style
Beuschel (Aust.) *BOY-shel*	veal lungs and heart
Bratwurst *BRAAT-voorst*	fried sausage
Bündnerfleisch (Swiss) *BEWND-nehr-fleyesh*	thinly sliced, air-dried beef
deutsches Beefsteak *DOY-ches BEEF-stayk*	Salisbury steak, hamburger
Eisbein *EYES-beyen*	pig's knuckle
Faschiertes (Aust.) *fah-SHEERT-es*	chopped meat
Fiakergulasch (Aust.) *fee-AHK-uh-goo-lahsh*	goulash topped with a fried egg
Frikadellen *fri-kah-DELL-en*	croquettes
gefülltes Kraut *geh-FEWLT-es krowt*	cabbage leaves stuffed with chopped meat, rice, eggs, and bread crumbs
Gehacktes *ge-HAHKT-es*	chopped meat

Geschnetzeltes (Swiss) *ge-SHNEH-tsel-tes* — braised meat tips

Geselchtes *ge-ZEHLKHT-es* — salty smoked meat

Gulasch *GOO-lahsh* — beef stew with spicy paprika gravy

Hackbraten *HAHK-braat-en* — meat loaf

Hackfleisch *HAHK-fleyesh* — chopped meat

Hammelbraten *HAHM-el-braat-en* — roast mutton

Hammelkeule, Hammelschlegel *HAHM-el-koyl-eh, HAHM-el-shlay-gel* — leg of mutton

Hammelrippchen *HAHM-el-rip-khen* — mutton chops

Herz *hehrts* — heart

Holsteiner Schnitzel *HOL-shteyen-uh SHNITS-el* — breaded veal cutlet topped with a fried egg and often with bits of toast, anchovies, vegetables, etc.

Jungfernbraten *YUNG-fehrn-braat-en* — a crunchy roast suckling pig

Kalbsbraten *KAHLPS-braat-en* — roast veal

Kalbsbrust *KAHLPS-brust* — breast of veal

Kalbshachse *KAHLPS-hahks-eh* — veal shank

Kalbsmilch *KAHLPS-milkh* — sweetbreads

Karbonade *kahr-bo-NAAD-eh* — fried rib pork chops

Klöße *KLERSS-eh*	meatballs
Klößchen, Klößlein *KLERSS-khen, KLERSS-leyen*	small meatballs
Kohl und Pinkel *kohl unt PINK-el*	smoked meat, cabbage, and potatoes
Kohlroulade *KOHL-roo-laad-eh*	stuffed cabbage
Königsberger Klops *KER-niks-behrg-uh klops*	meatballs in caper sauce
-kotelett *-kot-LET*	chop, cutlet
Krenfleisch (Aust.) *KRAYN-fleyesh*	pork (headcheese) with horseradish and shredded vegetables
Kutteln *KUT-ehln*	tripe
Lammkotelett *LAHM-kot-LET*	lamb chop
Leber *LAY-buh*	liver
Leberkäs *LAY-buh-kays*	meat loaf
Lendenbraten *LEHND-en-braat-en*	roast sirloin, tenderloin
Medaillons *mehd-EYE-yongs*	little discs of veal or pork
Naturschnitzel *nah-TOOR-shni-tsel*	thick, unbreaded veal cutlet
Nieren *NEER-en*	kidneys
Pöckelfleisch *PER-kel-fleyesh*	pickled meat

Rinderbraten *RIND-uh-braat-en*	roast beef
Rindsstück *RINTS-shtewk*	steak, slice of beef
Rippensteak *RIP-ehn-shtayk*	rib steak
Rouladen *roo-LAAD-en*	vegetables rolled up in thick slices of beef or veal
Rumpfstück *RUMPF-shtewk*	rump steak
Sauerbraten *ZOW-ehr-braat-en*	marinated pot roast in a spicy brown gravy
Saure Nieren *ZOW-reh NEER-en*	kidneys in a sauce containing vinegar
Schlachtplatte *SHLAHKHT-plaht-eh*	mixed sausages and cold meats
Schmorfleisch *SHMOHR-fleyesh*	stewed meat
Schnitzel *SHNITS-el*	cutlet (usually veal)
Schweinskotelett *SHVEYENS-kot-let*	pork chop
Spanferkel *SHPAAN-fehr-kel*	suckling pig
Speck *shpehk*	bacon
(Steierische) Brettjause *SHTEYE-uh-rish-eh BREHT-yowz-eh*	(Styrian) cold cuts on a wooden platter
Sülze *ZEWLTS-eh*	headcheese ("brawn" in Britain)
Tafelspitz *TAAF-el-shpits*	Viennese boiled beef

Tartarensteak	*tahr-TAAR-en-shtayk*	ground raw beef, seasoned variously
Wiener Schnitzel	*VEEN-uh SHNITS-el*	breaded veal cutlet
Zigeuner Schnitzel	*tsee-GOYN-uh SHNITS-el*	veal or pork cutlet in a sharp sauce
Zunge	*TSUNG-eh*	tongue

POULTRY, GAME

Backhuhn	*BAHK-hoon*	fried chicken
Brathuhn	*BRAAT-hoon*	roast chicken
Entenbraten	*EHNT-en-braat-en*	roast duck
Fasan	*fah-ZAAN*	pheasant
Gänsebraten	*GEHN-zeh-braat-en*	roast goose
Hähnchen	*HAYN-khen*	small chicken
Hasenbraten	*HAAZ-en-braat-en*	roast hare
Hasenpfeffer	*HAAZ-en-pfeh-fuh*	spicy rabbit stew
Hirschbraten	*HEERSH-braat-en*	venison
Hühnerbraten	*HEWN-ehr-braat-en*	roast chicken
Hühnerkeule, Hühnerschlegel *HEWN-ehr-koyl-eh*, *hewn-ehr-SHLAY gel*		drumstick, thigh
Kaninchen	*kah-NEEN-khen*	rabbit
Rebhuhn	*RAYP-hoon*	partridge

Rehrücken *RAY-rewk-en*	saddle of venison
Taube *TOW-beh*	pigeon, dove, squab
Truthahn *TROOT-haan*	turkey
Wachtel *VAHKHT-el*	quail
Wiener Backhendl *VEEN-uh BAHK-hen-del*	"southern fried chicken," Viennese style
Wildbraten *VILT-braat-en*	roast venison
Wildschweinrücken *VILT-shveyen-rewk-en*	saddle of wild boar

FISH, SEAFOOD

Aal *aal*	eel
Austern *OW-stern*	oysters
Barsch *bahrsh*	(lake) perch
Brachse, Brasse *BRAHKS-ehl, BRAHSS-eh*	bream (similar to carp)
Brathering *BRAAT-hayr-ing*	fried sour herring
Dorsch *dorsh*	cod
Felchen *FEHL-khen*	whiting
Fischfrikadellen *FISH-fri-kah-dehl-en*	fish dumplings (croquettes)
Forelle *for-EHL-eh*	trout
Flunder *FLUND-uh*	flounder

Garnelen *gahr-NAYL-en*	shrimp, prawns
Haifischsteak *HEYE-fish-shtayk*	shark steak
Hecht *hekht*	pike
Heilbutt *HEYEL-but*	halibut
Hering *HAY-ring*	herring
Hummer *HUM-uh*	lobster
Jakobsmuscheln *YAA-kops-mush-eln*	scallops
Junger Hecht *YUNG-uh hekht*	pickerel
Kabeljau *KAA-bel-yow*	cod
Karpfen *KAHR-pren*	carp
Kieler Sprotten *KEEL-uh SHPROT-en*	(Kiel) sprats
Krabben *KRAH-ben*	shrimp, prawn
Krebs *krayps*	crab
Lachs *lahks*	salmon
Languste *lahn-GOOST-eh*	spiny lobster
Makrele *mah-KRAY-leh*	mackerel
Muscheln *MUSH-eln*	clams, cockles, mussels
Neunauge *NOYN-owg-eh*	lamprey eel
Rauch-, Rächer- *rowkh-, ROY-khuh-*	smoked

Rogen *ROH-gen*	roe
Rotbarsch *ROHT-bahrsh*	red sea bass
Schellfisch *SHEHL-fish*	haddock
Scholle *SHOL-eh*	flatfish, plaice
Schwertfisch *SHVAYRT-fish*	swordfish
Seebarsch *ZAY-bahrsh*	sea bass
Seezunge *ZAY-tsung-eh*	sole
Sojawalfischsteak *ZOH-yah-vaal-fish-stayk*	soya whale steak
Steinbutt *SHTEYEN-but*	turbot
Stint *shtint*	smelt
Stör *shterr*	sturgeon
Tintenfisch *TINT-en-fish*	squid, cuttlefish
Weißfisch *VEYESS-fish*	whiting
Zander *TSAHND-uli*	pike/perch

Now, how would you like your fish?

With butter, lemon, and almonds	**Mit Butter, Zitrone, und Mandeln** *mit BUTT-uh tsi-TROHN-eh unt MAHN-deln*
Boiled	**Blau** *blow*
Baked	**Gebacken** *geh-BAH-ken*

Fried	**Gebraten** *geh-BRAA-ten*
Deep fried	**In schwimmendem Fett gebacken** *in SHVIM-end-em feht ge-BAHK-en*
Sautéed	**In Butter geschwenkt** *in BUT-uh geh-SHVEHNGKT*
Grilled	**Gegrillt** *geh-GRILT*
Steamed	**Gedämpft** *geh-DEHMPFT*

VEGETABLES

I am a vegetarian.	**Ich bin Vegetarier(in).** *ikh bin veh-geh-TAAR yehr(in)*
What can you recommend?	**Was können Sie mir empfehlen?** *vahs KERN-en zee meer emp-FAYL-en*

Auberginen *oh-behr-ZHEEN-en*	eggplant
Blumenkohl *BLOOM-en-kohl*	cauliflower
Bohnen *BOHN-en*	beans
Braunkohl *BROWN-kohl*	broccoli
Erbsen *EHRPS-en*	peas
Essiggurken *EHSS-ikh-goork-en*	sour pickles (gherkins)
Fisolen (Aust.) *fee-SOHL-en*	string beans, French beans
Gelbe Wurzeln *GEHLB-eh VOORTS-eln*	carrots

Gemischtes Gemüse *geh-MISHT-ehs ge-MEWZ-eh*	mixed vegetables
Grüne Bohnen *GREWN-eh BOHN-en*	green beans
Gurken *GOORK-en*	cucumbers
Häuptelsalat *HOYPT-el-zah-laat*	lettuce salad
Kabis, Kappes *KAHB-is, KAHP-es*	cabbage
Karfiol (Aust.) *kahr-fee-OHL*	cauliflower
Karotten *kahr-OT-en*	carrots
Knoblauch *KNOHP-lowkh*	garlic
Kohl, Kraut *kohl, krowt*	cabbage
Kren (Aust.) *krayn*	horseradish
Kürbis *KEWR-biss*	pumpkin
Kukuruz (Aust.) *KOOK-oor-oots*	corn, maize
Lauch *lowkh*	leeks
Leipziger Allerlei *LEYEPTS-eeg-uh AHL-uh-leye*	carrots, peas, and asparagus
Mais *meyess*	corn, maize
Meerrettich *MAYR-reh-tikh*	horseradish
Mohrrüben *MOHR-rewb-en*	carrots
Paradeiser (Aust.) *pah-rah-DEYEZ-uh*	tomatoes
Pfifferlinge *PFIF-ehr-ling-eh*	chanterelle mushrooms

Pilze *PILTS-eh*	mushrooms
Radieschen *rah-DEES-khen*	radishes
Rosenkohl *ROHZ-en-kohl*	brussels sprouts
Rote Beten (Rüben) *ROHT-eh BAYT-en (REWB-en)*	beets
Rotkohl (Rotkraut) *ROHT-kohl (ROHT-krowt)*	red cabbage
Rübenkraut *REWB-en-krowt*	turnip tops
Schnittbohnen *SHNIT-bohn-en*	French beans
Schwarzwurzeln *SHVAHRTS-voorts-eln*	salsify (vegetable oyster)
Spargelspitzen *SHPAARG-el-shpits-en*	asparagus tips
Spinat *shpeen-AAT*	spinach
Tomaten *to-MAAT-en*	tomatoes
Weiße Bohnen *VEYESS-eh BOHN-en*	white beans
Weiße Rüben *VEYESS-eh REWB-en*	turnips
Weißkohl *VEYESS-kohl*	cabbage
Zwiebeln *TSVEEB-eln*	onions

POTATOES, NOODLES

Bratkartoffeln *BRAAT-kahr-tof-eln*	fried potatoes
Geröstel *ge-RERST-el*	hash brown potatoes
Dampfnudeln *DAHMPF-nood-eln*	steamed noodles

Fadennudeln *FAAD-en-nood-eln*		vermicelli
Kartoffel(n) *kahr-TOF-el(n)*		potato(es)
■ **-bälle** *-behl-eh*		balls
■ **-brei** *-breye*		mashed
■ **-flocken** *-flok-en*		flakes (potato crisps)
■ **-klöße** *-klewss-eh*		dumplings
■ **-kroketten** *-kroh-keht-en*		croquettes
■ **-mus** *-moos*		mashed
■ **-puffer** *-puf-uh*		fritters, potato pancakes
Krautkrapfen *KROWT-krahp-fen*		cabbage fritters
Pellkartoffeln *PEHL-kahr-tof-eln*		unpeeled boiled potatoes
Petersilienkartoffeln *pay-tehr-ZEEL-yen-kahr-tof-eln*		parsleyed potatoes
Pommes frites *pom frit*		french fries
Röstkartoffeln *REWST-kahr-tof-eln*		fried potatoes
Rösti (Swiss) *REWST-ee*		hash brown potatoes
Salzkartoffeln *ZAHLTS-kahr-tof-eln*		boiled potatoes
Schlutzkrapfen (a South Tyrol specialty) *SHLUTS-krahpf-en*		ravioli filled with cottage cheese
Spätzle* *SHPEHTS-leh*		thick noodles or Swabian dumplings
Teigwaren *TEYEKH-vaar-en*		pasta products, noodles

CHEESES

We'll have the cheese platter, please.	**Wir nehmen den Käseteller, bitte.** *veer NAY-men dehn KAY-zeh-tell-uh BIT-eh*
Is the cheese soft or hard?	**Ist der Käse weich oder hart?** *ist dehr KAY-zeh veyekh OH-duh hahrt*
■ sharp or mild?	**scharf oder mild?** *shahrf OH-duh milt*

DESSERTS

I would like a:	**Ich möchte ein (eine)** *ikh MERKHT-eh eyen (EYEN-eh)*
■ strawberry ice cream	**Erdbeereis** *AYRT-bayr-eyess*
■ fruit-flavored berry pudding	**Rote Grütze** *ROHT-eh GREWTS-eh*
Is dessert included in my menu?	**Ist der Nachtisch in meinem Gedeck mit einbegriffen?** *ist dehr NAHKH-tish in MEYEN-em geh-DEHK mit EYEN-beh-grif-en*
What do you recommend?	**Was empfehlen Sie mir?** *vahs emp-FAYL-en zee meer*

Berliner *behr-LEEN-uh*		jelly doughnut
Bienenstich *BEEN-en-shtikh*		honey-almond cake (literally "bee sting")
Gugelhupf *GOOG-el-hupf*		a round pound cake often containing raisins and almonds
Hefekranz *HAY-feh-krahnts*		circular coffee cake

Mannheimer Dreck *MAHN-heyem-uh drehk* chocolate-covered almond paste

(Weihnachts) stollen *(VEYE-nahkhts)shtol-en* fruity (Christmas) coffee cake

Nothing more, thank you. **Nein danke, nichts mehr.** *neyen DAHNK-eh nikhts mayr*

Unfortunately, I can't eat any more. **Leider kann ich nichts mehr essen.** *LEYED-uh kahn ikh nikhts mayr ESS-en*

COFFEE AND TEA

I would like ____. **Ich möchte bitte ____.** *ikh MERKHT-eh BIT-eh*

■ a cup of coffee **eine Tasse Kaffee** *EYEN-eh TAHSS-eh KAH-fay*

■ with cream **mit Sahne** *mit ZAAN-eh*

■ with milk **einen Milchkaffee** *EYEN-en MILKH-kah-fay*

■ black coffee **einen Schwarzen** *EYEN-en SHVAHRTS-en*

■ coffee with cream **Braunen** *BROWN-en*

■ espresso **Espresso** *es-PREHSS-oh*

■ iced coffee **Eiskaffee** *EYES-kah-fay*

A cup of tea ____. **Eine Tasse Tee ____.** *EYEN-eh TAHSS-eh tay*

■ with milk **mit Milch** *mit milkh*

■ with lemon **mit Zitrone** *mit tsi-TROHN-eh*

FRUITS AND NUTS

Ananas *AHN-ah-nahss*	pineapple
Apfel *AHPF-el*	apple
Apfelsine *ahpf-el-ZEEN-eh*	orange
Aprikosen *ahp-ree-KOHZ-en*	apricots
Banane *bah-NAAN-eh*	banana
Birne *BEERN-eh*	pear
Blaubeeren *BLOW-bayr-en*	blueberries (bilberries)
Brombeeren *BROM-bayr-en*	blackberries
Erdbeeren *AYRT-bayr-en*	strawberries
Feigen *FEYEG-en*	figs
Gemischte Nüsse *geh-MISHT-eh NEWSS-eh*	mixed nuts
Granatapfel *grah-NAAT-ahpf-el*	pomegranate
Haselnüsse *HAAZ-el-newss-eh*	hazelnuts
Heidelbeeren *HEYED-el-bayr-en*	blueberries
Himbeeren *HIM-bayr-en*	raspberries
Holunderbeeren *hol-UND-uh-bayr-en*	elderberries

Johannisbeeren *yoh-HAHN-is-bayr-en*	currants
Kastanien *kahst-AAN-yen*	chestnuts
Kirschen *KEERSH-en*	cherries
Kokosnuß *KOHK-os-nuus*	coconut
Mandarine *mahn-dah-REEN-eh*	tangerine
Mandeln *MAHND-eln*	almonds
Marillen (Aust.) *mah-RIL-en*	apricots
Melone *meh-LOHN-eh*	cantaloupe
Nüsse *NEWSS-eh*	nuts
Pampelmuse *PAHMP-el-mooz-eh*	grapefruit
Pfirsich *PFEER-zikh*	peach
Pflaumen *PFLOW-men*	plums
Preiselbeeren *PREYE-zel-bayr-en*	cranberries
Quitte *KVIT-eh*	quince
Rauschbeeren *ROWSH-bayr-en*	cranberries, crawberries
Rhabarber *rah-BAHRB-uh*	rhubarb
Rosinen *roh-ZEEN-en*	raisins
Stachelbeeren *SHTAH-khel-bayr-en*	gooseberries

Studentenfutter *shtu-DENT-en-fut-uh*		"student fodder" (assorted nuts, raisins, seeds)
Südfrüchte *ZEWT-frewkht-eh*		tropical fruits
Trauben *TROWB-en*		grapes
Walnüsse *VAHL-newss-eh*		walnuts
Wassermelone *VAHSS-uh-meh-lohn-eh*		watermelon
Weichselkirschen *VEYEKS-el-keersh-en*		(sour) morello cherries
Weintrauben *VEYEN-trowb-en*		grapes
Zuckermelone *TSUK-uh-meh-lohn-eh*		honeydew melon
Zwetschgen *TSVEHTSH-gen*		plums

COMPLAINTS

Why is it taking so long?	**Warum dauert es so lange?** *vaar-UM DOW-ehrt ehs zoh LAHNG-eh*
This is dirty.	**Dies ist schmutzig.** *dees ist SHMUTS-ikh*
The food is ___.	**Das Essen ist ___.** *dahs ESS-en ist*
■ cold	**kalt** *kahlt*
■ not very hot	**nicht sehr heiß** *nikht zayer heyess*
■ not even warm	**nicht einmal warm** *nikht EYEN-mahl vahrm*

There's too much fat in it.	**Da ist zu viel Fett drin.** *dah ist tsoo feel fett drin*
This is too ____.	**Dies ist zu ____.** *dees ist tsoo*
■ salty	**salzig** *ZAHLTS-ikh*
■ dried out	**dürr** *dewr*
■ sweet	**süß** *zews*
■ sour	**sauer** *ZOW-uh*
■ bitter	**bitter** *BIT-uh*
The meat is ____.	**Das Fleisch ist ____.** *dahs fleyesh ist*
■ overdone	**zu stark gebraten** *tsoo shtahrk ge-BRAAT-en*
■ too tough	**zu zäh** *tsoo tsay*
■ too rare	**zu roh** *tsoo roh*
The milk is sour.	**Die Milch hat einen Stich.** *dee milkh haht EYEN-en shtikh*
The butter isn't fresh.	**Die Butter ist nicht frisch.** *dee BUT-uh ist nikht frish*

RESTRICTIONS

I can't have ____.	**Ich vertrage ____.** *ikh fehr-TRAAG-eh*
■ any dairy products	**keine Milchprodukte** *KEYEN-eh MILKH-pro-dookt-eh*
■ any alcohol	**keinen Alkohol** *KEYEN-en ahl-ko-HOHL*
■ any saturated fats	**keine gesättigten Fette** *KEYEN-eh geh-ZEHT-ikht-en FET-eh*
■ any seafood	**keine Meeresfrüchte** *KEYEN-eh MAYR-ehs-frewkht-eh*

■ any nuts	**keine Nüsse** *KEYEN-eh NEWSS-eh*
■ any MSG	**kein Glutamat** *keyen Gloot-ah-MAAT*
I'm looking for a dish ____.	**Ich suche ein ____ Gericht.** *ikh ZOOKH-eh eyen ____ geh-RICHT*
■ high in fiber	**ballaststoffreiches** *bah-LAHST-shtof-reyekh-es*
■ low in cholesterol	**cholesterinarmes** *ko-lest-ehr-EEN-ahrm-es*
■ low in fat	**fettarmes** *FETT-ahrm-es*
■ low in carbohydrates	**kohlenhydratarmes** *KOHL-en-hew-draat-ahrmes*
■ low in sodium	**natriumarmes** *NAA-tree-um-ahrm-es*
■ nondairy	**milchfreies** *MILKH-freyes-es*
■ salt-free	**salzfreies** *ZAHLTS-freye-es*
■ sugar-free	**zuckerfreies** *ZOOK-ehr-freye-es*
I'm looking for a dish/food without ____.	**Ich suche ein Gericht/Essen ohne ____.** *ikh ZOOKH-eh eyen geh-RIKHT/ESS-en OHN-eh*
■ preservatives	**Konservierungsmittel** *kohn-zayr-VEER-ungs-mit-el*
■ artificial coloring	**Kunstfarbstoff** *KOONST-fahrp-shtoff*

EATING IN

I need ____.	**Ich brauche ____.** *ikh BROWKH-eh*
■ bread	**Brot** *broht*
■ butter	**Butter** *BUT-uh*
■ cheese	**Käse** *KAYZ-eh*

cold cuts	**Kalter Aufschnitt** *KHALT-uh OWF-shnit*
cookies	**Kekse** *KAYKS-eh*
candy	**Konfekt** *kon-FEHKT*
a chocolate bar	**eine Tafel Schokolade** *EYEN-eh TAAF-el sho-ko-LAAD-eh*
a dozen eggs	**ein Dutzend Eier** *eyen DUTS-ent EYE-uh*
fruit	**Obst** *ohpst*
a bottle of milk	**eine Flasche Milch** *EYEN-eh FLAHSH-eh milkh*

MEETING PEOPLE

GREETINGS AND INTRODUCTIONS

What's your name?	**Wie heißen Sie?** *vee HEYESS-en zee*
My name is ____.	**Ich heiße ____.** *ikh HEYESS-eh*
Pleased to meet you.	**Sehr erfreut.** *zayr ehr-FROYT*
How do you do?	**Wie geht es Ihnen?** *vee gayt es EEN-en*
May I introduce ____?	**Darf ich ____ vorstelien?** *dahrf ikh ____ FOHR-shtehl-en*
my husband	**meinen Mann** *MEYEN-en mahn*
my wife	**meine Frau** *MEYEN-eh frow*
my son	**meinen Sohn** *MEYEN-en zohn*
my daughter	**meine Tochter** *MEYEN-eh TOKHT-uh*
my friend	**meinen Freund** *MEYEN-en froynd*

What's ___ name?	**Wie heißt ___?**	*vee heyesst*
■ your son's	**Ihr Sohn**	*eer zohn*
■ your daughter's	**Ihre Tochter**	*EER-eh TOKHT-uh*

CONVERSATION

We have children the same age as yours.	**Wir haben Kinder im selben Alter.**	*veer HAAB-en KIND-uh im ZEHLB-en AHLT-uh*
Where are you from?	**Wo sind Sie her?**	*voh zint zee hayr*
I'm ___.	**Ich bin ___.**	*ikh bin*
■ from America	**aus Amerika**	*owss ah-MAY-ree-kah*
■ from England	**aus England**	*ows EHNG-lahnt*
■ from Canada	**aus Kanada**	*ows KAH-nah-dah*
■ from Australia	**aus Australien**	*ows ows-TRAAL-yen*
This is my first time in Germany.	**Dies ist das erste Mal, das ich in Deutschland bin.**	*dees ist dahs EHRST-eh maal dahs ikh in DOYCH-lahnt bin*
I like many things.	**Mir gefällt vieles.**	*meer geh-FELT FEEL-es*
I think it's ___.	**Ich finde es ___.**	*ikh FIND-eh ehs*
■ a bit strange	**etwas komisch**	*ET-vahss KOHM-ish*
■ beautiful	**schön**	*shern*
■ interesting	**interessant**	*in-tehr-eh-SAHNT*
■ magnificent	**herrlich**	*HEHR-likh*
■ unique	**einzigartig**	*EYEN-tsikh-ahrt-ikh*

I will be staying ___.	**Ich bleibe ___.** *ikh BLEYEB-eh*
■ a few days	**einige Tage** *EYEN-ig-eh TAAG-eh*
■ a week	**eine Woche** *EYEN-eh VOKH-eh*
■ a month	**einen Monat** *EYEN-en MOHN-aat*

Is your hotel far?	**Ist Ihr Hotel weit entfernt?** *ist eer ho-TEL veyet ehnt-FEHRNT*

Would you like a picture?	**Möchten Sie ein Bild?** *MERKHT-en zee eyen bilt*

Stand here (there).	**Stellen sie sich dorthin.** *SHTEHL-en zee zikh dort hin*

Don't move.	**Keine Bewegung!** *KEYEN-eh beh-VAYG-ung*

Smile. That's it!	**Lächeln. Genau! (Richtig!)** *LEHKH-eln geh-NOW (RIKHT-ikh)*

Would you take a picture of me (us)?	**Wurden Sie mich (uns) photographieren?** *VEWRD-en zee mikh (uns) foh-toh-grah-FEER-en*

I'd like a picture of you, as a remembrance.	**Ich möchte ein Bild von Ihnen, als Andenken.** *ikh MERKHT-eh eyen bilt fon EEN-en, ahls AHN-denk-en*

DATING AND SOCIALIZING

Are you alone?	**Sind Sie allein?** *zint zee ah-LEYEN*
Or with your family?	**Oder mit der Familie?** *OHD-uh mit dehr fah-MEEL-yeh*

May I have this dance?	**Darf ich um diesen Tanz bitten?** *dahrf ikh um DEEZ-en tahnts BIT-en*
Would you like a drink (cigarette)?	**Möchten Sie ein Getränk (eine Zigarette)?** *MERKHT-en zee eyen geh-TREHNK (EYEN-eh tsi-gah-REHT-eh)*
Do you have a light?	**Haben Sie Feuer?** *HAAB-en zee FOY-uh*
Do you mind if I smoke?	**Macht es Ihnen etwas aus, wenn ich rauche?** *mahkht ehs EEN-en EHT-vahs ows vehn ikh ROWKH-eh*
Are you free this evening?	**Sind Sie heute Abend frei?** *zint zee HOYT-eh AAB-ent freye*
Would you like to go for a walk with me?	**Möchten Sie einen Spaziergang mit mir machen?** *MERKHT-en zee EYEN-en shpah-TSEER-gahng mit meer MAHKH-en*
What's your telephone number?	**Wie ist Ihre Telephonnummer?** *vee ist EER-eh TAY-leh-fohn-num-uh*
May I invite you for ___ ?	**Darf ich Sie zu ___ einladen?** *dahrf ikh zee tsoo ___ EYEN-laad-en*
■ a glass of wine	**einem Glas Wein** *EYEN-em glaass veyen*
■ a cup of coffee	**einer Tasse Kaffee** *EYEN-uh TASS-eh KAH-fay*
What is your profession?	**Was sind Sie von Beruf?** *vahs zint zee fon beh-ROOF*
I'm a ___ .	**Ich bin ___ .** *ikh bin*
■ doctor	**Arzt (Ärztin)** *ahrtst (EHRTST-in)*

■ accountant	**Buchhalter(in)** *BOOKH-hahlt-ehr(in)*
■ musician	**Musiker(in)** *MOOZ-ik-ehr(in)*
■ hairdresser	**Friseur (Friseuse)** *free-ZEWR (free-ZEWZ)*
■ police officer	**Polizeibeamte** *pol-its-EYE-beh-ahmt-uh*
■ engineer	**Ingenieur(in)** *in-jen-EWR(in)*
■ scientist	**Wissenschaftler(in)** *VISS-ent-shahft-lehr(in)*
■ clerk	**Verkäufer(in)** *fehr-KOYF-ehr(in)*
■ secretary	**Sekretär(in)** *zehk-reh-TAYR(in)*
■ manager	**Geschäftsführer(in)** *geh-SHEFTS-fewr-ehr(in)*
■ mechanic	**Mechaniker(in)** *meh-KHAA-ni-kehr(in)*
■ teacher	**Lehrer(in)** *LAY-rehr(in)*
■ lawyer	**Rechtsanwalt (Rechtsanwältin)** *REHKHTS-ahn-vahlt (REHKHTS-ahn-vehlt-in)*
■ gardener	**Gärtner(in)** *GEHRT-nehr(in)*
■ dentist	**Zahnarzt (Zahnärztin)** *TSAAN-aartst (TSAAN-ehrtst-in)*
■ writer	**Schriftsteller(in)** *SHRIFT-shteh-lehr(in)*
■ nurse	**Krankenpfleger(in)** *krahnk-en-PFLAY-gehr(in)*
■ secretary	**Sekretär(in)** *zeh-kreh-TAYR(in)*
■ salesperson	**Verkäufer(in)** *fehr-KOY-fehr(in)*
■ businessperson	**Geschäftsmann(frau)** *geh-SHEHFTS-mahn(frow)*
■ student	**Student(in)** *shtoo-DEHNT(in)*

Do you love music (the theater, films)?	**Lieben Sie Musik (Theater, Filme)?** *LEEB-en zee moo-ZEEK (TAY-aat-uh, FILM-eh)*
I'll pick you up at your house (hotel).	**Ich hole Sie in Ihrem Haus (Hotel) ab.** *ikh HOHL-eh zee in EER-em hows (ho-TEL) ahp*
I'll wait for you in front of the theater (café).	**Ich warte auf Sie vor dem Theater (Café).** *ikh VAART-eh owf zee for daym TAY-aat-uh (kah-FAY)*
I thank you for your wonderful hospitality.	**Ich danke Ihnen für Ihre wunderbare Gastfreundlichkeit.** *ikh DAHNK-eh EEN-en fewr EER-eh VUND-uh-baar-eh GAHST-froynt-likh-keyet*

SAYING GOOD-BYE

Nice to have met you.	**Nett, dass ich Sie kennen gelernt habe.** *neht dahss ikh zee KEHN-en-geh-lehrnt HAAB-eh*
Regards to ___.	**Grüße an ___.** *GREWSS-eh ahn*
I must go now.	**Ich muss jetzt gehen.** *ikh muss yehtst GAY-en*
We'd like to hear from you.	**Wir würden gerne von Ihnen hören.** *veer VEWRD-en GEHRN-eh fon EEN-en HER-en*
You must come to visit us.	**Sie müssen uns besuchen.** *zee MEWSS-en uns beh-ZOOKH-en*

Do you have a home page on the Internet?	**Haben Sie eine Home-Page im Internet?** *HAAB-en zee EYEN-eh hohm paych im IN-ter-net*
E-mail us often.	**E-mailen Sie uns oft!** *EE-mayl-en zee uns oft*

SHOPPING

GOING SHOPPING

I'm looking for ___.	**Ich suche ___.** *ikh ZOOKH-eh*
■ an antique shop	**ein Antiquitätengeschäft** *eyen ahn-ti-kvi-TAYT-en-geh-shehft*
■ an art dealer	**einen Kunsthändler** *EYEN-en KUNST-hehnt-luh*
■ a bookstore	**eine Buchhandlung** *EYEN-eh BOOKH-hahnt-lung*
■ a china shop	**einen Porzellanladen** *EYEN-en por-tseh-LAAN-laad-en*
■ a camera shop	**ein Photogeschäft** *eyen FOH-toh geh-shehft*
■ a bakery	**eine Bäckerei** *EYEN-eh beh-keh-REYE*
■ a butcher shop	**einen Fleischerladen** *EYEN-en FLEYESH-ehr-laa-den*
■ a candy store	**einen Süßwarenladen** *EYEN-en SEWSS-vaa-ren-laa-den*
■ a clothing store	**ein Bekleidungsgeschäft** *eyen beh-KLEYED-ungs-geh-shehft*
for children	**Kinderbekleidungsgeschäft** *KIND-ehr-beh-kleyed-ungs-geh-shehft*

for women	**Damenbekleidungsgeschäft** *DAH-men-beh-kleyed-ungs-geh-shehft*
for men	**Herrenbekleidungsgeschäft** *HEHR-en-beh-kleyed-ungs-geh-shehft*
■ a delicatessen	**ein Delikatessengeschäft** *eyen deh-li-kah-TEHSS-en-geh-shehft*
■ a department store	**ein Warenhaus** *eyen VAAR-en-hows*
■ a drugstore	**eine Drogerie/Apotheke** *EYEN-eh dro-geh-REE/ah-poh-TAYK-eh*
■ a dry cleaner's	**eine chemische Reinigung** *EYEN-eh KHAY-mi-sheh REYE-ni-gung*
■ a flower shop	**ein Blumengeschäft** *eyen BLOOM-en-geh-shehft*
■ a furrier	**einen Kürschner** *EYEN-en KEWRSH-nuh*
■ a gift (souvenir) shop	**einen Andenkenladen** *EYEN-en AHN-dehnk-en-laad-en*
■ a gourmet grocery store	**eine Feinkostwarenhandlung** *EYEN-eh FEYEN-kost-vaar-en-hahnt-lung*
■ a grocery store	**ein Lebensmittelgeschäft** *eyen LAYB-ens-mit-el-geh-shehft*
■ a hardware store	**eine Eisenwarenhandlung** *EYEN-eh EYEZ-en-vaar-en-hahnt-lung*
■ a health-food store	**ein Reformhaus** *eyen reh-FORM-hows*
■ a jewelry store	**einen Juwelier** *EYEN-en yu-veh-LEER*
■ a liquor store	**eine Spirituosenhandlung** *EYEN-eh shpee-ree-tu-OHZ-en-hahnt-lung*

■ a market	**einen Markt** *EYEN-en mahrkt*
■ a newsstand	**einen Zeitungsstand** *EYEN-en TSEYET-unks-shtahnt*
■ a pastry shop	**eine Konditorei** *EYEN-eh kon-dee-to-REYE*
■ a record store	**ein Schallplattengeschäft** *eyen SHAHL-plaht-en-geh-shehft*
■ a shoe store	**ein Schuhgeschäft** *eyen SHOO-geh-shehft*
■ a shopping center	**ein Einkaufszentrum** *eyen EYEN-kowfs-tsent-rum*
■ a supermarket	**einen Supermarkt** *EYEN-en ZOOP-uh-mahrkt*
■ a tobacco shop	**einen Tabakladen** *EYEN-en TAA-bahk-laad-en*
■ a toy shop	**ein Spielwarengeschäft** *eyen SHPEEL-vaar-en-geh-shehft*
■ a wine merchant	**eine Weinhandlung** *EYEN-eh VEYEN-hahnt-lung*

BOOKS

Where is the largest bookstore here?	**Wo ist hier die größte Buchhandlung?** *voh ist heer dee GRERST-eh BOOKH-hahnt-lung*
I'm looking for a copy of ___.	**Ich suche ein Exemplar von ___.** *ikh ZOOKH-eh eyen eks-ehm-PLAAR fon*
Do you have books (novels) in English?	**Haben Sie Bücher (Romane) in Englisch?** *HAAB-en zee BEWKH-uh (roh-MAAN-eh) in EHNG-lish*

I need a guidebook.	**Ich brauche einen Reiseführer.** *ikh BROWKH-eh EYEN-en REYEZ-eh-fewr-uh*
Can you recommend a good grammar book to me?	**Können Sie mir eine gute Grammatik empfehlen?** *KERN-en zee meer EYEN-eh GOOT-eh grah-MAH-tik ehmp-FAYL-en*
I'm looking for ___.	**Ich suche ___.** *ikh ZOOKH-eh*
■ a pocket dictionary	**ein Taschenwörterbuch** *eyen TAHSH-en-vert-ehr-bookh*
■ a German-English dictionary	**ein deutsch-englisches Wörterbuch** *eyen doytsh-EHNG-lishes vert-ehr-bookh*
■ a map of the city	**einen Stadtplan** *EYEN-en SHTAHT-plaan*

CLOTHING

Please show me ___.	**Zeigen Sie mir bitte ___.** *TSEYEG-en zee meer BIT-eh*
■ a belt	**einen Gürtel** *EYEN-en GEWRT-el*
■ a blouse	**eine Bluse** *EYEN-eh BLOOZ-eh*
■ a cap	**eine Mütze** *EYEN-eh MEWTS-eh*
■ a brassiere	**einen Büstenhalter** *EYEN-en BEWST-en-hahlt-uh*
■ a coat	**einen Mantel** *EYEN-en MAHNT-el*
■ a dress	**ein Kleid** *eyen kleyet*
■ furs	**Pelze** *PELTS-eh*
■ an evening gown	**ein Abendkleid** *eyen AAB-ent-kleyet*

▪ gloves	**Handschuhe** *HAHNT-shoo-eh*
▪ a hat	**einen Hut** *EYEN-en hoot*
▪ a jacket	**eine Jacke** *EYEN-eh YAHK-eh*
▪ knitwear	**Stricksachen** *SHTRIK-zahkh-en*
▪ lingerie	**Damenunterwäsche** *DAAM-en-un-tehr-vehsh-eh*
▪ pants	**eine Hose** *EYEN-eh HOHZ-eh*
▪ a mink coat	**einen Nerzmantel** *EYEN-en NEHRTS-mahn-tel*
▪ panties	**einen Schlüpfer** *EYEN-en SHLEWPF-uh*
▪ panty hose	**eine Strumpfhose** *EYEN-eh SHTRUMPF-hohz-eh*
▪ a raincoat	**einen Regenmantel** *EYEN-en RAYG-en-mahn-tel*
▪ a scarf	**ein Halstuch** *eyen HAHLS-tookh*
▪ a shirt	**ein Hemd** *eyen hemt*
▪ a pair of shoes	**ein Paar Schuhe** *eyen paar SHOO-eh*
▪ shorts	**kurze Unterhosen** *KURTS-eh UN-tehr-hohz-en*
▪ a skirt	**einen Rock** *EYEN-en rok*
▪ a slip	**einen Unterrock** *EYEN-en UN-tehr-rok*
▪ slippers	**Hausschuhe** *HOWS-shoo-eh*
▪ socks	**Socken** *ZOK-en*
▪ stockings	**Strümpfe** *SHTREWMPF-eh*
▪ a man's suit	**einen Anzug** *EYEN-en AHN-tsook*
▪ a woman's suit	**ein Kostüm** *eyen kos-TEWM*
▪ a sweater	**einen Pullover** *EYEN-en pul-OHV-uh*

■ a tie	**eine Krawatte** *EYEN-eh krah-VAHT-eh*
■ an undershirt	**ein Unterhemd** *eyen UN-tehr-hehmt*
■ underwear	**Unterwäsche** *UN-tehr-vehsh-eh*

Is there a sale today?	**Gibt's heute einen Verkauf?** *gipts HOYT-eh EYEN-en fehr-KOWF*
Do you have the same thing with short (long) sleeves?	**Haben Sie dasselbe mit kurzen (langen) Ärmeln?** *HAAB-en zee dahs-ZELB-eh mit KOORTS-en (LAHNG-en) EHRM-ehln*
I'd like something ____.	**Ich möchte etwas ____.** *ikh MERKHT-eh EHT-vahs*
■ less expensive	**Billigeres** *BIL-ig-ehr-es*
■ more elegant	**Eleganteres** *eh-lay-GAHNT-ehr-es*
■ of better quality	**von besserer Qualität** *fon BEHSS-ehr-uh kvah-li-TAYT*
■ more cheerful	**Heitereres** *HEYET-ehr-ehr-es*
■ more youthful	**Jugendlicheres** *YOOG-ent-li-kher-es*
■ else	**anderes** *AHND-ehr-es*
■ bigger	**Größeres** *GRERSS-ehr-es*
■ smaller	**Kleineres** *KLEYEN-ehr-es*

I (don't) like it.	**Es gefällt mir (nicht).** *ehs geh-FEHLT meer (nikht)*
This is too ____.	**Dies ist zu ____.** *deess ist tsoo*
■ thick	**dick** *dik*
■ thin	**dünn** *dewn*
■ expensive	**teuer** *TOY-uh*

■ dark	**dunkel** *DUNK-el*
■ light	**hell** *hel*

It's very elegant, but I don't want to spend a fortune on it.
Es ist sehr elegant, aber ich will kein Vermögen dafür ausgeben.
ehs ist zayr eh-lay-GAHNT AAB-uh ikh vil keyen fehr-MERG-en dah-FEWR OWS-gay-ben

COLORS

I like the material, but I don't like the color.
Der Stoff gefällt mir, aber nicht die Farbe. *dehr shtof geh-FEHLT meer, AAB-uh nikht die FAARB-eh*

Would you have it in ____?
Hätten Sie es vielleicht in ____?
HEHT-en zee ehs fee-LEYEKHT in

■ black	**schwarz** *shvaarts*
■ blue	**blau** *blow*
■ brown	**braun** *brown*
■ gray	**grau** *grow*
■ green	**grün** *grewn*
■ pink	**rosa** *ROH-zaa*
■ red	**rot** *roht*
■ white	**weiß** *veyess*
■ yellow	**gelb** *gehlp*

FIT, ALTERATIONS

Please take my measurements (for a dress).
Bitte nehmen Sie mir Maß (zu einem Kleid). *BIT-eh NAYM-en zee meer maass (tsoo EYEN-em kleyet)*

I think my size is 40.
Ich glaube, ich habe Größe vierzig.
ikh GLOWB-eh ikh HAAB-eh GRERSS-eh FEER-tsikh

I'd like to try it on.	**Ich möchte es anprobieren.** *ikh MERKHT-eh ehs AHN-proh-beer-en*
It fits badly in the shoulders.	**Es sitzt schlecht in den Schultern.** *ehs zitst shlehkht in dayn SHUL-tehrn*
The sleeves are too narrow (wide).	**Die Ärmel sind zu eng (weit).** *dee EHRM-el zint tsoo ehng (veyet)*
It needs alterations.	**Es braucht Änderungen.** *ehs browkht EHND-eh-rung-en*
Can you alter it?	**Können Sie es ändern?** *KERN-en zee ehs EHND-ehrn*
Can I return this?	**Kann ich dies zurückgeben?** *kahn ikh dees tsoo-REWK-gayb-en*
It fits very well.	**Es passt sehr gut.** *ehs pahsst zayr goot*
It doesn't fit.	**Es passt nicht.** *ehs pahsst nikht*
I'll take it.	**Ich nehm's.** *ikh naymss*
Please wrap it well.	**Bitte packen Sie es gut ein.** *BIT-eh PAHK-en zee ehs goot eyen*
Please giftwrap it.	**Bitte packen Sie es als Geschenk ein.** *BIT-eh PAHK-en zee ehs ahls geh-SHEHNK eyen*

JEWELRY

Please show me ___.	**Zeigen Sie mir bitte ___.** *TSEYEG-en zee meer BIT-eh*
■ a bracelet	**ein Armband** *eyen AHRM-bahnt*

■ a brooch	**eine Brosche** *EYEN-eh BROSH-eh*
■ a chain	**ein Kettchen** *eyen KET-khen*
■ cuff links	**Manschettenknöpfe** *mahn-SHEHT-en-knerpf-eh*
■ a goblet	**einen Becher** *EYEN-en BEHKH-uh*
■ earrings	**Ohrringe** *OHR-ring-eh*
■ a necklace	**eine Halskette** *EYEN-eh HAHLS-ket-eh*
■ a pin	**eine Anstecknadel** *EYEN-eh AHN-shtehk-naad-el*
■ a ring	**einen Ring** *EYEN-en ring*
■ an engagement ring	**einen Verlobungsring** *EYEN-en fehr-LOHB-unks-ring*
■ a wedding ring	**einen Ehering** *EYEN-en AY-eh-ring*
■ a tie pin	**eine Krawattennadel** *EYEN-eh krah-VAHT-en-naad-el*
■ a tiara	**eine Tiara** *EYEN-eh tee-AAR-ah*
■ a wristwatch	**eine Armbanduhr** *EYEN-eh AHRM-bahnt-oor*
Is this ___?	**Ist dies in ___?** *ist dees in*
■ gold	**Gold** *golt*
■ platinum	**Platin** *plah-TEEN*
■ silver	**Silber** *ZILB-uh*
■ stainless steel	**rostfreiem Stahl** *ROST-freye-em shtahl*
Is it gold or just gold plate?	**Ist es in Gold oder nur vergoldet?** *ist ehs in golt OHD-uh noor fehr-GOLD-et*
■ silver plate	**versilbert** *fehr-ZILB-ehrt*

How many carats is it?	**Wieviel Karat hat es?** *VEE-feel kah-RAAT haht ehs*
I collect precious stones.	**Ich sammle Edelsteine.** *ikh ZAHM-leh AY-del-shteyen-eh*
■ semiprecious stones, too	**Halbedelsteine auch** *HAHLP-ay-del-shteyen-eh owkh*
I'm looking for ___.	**Ich suche ___.** *ikh ZOOKH-eh*
■ amber jewelry	**Bernsteinschmuck** *BEHRN-shteyen-shmuk*
■ an amethyst	**einen Amethyst** *EYEN-en ah-meh-THEWST*
■ diamonds	**Diamanten** *dee-ah-MAHNT-en*
■ emeralds	**Smaragde** *smah-RAHKT-eh*
■ hematite	**Blutstein** *BLOOT-shteyen*
■ ivory	**Elfenbein** *EHLF-en-beyen*
■ jade	**Jade** *YAAD-eh*
■ onyx	**Onyx** *OH-niks*
■ pearls	**Perlen** *PEHRL-en*
■ rubies	**Rubine** *ru-BEEN-eh*
■ sapphires	**Saphire** *zah-FEER-eh*
■ topazes	**Topase** *toh-PAAZ-eh*
■ turquoises	**Türkise** *tewr-KEEZ-eh*

MUSIC EQUIPMENT

Is there an audio/video store in the neighborhood?	**Gibt es einen Audiovisuell-Laden hier in der Gegend?** *gipt ehs EYEN-en OW-dee-o-viz-oo-el-laad-en heer in dehr GAYG-ent*

I'm looking for a CD by ___.	**Ich suche eine CD von ___.** *ikh ZOOKH-eh EYEN-eh tsey-day fon*
I'm interested in ___.	**Ich interessiere mich für ___.** *ikh in-teh-reh-SEER-eh mikh fewr*
■ brass-band music	**Blasmusik** *BLAAS-moo-zeek*
■ chamber music	**Kammermusik** *KAHM-uh-moo-zeek*
■ classical music	**klassische Musik** *KLAHS-ish-eh moo-ZEEK*
■ folk music	**Volksmusik** *FOLKS-moo-zeek*
■ folksongs (dances)	**Volkslieder (tänze)** *FOLKS-leed-uh (TEHNTS-eh)*
■ the latest hits	**die allerneusten Schlager** *die AHL-ehr-noyst-en SHLAAG-uh*
■ golden oldies	**"Evergreens"** *Evergreens*
■ easy listening	**Unterhaltungsmusik** *UNT-ehr-hahlt-unks-moo-zeek*
■ pop music	**Pop-Musik** *POP-moo-zeek*

VIDEO EQUIPMENT

I need ___.	**Ich brauche ___.** *ikh BROWKH-eh*
■ a camcorder	**einen Camcorder** *EYEN-en KAHM-kord-uh*
■ DVD movies	**DVD Spielfilme** *day vay day SHPEEL-film-eh*
■ videofilm	**Videofilm** *VEE-day-oh-film*
■ VCR tape	**VCR-Tonband** *vay-tsay-ehr TOHN-bahnt*
Do you have VCR or DVD movies with subtitles in English?	**Haben sie VCR oder DVD Spielfilme mit englischen Untertiteln?** *HAAB-en zee vay-tsay-ehr OHD-uh day-vay-day SHPEEL-film-eh mit EHNG-lish-en UNT-ehr-teet-eln*

PHOTOGRAPHIC EQUIPMENT

Where can I find a camera shop?	**Wo finde ich ein Fotogeschäft?** *voh FIND-eh ikh eyen FOH-toh-geh-sheft*
I would like ___.	**Ich möchte ___.** *ikh MERKHT-eh*
■ black-and-white film	**Schwarzweißfilm** *SHVAHRTS-veyess-film*
■ a camera bag	**eine Kameratasche** *EYEN-eh KAHM-eh-raa-tah-she*
■ camera batteries	**Kamerabatterien** *KAHM-eh-raa-bah-tehr-ee-en*
■ camera film	**Kamerafilm** *KAHM-eh-raa-film*
■ digital camera film	**digitalen Kamerafilm** *di-gi-taal-en KAHM-eh-raa-film*
■ a disposable camera	**eine Einwegkamera** *EYEN-eh EYEN-vayk-kahm-eh-raa*
■ film	**Film** *film*
■ a flash	**ein Blitzlicht** *eyen BLITS-likht*
■ a lens	**ein Objektiv** *eyen ob-yek-TEEF*
■ a point-and-shoot camera	**eine Richt-und-Knips-Kamera** *EYEN-eh rikht-unt-knips-kahm-eh-raa*
■ slide film	**Diafilm** *DEE-ah-film*
■ an SLR camera	**eine Spiegelreflexkamera** *EYEN-eh SHPEEG-el-reh-flex-kahm-eh-raa*
■ a tripod	**ein Stativ** *eyen shtaht-EEF*
How quickly can you develop these films?	**Wie schnell können Sie diese Filme entwickeln?** *vee shnel KERN-en zee DEEZ-eh FILM-eh ehnt-VIK-ehln*

Here are a black-and-white and two color films.	**Hier haben Sie einen schwarz-weißen und zwei Farbfilme.** *heer HAAB-en zee EYEN-en SHVAHRTS-veyess-en unt tsveye-FAHRP-film-eh*
I want a print of each negative.	**Ich möchte einen Abzug von jedem Negativ.** *ikh MERKHT-eh EYEN-en AHP-tsook fon YAYD-em NEH-gah-teef*
I want this picture enlarged.	**Ich möchte dieses Bild vergrößern lassen.** *ikh MERKHT-eh DEEZ-es bilt fehr-GRERSS-ehrn LASS-en*

■ with a glossy finish **Hochglanz** *HOHKH-glahnts*
■ with a matte finish **matt** *maht*

Is there an extra charge for developing?	**Kostet das Entwickeln extra?** *KOST-et dahs ehnt-VIK-eln EKS-traa*
I want prints only of the exposures that turned out well.	**Ich möchte nur von den gut gelungenen Aufnahmen Abzüge haben.** *ikh MERKHT-eh noor fon dayn goot geh-LUNG-en-en OWF-naam-en AHP-tsewg-eh HAAB-en*

NEWSPAPERS, MAGAZINES, AND POSTCARDS

Do you have stamps?	**Haben Sie auch Briefmarken?** *HAAB-en zee owkh BREEF-maark-en*
Do you sell booklets of tickets for the streetcars?	**Verkaufen Sie Fahrscheinhefte für die Straßenbahnen?** *fehr-KOW-fen zee FAAR-sheyen-heft-eh fewr dee SHTRAASS-en-baan-en*

Do you have newspapers (magazines, periodicals) in English?

Haben Sie Zeitungen (Illustrierten, Zeitschriften) in Englisch? *HAAB-en zee TSEYET-ung-en (il-us-TREERT-en, TSEYET-shrift-en) in EHNG-lish*

How much is that?

Was macht das? *vahs mahkht dahs*

HANDICRAFTS, TOYS, SOUVENIRS

I'd like to buy a gift (souvenir).

Ich möchte gerne ein Geschenk (Andenken) kaufen. *ikh MERKHT-eh GEHRN-eh eyen geh-SHENK (AHN-dehnk-en) KOWF-en*

I don't want to spend more than ___ on it.

Ich will nicht mehr als ___ dafür ausgeben. *ikh vil nikht mayr ahls ___ dah-FEWR OWS-gayb-en*

What do you have in ___?

Was haben Sie an ___? *vahs HAAB-en zee ahn*

■ leather goods

Lederwaren *LAYD-uh-vaar-en*

■ glassware

Glaswaren *GLAAS-vaar-en*

Are these little spoons genuine silver?

Sind diese Löffelchen echt Silber? *zint DEEZ-eh LERF-el-khen ehkht ZILB-uh*

Is this ___ ?

Ist dies ___? *ist dees*

■ handcarved

handgeschnitzt *HAHNT-geh-shnitst*

■ handpainted

handgemalt *HAHNT-geh-maalt*

How much is this little cup?

Was kostet dieses Tässchen? *vahs KOST-et DEEZ-es TEHS-khen*

Do you have dolls in peasant costumes?

Haben Sie Puppen in Trachten? *HAAB-en zee PUP-en in TRAHKHT-en*

Is this made of wood (paper, metal, copper, pewter)?	**Ist dies aus Holz (Papier, Metall, Kupfer, Zinn)?** *ist dees ows holts (pah-PEER, meh-TAHL, KUP-fuh, tsin)*
What kinds of toys do you have?	**Was für Spielzeuge haben Sie?** *vahs fewr SHPEEL-tsoyg-eh HAAB-en zee*
■ For a ten-year-old child.	**Für ein zehnjähriges Kind.** *fewr eyen TSAYN-yay-rig-es kint*
■ Nothing dangerous!	**Nichts Gefährliches!** *nikhts geh-FAYR-likh-es*

STATIONERY ITEMS

I'm looking for ___.	**Ich suche ___.** *ikh ZOOKH-eh*
■ ball-point pens	**Kugelschreiber** *KOOG-el-shreyeb-uh*
■ a deck of playing cards	**Spielkarten** *SHPEEL-kaart-en*
■ envelopes	**Umschläge** *UM-shlayg-eh*
■ an eraser	**einen Radiergummi** *EYEN-en rah-DEER-gu-mee*
■ glue	**Leim** *leyem*
■ notebooks	**Notizhefte** *noh-TEETS-hehft-eh*
■ pencils	**Bleistifte** *BLEYE-shtift-eh*
■ a ruler	**ein Lineal** *eyen lee-nay-AAL*
■ tape	**Klebestreifen** *KLAYB-eh-shtreyef-en*
■ some string	**Schnur** *schnoor*
■ thumbtacks	**Reißzwecken** *REYESS-tsvehk-en*
■ typing paper	**Schreibmaschinenpapier** *SHREYEP-mah-sheen-en-pah-peer*
■ a writing pad	**einen Schreibblock** *EYEN-en SHREYEP-blok*

- airmail writing paper

  Luftpost Briefpapier *LUFT-post BREEF-pah-peer*

- Scotch tape

  Tesafilm *TAY-zaa-film*

TOBACCO

Can you give me change for the machine?

Können Sie mir Kleingeld für den Automaten geben? *KERN-en zee meer KLEYEN-gehlt fewr dayn ow-toh-MAAT-en GAYB-en*

I'd like a pack (carton) of cigarettes.

Ich möchte eine Schachtel (Stange) Zigaretten. *ikh MERKHT-eh EYEN-eh SHAHKHT-el (SHTAHNG-eh) tsee-gah-REHT-en*

- filtered

  mit Filter *mit FILT-uh*

- unfiltered

  ohne Filter *OHN-eh FILT-uh*

- menthol

  Mentholzigaretten *mehn-TOHL-tsee-gah-REHT-en*

- king-size

  extra lang *EKS-traa lahng*

- reduced nicotine

  nikotinarm *ni-koh-TEEN-ahrm*

What American cigarettes do you have?

Was für amerikanische Zigaretten haben Sie? *vahs fewr ah-meh-ree-KAAN-ish-eh tsee-gah-REHT-en HAAB-en zee*

Do you carry Cuban cigars?

Führen Sie Havannas? *FEWR-en zee hah-VAHN-ahs*

FOOD AND HOUSEHOLD ITEMS

I'd like ___.

Ich möchte ___. *ikh MERKHT-eh*

- a bar of soap

  ein Stück Seife *eyen shtewk ZEYEF-eh*

■ a bottle of juice	**eine Flasche Saft** *EYEN-eh FLAHSH-eh zahft*
■ a box of cereal	**ein Karton Müsli** *eyen kahr-TONG MEWS-lee*
■ a can (tin) of tomato sauce	**eine Dose Tomatensoße** *EYEN-eh DOHZ-eh toh-MAAT-en-zohss-eh*
■ a dozen eggs	**ein Dutzend Eier** *eyen DUTS-ehnt EYE-uh*
■ a jar of coffee	**ein Glas Kaffee** *eyen glahs KAH-fay*
■ a kilo of potatoes (just over 2 pounds)	**ein Kilo Kartoffeln** *eyen KEE-loh kahr-TOF-eln*
■ a half-kilo of cherries (just over 1 pound)	**ein halbes Kilo Kirschen** *eyen HAHLB-es KEE-loh KEERSH-en*
■ a liter of milk (about 1 quart)	**ein Liter Milch** *eyen LEET-uh milkh*
■ a package of candies	**ein Paket Bonbons** *eyen pah-KAYT bohn-BOHNS*
■ 100 grams of cheese (about $\frac{1}{4}$ pound)	**hundert Gramm Käse** *HUN-dehrt grahm KAYZ-eh*
■ a roll of toilet paper	**eine Rolle Toilettenpapier** *EYEN-eh ROL-eh toy-LEHT-en-pah-peer*
■ a kilo of butter	**ein Kilo Butter** *eyen KEE-loh BUT-uh*
■ 200 grams (about $\frac{1}{2}$ pound) of cookies	**zweihundert Gramm Kekse** *TSVEYE-hun-dehrt grahm KAYKS-eh*
■ 100 grams of bologna	**hundert Gramm Fleischwurst** *HUN-dehrt grahm FLEYESH-voorst*

TOILETRIES

I'm looking for ___.	**Ich suche ___.**	*ikh ZOOKH-eh*
a brush	**eine Bürste**	*EYEN-eh BEWRST-eh*
cleansing cream	**Reinigungscreme**	*REYEN-ig ungs-kraym*
cologne	**Kölnisch Wasser**	*KERLN-ish VAHS-uh*
condoms	**Kondome** **Präservative**	*KON-dohm-eh pray-zayr-vah-TEEV-eh*
dental floss	**Zahnseide**	*TSAAN-zeyed-eh*
(disposable) diapers	**(wegwerfbare) Windeln**	*(VEHK-vehrf-baar-eh) VIND-eln*
a file	**eine Feile**	*EYEN-eh FEYEL-eh*
eyeliner	**einen Lidstift**	*EYEN-en LEED-shtift*
eye shadow	**einen Lidschatten**	*EYEN-en LEED-shaht-en*
an eyebrow pencil	**einen Augenbrauenstift**	*EYEN-en OWG-en-brow-en-shtift*
foot powder	**Fußpuder**	*FOOSS-pood-uh*
hairpins	**Haarklemmen**	*HAAR-klem-en*
hair spray	**Haarspray**	*HAAR-shpray*
lipstick	**einen Lippenstift**	*EYEN-en LIP-en-shtift*
mascara	**Wimperntusche**	*VIMP-ehrn-tush-eh*
a mirror	**einen Spiegel**	*EYEN en SHPEEG-el*
mouthwash	**Mundwasser**	*MUNT-vahs-uh*
nail clippers	**eine Nagelzange**	*EYEN-eh NAAG-el-tsahng-eh*

- nail polish — **Nagellack** *NAAG-el-lahk*
- nail polish remover — **Nagellackentferner** *NAAG-el-lahk-ehnt-fehrn-uh*
- nail scissors — **eine Nagelschere** *EYEN-eh NAAG-el-shayr-eh*
- a razor — **einen Rasierapparat** *EYEN-en rah-ZEER-ah-pah-raat*
- razor blades — **Rasierklingen** *rah-ZEER-kling-en*
- rouge — **Schminke, Rouge** *SHMINK-eh, roozh*
- sanitary napkins — **Damenbinden** *DAAM-en-bind-en*
- shampoo — **ein Haarwaschmittel** *eyen HAAR-vahsh-mit-el*
- shaving lotion — **Rasierwasser** *rah-ZEER-vahs-uh*
- shaving cream — **Rasiercreme** *rah-ZEER-kraym*
- soap — **Seife** *ZEYEF-eh*
- a sponge — **einen Schwamm** *EYEN-en shvahm*
- tissues — **Papiertücher** *pah-PEER-tewkh-uh*
- toilet paper — **Toilettenpapier** *toy-LEHT-en-pah-peer*
- a toothbrush — **eine Zahnbürste** *EYEN-eh TSAAN-bewrst-eh*
- toothpaste — **Zahnpaste** *TSAAN-pahs-teh*
- tweezers — **eine Pinzette** *EYEN-eh pin-TSEHT-eh*

PERSONAL CARE AND SERVICES

THE BARBER SHOP

| I must go to the barber. | **Ich muss zum Friseur.** *ikh muss tsoom free-ZEHR* |

Is there one in the hotel?	**Gibt's einen im Hotel?** *gipts EYEN-en im ho-TEL*	
I don't want to wait long.	**Ich will nicht lange warten.** *ikh vil nikht LAHNG-eh VAART-en*	
Give me a shave, please.	**Rasieren, bitte.** *rah-ZEER-en BIT-eh*	
I want a haircut, please.	**Haare schneiden, bitte.** *HAAR-eh SHNEYED-en BIT-eh*	
(Not too) short in back, long in front.	**(Nicht zu) kurz hinten, lang vorne.** *(nikht tsoo) koorts HINT-en, lahng FORN-eh*	
Take a little more off on top.	**Nehmen Sie oben ein bisschen mehr weg.** *NAYM-en zee OHB-en eyen BISS-khen mayr vehk*	
Nothing more on the sides.	**Nichts mehr an den Seiten.** *nikhts mayr ahn dayn ZEYET-en*	
That's enough.	**Das genügt.** *dahs ge-NEWKT*	
Just use the scissors, please.	**Nur mit der Schere, bitte.** *noor mit dehr SHAYR-eh BIT-eh*	
Don't use the machine.	**Keine Maschine, bitte.** *KEYEN-eh mah-SHEEN-eh BIT-eh*	
Please, just a light trim.	**Bitte nur ausputzen.** *BIT-eh noor OWS-puts-en*	
Please trim my ____.	**Bitte stutzen Sie mir ____.** *BIT-eh SHTUTS-en zee meer*	

- beard   **den Bart** *dayn baart*
- moustache   **den Schnurrbart** *dayn SCHNOOR-baart*
- sideburns   **die Koteletten** *dee kot-eh-LEHT-en*

Please bring me a hand mirror.	**Bringen Sie mir bitte einen Handspiegel.** *BRING-en zee meer BIT-eh EYEN-en HAHNT-shpeeg-el*
How much do I owe you?	**Was schulde ich Ihnen?** *vahs SHULD-eh ikh EEN-en*

THE BEAUTY PARLOR

Is there a beauty parlor around here?	**Gibt es einen Damensalon hier in der Nähe?** *gipt ehs EYEN-en DAAM-en-zaa-long heer in dehr NAY-eh*
I'd like to make an appointment for today (tomorrow).	**Ich möchte mich für heute (morgen) anmelden.** *ikh MERKHT-eh mikh fewr HOYT-eh (MORG-en) AHN meld en*
I'd like ____.	**Ich möchte ____.** *ikh MERKHT-eh*
Can you give me ____?	**Können Sie mir ____ geben?** *KERN-en zee meer ____ GAYB-en*
▪ a color rinse	**eine Farbspülung** *EYEN-eh FAHRP-shpewl-ung*
▪ a face pack	**eine Gesichtsmaske** *EYEN-eh geh-ZIKHTS-mahsk-eh*
▪ a manicure (pedicure)	**eine Maniküre (Pediküre)** *EYEN-eh MAHN-i-kewr-eh (PAYD-i-kewr-eh)*
▪ a mudbath	**ein Schlammbad** *eyen SHLAHM-baat*
▪ a facial massage	**eine Gesichtsmassage** *EYEN-eh geh-ZIKHTS-mah-sazh-eh*
▪ a permanent	**eine Dauerwelle** *EYEN-eh DOW-uh-vehl-eh*

■ a touch up · **eine Auffrischung** *EYEN-eh OWF-frish-ung*

Just a shampoo and set, please. · **Nur Waschen und Legen, bitte.** *noor VAHSH-en unt LAYG-en BIT-eh*

No, don't cut it. · **Nein, nicht schneiden.** *neyen, nikht SHNEYED-en*

I don't like the color anymore. · **Die Farbe gefällt mir nicht mehr.** *dee FAARB-eh geh-FEHLT meer nikht mayr*

This time I'm going to try ____. · **Diesmal versuche ich ____.** *DEES-maal fehr-ZOOKH-eh ikh*

■ auburn · **kastanienbraun** *kahs-TAAN-yen-brown*

■ light blond · **hellblond** *hel blont*

■ dark blond · **dunkelblond** *DUNK-el blont*

■ brunette · **braun** *brown*

■ a darker color · **eine dunklere Farbe** *EYEN-eh DUNK-lehr-eh FAARB-eh*

■ a lighter color · **eine hellere Farbe** *EYEN-eh HEL-ehr-eh FAARB-eh*

■ the same color · **dieselbe Farbe** *DEE-zehlb-eh FAARB-eh*

■ something exotic · **etwas Exotisches** *EHT-vahs eks-OHT-ish-es*

I'd like to look at the color chart again. · **Ich möchte mir nochmal die Farbtabelle ansehen.** *ikh MERKHT-eh meer NOKH-maal dee FAARP-tah-bel-eh AHN-zay-en*

Not too much hair spray. · **Nicht zu viel Haarspray.** *nikht tsoo feel HAAR-shpray*

No hair spray, please. **Kein Haarspray, bitte.** *keyen HAAR-shpray BIT-eh*

More hair spray. **Mehr Haarspray.** *mayr HAAR-shpray*

Do you carry wigs? **Führen Sie Perücken?** *FEWR-en zee peh-REWK-en*

I want a new hairdo. **Ich will eine neue Frisur.** *ikh vil EYEN-eh NOY-eh free-ZOOR*

Something striking. **Etwas Auffallendes.** *EHT-vahs OWF-fahl-ehnd-es*

Something wild. **Etwas ganz Tolles.** *EHT-vahs gahnts TOL-es*

With curls. **Mit Löckchen.** *mit LERK-khen*

With waves. **Mit Wellen.** *mit VEL-en*

In a bun on top or behind. **In einem Knoten oben oder hinten.** *in EYEN-em KNOHT-en OHB-en OHD-uh HINT-en*

SHOE REPAIRS

Can you fix these shoes (boots) right now? **Können Sie gleich jetzt diese Schuhe (Stiefel) reparieren?** *KERN-en zee gleyekh yetst DEEZ-eh SHOO-eh (SHTEEF-el) reh-pah-REER-en*

They need new (half) soles and heels. **Sie brauchen neue (Halb)sohlen und Absätze.** *zee BROWKH-en NOY-eh (hahlp)ZOHL-en unt AHP-zehts-eh*

I can come back in an hour.	**Ich kann in einer Stunde zurückkommen.** *ikh kahn in EYEN-uh SHTUND-eh tsoo-REWK-kom-en*
Please shine them also.	**Bitte putzen Sie sie auch.** *BIT-en PUTS-en zee zee owkh*
Will they be ready by Friday?	**Sind sie bis Freitag fertig?** *zint zee bis FREYE-taak FEHRT-ikh*

LAUNDRY AND DRY CLEANING

Is there a laundry (dry cleaner's) nearby?	**Gibt es eine Wäscherei (chemische Reinigung) in der Nähe?** *gipt ehs EYEN-eh vehsh-eh-REYE (KHAY-mi-sheh REYE-ni-gung) in dehr NAY-eh?*
Can these clothes be washed (ironed, cleaned) for me?	**Kann man mir diese Kleider waschen (bügeln, reinigen)?** *kahn mahn meer DEEZ-eh KLEYED-uh VAHSH-en BEWG-eln, REYE-nig-en)*
Could I have it today (tomorrow, the day after tomorrow)?	**Könnte ich's schon heute (morgen, übermorgen) haben?** *KERNT-eh ikhs shon HOYT-eh (MORG-en, EWB-uh-morg-en) HAAB-en*
I absolutely must have it ____.	**Ich muss es unbedingt ____ haben.** *ikh muss ehs UN-beh-dingt ____ HAAB-en*
■ as soon as possible	**so bald wie möglich** *zoh bahlt vee MERG-likh*
■ tonight	**vor heute Abend** *for HOYT-eh AAB-ehnt*
■ tomorrow	**vor morgen** *for MORG-en*
■ next week	**vor nächste Woche** *for NAYKHST-eh VOKH-eh*
■ the day after tomorrow	**vor übermorgen** *for EWB-uh-morg-en*

When will you bring it (them) back?	**Wann werden Sie es (sie) zurückbringen?** *vahn VEHRD-en zee ehs (zee) tsoo-REWK-bring-en*
When will it be ready?	**Wann wird es fertig sein?** *vahn virt ehs FEHR-tikh zeyen*
This isn't my laundry.	**Dies ist nicht meine Wäsche.** *dees ist nikht MEYEN-eh VEHSH-eh*

WATCH REPAIRS

I need ____.	**Ich brauche ____.** *ikh BROWKH-eh*
■ a glass	**ein Glas** *eyen glaass*
■ a stem	**ein Rad** *eyen raat*
■ a battery	**eine Batterie** *EYEN-eh bah-teh-REE*
I dropped it.	**Ich habe sie fallen lassen.** *ikh HAAB-eh zee FAHL-en LASS-en*
It often stops.	**Sie bleibt oft stehen.** *zee bleyept oft SHTAY-en*
It's often fast (slow).	**Sie geht oft vor (nach).** *zee gayt oft fohr (nahkh)*
How long do you need for that?	**Wie lange brauchen Sie dafür?** *vee LAHNG-eh BROWKH-en zee dah-FEWR*

CAMERA REPAIRS

Can you fix this (movie) camera?	**Können Sie diese (Film) Kamera reparieren?** *KERN-en zee DEEZ-eh (film) KAH-meh-raa reh-pah-REER-en*

How much would it cost to have this camera repaired?	**Wieviel würde es kosten, diese Kamera reparieren zu lassen?** *VEE-feel VEWRD-eh ehs KOST-en DEEZ-eh KAH-meh-raa reh-pah-REER-en tsoo LASS-en*
Would it take long?	**Würde es lange dauern?** *VEWRD-eh ehs LAHNG-eh DOW-ehrn*
The film doesn't advance.	**Der Film dreht sich nicht weiter.** *dayr film drayt zikh nikht VEYET-uh*
I think I need new batteries.	**Ich denke, ich brauche neue Batterien.** *ikh DEHNK-eh ikh BROWKH-eh NOY-eh bah-teh-REE-en*
May I have an estimate?	**Können Sie mir einen Kostenanschlag geben?** *KERN-en zee meer EYEN-en KOST-en-ahn-shlaak GAYB-en*
May I have a receipt?	**Darf ich eine Quittung haben?** *dahrf ikh EYEN-eh KVIT-ung HAAB-en*
When can I come and get it?	**Wann kann ich sie wieder abholen?** *vahn kahn ikh zee VEED-uh AHP-hohl-en*
I need it as soon as possible.	**Ich brauche sie sobald wie möglich.** *ikh BROWKH-eh zee zoh-BAHLT vee MERG-likh*

MEDICAL CARE

AT THE PHARMACY

Where can I find the nearest (all-night) pharmacy?	**Wo finde ich die nächste Apotheke (mit Nachtdienst)?** *voh FIND-eh ikh dee NAYKST-eh ah-poh-TAYK-eh (mit NAHKHT-deenst)*

At what time does it open (close)?	**Um wieviel Uhr wird geöffnet (geschlossen)?** *um VEE-feel oor veert geh-ERF-net (geh-SHLOSS-en)*
I'm looking for something for ____.	**Ich suche etwas gegen ____.** *ikh ZOOKH-eh EHT-vahs GAYG-en*
■ a cold	**eine Erkältung** *EYEN-eh ehr-KEHLT-ung*
■ lack of appetite	**Appetitlosigkeit** *ah-peh-TEET-loh-zikh-keyet*
■ constipation	**Verstopfung** *fehr-SHTOPF-ung*
■ a cough	**Husten** *HOOST-en*
■ a fever	**Fieber** *FEEB-uh*
■ diarrhea	**Durchfall** *DOORKH-fahl*
■ a hangover	**Kater** *KAAT-uh*
■ indigestion	**Magenverstimmung** *MAAG-en-fehr-shtim-ung*
■ hay fever	**Heuschnupfen** *HOY-shnupf-en*
■ headache	**Kopfschmerzen** *KOPF-shmehrts-en*
■ insomnia	**Schlaflosigkeit** *SHLAAF-loh-zikh-keyet*
■ motion sickness	**Reisekrankheit** *REYEZ-eh-krahnk-heyet*
■ insect bites	**Insektenstiche** *in-ZEHKT-en-shtikh-eh*
■ prickly heat	**Hitzblattern** *HITS-blaht-ehrn*
■ a blister	**eine Blase** *EYEN-eh BLAAZ-eh*
■ a burn	**eine Brandwunde** *EYEN-eh BRAHNT-vund-eh*
■ sunburn	**Sonnenbrand** *ZON-en-brahnt*
■ a toothache	**Zahnschmerzen** *TSAAN-shmehrts-en*

Must I have a prescription for the medicine?	**Muss ich ein Rezept für das Medikament haben?** *muss ikh eyen reh-TSEPT fewr dahs may-di-kaa-MENT HAAB-en*
Is there a German equivalent for this medicine?	**Gibt es ein deutsches Äquivalent für dieses Medikament?** *gipt ehs eyer DOYTSH-es ay-kvi-vah-LENT fewr DEEZ-es may-di-kaa-MENT*
Is there something similar?	**Gibt es etwas Ähnliches?** *gipt ehs EHT-vahs AYN-likh-es*
Please look it up for me.	**Bitte schlagen Sie es nach.** *BIT-eh SHLAAG-en zee ehs nahkh*
Can you fill this prescription for me now?	**Können Sie mir dieses Rezept jetzt machen?** *KERN-en zee meer DEEZ-es reh-TSEPT yetst MAAKH-en*
It's urgent.	**Es ist dringend.** *ehs ist DRING-ent*
How long will it take?	**Wie lange wird's dauern?** *vee LAHNG-eh veerts DOW-ehrn*
I'll wait.	**Ich warte darauf.** *ikh VAART-eh dah-ROWF*
When can I pick it up?	**Wann kann ich's abholen?** *vahn kahn ikhs AHP-hohl-en*
I need ____.	**Ich brauche ____.** *ikh BROWKH-eh*
■ an antacid	**Magentabletten** *MAAG-en-tahb-leht-en*
■ an antiseptic	**ein Antiseptikum** *even ahn-tee-ZEP-ti-kum*
■ aspirin	**Aspirin** *ah-spee-REEN*

■ bandages	**Verbandzeug**	*fehr-BAHNT-tsoyk*
■ Band Aids	**Heftpflaster**	*HEHFT-pflahst-uh*
■ a contraceptive	**ein Verhütungsmittel**	*eyen fehr-HEWT-ungs-mit-el*
■ corn plasters	**Hühneraugenpflaster**	*HEWN-ehr-owg-en-pflahst-uh*
■ cotton balls	**Wattebäusche**	*VAHT-eh-boysh-eh*
■ cough drops	**Hustenbonbons**	*HOOST-en-bohn-BOHNS*
■ eardrops	**Ohrentropfen**	*OHR-en-tropf-en*
■ eyedrops	**Augentropfen**	*OWG-en-tropf-en*
■ herbal teas	**Kräutertees**	*KROY-tehr-tayss*
■ first-aid kit	**einen Verbandkasten**	*EYEN-en fehr BAHNT-kahst-en*
■ iodine	**Jod**	*yoht*
■ an (herbal) laxative	**ein (Kräuter) Abführmittel**	*eyen (KROYT-ehr) AHP-fewr-mit-el*
■ talcum powder	**Talkumpuder**	*TAHLK-um-pood-uh*
■ a thermometer	**ein Thermometer**	*eyen tehr-mo-MAYT-uh*
■ throat lozenges	**Halspastillen**	*HAHLS-pahs-til-en*
■ tranquilizers	**ein Beruhigungsmittel**	*eyen beh-ROO-i-gungs-mit-el*
■ vitamins	**Vitamine**	*vee-taa-MEEN-eh*

WITH THE DOCTOR

I don't feel well.	**Ich fühle mich nicht wohl.**	*ikh FEWL-eh mikh nikht vohl*
I need a doctor.	**Ich brauche einen Arzt.**	*ikh BROWKH-eh EYEN-en ahrtst*

Is there a doctor here who speaks English?	**Gibt's hier einen Arzt, der Englisch spricht?** *gipts heer EYEN-en ahrtst dehr EHNG-lish shprikht*
Where is his office?	**Wo ist seine Praxis?** *voh ist SEYEN-eh PRAHK-siss*
What are his office hours?	**Was sind seine Sprechstunden?** *vahs zint ZEYEN-eh SHPREKH-shtund-en*
Could the doctor come to me in my hotel?	**Könnte der Arzt zu mir ins Hotel kommen?** *KERNT-eh dehr ahrtst tsoo meer ins ho-TEL KOM-en*
I feel dizzy (nauseated).	**Mir ist schwindlig (übel).** *meer ist SHVIND-likh (EWB-el)*
I feel weak.	**Ich fühle mich schwach.** *ikh FEWL-eh mikh shvahkh*
I have ____.	**Ich habe ____.** *ikh HAAB-eh*
■ an abscess	**einen Abszess** *EYEN-en ahps-TSESS*
■ a broken leg	**einen Beinbruch** *EYEN-en BEYEN-brukh*
■ a bruise	**eine Quetschung** *EYEN-eh KVETSH-ung*
■ a burn	**eine Brandwunde** *EYEN-eh BRAHNT-vund-eh*
■ a cold	**eine Erkältung** *EYEN-eh ehr-KEHLT-ung*
■ constipation	**Verstopfung** *fehr-SHTOPF-ung*
■ cramps	**Krämpfe** *KREHMPF-eh*
■ a cut	**eine Schnittwunde** *EYEN-eh SHNIT-vund-eh*
■ diarrhea	**Durchfall** *DOORKH-fahl*

■ dysentery	**Ruhr** *roor*
■ fever	**Fieber** *FEEB-uh*
■ a fracture	**einen Bruch** *EYEN-en brookh*
■ an eye inflammation	**eine Augenentzündung** *EYEN-eh OWG-en-ehnt-tsewnd-ung*
■ a lump	**eine Beule** *EYEN-eh BOYL-eh*
■ a sore throat	**Halsschmerzen** *HAHLS-shmehrts-en*
■ a skin disease	**eine Hautkrankheit** *EYEN-eh HOWT-krahnk-heyet*
■ a stomach ulcer	**ein Magengeschwür** *eyen MAAG-en-geh-shvewr*
■ a sty	**einen Augenliderbrand** *EYEN-en OWG-en-leed-ehr-brahnt*
■ a swelling	**eine Schwellung** *EYEN-eh SHVEL-ung*
■ a wound	**eine Wunde** *EYEN-eh VUND-eh*
■ a venereal disease	**eine Geschlechtskrankheit** *EYEN-eh geh-SHLEKHTS-krahnk-heyet*
■ a head (back) ache	**Kopf (Rücken) schmerzen** *kopf (REWK-en) SHMERTS-en*
I have chills.	**Mich fröstelt.** *mikh FRERST-elt*
It hurts me here.	**Hier tut es weh.** *heer toot ehs vay*
I hurt all over.	**Es tut mir überall weh.** *ehs toot meer EWB-ehr-ahl vay*
My ____ hurts (hurt).	**Mein(e) ____ tut (tun) mir weh.** *meyen(eh) ____ toot (toon) meer vay*
■ my ankle	**mein Knöchel** *meyen KNERKH-el*
■ my arm	**mein Arm** *meyen ahrm*

- my ear **mein Ohr** *meyen ohr*
- my eye **mein Auge** *meyen OWG-eh*
- my face **mein Gesicht** *meyen geh-ZIKHT*
- my finger **mein Finger** *meyen FING-uh*
- my foot **mein Fuß** *meyen fooss*
- my glands **meine Drüsen** *MEYEN-eh DREWZ-en*
- my hand **meine Hand** *MEYEN-eh hahnt*
- my hip joint **mein Hüftgelenk** *meyen HEWFT-geh-lehnk*
- my heel **meine Ferse** *MEYEN-eh FEHRZ-eh*
- my leg **mein Bein** *meyen beyen*
- my nose **meine Nase** *MEYEN-eh NAAZ-eh*
- my ribs **meine Rippen** *MEYEN-eh RIP-en*
- my shoulder **meine Schulter** *MEYEN-eh SHULT-uh*
- my stomach **mein Magen** *meyen MAAG-en*
- my toe **meine Zehe** *MEYEN-eh TSAY-eh*
- my wrist **mein Handgelenk** *meyen HAHNT-geh-lenk*

I've had this pain since yesterday.	**Seit gestern habe ich diese Schmerzen.** *zeyet GEHST-ehrn HAAB-eh ikh DEEZ-eh SHMEHRTS-en*
I've been suffering from this disease for some time.	**Seit einiger Zeit leide ich an dieser Krankheit.** *zeyet EYE-ni-guh tseyet LEYED-eh ikh ahn DEEZ-uh KRAHNK-heyet*
Can you prescribe sleeping pills for me?	**Können Sie mir Schlaftabletten verschreiben?** *KERN-en zee meer SHLAAF-tah-blet-en fehr-SHREYEB-en*

I have heart trouble.	**Ich bin herzkrank.** *ikh bin HEHRTS-krahnk*
Do I have to go to the hospital?	**Muss ich ins Krankenhaus?** *muss ikh ins KRAHNK-en-howss*
When can I continue my trip?	**Wann kann ich meine Reise fort-setzen?** *vahn kahn ikh MEYEN-eh REYEZ-eh FORT-zets-en*

IN THE HOSPITAL

Help me, quick!	**Helfen Sie mir, schnell!** *HELF-en zee meer shnel*
It's urgent.	**Es ist dringend.** *ehs ist DRING-ehnt*
Call a doctor immediately.	**Rufen Sie sofort einen Arzt.** *ROOF-en zee zoh-FORT EYEN-en ahrtst*
Get an ambulance.	**Holen Sie einen Krankenwagen.** *HOHL-en zee EYEN-en KRAHNK-en-vaag-en*
Take me (him) to the hospital.	**Bringen Sie mich (ihn) ins Kran-kenhaus.** *BRING-en zee mikh (een) ins KRAHNK-en-howss*
I need first aid.	**Ich brauche erste Hilfe.** *ikh BROWKH-eh EHRST-eh HILF-eh*
I'm bleeding.	**Ich blute.** *ikh BLOOT-eh*
I've (he's) lost a lot of blood.	**Ich habe (er hat) viel Blut verloren.** *ikh HAAB-eh (ehr haht) feel bloot fehr-LOHR-en*

I think something is broken (dislocated).	**Ich glaube, es ist etwas gebrochen (verrenkt).** *ikh GLOWB-eh ehs ist EHT-vahs geh-BROKH-en (fehr-REHNKT)*

SPECIAL NEEDS

Where can I get ____?	**Wo bekomme ich ____?** *voh beh-KOM-eh ikh*
■ a cane	**einen Stock** *EYEN-en shtok*
■ crutches	**Krücken** *KREWK-en*
■ a hearing aid	**ein Hörgerät** *eyen HEWR-geh-RAYT*
■ a walker	**einen Laufstuhl** *EYEN-en LOWF-shtool*
■ a wheelchair	**einen Rollstuhl** *EYEN-en ROL-shtool*
Is there a toilet for disabled persons?	**Gibt es ein WC für Behinderte?** *gipt ehs eyen vay-tsay fewr beh-HIN-dehrt-eh*
Is the building/the theater/the place/ the bus/the train also easily accessible to the handicapped?	**Ist das Gebäude/das Theater/ das Lokal/der Bus/der Zug auch für Behinderte leicht zugänglich?** *ist dahs geh-BOY-duh/dahs tay-AAT-uh/dahs loh-KAAL/dehr bus/dehr tsook owkh fewr beh-HIN-dehrt-eh leyekht TSOO-geng-likh*
Is there a ramp/an elevator for people in wheelchairs?	**Gibt es eine Rampe/einen Aufzug für Rollstuhlfahrer?** *gipt ehs EYEN-eh RAHM-peh/EYEN-eh OWF-tsook fewr ROL-shtool-FAAR-uh*

AT THE DENTIST

Unfortunately, I must go to the dentist. **Leider muss ich zum Zahnarzt.** *LEYED-uh muss ikh tsoom TSAAN-ahrtst*

Do you know a good one? **Kennen Sie einen guten?** *KEN-en zee EYEN-en GOOT-en*

I have a toothache that's driving me crazy. **Ich habe wahnsinnige Zahnschmerzen.** *ikh hahp VAAN-zi-nig-eh TSAAN-shmehrts-en*

I've lost a filling (crown). **Ich habe eine Plombe (Krone) verloren.** *ikh hahp EYEN-eh PLOMB-eh (KROHN-eh) fehr-LOHR-en*

I broke a tooth on hard nuts. **Ich habe mir an harten Nüssen einen Zahn ausgebissen.** *ikh hahp meer ahn HAHRT-en NEWSS-en EYEN-en tsaan OWSS-geh-biss-en*

I can't chew. **Ich kann nicht kauen.** *ikh kahn nikht KOW-en*

My gums are bleeding. **Das Zahnfleisch blutet.** *dahs TSAAN-fleyesh BLOOT-et*

Do I have an abscess? **Habe ich einen Abszess?** *hahb ikh EYEN-en ahps-TSESS*

Can the tooth be saved? **Ist der Zahn noch zu retten?** *ist dehr tsaan nokh tsoo RET-en*

I won't have it pulled. **Ich will ihn nicht ziehen lassen.** *ikh vil een nikht TSEE-en LAHSS-en*

I will wait and ask my dentist at home. **Ich warte, und frage meinen Zahnarzt zu Hause.** *ikh VAART-eh unt FRAAG-eh MEYEN-en TSAAN-ahrtst tsoo HOWZ-eh*

I just want a temporary filling (treatment).	**Ich möchte nur eine provisorische Füllung (Behandlung).** *ikh MERKHT-eh noor EYEN-eh pro-vee-ZOR-ish-eh FEWL-ung (beh-HANT-lung)*
Can you fix ____?	**Können Sie ____ reparieren?** *KERN-en zee ____ reh-pah-REER-en*
■ this denture	**dieses Gebiss** *DEEZ-es geh-BISS*
■ these false teeth	**diesen Zahnersatz** *DEEZ-en TSAAN-ehr-zahts*
How much do I owe you for your services?	**Wieviel bin ich Ihnen schuldig?** *VEE-feel bin ikh EEN-en SHULD-ikh*

WITH THE OPTICIAN

I'd like to get these glasses repaired.	**Diese Brille möchte ich reparieren lassen.** *DEEZ-eh BRIL-eh MERKHT-eh ikh reh-pah-REER-en LAHSS-en*
Can you put in a new lens for the broken one?	**Können Sie das gebrochene Glas auswechseln?** *KERN-en zee dahs geh-BROKH-en-eh glaas OWSS-vehks-eln*
The screw must be replaced.	**Die Schraube muss ersetzt werden.** *dee SHROWB-eh muss ehr-ZETST VAYRD-en*
It fell out.	**Sie ist herausgefallen.** *zee ist hehr-OWSS-geh-fahl-en*
Could you repair them right away?	**Können Sie sie gleich jetzt reparieren?** *KERN-en zee zee gleyekh yetst reh-pah-REER-en*

| I can wait. | **Ich kann warten.** *ikh kahn VAART-en* |

COMMUNICATIONS

POST OFFICE

I must mail some letters.	**Ich muss einige Briefe auf die Post tragen.** *ikh muss EYE-ni-geh BREEF-eh owf dee post TRAAG-en*
I want to send (mail) these postcards home.	**Ich will diese Postkarten mit der Post nach Hause schicken.** *ikh vil DEEZ-eh POST-kart-en mit dehr post nahkh HOWZ-eh SHIK-en*
I want to mail these packages home.	**Ich möchte diese Pakete mit der Post nach Hause schicken.** *ikh MERKHT-eh DEEZ-eh pah-KAYT-eh mit dehr post nahkh HOWZ-eh SHIK-en*
Where is the post office?	**Wo ist das Postamt?** *voh ist dahs POST-ahmt*
Where can I find a mailbox?	**Wo finde ich einen Briefkasten?** *voh FIND-eh ikh EYEN-en BREEF-kahst-en*
What is the postage on ____ to the U.S. (England, Canada, Australia)?	**Was kostet ____ nach USA (England, Kanada, Australien)?** *vahs KOST-et ____ nahkh oo-ess-aa (EHNG-lahnt, KAA-naa-dah, owss-TRAAL-yen)*
▪ a letter	**ein Brief** *eyen breef*
▪ an airmail letter	**ein Luftpostbrief** *eyen LUFT-post-breef*

■ a registered letter	**ein Einschreibebrief** *eyen EYEN-shreyeb-eh-breef*
■ a special delivery letter	**ein Eilbrief** *eyen EYEL-breef*
■ a postcard	**eine Postkarte** *EYEN-eh POST-kaart-eh*
■ this package	**dieses Paket** *DEEZ-es pah-KAYT*
Can I have this letter (this package) insured?	**Kann ich diesen Brief (dieses Paket) versichern lassen?** *kahn ikh DEEZ-en breef (DEEZ-es pah-KAYT) fehr-ZIKH-ehrn LAHSS-en*
When will it arrive?	**Wann wird's ankommen?** *vahn veerts AHN-kom-en*
Where is the ____ window?	**Wo ist der Schalter für ____?** *voh ist dehr SHAHLT-uh fewr*
■ general delivery	**postlagernde Sendungen** *POST-laa-gehrnd-eh ZEHND-ung-en*
■ money orders	**Postanweisungen** *POST-ahn-veyez-ung-en*
■ philately	**Briefmarkensammler** *BREEF-mahrk-en-zahm-luh*
■ stamps	**Briefmarken** *BREEF-mahrk-en*
Please let me have ____.	**Geben Sie mir bitte ____.** *GAYB-en zee meer BIT-eh*
■ eight envelopes	**acht Umschläge** *ahkht UM-shlayg-eh*
■ twelve postcards	**zwölf Postkarten** *tsverlf POST-kaart en*
■ twenty (airmail) stamps	**zwanzig (Luftpost) Briefmarken** *TSVAHN-tsikh (LUFT-post) BREEF-mahrk-en*

Are there any letters for me?	**Ist Post für mich da?** *ist post fewr mikh daa*
My name is ____.	**Ich heiße ____.** *ikh HEYESS-eh*

FAX

Do you have a fax machine?	**Haben Sie ein Faxgerät?** *HAAB-en zee eyen FAHKS-geh-RAYT*
What is your fax number?	**Wie ist Ihre Faxnummer?** *vee ist EER-eh FAHKS-noom-uh*
I want to send a fax.	**Ich will ein Fax senden.** *ikh vil eyen fahks SEHND-en*
Fax it to me.	**Faxen Sie es mir.** *FAHKS-en zee ehs meer*
I didn't get your fax.	**Ihr Fax hab ich nicht bekommen.** *eer fahks haab ikh nikht beh-KOM-en*
Did you receive my fax?	**Haben Sie mein Fax bekommen?** *HAAB-en zee meyen fahks beh-KOM-en*
Your fax is illegible.	**Ihr Fax ist unleserlich.** *eer fahks ist un-LAYZ-uh-likh*
Please send it again.	**Bitte senden Sie es wieder.** *BIT-eh ZEND-en zee ehs VEED-uh*

COMPUTERS

Do you have ____?	**Haben Sie ____?** *Haab-en zee*
■ a Macintosh computer	**einen Macintosh Computer** *EYEN-en MEHK-in-tosh com-PYOOT-uh*

■ a PC   **einen PC** *EYEN-en pay-tsay*

What operating system are you using?   **Welches Betriebssystem benutzen Sie?** *VELKH-es beh-TREEPS-sewss-TAYM beh-nutz-en zee*

What word processing program are you using?   **Welches Textverarbeitungs-programm benutzen Sie?** *VELKH-es text-fehr-AHR-beyet-ungs-proh-grahm beh-NUTZ-en zee*

Are our systems compatible?   **Sind unsere Systeme kompatibel?** *zint UNZ-ehr-eh sewss-TAYM-eh kom-pah-TEE-bel*

What is your e-mail address?   **Wie ist Ihre E-Mail Adresse?** *vee ist EER-eh ee-mayl ah-DREHSS-eh*

TELEPHONES

I'm looking for ____.   **Ich suche ____.** *ikh ZOOKH-eh*

■ a telephone booth   **eine Telefonzelle** *EYEN-eh tay-leh-FOHN-tsel-eh*

■ a telephone directory   **ein Telefonbuch** *eyen tay-leh-FOHN-bookh*

May I use your phone?   **Darf ich Ihr Telefon benutzen?** *dahrf ikh eer tay-leh-FOHN beh-NUTS-en*

Here is the number.   **Hier ist die Nummer.** *heer ist dee NUM-uh*

I don't know the area code.   **Ich weiß die Vorwahlnummer nicht.** *ikh veyes dee FOHR-vaal-num-uh nikht.*

Can you help me?	**Können Sie mir helfen?** *KERN-en zee meer HELF-en*
It's a local call.	**Es ist ein Ortsgespräch.** *ehs ist eyen ORTS-geh-shpraykh*
■ a long-distance call	**ein Ferngespräch** *eyen FEHRN-geh-shpraykh*
Where can I buy a telephone card?	**Wo kann ich eine Telefonkarte kaufen?** *voh kahn ikh EYEN-eh TAY-leh-FOHN-kaart-eh KOWF-en*
Do you sell telephone cards?	**Verkaufen Sie Telefonkarten?** *fehr-KOWF-en zee TAH-leh-FOHN-kaart-en*
How many units is it good for?	**Wie viele Einheiten sind darauf?** *vee FEEL-eh EYEN-heyet-en zint dah-ROWF*
How much does this card cost?	**Was kostet diese Karte?** *vahss KOST-et DEEZ-eh KAART-eh*
■ a person-to-person call	**ein Gespräch mit Voranmeldung** *eyen geh-SHPRAYKH mit FOHR-ahn-mehld-ung*
■ a collect call	**ein R-Gespräch** *eyen ehr-geh-SHPRAYKH*
May I speak to Mr. (Mrs., Miss) ____?	**Darf ich bitte Herrn (Frau, Fräulein) ____ sprechen?** *dahrf ikh BIT-eh hehrn (frow, FROY-leyen) SHPREHKH-en*
Speaking.	**Am Apparat.** *ahm ah-pah-RAAT*
Hello.	**Hallo.** *hah-LOH*
This is ____.	**Hier ist ____.** *heer ist*

Speak louder (more slowly).	**Sprechen Sie lauter (langsamer).** *SHPREHKH-en zee LOWT-uh (LAHNG-zaam-uh)*
Don't hang up.	**Bleiben Sie am Apparat.** *BLEYEB-en zee ahm ah-pah-RAAT*
There's no answer.	**Es meldet sich niemand.** *ehss MEHLD-et zikh NEE-mahnt*
The line is busy.	**Die Leitung ist besetzt.** *dee LEYET-ung ist beh-ZEHTST*
You gave me the wrong number.	**Sie haben mich falsch verbunden.** *zee HAAB-en mikh fahlsh fehr-BUND-en*
I'll call again later.	**Später rufe ich noch einmal an.** *SHPAYT-uh roof ikh nokh EYEN-maal ahn*
I'd like to leave a message.	**Ich möchte etwas ausrichten lassen.** *ikh merkht EHT-vahs OWSS-rikht-en LAHSS-en*

TELEGRAMS

Telegrams are sent from post offices.

| I'd like to send a telegram to ____. | **Ich möchte ein Telegramm nach ____ aufgeben.** *ikh MERKHT-eh eyen tay-leh-GRAHM nakh ____ OWF-gayb-en* |
| How much is it per word? | **Was kostet es pro Wort?** *vahs KOST-et ehs proh vort* |

| Please let me have a form. | **Geben Sie mir bitte ein Formular.** *GAYB-en zee meer BIT-eh eyen for-mu-LAAR* |

GENERAL INFORMATION

TELLING TIME

What time is it?	**Wieviel Uhr ist es?** *VEE-feel oor ist ehs*
▣ hour	**Stunde** *SHTUND-eh*
▣ minute	**Minute** *mi-NOOT-eh*
▣ second	**Sekunde** *zeh-KUN-deh*
▣ half an hour	**eine halbe Stunde** *EYEN-eh HAHLB-eh SHTUND-eh*
▣ an hour and a half	**anderthalb Stunden** *AHN-dehrt-haalp SHTUND-en*
At what time shall we meet?	**Um wieviel Uhr treffen wir uns?** *um VEE-feel oor TREHF-en veer uns*

Telling time in conversation is done as in English.

| We'll eat at eight (o'clock). | **Wir essen um acht (Uhr).** *veer ESS-en um ahkht (oor)* |

12:20 can be expressed as

| twenty after twelve | **zwanzig nach zwölf** *TSVAHNTS-ikh nahkh tsverlf* |

or

| twelve twenty | **zwölf Uhr zwanzig** *tsverlf oor TSVAHNTS-ikh* |

The easiest way for you to tell the time in German is to state the hour (**ein Uhr, zwei Uhr, drei Uhr,** etc.) and then the minutes (from 1 to 60).

| 9:37 | **neun Uhr siebenunddreißig** *noyn oor ZEEB-en-unt-dreyess-ikh* |

Nach (after) and **vor** (to, before) are not difficult either.

eight to three (2:52)	**acht vor drei** *ahkht for drey*
five to seven (6:55)	**fünf vor sieben** *fewnf for ZEEB-en*
nine after four (4:09)	**neun nach vier** *noyn nahkh feer*
a quarter after three (3:15)	**viertel nach drei** *FEERT-el nahkh dreye*

Timetables use the 24-hour clock, so that the next hour after 12 noon is 13 (1:00 P.M.). Thus 2:00 P.M. is **vierzehn Uhr,** and so on.

| My train leaves at 8:20 P.M. | **Mein Zug fährt um zwanzig Uhr zwanzig.** *meyen tsook fayrt um TSVAHN-tsikh oor TSVAHN-tsikh* |

DAYS OF THE WEEK

Today is ____.	**Heute ist ___.** *HOYT-eh ist*
■ Monday	**Montag** *MOHN-taak*
■ Tuesday	**Dienstag** *DEENS-taak*
■ Wednesday	**Mittwoch** *MIT-vokh*
■ Thursday	**Donnerstag** *DON-ehrs-taak*

■ Friday	**Freitag** *FREYE-taak*
■ Saturday	**Samstag/Sonnabend** *ZAHMS-taak/ ZON-aab-ent*
■ Sunday	**Sonntag** *ZON-taak*
yesterday	**gestern** *GEST-ehrn*
the day before yesterday	**vorgestern** *FOHR-gest-ehrn*
tomorrow	**morgen** *MORG-en*
the day after tomorrow	**übermorgen** *EWB-ehr-morg-en*
in the morning (afternoon, evening)	**am Morgen (Nachmittag, Abend)** *ahm MORG-en (NAHKH-mit-taak, AAB-ent)*
mornings	**morgens** *MORG-ens*
evenings	**abends** *AAB-ents*
all day	**den ganzen Tag** *dayn GAHNTS-en taak*
tonight	**heute Abend** *HOYT-eh AAB-ent*
this afternoon	**heute nachmittag** *HOYT-eh NAHKH-mit-taak*
every day	**jeden Tag** *YAYD-en taak*

MONTHS OF THE YEAR

January	**Januar/Jänner** (Austria) *YAA-noo-aar/YEH-nehr*

February	**Februar** *FAY-broo-aar*	
March	**März** *mehrts*	
April	**April** *ah-PRIL*	
May	**Mai** *meye*	
June	**Juni** *YOON-ee*	
July	**Juli** *YOOL-ee*	
August	**August** *ow-GUST*	
September	**September** *zep-TEHM-buh*	
October	**Oktober** *ok-TOH-buh*	
November	**November** *no-VEHM-buh*	
December	**Dezember** *deh-TSEHM-buh*	

What is today's date?	**Der Wievielte ist heute?** *dehr VEE-feelt-eh ist HOYT-eh*
Today is May 3.	**Heute ist der 3. Mai.** *HOYT-eh ist dehr DRIT-eh meye*
■ March 8	**der 8. März** *dehr AHKHT-eh mehrts*
monthly	**monatlich** *MOHN aat-likh*
this month	**in diesem Monat** *in DEEZ-em MOHN-aat*
next month	**im nächsten Monat** *im NAYKHST-en MOHN-aat*
last month	**im letzten Monat** *im LETST-en MOHN-aat*

two months ago	**vor zwei Monaten** *for tsveye MOHN-aaten*

THE FOUR SEASONS

spring	**der Frühling** *dehr FREW-ling*
summer	**der Sommer** *dehr ZOM-uh*
autumn	**der Herbst** *dehr hehrpst*
winter	**der Winter** *dehr VINT-uh*
during the spring	**während des Frühlings** *VEHR-ent dehs FREW-lings*
every summer	**jeden Sommer** *YAYD-en ZOM-uh*
in the winter	**im Winter** *im VINT-uh*

THE WEATHER

How is the weather today?	**Wie ist das Wetter heute?** *vee ist dahs VEHT-uh HOYT-eh*
The weather is good (bad).	**Es ist gutes (schlechtes) Wetter.** *ehs ist GOOT-es (SHLEHKHT-es) VEHT-uh*
It is ____.	**Es ist ____.** *ehs ist*
■ hot	**heiss** *heyess*
■ warm	**warm** *vaarm*
■ cold	**kalt** *kahlt*
■ cool	**kühl** *kewl*

■ sunny	**sonnig**	*ZON-ikh*
■ windy	**windig**	*VIND-ikh*

It's raining (snowing).   **Es regnet (schneit).**   *ehs RAYG-net (shneyet)*

IMPORTANT SIGNS

Abfahrten	Departures
Achtung	Attention
Angebot	Featured item (in a sale)
Aufzug	Elevator
Ausfahrt	Highway exit
Ausgang	Exit
Auskunft	Information
Ausverkauf	Clearance sale
Ausverkauft	Sold out
Baden verboten	No swimming
Belegt	Filled up
Besetzt	Occupied
Betreten des Rasens verboten	Keep off the grass

Damentoilette	Ladies' room
Drücken	Push
Einfahrt	Highway entrance
Eingang	Entrance
Eintritt frei	No admission charge
Frei	Vacant
Für Unbefugte verboten	No trespassing
Gefahr	Danger
Geöffnet von ____ bis ____	Open from ____ to ____
Geschlossen	Closed
Geschlossene Gesellschaft	Private party
Heiß	Hot
Kalt	Cold
Herrentoilette	Men's room
Kasse	Cashier
Kein Zutritt	No entry
Lebensgefahr	Mortal danger

Lift	Elevator
Nicht berühren	Do not touch
Nichtraucher	Nonsmoking compartment (section)
Notausgang	Emergency exit
Privatstrand	Private beach
Privatweg	Private road
Rauchen verboten	No smoking
Raucher	Smoking compartment
Reserviert	Reserved
Schlussverkauf	Final sale
Unbefugtes Betreten verboten	No tïrespassing
____ verboten	____ prohibited
Vorsicht	Caution
Vorsicht, Bissiger Hund	Beware of the dog
Ziehen	Pull
Zimmer frei	Room(s) to let
Zu den Bahnsteigen	To the railroad platforms

COMMON ABBREVIATIONS

Abt.	**Abteilung**	compartment
ACS	**Automobil-Club der Schweiz**	Automobile Association of Switzerland
ADAC	**Allgemeiner Deutscher Automobil Club**	General Automobile Association of Germany
Bhf	**Bahnhof**	railway station
BRD	**Bundesrepublik Deutschland**	Federal Republic of Germany
CDU	**Christlich-Demokratische Union**	Christian Democratic Union
DB	**Deutsche Bahn**	German Rail
DP	**Deutsche Post**	German Postal Service
DZT	**Deutsche Zentrale für Tourismus**	German National Tourist Board
d.h.	**das heißt**	that is (i.e.)
e.V.	**eingetragener Verein**	registered association (corporation)
FKK	**Freikörperkultur**	Free Physical Culture (nudism)

Frl.	**Fräulein**	Miss
GmbH	**Gesellschaft mit beschränkter Haftung**	limited-liability corporation
Hr.	**Herr**	Mr.
JH	**Jugendherberge**	youth hostel
km	**Kilometer**	kilometer
KG	**Kommandit- gesellschaft**	limited partnership
LKW	**Lastkraftwagen**	truck
Mill.	**Million**	million
ÖAMTC	**Österreichischer Automobil- Motorrad- und Touring- Club**	Austrian Automobile, Motorcycle, and Touring Association
ÖBB	**Österreichische Bundesbahnen**	Austrian Federal Railroad
PKW	**Personenkraftwagen**	passenger car
PTT	**Post, Telefon, Telegraph**	Postal, Telephone, and Telegraph Office
SBB	**Schweizerische Bundesbahnen**	Swiss Federal Railways
SPD	**Sozialdemokrat- ische Partei Deutschlands**	Social Democratic Party of Germany

Str.	Straße	street
TCS	Touring-Club der Schweiz	Swiss Touring Association
usf/usw.	und so fort/und so weiter	et cetera (etc.)
Ztg.	Zeitung	newspaper
z.Z.	zur Zeit	at the present time

ITALIAN

QUICK PRONUNCIATION GUIDE

ITALIAN LETTER(S)	SOUND IN ENGLISH	EXAMPLE
VOWELS		
a	ah (y<u>a</u>cht)	**casa** (*kAH-sah*), house
è	eh (n<u>e</u>t)	**lèggere** (*lEH-jeh-reh*), to read
e	ay (h<u>ay</u>)	**mela** (*mAY-lah*), apple
i	ee (f<u>ee</u>t)	**libri** (*lEE-bree*), books
o	oh (r<u>o</u>pe)	**boccone** (*boh-kOH-neh*), mouthful
u	oo (c<u>oo</u>l)	**tutto** (*tOOt-toh*), everything
CONSONANT SOUNDS		
ci	chee (<u>chee</u>se)	**cinema** (*chEE-nay-mah*), movies
ce	chay (<u>ch</u>air)	**piacere** (*pee-ah-chAY-reh*), pleasure
ca	kah (<u>c</u>ot)	**casa** (*kAH-sah*), house
co	koh (<u>c</u>old)	**cotto** (*kOHt-toh*), cooked
che	kay (<u>k</u>ent)	**perché** (*pehr-kAY*), because
chi	key (<u>key</u>)	**pochi** (*pOH-key*), few
gi	jee (<u>j</u>eep)	**giro** (*jEE-roh*), turn
ge	jay (<u>ge</u>neral)	**generale** (*jay-nay-rAH-leh*), general
gh	gh (spa<u>gh</u>etti)	**spaghetti** (*spah-ghAYt-tee*)
gli	ll (mi<u>lli</u>on)	**egli** (*AY-ly-ee*), he **bottiglia** (*boht-tEE-ly-ee-ah*), bottle
gn	ny (can<u>yo</u>n)	**magnifico** (*mah-ny-EE-fee-koh*), magnificent

ITALIAN LETTER(S)	SOUND IN ENGLISH	EXAMPLE
qu	koo (<u>qu</u>iet)	**àquila** (*AH-koo-ee-lah*), eagle
sce	sh (fi<u>sh</u>)	**pesce** (*pAY-sheh*), fish
sci	sh (fi<u>sh</u>)	**sciòpero** (*shee-OH-peh-roh*), strike
z or zz	ts (ea<u>ts</u>)	**pizza** (*pEE-tsah*), pizza **zero** (*tsEH-roh*), zero

THE BASICS FOR GETTING BY

MOST FREQUENTLY USED EXPRESSIONS

Yes	**Sì**	*see*
No	**No**	*noh*
Maybe	**Forse**	*fOHr-seh*
Please	**Per piacere**	*pehr pee-ah-chAY-reh*
Thank you (very much)	**(Mille) grazie**	*(mEEl-leh) grAH-tsee-eh*
You're welcome	**Prego**	*prEh-goh*
Excuse me	**Mi scusi**	*mee skOO-see*
I'm sorry	**Mi dispiace**	*mee dee-spee-AH-cheh*
Just a second	**Un momento**	*oon moh-mEHn-toh*
That's all right, okay	**Va bene**	*vah bEH-neh*
It doesn't matter	**Non importa**	*nohn eem-pOHr-tah*
Good morning (afternoon)	**Buon giorno**	*boo-Ohn jee-Ohr-noh*

Good evening (night)	**Buona sera (notte)**	*boo-Oh-nah sAY-rah (nOHt-teh)*
Sir	**Signore**	*see-ny-OH-reh*
Madame	**Signora**	*see-ny-OH-rah*
Miss	**Signorina**	*see-ny-oh-rEE-nah*
Good-bye	**Arrivederci**	*ahr-ree-veh-dAYr-chee*
See you later (so long)	**A più tardi (ciao)**	*ah pee-OO tAHr-dee (chee-AH-oh)*
See you tomorrow	**A domani**	*ah doh-mAH-nee*
Do you speak English?	**Parla inglese?**	*pAHr-lah een-glAY-seh*

I don't speak Italian. **Io non parlo italiano.** *EE-oh nohn pAHr-loh ee-tah-lee-AH-noh*

I speak a little Italian. **Parlo poco l'italiano.** *pAHr-loh pOH-koh lee-tah-lee-AH-noh*

Is there anyone here who speaks English? **C'è qualcuno qui che parla inglese?** *chEH koo-ahl-kOO-noh koo-EE kay pAHr-lah een-glAY-seh*

Do you understand? **Capisce? (ha capito?)** *kah-pEE-sheh (ah kah-pEE-toh)*

I understand. **Capisco (ho capito).** *kah-pEE-skoh (oh kah-pEE-toh)*

I don't understand. **Non capisco (non ho capito).** *nohn kah-pEE-skoh (nohn oh kah-pEE-toh)*

What does that mean? **Che cosa significa (quello)?** *kay kOH-sah see-ny-EE-fee-kah (koo-Ayl-loh)*

What? What did you say? **Che? Che cosa ha detto?** *kAY kay kOH-sah ah dAYt-toh*

What do you call this (that) in Italian? **Come si chiama questo (quello) in italiano?** *kOH-meh see key-AH-mah koo-AYs-toh (koo-Ayl-loh) een ee-tah-lee-AH-noh*

Please speak slowly. **Per piacere parli lentamente.**
pehr pee-ah-chAY-reh pAHr-lee lehn-tah-mEHn-teh

Please repeat that. **Lo ripeta per favore.** *loh ree-pEH-tah pehr fah-vOH-reh*

INTRODUCTIONS

I'm American (English) (Australian) (Canadian). **Sono americano(a) (inglese) (australiano [a]) (canadese).** *sOH-noh ah-meh-ree-kAH-noh (nah) (een-glAY-seh) (ah-oos-trah-lee-AH-noh [nah]) (kah-nah-dAY-seh)*

My name is _____. **Mi chiamo _____.** *mee kee-AH-moh*

What's your name? **Lei, scusi, come si chiama?** *lEH-ee skOO-see kOH-meh see key-AH-mah*

How are you? **Come sta?** *kOH-meh stAH*

How's everything? **Come va?** *kOH-meh vAH*

Very well, thanks. And you? **Molto bene, grazie. E lei?** *mOHl-toh bEH-neh grAH-tsee-eh Ay lEH-ee*

LOCATIONS

Where is _____? **Dove si trova _____?** *dOH-veh see trOH-vah*

■ the bathroom **un gabinetto (una toilette)** *oon gah-bee-nAYt-toh (OO-nah too-ah-lEHt)*

■ the dining room (restaurant) **un ristorante** *oon rees-toh-rAHn-teh*

■ the entrance **l'ingresso** *leen-grEHs-soh*

■ the exit **l'uscita** *loo-shEE-tah*

■ the telephone **un telefono** *oon teh-lEH-phoh-noh*

I'm lost.	**Non so dove mi trovo.** *nohn sOH dOH-veh mee trOH-voh*
We are lost.	**Non sappiamo dove ci troviamo.** *nohn sahp-pee-AH-moh dOH-veh chee troh-vee-AH-moh*
Where are _____?	**Dove sono _____?** *dOH-veh sOH-noh*
I am looking for _____.	**Sto cercando _____.** *stOH chehr-kAHn-doh*
Which way do I go?	**In che direzione devo andare?** *een-kAY dee-reh-tsee-OH-neh dAY-voh ahn-dAH-reh*
■ to the left	**a sinistra** *ah see-nEE-strah*
■ to the right	**a destra** *ah dEH-strah*
■ straight ahead	**sempre diritto** *sehm-preh dee-rEEt-toh*
■ around the corner	**all'angolo (della via)** *ahl-lAHn-goh-loh (dAYl-lah vEE-ah)*
■ the first street on the right	**la prima strada a destra** *lah prEE-mah strAH-dah ah dEH-strah*

MISCELLANEOUS

I'm hungry.	**Ho fame.** *oh fAH-meh*
I'm thirsty.	**Vorrei bere (ho sete).** *vohr-rEH-ee bAY-reh (oh sAY-teh)*
I'm tired.	**Mi sento stanco(a).** *mee sEHn-toh stAHn-koh(ah)*
What's that?	**Che cos'è quello(a)?** *kay ko-sEH koo-AYl-loh (lah)*
What's up?	**(Che) cosa succede?** *(kay) kOH-sah soo-chEH-deh*
I (don't) know.	**(Non) lo so.** *(nohn) loh sOH*

QUESTIONS

Where is _____?	**Dov'è _____?**	*doh-vEH*
When?	**Quando?**	*koo AHn-doh*
How?	**Come?**	*kOH-meh*
How much?	**Quanto?**	*koo-AHn-toh*
Who?	**Chi?**	*key*
Why?	**Perchè?**	*pehr-kAY*
Which?	**Quale?**	*koo-AH-leh*

PROBLEMS, PROBLEMS, PROBLEMS (EMERGENCIES)

Watch out! Be careful!	**Attenzione! Stia attento(a)!** *ah-tehn-tsee-OH-neh stEE-ah aht-tEHn-toh(ah)*
Hurry up!	**Si sbrighi!** *see sbrEE-ghee*
Look!	**Guardi!** *goo-AHr-dee*
Wait!	**Aspetti un momento!** *ah-spEHt-tee oon moh-mEHn-toh*
Fire!	**Al fuoco!** *Ahl foo-OH-koh*
Go away!	**Se ne vada!** *say nay vAH-dah*
Leave me alone!	**Mi lasci in pace!** *mee lAH-shee een pAH-cheh*
Help, police!	**Aiuto, polizia!** *ah-ee-OO-toh poh-lee-tsEE-ah*

That (one) is a thief!	**Quello è un ladro!** *koo-AYl-loh EH oon lAH-droh*
He has snatched my bag!	**Mi ha scippato la borsa!** *mee ah sheep-pAH-toh lah bOHr-sah*
He has stolen _____.	**Mi ha rubato _____.** *mee ah roo-bAH-toh*
I have lost _____.	**Ho perduto _____.** *oh pehr-dOO-toh*

- my car   **la (mia) auto** *lah (mEE-ah) AH-oo-toh*
- my passport   **il (mio) passaporto** *eel (mEE-oh) pahs-sah-pOHr-toh*
- my purse   **la (mia) borsa** *lah (mEE-ah) bOHr-sah*
- my suitcase   **la (mia) valigia** *lah (mEE-ah) vah-lEE-jee-ah*
- my wallet   **il (mio) portafoglio** *eel (mEE-oh) pohr-tah-fOH-ly-ee-oh*
- my watch   **l'orologio (il mio orologio)** *loh-roh-lOH-jee-oh (eel mEE-oh oh-roh-lOH-jee-oh)*

| I want to go _____. | **Voglio andare ___.** *vOH-ly-ee-oh ahn-dAH-reh* |

- to the American (British) (Australian) (Canadian) Consulate.   **al Consolato Americano (Inglese) (Australiano) (Canadese).** *ahl kohn-soh-lAH-toh ah-meh-ree-kAH-noh (een-glAY-seh) (ah-oo-strah-lee-ah-noh) (kah-nah-dAY-seh)*

- to the police station.   **all'ufficio di polizia (al Commissariato)** *ahl-loof-fEE-chee-oh dee poh-lee-tsEE-ah (ahl kohm-mees-sah-ree-AH-toh)*

I need help, quick!	**Ho bisogno d'aiuto, subito!** *oh bee-sOH-ny-oh dah-ee-OO-toh sOO-bee-toh*
Can you help me, please?	**Può aiutarmi, per favore?** *poo-OH ah-ee-oo-tAHr-mee pehr fah-vOH-reh*
Does anyone here speak English?	**Qui c'è qualcuno che parla inglese?** *koo-EE chEH koo-ahl-kOO-noh kay pAHr-lah een-glAY-seh*

NUMBERS

CARDINAL NUMBERS

0	**zero**	*tsEH-roh*
1	**uno**	*OO-noh*
2	**due**	*dOO-eh*
3	**tre**	*trEH*
4	**quattro**	*koo-AHt-troh*
5	**cinque**	*chEEn-koo-eh*
6	**sei**	*sEH-ee*
7	**sette**	*sEHt-teh*
8	**otto**	*OHt-toh*
9	**nove**	*nOH-veh*
10	**dieci**	*dee-EH-chee*
11	**undici**	*OOn-dee-chee*
12	**dodici**	*dOH-dee-chee*
13	**tredici**	*trEH-dee-chee*
14	**quattordici**	*koo-aht-tOHr-dee-chee*
15	**quindici**	*koo-EEn-dee-chee*
16	**sedici**	*sAY-dee-chee*
17	**diciassette**	*dee-chee-ahs-sEHt-teh*
18	**diciotto**	*dee-chee-OHt-toh*

19	**diciannove**	*dee-chee-ahn-nOH-veh*
20	**venti**	*vAYn-tee*
■ 21	**ventuno**	*vayn-tOO-noh*
■ 22	**ventidue**	*vayn-tee-dOO-eh*
■ 23	**ventitrè**	*vayn-tee-trEH*
■ 24	**ventiquattro**	*vayn-tee-koo-AHt-troh*
■ 25	**venticinque**	*vayn-tee-chEEn-koo-eh*
■ 26	**ventisei**	*vayn-tee-sEH-ee*
■ 27	**ventisette**	*vayn-tee-sEHt-teh*
■ 28	**ventotto**	*vayn-tOHt-toh*
■ 29	**ventinove**	*vayn-tee-nOH-veh*
30	**trenta**	*trEHn-tah*
40	**quaranta**	*koo-ah-rAHn-tah*
50	**cinquanta**	*cheen-koo-AHn-tah*
60	**sessanta**	*sehs-sAHn-tah*
70	**settanta**	*seht-tAHn-tah*
80	**ottanta**	*oht-tAHn-tah*
90	**novanta**	*noh-vAHn-tah*
100	**cento**	*chEHn-toh*
■ 101	**centouno**	*chEHn-toh OO-noh*
■ 102	**centodue**	*chEHn-toh dOO-eh*
200	**duecento**	*doo-eh-chEHn-toh*
300	**trecento**	*treh-chEHn-toh*
400	**quattrocento**	*koo-aht-troh-chEHn-toh*
500	**cinquecento**	*cheen-koo-eh-chEHn-toh*
600	**seicento**	*seh-ee-chEHn-toh*
700	**settecento**	*seht-teh-chENn-toh*
800	**ottocento**	*oht-toh-chEHn-toh*
900	**novecento**	*noh-veh-chEHn-toh*
1.000	**mille**	*mEEl-leh*

■	1.001	**mille e uno**	*mEEl-leh eh OO-noh*
■	1.100	**mille e cento**	*mEEl-leh eh chEHn-toh*
■	1.200	**mille e duecento**	*mEEl-leh eh doo-eh-chEHn-toh*
■	1.350	**mille trecento cinquanta**	*mEE-leh treh-chEHn-toh cheen-koo-AHn-tah*
	2.000	**duemila**	*dOO-eh mEE-lah*
	5.000	**cinque mila**	*chEEn-koo-eh mEEl-lah*
	10.000	**dieci mila**	*dee-EH-chee mEEl-lah*
	100.000	**cento mila**	*ch-EHn-toh mEEl-lah*
	1.000.000	**un milione**	*oon mee-lee-OH-neh*
	2.000.000	**due milioni**	*dOO-eh mee-lee-OH-nee*
	1991	**mille novecento novantuno**	*mEEl-leh noh-veh-chEHn-toh noh-vAHn-tOOn-noh*
	2000	**due mila**	*dOO-eh mEEl-lah*

ORDINAL NUMBERS

first	**primo**	*prEE-moh*
second	**secondo**	*seh-kOHn-doh*
third	**terzo**	*tEHr-tsoh*
fourth	**quarto**	*koo-AHr-toh*
fifth	**quinto**	*koo-EEn-toh*
sixth	**sesto**	*sEHs-toh*
seventh	**settimo**	*sEHt-tee-moh*
eighth	**ottavo**	*oht-tAH-voh*
ninth	**nono**	*nOH-noh*
tenth	**decimo**	*dEH-chee-moh*
the last one	**l'ultimo**	*lOOl-tee-moh*
once	**una volta**	*oo-nah vOHl-tah*
twice	**due volte**	*dOO-eh vOHl-teh*
three times	**tre volte**	*trEH vOHl-teh*

half of _____.	la metà di _____.	*lah meh-tAH dee*
■ half of the money	la metà dei soldi	*lah meh-tAH day-ee sOHl-dee*
half a _____.	mezzo	*mEH-tsoh*
■ half a kilo	mezzo chilo	*mEH-tsoh kEE-loh*
a fourth (quarter)	un quarto	*oon koo-AHr-toh*
a dozen	una dozzina	*OO-nah doh-tsEE-nah*
■ a dozen oranges	una dozzina d'arance	*OO-nah doh-tsEE-nah dah-rAHn-cheh*
100 grams	un etto	*oon EHt-toh*
200 grams	due etti	*dOO-eh EHt-tee*
350 grams	tre etti e mezzo	*treh EHt-tee ay mEH-tsoh*
■ a pair of shoes	un paio de scarpe	*oon pAH-ee-oh dee skAHr-peh*

WHEN YOU ARRIVE

PASSPORT AND CUSTOMS

| My name is _____. | Mi chiamo _____. | *mee key-AH-moh* |

I'm American (British) (Australian) (Canadian). **Sono americano(a) (inglese) (australiano[a] (canadese).** *sOH-noh ah-meh-ree kAH-noh(ah) (een-glAY-seh) (ah-oo-strah-lee-AH-noh[ah]) (kah-nah-dAY-seh)*

| My address is _____. | Il mio indirizzo è _____. | *eel mEE-oh een-dee-rEE-tsoh EH* |

| I'm staying at _____. | Starò a _____. | *stah-rOH ah* |

| Here is (are) _____. | Ecco _____. | *EHk-oh* |
| ■ my documents | i (miei) documenti | *ee (mee-EH-ee) doh-koo-mEHn-tee* |

■ my passport   **il (mio) passaporto**   *eel (mEE-oh) pahs-sah-pOHr-toh*

■ my I.D. card   **la (mia) carta d'identità** *lah (mEE-ah) kAHr-tah dee-dehn-tee-tAH*

I'm _____.   **Sono _____.**   *sOH-noh*

■ on a business trip   **in viaggio d'affari**   *een vee-AH-jee-oh dahf-fAH-ree*

■ on vacation   **in vacanza**   *een vah-kAHn-tsah*

■ visiting relatives (friends)   **venuto(a) a trovare i parenti (gli amici)** *vay-nOO-toh(ah) ah troh-vAH-reh ee pah-rEHn-tee (ly-ee ah-mEE-chee)*

■ just passing through   **solo di passaggio**   *sOH-loh dee pahs-sAH-jee-oh*

I'll be staying here for _____.   **Resterò qui per _____.**   *ray-steh-rOH koo-EE pehr*

■ a few days   **alcuni giorni**   *ahl-kOO-nee jee-OHr-nee*

■ a few weeks   **alcune settimane**   *ahl-kOO-neh seht-tee-mAH-neh*

■ a week   **una settimana**   *OO-nah seht-tee-mAH-nah*

■ a month   **un mese**   *oon mAY-seh*

I'm traveling _____.   **Sto viaggiando _____.**   *stOH vee-ah-jee-AHn-doh*

■ alone   **da solo(a)**   *dah sOH-loh(ah)*

■ with my husband   **con mio marito**   *kohn mEE-oh mah-rEE-toh*

■ with my wife   **con mia moglie**   *kohn mEE-ah mOH-ly-ee-eh*

■ with my family   **con la mia famiglia**   *kohn lah mEE-ah fah-mEE-ly-ee-ah*

■ with my friend **con il mio amico (la mia amica)** *kohn eel mEE-oh ah-mEE-koh (lah mEE-ah ah-mEE-kah)*

These are my bags. **Queste sono le mie valigie.** *koo-AYs-teh sOH-noh leh mEE-eh vah-lEE-jee-eh*

I have nothing to declare. **Non ho nulla da dichiarare.** *nohn oh nOOl-lah dah dee-key-ah-rAH-reh*

I only have _____. **Ho solo _____.** *oh sOH-loh*

■ a carton of cigarettes **una stecca di sigarette** *OO-nah stAYk-kah dee see-gah-rAYt-teh*

■ a bottle of whisky **una bottiglia di whisky** *OO-nah boht-tEE-ly-ee-ah dee oo-EE-skey*

They're gifts. **Sono regali.** *sOH-noh reh-gAH-lee*

They're for my personal use. **Sono cose di uso personale.** *sOH-noh kOH-seh dee OO-soh pehr-soh-nAH-leh*

Do I have to pay duty? **Devo pagare dogana?** *dAY-voh pah-gAH-reh doh-gAH-nah*

BAGGAGE AND PORTERS

Where can I find a baggage cart? **Dove posso trovare un carrello portabagagli?** *dOH-veh pOHs-soh troh-vAH-reh oon kahr-rEHl-loh pohr-tah-bah-gAH-ly-ee*

I need a porter. **Ho bisogno di un portabagagli.** *oh bee-sOH-ny-oh dee oon pohr-tah-bah-gAH-ly-ee*

Porter! **Portabagagli! Facchino!** *pohr-tah-bah-gAH-ly-ee fahk-kEE-noh*

These are our (my) bags.	**Queste sono le nostre (mie) valigie.** *koo-AYs-teh sOH-noh leh nOH-streh (mEE-eh) van-lEE-jee-eh*
That big (little) one.	**Quella grande (piccola).** *koo-AYl-lah grAHn-deh (pEEk-koh-lah)*
These two black (green) ones.	**Queste due nere (verdi).** *koo-AYs-teh dOO-eh nAY-reh (vAYr-dee)*
Put them here (there).	**Le metta qui (lì).** *leh mAYt-tah koo-EE (lEE)*
Be careful with that one!	**Stia attento a quella lì!** *stEE-ah aht-tEHn-toh ah koo-AYl-lah lEE*
I'll carry this one myself.	**Questa la porto io.** *koo-AYs-tah lah pOHr-toh ee-oh*
I'm missing a suitcase.	**Mi manca una valigia.** *mee mAHn-kah OO-nah vah-lEE-jee-ah*
How much do I owe you?	**Quanto le devo?** *koo-AHn-toh leh dAY-voh*

BANKING AND MONEY MATTERS

EXCHANGING MONEY

Where is the currency exchange (bank)?	**Dov'è l'ufficio di cambio (la banca)?** *doh-vEH loof-fEE-chee-oh dee kAHm-bee-oh (lah bAHn-kah)*
I wish to change ____.	**Desidero cambiare ____.** *day-sEE-deh-roh kahm-bee-AH-reh*
■ money	**il denaro** *eel deh-nAH-roh*

■ dollars | **i dollari** *ee-dOHl-lah-ree*

■ travelers' checks | **travelers' checks (assegni da viaggiatori)** *(ahs-sAY-ny dah vee-ah-jee-ah-tOH-ree)*

May I cash a personal check? | **Posso cambiare un assegno personale?** *pOHs-soh kahm-bee-AH-reh oon ahs-sAY-ny-ee-oh pehr-soh-nAH-leh*

What time do they open (close)? | **A che ora aprono (chiudono)?** *ah kay OH-rah AH-proh-noh (key-OO-doh-noh)*

Where is the cashier's window? | **Dov'è lo sportello del cassiere?** *doh-vEH loh spohr-tEHl-loh dayl kahs-see-AY-reh*

What's the current exchange rate for dollars? | **Qual è il cambio corrente del dollaro?** *koo-ahl-EH eel kAHm-bee-oh kohr-rEHn-teh dayl dOHl-lah-roh*

What commission do you charge? | **Quale percentuale vi fate pagare?** *koo-AH-leh pehr-chehn-too-AH-leh vee fAH-teh pah-gAH-reh*

Where do I sign? | **Dove debbo firmare?** *dOH-veh dAYb-boh feer-mAH-reh*

I'd like the money ____. | **Vorrei i soldi ____.** *vohr-rEH-ee ee sOHl-dee*

■ in large (small) bills | **in grosse (piccole) banconote** *een grOHs-seh (pEEk-oh-leh) bahn-koh-nOH-teh*

■ in small change | **in spiccioli** *een spee-chee-oh-lee*

Give me two twenty-euro bills.	**Mi dia due biglietti da venti euro.** *mee dEE-ah dOO-eh bee-ly-ee-AYt-tee dah vayn-tee EH-oo-roh*
■ fifty euros	**cinquanta euro** *cheen-koo-AHn-tah EH-oo-roh*
■ one hundred euros	**cento euro** *chehn-toh EH-oo-roh*
Do you accept credit cards?	**Si accettano carte di credito?** *see ah-chEHt-tah-noh kAHr-teh dee krEH-dee-toh*

AT THE HOTEL

CHECKING IN

I'd like a single (double) room for tonight.	**Vorrei una camera singola (doppia) per stanotte.** *vohr-rEH-ee OO-nah kAH-meh-rah sEEn-goh-lah (dOHp-pee-ah) pehr stah-nOHt-teh*
How much is the room _____?	**Quant'è la camera _____?** *koo-ahn-tEH lah kAH-meh-rah*
■ with a shower	**con doccia** *kohn dOH-chee-ah*
■ with a private bath	**con bagno proprio (privato)** *kohn bAH-ny-oh prOH-pree-oh (pree-vAH-toh)*
■ with a balcony	**con terrazzino** *kohn tehr-rah-tsEE-noh*
■ facing the sea	**che dia sul mare** *kay dEE-ah sool mAH-reh*
■ facing (away from) the street	**che (non) dia sulla strada** *kay (nohn) dEE-ah sOOl-lah strAH-dah*

■ facing the courtyard   **che dia sul cortile**   *kay dEE-ah sOOl kohr-tEE-leh*

Does it have _____?   **Ha _____?**   *ah*

■ air-conditioning   **l'aria condizionata** *lAH-ree-ah kohn-dee-tsee-oh-nAH-tah*

■ hot water   **l'acqua calda**   *lAH-koo-ah kAHl-dah*

■ television   **la televisione**   *lah teh-leh-vee-see-OH-neh*

Can I get video games?   **Si possono avere videogiochi?** *see pOHs-soh-noh ah-vAY-reh vee-deh-oh-jee-OH-key*

Can I rent movies?   **È possibile affittare dei film?** *EH pohs-sEE-bee-leh ahf-feet-tAH-reh dAY-ee fEElm*

Do you receive satellite programs?   **Ricevete i programmi via satellite?** *ree-chay-vAY-teh ee proh-grAHm-mee VEE-ah sah-tehl-lee-teh*

Do you have cable TV?   **Avete i programmi cable (via cavo)?** *ah-vAY-teh ee proh-grAHm-mee kAH-bleh (vEE-ah kAH-voh)*

Do you get CNN?   **Ricevete le trasmissioni CNN?** *ree-chay-vAY-teh leh trahs-mees-see-OH-nee CNN*

Are there any programs in English?   **Ci sono programmi in inglese?** *chee sOH-noh proh-grAHm-mee een een-glAY-seh*

Are there programs that should be blocked from children?   **Ci sono programmi che dovrebbero essere bloccati ai bambini?**   *chee sOH-noh proh-grAHm-mee kay doh-vrAYb-beh-roh EHs-seh-reh bloh-kAH-tee ah-ee bahm-bEE-nee*

At what time are the adult programs?	**A che ora ci sono i programmi/ spettacoli pornografici?** *ah kay OH-rah chee sOH-noh ee proh- grAHm-mee/speht-tAH-koh-lee pohr- noh-grAH-fee-chee*
Do you have automatic checkout?	**Si può pagare il conto automaticamente e andarsene?** *see poo-OH pah-gAH-reh eel kOHn- toh ah-oo-toh-mah-tee-kah-mEHn-teh ay ahn-dAHr-seh-neh*
I (don't) have a reservation.	**(Non) ho prenotazione.** *(nohn) oh preh-noh-tah-tsee-OH-neh*
I (don't) like it.	**(Non) mi piace.** *(nohn) mee pee- AH-cheh*
Do you have some- thing _____?	**Ha qualche cosa _____?** *ah koo- AHl-keh kOH-sah*
■ better	**di meglio** *dee mEH-ly-ee-oh*
■ larger	**più grande** *pee-OO grAHn-deh*
■ smaller	**più piccolo** *pee-OO pEEk-koh-loh*
■ cheaper	**meno costoso** *mAY-noh koh- stOH-soh*
■ quieter	**più quieto (tranquillo)** *pee-OO quee-EH-toh (trahn-hoo-EEl-loh)*
What floor is it on?	**A che piano è?** *ah kay pee-AH- noh EH*
Is there an elevator (lift)?	**C'è l'ascensore?** *chEH lah-shehn- sOH-reh*
How much is the room _____?	**Quanto si paga per una camera _____?** *koo-AHn-toh see pAH-gah pehr OO-nah kAH-meh-rah*
■ with the American plan (three meals a day)	**con pensione completa** *kohn pehn-see-OH-neh kohm-plEH-tah*

■ with breakfast	**con colazione** *kohn koh-lah-tsee-OH-neh*
■ with no meals	**senza i pasti** *sEHn-tsah ee pAH-stee*
Is everything included?	**È tutto compreso?** *EH tOOt-toh kohm-prAY-soh*
The room is very nice. I'll take it.	**La camera è molto bella. La prendo.** *lah kAH-meh-rah EH mOHl-toh bEHl-lah lah prAYn-doh*
We'll be staying ____.	**Resteremo ____.** *rehs-teh-rAY-moh*
■ one night	**una notte** *OO-nah nOHt-teh*
■ a few nights	**alcune notti** *ahl-kOO-neh nOHt-tee*
■ one week	**una settimana** *OO-nah seht-tee-mAH-nah*
How much do you charge for children?	**Quanto fanno pagare per i bambini?** *koo-AHn-toh fAHn-noh pah-gAH-reh pehr ee bahm-bEE-nee*
Could you put another bed in the room?	**Si potrebbe avere un altro letto nella camera?** *see poh-trAYb-beh ah-vAY-reh oon AHl-troh lEHt-toh nAYl-lah kAH-meh-rah*
Is there a charge? How much?	**C'è da pagare? Quanto?** *chEH dah pah-gAH-reh koo-AHn-toh*

OTHER ACCOMMODATIONS

I'm looking for ____.	**Sto cercando ____.** *stOH chehr-kAHn-doh*
■ a boardinghouse	**una pensione** *OO-nah pehn-see-OH-neh*

■ a private house	**una casa privata (un villino)** *OO-nah kAH-sah pree-vAH-tah (oon veel-lEE-noh)*
How much is the rent?	**Quant'è d'affitto?** *koo-ahn-teh dahf-fEEt-toh*
I'll be staying here for ____.	**Resterò qui per ____.** *rehs-teh-rOH koo-EE pehr*
■ two weeks	**due settimane** *dOO-eh seht-tee-mAH-neh*
■ one month	**un mese** *oon mAY-seh*
■ the whole summer	**tutta l'estate** *tOOt-tah leh-stAH-teh*
I want a place ____.	**Voglio abitare ____.** *vOH-ly-ee-oh ah-bee-tAH-reh*
■ that's centrally located	**al centro** *ahl chAYn-troh*
■ near public transportation	**vicino ai servizi di trasporti pubblici** *vee-chEE-noh AH-ee sayr-vEE-tsee dee trah-spOHr-tee pOOb-blee-chee*
■ in a safe neighborhood	**in un vicinato tranquillo e sicuro** *een oon vee-chee-nAH-toh trahn-koo-EEl-loh ay see-kOO-roh*
Is there a youth hostel around here?	**C'è un ostello per la gioventù qui vicino?** *chEH oon oh-stAYl-loh pehr lah jee-oh-vehn-tOO koo-EE vee-chEE-noh*

TRAVELERS WITH SPECIAL NEEDS

Do you have facilities for the disabled?	**Ci sono servizi per disabili?** *chee sOH-noh sayr-vEE-tzee pehr dee-sAH-bee-lee*

Is there a special rate for the handicapped?	**Ci sono tariffe speciali per disabili?** *chee sOH-noh tah-rEEf-feh speh-chee-AH-lee pehr dee-sAH-bee-lee*
Can you provide _____?	**È possibile avere _____?** *EH pohs-sEE-bee-leh ah-vAY-reh*
■ a wheelchair	**una sedia a rotelle** *OO-nah seh-dee-ah ah roh-tEHl-leh*
■ an assistant	**un assistente** *OOn ahs-see-stEHn-teh*
Is there room in the elevator for a wheelchair?	**C'è posto in ascensore per una sedia a rotelle?** *chEH pOHs-toh een ah-shayn-sOH-reh pehr OO-nah seh-dee-ah roh-tEHl-leh*
Do you allow seeing-eye dogs?	**È permesso avere un cane da guida?** *EH pehr-mAYs-soh ah-vAY-reh oon KAH-neh dah goo-EE-dah*
I have asthma (heart problems).	**Ho l'asma (problemi cardiaci).** *oh lAHs-mah (proh-blEH-mee kahr-dEE-ah-chee)*
I'm epileptic.	**Sono epilèttico.** *sOH-noh eh-pee-lEHt-tee-koh*
I'm diabetic.	**Sono diabetico.** *sOH-noh dee-ah-bEH-tee-koh*
I'm allergic to _____.	**Sono allergico _____.** *sOH-noh ahl-lEHr-jee-koh*
■ dairy products	**ai latticini** *AH-ee laht-tee-chEE-nee*
■ meat	**alla carne** *AHl-lah kAHr-neh*
■ mold	**alla muffa** *AHl-lah mOOf-fah*
■ peanuts	**alle noccioline americane** *AHl-leh noh-chee-oh-lEE-neh ah-meh-ree-kAH-neh*

- pork **alla carne di maiale** *AHl-lah kAHr-neh dee mah-ee-AH-leh*

- salt **al sale** *AHl sAH-leh*

- shellfish **ai crostacei** *AH-ee kroh-stAH-cheh-ee*

I wanted it without _____. **Lo volevo senza _____.** *loh voh-lAY-voh sEHn-tsah*

- alcohol **alcol** *AHl-cohl*

- caffeine **caffeina** *kahf-feh-EE-nah*

- meat **carne** *kAHr-neh*

- sugar **zucchero** *tsOO-keh-roh*

I am a vegetarian. **Sono vegetariano (a).** *sOH-noh veh-jeh-tah-ree-AH-noh (nah)*

Do you have food _____? **C'è cibo _____?** *chEH chEE-boh*

- low in calories **con poche calorie** *kohn pOH-keh kah-loh-rEE-eh*

- low in cholesterol **con poco colesterolo** *kohn pOH-koh koh-leh-steh-rOH-loh*

- low in fat **con poco grasso** *kohn pOH-koh grAHs-soh*

Do you have _____? **C'è _____?** *chEH*

- an artificial sweetener **qualche dolcificante artificiale** *koo-AHl-keh dohl-chee-fee-kAHn-teh ahr-tee-fee-chee-AHl-eh*

- saccharin **della saccarina** *dΛYl-lah sahk-kah-rEE-nah*

- Sweet 'n Low **dello sweet e low** *dΛYl-loh soo-EEt ay lOH*

We need a _____.	**Abbiamo bisogno di _____.** *ahb-bee-AH-moh bee-sOH-ny-oh dee*
■ cane	**un bastone** *oon bah-stOH-neh*
■ crutch	**una stambella** *OO-nah stahm-bEHl-lah*
■ pair of crutches	**un paio di stambelle** *oon pAH-ee-oh dee stahm-bEHl-leh*
■ walker	**un girello** *oon jee-rEHl-loh*
Are there any _____?	**Ci sono _____?** *chee sOH-noh*
■ escalators	**scale mobili** *skAH-leh mOH-bee-lee*
■ ramps	**rampe** *rAHm-peh*
Are there any _____ we can contact in case of emergency?	**Ci sono _____ che possiamo contattare in caso d'emergenza?** *chee sOH-noh _____ kay pohs-see-AH-moh kohn-taht-tAH-reh een kAH-soh deh-mehr-jEHn-tzah*
■ agencies	**agenzie** *ah-jehn-tzEE-eh*
■ drugstores	**farmacie** *fahr-mah-chEE-eh*
■ emergency rooms	**sale di pronto soccorso** *sAH-leh dee prOHn-toh soh-k-kOHr-soh*
Is there a(n) _____ available?	**C'è _____ disponibile?** *chEH _____ dees-poh-nEE-bee-leh*
■ ambulance	**un'ambulanza** *oon-ahm-boo-lAHn-tzah*
■ car service	**un servizio noleggio** *oon sayr-vEE-tzee-oh noh-LAY-jee-oh*
■ taxi	**un taxi** *oon tahs-sEE*
Is there a doctor in the hotel?	**C'è un dottore nell'hotel?** *chEH oon doht-tOH-reh nayl-loh-tEHl*

ORDERING BREAKFAST

We'll have breakfast in the room.	**Faremo colazione in camera.** *fah-rAY-moh koh-lah-tsee-OH-neh een kAH-meh-rah*
Please send up _____.	**Per favore mandino _____.** *pehr fah-vOH-reh mAHn-dee-noh*
■ one (two) coffee(s)	**un (due) caffè** *oon (dOO-eh) kahf-fEH*
■ tea	**un tè** *oon tEH*
■ hot chocolate	**una cioccolata calda** *OO-nah chee-oh-koh-lAH-tah kAHl-dah*
■ a sweet roll (brioche)	**un berlingozzo (una brioche)** *oon behr-leen-gOH-tsoh (oon-ah brEE-osh)*
■ fruit (juice)	**(un succo di) frutta** *(oon sOO-koh-dee) frOOt-tah*
I'll eat breakfast downstairs.	**Mangerò la colazione giù.** *mahn-jeh-rOH lah koh-lah-tsee-OH-neh jee-OO*
We'd both like _____.	**Noi due desideriamo _____.** *nOH-ee dOO-eh deh-see-deh-ree-AH-moh*
■ bacon and eggs	**uova al tegamino con pancetta** *oo-OH-vah ahl teh-gah-mEE-noh kohn pahn-chAYt-tah*
■ scrambled (fried, boiled) eggs	**uova al tegamino strapazzate (fritte, alla coque)** *oo-OH-vah ahl teh-gah-mEE-noh strah-pah-tsAH-teh (frEEt-teh ahl-lah kOHk)*
■ toast	**pan tostato** *pAHn toh-stAH-toh*
■ jam	**marmellata** *mahr-mehl-lAH-tah*

HOTEL SERVICES

Where is _____?	**Dov'è _____?** *doh-vEH*
■ the dining room	**la sala da pranzo** *lah sAH-lah dah prAHn-tsoh*
■ the bathroom	**il bagno (la toilette)** *eel bAH-ny-oh (lah too-ah lEHt)*
■ the elevator (lift)	**l'ascensore** *lah-shehn-sOH-reh*
■ the phone	**il telefono** *eel teh-lEH-foh-noh*
What is my room number?	**Qual è il numero della mia camera?** *koo-ah-lEH eel nOO-meh-roh dAYl-lah mEE-ah kAH-meh-rah*
May I please have my key?	**Può darmi la chiave, per favore?** *poo-OH dAHr-mee lah key-AH-veh pehr fah-vOH-reh*
I've lost my key.	**Ho perduto la chiave.** *oh pehr-dOO-toh lah key-AH-veh*
I need _____.	**Ho bisogno di _____.** *oh bee-sOH-ny-oh dee*
■ a bellhop	**un fattorino** *oon faht-toh-rEE-noh*
■ a chambermaid	**una cameriera** *OO-nah kah-meh-ree-EH-rah*
Please send _____ to my room.	**Per piacere mi mandi _____ in camera.** *pehr pee-ah-chAY-reh mee mAHn-dee _____ een kAH-meh-rah*
■ a towel	**un asciugamano** *oon ah-shoo-gah-mAH-noh*
■ a bar of soap	**una saponetta** *OO-nah sah-poh-nAYt-tah*

- some hangers **delle grucce (degli attaccapanni)** *dAYl-lay grOO-cheh (dAY-ly-ee aht-AHk-kah-pAHn-nee)*

- a pillow **un cuscino** *oon koo-shEE-noh*

- a blanket **una coperta** *OO-nah koh-pEHr-tah*

- some ice cubes **dei cubetti di ghiaccio** *dAY-ee koo-bAYt-tee dee ghee-AH-chee-oh*

- some ice water **dell'acqua ghiacciata** *dayl-lAH-koo-ah ghee-ah-chee-AH-tah*

- a bottle of mineral water **una bottiglia d'acqua minerale** *OO-nah boht-tEE-ly-ee-ah dAH-koo-ah mee-neh-rAH-leh*

- an ashtray **un portacenere** *oon pohr-tah-chAY-nay-reh*

- toilet paper **della carta igienica** *dAYl-lah kAHr-tah ee-jee-EH-nee-kah*

- a reading lamp **una lampada per la lettura** *OO-nah lAHm-pah-dah pehr lah leht-tOO-rah*

- an electric adapter **un trasformatore elettrico** *oon trahs-fohr-mah-tOH-reh ay-lEHt-tree-koh*

COMPLAINTS

There is no _____. **Manca _____.** *mAHn-kah*

- running water **l'acqua corrente** *lAH-koo-ah kohr-rEHn-teh*

- hot water **l'acqua calda** *lAH-koo-ah kAHl-dah*

- electricity **la luce elettrica** *lah lOO-cheh eh-lEHt-tree-kah*

The _____ doesn't work. **_____ non funziona.** *_____ nohn foon-tsee-OH-nah*

- air-conditioning **l'aria condizionata** *lAH-ree-ah kohn-dee-tsee-oh-nAH-tah*

■ fan **il ventilatore** *eel vehn-tee-lah-tOH-reh*

■ faucet **il rubinetto** *eel roo-bee-nAYt-toh*

■ light **la luce** *lah lOO-cheh*

■ radio **la radio** *lah rAH-dee-oh*

■ electric socket **la presa della corrente** *lah prAY-sa dehl-lah kohr-rEHn-teh*

■ light switch **l'interruttore** *leen-tehr-root-tOH-reh*

■ television **la televisione** *lah teh-leh-vee-see-OH-neh*

Can you fix it? **Può farlo(la) riparare?** *poo-OH fAHr-loh(ah) ree-pah-rAH-reh*

The room is dirty. **La camera è sporca.** *lah kAH-meh-rah EH spOHr-kah*

Can you clean it _____? **Può farla pulire _____?** *poo-OH fAHr-lah poo-lEE-reh*

■ now **subito** *sOO-bee-toh*

■ as soon as possible **il più presto possibile** *eel pee-OO prEH-stoh pohs-sEE-bee-leh*

AT THE DESK

Are there (any) _____ for me? **Ci sono _____ per me?** *chee sOH-noh _____ payr mAY*

■ letters **(delle) lettere** *(dAYl-leh) lAYt-teh-reh*

■ messages **(dei) messaggi** *(dAY-ee) mehs-sAH-jee*

■ packages **(dei) pacchi** *(dAY-ee) pAH-key*

■ postcards **(delle) cartoline postali** *(dAYl-leh) kahr-toh-lEE-neh poh-stAH-lee*

Did anyone call for me? **Mi ha cercato qualcuno?** *mee-AH chehr-kAH-toh koo-ahl-kOO-noh*

CHECKING OUT

I'd like the bill, please.

Vorrei il conto per favore. *vohr-rEH-ee eel kOHn-toh pehr fah-vOH-reh*

I'll be checking out today (tomorrow).

Pagherò e partirò oggi (domani). *pah-gheh-rOH ay pahr-tee-rOH OH-jee (doh-mAH-nee)*

Please send someone up for our baggage.

Per favore mandi qualcuno a prendere le valigie. *pehr fah-vOH-reh mAHn-dee koo-ahl-kOO-noh ah prAYn-deh-reh leh vah-lEE-jee-eh*

GETTING AROUND TOWN

THE SUBWAY (UNDERGROUND)

Is there a subway (underground) in this city?

C'è una metropolitana in questa città? *chEH OO-nah meh-troh-poh-lee-tAH-nah een koo-AYs-tah cheet-tAH*

Do you have a map showing the stops?

Ha una cartina che indica le fermate della metropolitana? *ah OO-nah kahr-tEE-nah kay EEn-dee-kah lay fayr-mAH-teh dAYl-lah meh-troh-poh-lee-tAH-nah*

Where is the closest subway (underground) station?

Dov'è la stazione più vicina della metropolitana? *doh-vEH lah stah-tsee-OH-neh pee-OO vee-chEE-nah dAYl-lah meh-troh-poh-lee-tAH-nah*

How much is the fare?

Quanto costa il biglietto? *koo-AHn-toh kOHs-tah eel bee-ly-ee-AYt-toh*

Where can I buy a token (a ticket)?	**Dove posso comprare un gettone (un biglietto)?** *dOH-veh pOHs-soh kohm-prAH-reh oon jee-eht-tOH-neh (oon bee-ly-ee-AYt-toh)*
Which is the train that goes to ____?	**Qual è il treno che va a ____?** *koo-ah-lEH eel trEH-noh keh vah ah*
Does this train go to ____?	**Questo treno va a ____?** *koo-AYs-toh trEH-noh vAH ah*
How many more stops?	**Quante fermate ancora?** *koo-AHn-teh fehr-mAH-teh ahn-kOH-rah*
What's the next station?	**Qual è la prossima stazione?** *koo-ah-lEH lah prOHs-see-mah stah-tsee-OH-neh*
Where should I get off?	**Dove dovrei scendere?** *dOH-vay doh-vrEH-ee shAYn-deh-reh*
Do I have to change trains?	**Devo cambiare treno?** *dAY-voh kahm-bee-AH-reh trEH-noh*
Can you tell me when we get there?	**Può farmi sapere quando siamo arrivati(e)?** *poo-OH fAHr-mee sah-pAY-reh koo-AHn-doh see-AH-moh ahr-rEE-vah-tee(eh)*

THE BUS (STREETCAR, TRAM)

Where is the bus stop (bus terminal)?	**Dov'è la fermata dell'autobus (il capolinea)?** *doh-vEH lah fehr-mAH-tah dayl-lAH-oo-toh-boos (eel kah-poh-lEE-neh-ah)*
Which bus (trolley) do I take to get to ____?	**Quale autobus (tram) devo prendere per andare a ____?** *koo-AH-leh AH-oo-toh-boos (trAH-m) dAY-voh prAYn-deh-reh pehr ahn-dAH-reh ah*

In which direction do I have to go?	**In quale direzione devo andare?** *een koo-AH-leh dee-reh-tsee-OH-neh dAY-voh ahn-dAH-reh*
How often do the buses run?	**Ogni quanto tempo passano gli autobus?** *OH-ny-ee koo-AHn-toh tEHm-poh pAHs-sah-noh ly-ee AH-oo-toh-boos*
Do you go to _____?	**Va a _____?** *vAH ah*
I want to go to _____.	**Voglio andare a _____.** *vOH-ly-ee-oh ahn-dAH-reh ah*
Is it far from here?	**È lontano da qui?** *EH lohn-tAH-noh dah koo-EE*
How many stops are there?	**Quante fermate ci sono?** *koo-AHn-teh fehr-mAH-teh chee sOH-noh*
Do I have to change buses?	**Devo cambiare autobus?** *dAY-voh kahm-bee-AH-reh AH-oo-toh-boos*
How much is the fare?	**Quanto costa il biglietto?** *koo-AHn-toh kOH-stah eel bee-ly-ee-AYt-toh*
Where do I get off?	**Dove devo scendere?** *dOH-vay dAY-voh shAYn-deh-reh*
Can you tell me where to get off?	**Può dirmi dove devo scendere?** *poo-OH dEEr-mee dOH-veh dAY-voh shAYn-deh-reh*

TAXIS

Is there a taxi stand near here?	**C'è un posteggio dei taxi qui vicino?** *chEH oon poh-stAY-jee-oh dAY-ee tahs-sEE koo-EE vee-chEE-noh*

Please get me a taxi.	**Per favore mi chiami un taxi.** *pehr fah-vOH-reh mee key-AH-mee oon tahs-sEE*
Taxi! Are you free?	**Taxí! È libero?** *tahs-sEE EH lEE-beh-roh*
Take me (I want to go) ____.	**Mi porti (voglio andare) ____.** *mee pOHr-tee (vOH-ly-ee-oh ahn-dAH-reh)*
■ to the airport	**all'aeroporto** *ahl-lah-eh-roh-pOHr-toh*
■ to this address	**a questo indirizzo** *ah koo-AYs-toh een-dee-rEE-tsoh*
■ to the station	**alla stazione** *AHl-lah stah-tsee-OH-neh*
■ to ____ Street	**in via ____** *een vEE-ah*
Do you know where it is?	**Sa dove si trova?** *sah dOH-veh see trOH-vah*
How much is it to ____?	**Qual è la tariffa per ____?** *koo-ah-lEH lah tah-rEEf-fah pehr*
Faster! I'm in a hurry.	**Più presto (veloce)! Ho fretta.** *pee-OO prEH-stoh (veh-lOH-cheh) oh frAYt-tah*
Please drive more slowly.	**Per cortesia guidi più piano.** *pehr kohr-tay-sEE-ah goo-EE-dee pee-OO pee-AH-noh*
Stop here at the corner.	**Si fermi qui all'angolo.** *see fAYr-mee koo-EE ahl-lAHn-goh-loh*
Stop at the next block.	**Si fermi alla prossima via.** *see fAYr-mee AHl-lah prOHs-see-mah vEE-ah*

How much do I owe you?	**Quanto le devo?** *koo-AHn-toh leh dAY-voh*
This is for you.	**Questo è per lei.** *koo-AYs-toh EH pehr lEH-ee*

SIGHTSEEING AND TOURS

Where is the Tourist Information Office?	**Dov'è l'Ente Locale (Nazionale) per il Turismo?** *doh-vEH lEHn-teh loh-kAH-leh (nah-tsee-oh-nAH-leh) pehr eel too-rEEs-moh*
Where can I buy an English guidebook?	**Dove posso comprare una guida turistica in inglese?** *dOH-veh pOHs-soh kohm-prAH-reh OO-nah goo-EE-dah too-rEEs-tee-kah een een-glAY-seh*
I need an English-speaking guide.	**Ho bisogno di una guida che parli inglese.** *oh bee-sOH-ny-oh dee OO-nah goo-EE-dah kay pAHr-lee een-glAY-seh*
How much does he charge ____?	**Quanto si fa pagare ____?** *koo-AHn-toh see fah pah-gAH-reh*
■ per hour	**all'ora** *ahl-lOH-rah*
■ per day	**al giorno** *ahl jee-OHr-noh*
When does the tour begin?	**Quando inizia il tour (la gita)?** *koo-AHn-doh ee-nEE-tsee-ah eel tOOr (lah jEE-tah)*
How long is the tour?	**Quanto dura il tour (la gita)?** *koo-AHn-toh dOO-rah eel tOOr (lah jEE-tah)*
There are two (four, six) of us.	**Siamo in due (quattro, sei).** *see-AH-moh een-dOO-eh (koo-AHt-troh sEH-ee)*

We are here for one (two) day(s) only.	**Saremo qui un giorno (due giorni) soltanto.** *sah-rAY-moh koo-EE oon jee-OHr-noh (dOO-eh jee-OHr-nee) sohl-tAHn-toh*
Are there trips through the city?	**Si fanno (dei tour) delle gite turistiche della città?** *see fAHn-noh (dAY-ee tOOr) dAYl-leh jEE-teh too-rEE-stee-keh dAHl-lah cheet-tAH*
Where do they leave from?	**Da dove iniziano i tour (le gite)?** *dah dOH-veh ee-nEE-tsee-ah-noh ee tOOr (leh jEE-teh)*
We want to see ____.	**Vogliamo vedere ____.** *voh-ly-ee-AH-moh vay-dAY-reh*
■ the botanical garden	**il giardino botanico** *eel jee-ahr-dEE-noh boh-tAH-nee-koh*
■ the business center	**il centro commerciale** *eel chAYn-troh kohm-mehr-chee-AH-leh*
■ the castle	**il castello** *eel kahs-tEHl-loh*
■ the cathedral	**la cattedrale** *lah kaht-teh-drAH-leh*
■ the church	**la chiesa** *lah key-EH-sah*
■ the concert hall	**la sala dei concerti** *lah sAH-lah dAY-ee kohn-chEHr-tee*
■ the downtown area	**la zona del centro** *lah tsOH-nah dayl chAYn-troh*
■ the fountains	**le fontane** *leh fohn-tAH-neh*
■ the library	**la biblioteca** *lah bee-blee-oh-tEH-kah*
■ the main park	**il parco principale** *eel pAHr-koh preen-chee-pAH-leh*
■ the main square	**la piazza principale** *lah pee-AH-tsah preen-chee-pAH-leh*
■ the market	**il mercato** *eel mehr-kAH-toh*
■ the mosque	**la moschea** *lah moh-skEH-ah*
■ the museum (of fine arts)	**il museo (delle belle arti)** *eel moo-sEH-oh (dAYl-leh bEHl-leh AHr-tee)*

■ a nightclub	**un night club (locale notturno)** *oon nAH-eet klOOb (loh-kAH-leh noht-tOOr-noh)*
■ the old part of town	**la parte vecchia della città** *lah pAHr-teh vEHk-key-ah dAYl-la cheet-tAH*
■ the opera	**il teatro dell'opera** *eel teh-AH-troh dayl-lOH-peh-rah*
■ the palace	**il palazzo** *eel pah-lAH-tsoh*
■ the stadium	**lo stadio** *loh stAH-dee-oh*
■ the synagogue	**la sinagoga** *lah see-nah-gOH-gah*
■ the university	**l'università** *loo-nee-vehr-see-tAH*
■ the zoo	**il giardino zoologico (lo zoo)** *eel jee-ahr-dEE-no tsoh-oh-lOH-jee-koh (loh tsOH-oh)*
Is it all right to go in now?	**Si può entrare adesso?** *see poo-OH ehn-trAH-reh ah-dEHs-soh*
Is it open (closed)?	**È aperto (chiuso)?** *EH ah-pEHr-toh (key-OO-soh)*
At what time does it open (close)?	**A che ora aprono (chiudono)?** *ah kay OH-rah AH-proh-noh (key-OO-doh-noh)*
What's the admission price?	**Quant'è l'entrata?** *koo-ahn-tEH lehn-trAH-tah*
How much do children pay?	**Quanto pagano i bambini?** *koo-AHn-toh pAH-gah-noh ee bahm-bEE-nee*
Can they go in free? Until what age?	**Possono entrare gratis? Fino a quale età?** *pOHs-soh-noh ehn-trAH-reh grAH-tees fEE-noh ah koo-AH-leh eh-tAH*

Is it all right to take pictures?	**Si possono fare fotografie?** *see pOHs-soh-noh fAH-reh foh-toh-grah-fEE-eh*
How much extra does it cost to take pictures?	**Quanto costa in più per fare delle fotografie?** *koo-AHn-toh kOHs-tah een pee-OO pehr fAH-reh dAYl-leh foh-toh-grah-fEE-eh*
I do (not) use a flash.	**Io (non) uso il flash.** *EE-oh (nohn) OO-soh eel flEH-sh*

PLANNING A TRIP

AIR SERVICE

When is there a flight to _____?	**Quando c'è un volo per _____?** *koo-AHn-doh chEH oon vOH-loh pehr*
I would like _____.	**Vorrei _____.** *vohr-rEH-ee*
■ a round-trip (one-way) ticket _____.	**un biglietto di andata e ritorno (di andata)** *oon bee-ly-ee-AYt-toh dee ahn-dAH-tah ay ree-tOHr-noh (dee ahn-dAH-tah)*
■ in tourist class	**in classe turistica** *een klAHs-seh too-rEE-stee-kah*
■ in first class	**in prima classe** *een prEE-mah klAHs-seh*
Can I use this ticket for frequent flyer miles?	**Posso usare questo biglietto per il club "Mille miglia," frequent flyer miles?** *pOHs-soh oo-sAH-reh koo-AYs-toh bee-ly-AYt-toh pehr eel kloob mEEl-leh mEE-ly-ee-ah frequent flyer miles*

I would like a seat ____.	**Vorrei un posto ____.** *vohr-rEH-ee OOn pOH-stoh*
■ in the (non) smoking section	**tra i (non)fumatori** *trAH ee (nohn)foo-mah-tOH-ree*
■ next to the window	**accanto al finestrino** *ah-kAHn-toh ahl fee-neh-strEE-noh*
■ on the aisle	**vicino al corridoio** *vee-chEE-noh ahl kohr-ree-dOH-ee-oh*
What is the fare?	**Qual è il prezzo del biglietto?** *koo-ah-lEH eel prEH-tsoh dAYl bee-ly-ee-EHt-toh*
Are meals served?	**Sono inclusi i pasti?** *sOH-noh een-klOO-see ee pAH-stee*
When does the plane leave (arrive)?	**A che ora parte (arriva) l'aereo?** *ah kay OH-rah pAHr-teh (ahr-ree-vAH) lah-EH-reh-oh*
When must I be at the airport?	**Quando dovrò trovarmi all'aeroporto?** *koo-AHn-doh doh-vrOH troh-vAHr-mee ahl-lah-eh-roh-pOHr-toh*
What is my flight number?	**Qual è il (mio) numero di volo?** *koo-AH-lEH eel (mEE-oh) nOO-meh-roh dee vOH-loh*
What gate do we leave from?	**Qual è la nostra porta d'uscita?** *koo-ah-lEH lah nOH-strah pOHr-tah doo-shEE-tah*
I want to confirm (cancel) my reservation for flight ____.	**Desidero confermare (cancellare) la mia prenotazione per il volo ____.** *day-sEE-deh-roh kohn-fayr-mAH-reh (kahn-chehl-lAH-reh) lah mEE-ah preh-noh-tah-tsee-OH-neh pehr eel vOH-loh*
I'd like to check my bags.	**Vorrei consegnare le valigie.** *vohr-rEH-ee kohn-say-ny-AH-reh leh vah-lEE-jee-eh*

I have only carry-on baggage.

Ho soltanto bagagli a mano.
oh sohl-tAHn-toh bah-gAH-ly-ee ah MAH-noh

Please pass my film (camera) through by hand.

Per piacere mi passi il rollino (la macchina fotografica) a mano.
pehr pee-ah-chAY-reh mee pAHs-see eel rohl-lEE-noh (lah mAH-kee-nah foh-toh-grAH-fee-koh) ah MAH-noh

TRAIN SERVICE

Where is the train station?

Dov'è la stazione ferroviaria?
doh-vEH lah stah-tsee-OH-neh fehr-roh-vee-AH-ree-ah

When does the train leave (arrive) for (from) _____?

Quando parte (arriva) il treno per (da) _____? *koo-AHn-doh pAHr-teh (ahr-rEE-vah) eel trEH-noh pehr (dah)*

Does this train stop at _____?

Questo treno si ferma a _____?
koo-AYs-toh trEH-noh see fAYr-mah ah

I would like _____.

Vorrei _____. *vohr-rEH-ee*

■ a first- (second-) class ticket for _____.

un biglietto di prima (seconda) classe per _____. *oon bee-ly-ee-AYt-toh dee prEE-mah (say-kOHn-dah) klAHs-seh pehr*

■ a half-price ticket

un biglietto a tariffa ridotta
oon bee-ly-ee-AYt-toh ah tah-rEEf-fah ree-dOHt-tah

■ a one-way (round-trip) ticket

un biglietto di andata (andata e ritorno) *oon bee-ly-ee-AYt-toh dee ahn-dAH-tah (ahn-dAH-tah ay ree-tOHr-noh)*

■ with supplement for the rapid train

con supplemento rapido *kohn soop-pleh-mEHn-toh rAH-pee-doh*

■ with reserved seat	**con prenotazione**	*kohn prey-noh-tAH-tzee-oh-neh*
Are there discounts for ____?	**Ci sono sconti per ____?**	*chee sOH-no skOHn-tee pehr*
■ seniors	**anziani**	*ahn-tzee-AH-nee*
■ youths	**giovani**	*jee-OH-vah-nee*
■ groups	**gruppi**	*grOOp-pee*
■ travelers with special needs	**disabili**	*dee-sAH-bee-lee*
How can I obtain a refund?	**Come posso ottenere il rimborso?**	*kOH-meh pOHs-soh oht-ten-nAY-reh eel reem-bOHr-soh*
Are there special passes?	**Ci sono sconti speciali?**	*chee sOH-noh skOHn-tee speh-chee-AH-lee*
■ weekly	**settimanali**	*seht-tee-mah-nAH-lee*
■ monthly	**mensili**	*mehn-sEE-lee*
■ for groups	**per gruppi**	*pehr grOOp-pee*
■ for tourists	**per turisti**	*pehr too-rEEs-tee*
Is the train late?	**Il treno è in ritardo?**	*eel trEH-noh EH een ree-tAHr-doh*
How long does it stop?	**Quanto tempo si ferma?**	*koo-AHn-toh tEHm-poh see fAYr-mah*
Is there time to get a bite?	**C'è tempo per comprare un boccone?**	*chEH tEHm-poh pehr kohm-prAH-reh oon boh-kOH-neh*
Is there a dining car (a sleeping car)?	**C'è un vagone ristorante (un vagone letto)?**	*chEH oon vah-gOH-neh ree-stoh-rAHn-teh (oon vah-gOH-neh lEHt-toh)*
Is this an express (local) train?	**È questo un treno rapido (locale)?**	*EH koo-AYs-toh oon trEH-noh rAH-pee-doh (loh-kAH-leh)*

Do I have to change trains?	**Debbo cambiar treno?** *dAYb-boh kahm-bee-AHr trEH-noh*
Is this seat taken?	**È occupato questo posto?** *EH oh-koo-pAH-toh koo-AYs-toh pOH-stoh*
Excuse me, but you are in my seat.	**Mi scusi ma lei ha occupato il mio posto.** *mee skOO-see mah lEH-ee ah oh-koo-pAH-toh eel mEE-oh pOHs-toh*
Where is the train station?	**Dov'è la stazione ferroviaria?** *doh-vEH lah stah-tsee-OH-neh fehr-roh-vee-AH-ree-ah*

SHIPBOARD TRAVEL

Where is the port (dock)?	**Dov'è il porto (molo)?** *doh-vEH eel pOHr-toh (mOH-loh)*
When does the next boat leave for ____?	**Quando parte il prossimo battello per ____?** *koo-AHn-doh pAHr-teh eel prOHs-see-moh baht-tEHl-loh pehr*
How long does the crossing take?	**Quanto dura la traversata?** *koo-AHn-toh dOO-rah lah trah-vehr-sAH-tah*
Do we stop at any other ports?	**Ci fermiamo in qualche altro porto?** *chee fayr-mee-AH-moh een koo-AHl-keh AHl-troh pOHr-toh*
How long will we remain in port?	**Quanto tempo resteremo in porto?** *koo-AHn-toh tEHm-poh reh-stay-rEH-moh een pOHr-toh*
When do we land?	**Quando sbarcheremo?** *koo-AHn-do sbahr-keh-rAY-moh*
At what time do we have to go back on board?	**A che ora ritorniamo a bordo?** *ah kay OH-rah-ree-tohr-nee-AH-moh ah bOHr-doh*

DRIVING A CAR

CAR RENTALS

Where can I rent _____?	**Dove posso noleggiare _____?** *dOH-veh pOHs-soh noh-leh-jee-AH-reh*
■ a car	**una macchina** *OO-nah mAHk-kee-nah*
■ a motorcycle	**una motocicletta** *OO-nah moh-toh-chEE-klAYt-tah*
■ a motor scooter	**una vespa (una lambretta)** *OO-nah vEH-spah (OO-nah lahm-brAYt-tah)*
■ a moped	**un motorino** *oon moh-toh-rEE-noh*
■ a bicycle	**una bicicletta** *OO-nah bee-chee-klAYt-tah*
I want (I'd like) _____.	**Voglio (Vorrei) _____.** *vOH-ly-ee-oh (vohr-rEH-ee)*
■ a small car	**una macchina piccola** *OO-nah mAHk-kee-nah pEE-koh-lah*
■ a large car	**una macchina grande** *OO-nah mAHk-kee-nah grAHn-deh*
■ a sports car	**una macchina sportiva** *OO-nah mAHk-kee-nah spohr-tEE-vah*
I prefer automatic transmission.	**Preferisco il cambio automatico.** *preh-feh-rEE-skoh eel kAHm-bee-oh ah-oo-toh-mAH-tee-koh*
How much does it cost _____?	**Quanto costa _____?** *koo-AHn-toh kOH-stah*
■ per day	**al giorno** *ahl jee-OHr-noh*
■ per week	**alla settimana** *AHl-lah seht-tee-mAH-nah*

■ per kilometer

per chilometro *pehr key-lOH-meh-troh*

■ for unlimited mileage

a chilometraggio illimitato *ah key-loh-meh-trAH-jee-oh eel-lee-mee-tAH-toh*

How much is the (complete) insurance?

Quant'è l'assicurazione (completa)? *koo-ahn-tEH lahs-see-koo-rah-tsee-OH-neh (kohm-plEH-tah)*

Is gas included?

È inclusa la benzina? *EH een-klOO-sah lah behn-tsEE-nah*

Do you accept credit cards?

Accetta(no) carte di credito? *ah-chEHt-tah(noh) kAHr-teh dee krEH-dee-toh*

Here's my (international) driver's license.

Ecco la mia patente (internazionale) di guida. *EHk-koh lah mEE-ah pah-tEHn-teh (een-tehr-nah-tsEE-oh-nAH-leh) dee goo-EE-dah*

Do I have to leave a deposit?

Devo lasciare un acconto (un deposito)? *dAY-voh lah-shee-AH-reh oon ahk-kOHn-toh (oon day-pOH-see-toh)*

Is there a drop-off charge?

C'è un supplemento per la consegna dell'auto? *chEH oon soop-pleh-mEHn-toh pehr lah kohn-sEH-ny-ee-ah dayl-lAH-oo-toh*

I want to rent the car here and leave it in Turin.

Desidero noleggiare l'auto qui e consegnarla a Torino. *day-sEE-deh-roh noh-lay-jee-AH-reh lAH-oo-toh koo-EE ay kohn-say-ny-ee-AHr-lah ah toh-rEE-noh*

What kind of gasoline does it take?

Che tipo di carburante usa? *kay tEE-poh dee kahr-boo-rAHn-teh OO-sah*

ON THE ROAD

Excuse me. Can you tell me _____?	**Mi scusi. Può dirmi _____?** *mee skOO-see poo-OH dEEr-mee*
■ which way is it to _____	**qual'è la via per _____** *koo-ah-lEH lah vEE-ah pehr*
■ how I get to _____	**come potrei raggiungere _____** *kOH-meh poh-trEH-ee rah-jee-OOn-jeh-reh*
I think we're lost.	**Penso che ci siamo perduti(e).** *pEHn-soh kay chee see-AH-moh pehr-dOO-tee(eh)*
Is this the road (way) to _____?	**È questa la strada (via) per _____?** *EH koo-AYs-tah lah strAH-dah (vEE-ah) pehr*
Where does this road go?	**Dove porta questa strada?** *dOH-veh pOHr-tah koo-AYs-tah strAH-dah*
How far is it from here to the next town?	**Quanto dista da qui la prossima città?** *koo-AHn-toh dEE-stah dah koo-EE lah prOHs-see-mah cheet-tAH*
How far away is _____?	**Quanto dista _____?** *koo-AHn-toh dEE-stah*
Do you have a road map?	**Ha una cartina stradale?** *AH OO-nah kahr-tEE-nah strah-dAH-leh*
Can you show it to me on the map?	**Può indicarmelo sulla cartina?** *poo-OH een-dee-kAHr-meh-loh sOOl-lah kahr-tEE-nah*
Is it a good road?	**È buona la strada?** *EH boo-OH-nah lah strAH-dah*

Guarded railroad crossing

Yield

Stop

Right of way

Dangerous intersection ahead

Gasoline (petrol) ahead

Parking

No vehicles allowed

Dangerous curve

Pedestrian crossing

Oncoming traffic has right of way

No bicycles allowed

No parking allowed

No entry

No left turn

No U-turn

No passing

Border crossing

Traffic signal ahead

Speed limit

Traffic circle (roundabout) ahead

Minimum speed limit

All traffic turns left

End of no passing zone

SENSO UNICO

One-way street

DEVIAZIONE

Detour

Danger ahead

Entrance to expressway

Expressway ends

Is this the shortest way?	**È questa la via più corta?** *EH koo-AYs-tah lah vEE-ah pee-OO kOHr-tah*
Are there any detours?	**Ci sono deviazioni?** *chee sOH-noh day-vee-ah-tsee-OH-nee*
Do I go straight?	**Posso proseguire diritto?** *pOHs-soh proh-seh-goo-EE-reh dee-rEEt-toh*
Turn to the right (to the left).	**Giri a destra (a sinistra).** *jEE-ree ah dEH-strah (ah see-nEE-strah)*

AT THE SERVICE STATION

Where is there a gas (petrol) station?	**Dov'è una stazione di servizio?** *doh-vEH OO-nah stah-tsee-OH-neh dee sayr-vEE-tsee-oh*
Give me 15 (25) liters.	**Mi dia quindici (venticinque) litri.** *mee dEE-ah koo-EEn-dee-chee (vayn-tee-chEEn-koo-eh) lEE-tree*
Fill'er up with _____.	**Faccia il pieno di _____ .** *fAH-chee-ah eel pee-AY-noh dee*
■ diesel	**diesel** *dEE-eh-sehl*
■ regular (standard)	**normale** *nohr-mAH-leh*
■ super (premium)	**super** *sOO-pehr*
Please check _____.	**Per favore mi controlli _____.** *pehr fah-vOH-reh mee kohn-trOHl-lee*
■ the antifreeze	**l'acqua** *lAH-koo-ah*
■ the battery	**la batteria** *lah baht-teh-rEE-ah*
■ the carburetor	**il carburatore** *eel kahr-boo-rah-tOH-reh*
■ the oil	**l'olio** *lOH-lee-oh*

■ the spark plugs	**le candele** *leh kahn-dAY-leh*
■ the tires	**i pneumatici (le gomme)** *ee pneh-oo-mAH-tee-chee* *(leh gOHm-meh)*
■ the tire pressure	**la pressione delle gomme** *lah prehs-see-OH-neh dAYl-leh* *gOHm-meh*

Change the oil (please).	**Mi cambi l'olio (per favore).** *mee kAHm-bee lOH-lee-oh (pehr* *fah-vOH-reh)*
Lubricate the car (please).	**Mi lubrifichi la macchina (per favore).** *mee loo-brEE-fee-key* *lah mAHk-kee-nah (pehr fah-vOH-reh)*
Charge the battery.	**Mi carichi la batteria.** *mee kAH-ree-key lah baht-teh-rEE-ah*
Change this tire.	**Mi cambi questa ruota.** *mee kAHm-bee koo-AYs-tah roo-OH-tah*
Wash the car.	**Mi faccia il lavaggio alla macchina.** *mee fAH-chee-ah eel lah-vAH-jee-oh* *AHl-lah mAHk-kee-nah*
Where are the restrooms?	**Dove sono i gabinetti?** *dOH-veh* *sOH-noh ee gah-bee-nAYt-tee*

ACCIDENTS AND REPAIRS

| My car has broken down. | **Mi si è guastata la macchina.**
mee see-EH goo-ah-stAH-tah lah
mAHk-kee-nah |
| It overheats. | **Si surriscalda.**   *see soor-ree-skAHl-dah* |

It doesn't start.	**Non si avvia.**	*nohn see ahv-vEE-ah*
I have a flat tire.	**Ho una gomma bucata.**	*oh OO-nah gOHm-mah boo-kAH-tah*
The radiator is leaking.	**Il radiatore perde acqua.**	*eel rah-dee-ah-tOH-reh pEHr-deh AH-koo-ah*
The battery is dead.	**La batteria è scarica.**	*lah baht-teh-rEE-ah EH skAH-ree-kah*
The keys are locked inside the car.	**Le chiavi sono rimaste chiuse in macchina.**	*leh key-AH-vee sOH-noh ree-mAH-steh key-OO-seh een mAHk-kee-nah*
Is there a garage near here?	**C'è un'autorimessa qui vicino?**	*chEH oon-ah-oo-toh-ree-mEHs-sah koo-EE vee-chEE-noh*
I need a mechanic (tow truck).	**Ho bisogno di un meccanico (carroattrezzi).**	*oh bee-sOH-ny-oh dee oon mehk-kAH-nee-koh (kAHr-roh-aht-trAY-tsee)*
Can you give me a push?	**Può darmi una spinta?**	*poo-OH dAHr-mee OO-nah spEEn-tah*
I don't have any tools.	**Non ho gli attrezzi.**	*nohn-OH ly-ee aht-trAY-tsee*
Can you lend me _____?	**Può prestarmi _____?**	*poo-OH preh-stAHr-mee*
■ a flashlight	**una lampadina tascabile**	*OO-nah lahm-pah-dEE-nah tah-skAH-bee-leh*
■ a hammer	**un martello**	*oon mahr-tEHl-loh*
■ a jack	**un cricco**	*oon krEEk-koh*
■ a monkey wrench	**una chiave inglese**	*OO-nah key-AH-veh een-glAY-seh*

■ pliers | **delle pinze**   *dAYl-leh pEEn-tseh*
■ a screwdriver | **un cacciavite**   *oon kah-chee-ah-vEE-teh*

I need _____. | **Ho bisogno di _____.**   *oh bee-sOH-ny-oh dee*

■ a bulb | **una lampadina**   *OO-nah lahm-pah-dEE-nah*
■ a filter | **un filtro**   *oon fEEl-troh*
■ a fuse | **un fusibile**   *oon foo-sEE-bee-leh*

Can you fix the car? | **Può ripararmi la macchina?**
poo-OH ree-pah-rAHr-mee lah mAHk-kee-nah

Can you repair it temporarily? | **Può farmi una riparazione provvisoria?**   *poo-OH fAHr-mee OO-nah ree-pah-rah-tsee-OH-neh prohv-vee-sOH-ree-ah*

Do you have the part? | **Ha il pezzo di recambio?**   *ah eel pEH-tsoh dee ree-kAHm-bee-oh*

I think there's something wrong with _____. | **Penso che ci sia un guasto _____.**
pEHn-soh kay chee sEE-ah oon goo-AH-stoh

■ the antilock brake system (ABS) | **al l'antibloccaggio Abs**   *ahl lahn-tee-blohk-kAH-jee-oh ah-bee-EHs-seh*
■ the automatic transmission | **al cambio automatico a controllo elettronico**   *ahl kAHm-bee-oh ah-oo-toh-mAH-tee-koh ah kohn-trOHl-loh eh-leht-trOH-nee-koh*
■ the defogger/defroster | **al lo sbrinatore**   *ahl loh sbree-nah-tOH-reh*
■ the directional signal | **alla freccia**   *AHl-lah frAY-chee-ah*
■ the electrical system | **all'impianto elettrico**   *ahl-leem-pee-AHn-toh eh-lEHt-tree-koh*

■ the fan   **alla ventola**   *AHl-lah vEHn-toh-lah*

■ the fan belt   **alla cinghia del ventilatore**   *AHl-lah chEEn-ghee-ah dayl vehn-tee-lah-tOH-reh*

■ the fog lights   **al fendinebbia**   *ahl fEHn-dee-nAYb-bee-ah*

■ the fuel pump   **alla pompa della benzina**   *AHl-lah pOHm-pah dAHl-lah behn-tsEE-nah*

■ the gear shift   **al cambio**   *ahl kAHm-bee-oh*

■ the headlights   **agli abbaglianti**   *AH-ly-ee ahb-bah-ly-ee-AHn-tee*

■ the horn   **al clacson**   *ahl klAH-ksohn*

■ the ignition   **all'accensione**   *ahl-lah-chehn-see-OH-neh*

■ the power windows   **agli alzacristalli elettrici**   *AH-ly-ee AHl-tsah-kree-stAHl-lee ay-lEHt-tree-chee*

■ the radio   **alla radio**   *AHl-lah rAH-dee-oh*

■ the starter   **al motorino d'avviamento**   *ahl moh-toh-rEE-noh dahv-vee-ah-mEHn-toh*

■ the steering wheel   **al volante**   *ahl voh-lAHn-teh*

■ the taillight   **al fanalino posteriore**   *ahl fah-nah-lEE-noh poh-steh-ree-OH-reh*

■ the transmission   **alla trasmissione**   *AHl-lah trah-smees-see-OH-neh*

■ the water pump   **alla pompa dell'acqua**   *AHl-lah pOHm-pah dayl-AH-koo-ah*

■ the windshield (windscreen) wiper   **al tergicristallo**   *ahl tehr-jee-kree-stAHl-loh*

What's the matter?   **Che cosa c'è che non va?**   *kay kOH-sah chEH kay nohn vAH*

Is it possible to (can you) fix it today?	**È possibile (può) aggiustarlo oggi?** *EH pohs-sEE-bee-leh (poo-OH) ah-jee-oo-stAHr-loh OH-jee*
How long will it take?	**Quanto tempo ci vorrà?** *koo-AHn-toh tEHm-poh chee vohr-rAH*
How much do I owe you?	**Quanto le devo?** *koo-AHn-toh leh dAY-voh*

ENTERTAINMENT AND DIVERSIONS

MOVIES, THEATER, CONCERTS, OPERA, BALLET

Let's go to the _____.	**Andiamo al _____.** *ahn-dee-AH-moh ahl*
■ movies (cinema)	**cinema** *chEE-neh-mah*
■ theater	**teatro** *teh-AH-troh*
What are they showing today?	**Che spettacoli ci sono oggi?** *kay speht-tAH-koh-lee chee sOH-noh OH-jee*
Is it a _____?	**È _____?** *EH*
■ mystery	**un giallo** *oon jee-AHl-loh*
■ comedy	**una commedia** *OO-nah kohm-mEH-dee-ah*
■ drama	**un dramma** *oon drAHm-mah*
■ musical	**un'operetta** *oo-noh-peh-rAYt-tah*
■ romance	**un romanzo** *oon roh-mAHn-tsoh*
■ Western	**un western** *oon oo-EH-stehrn*
■ war film	**un film di guerra** *oon fEElm dee goo-EHr-ra*

■ science fiction film	**un film di fantascienza** *oon fEElm dee fahn-tah-shee-EHn-tsah*
Is it in English?	**È parlato in inglese?** *EH pahr-lAH-toh een een-glAY-seh*
Has it been dubbed?	**È stato doppiato?** *EH stAH-toh dohp-pee-AH-toh*
Where is the box office?	**Dov'è il botteghino?** *doh-vEH eel boht-tay-ghEE-noh*
What time does the (first) show begin?	**A che ora comincia lo (il primo) spettacolo?** *ah kay OH-rah koh-mEEn-chee-ah loh (eel prEE-moh) speht-tAH-koh-loh*
What time does the (last) show end?	**A che ora finisce lo (l'ultimo) spettacolo?** *ah kay OH-rah fee-nEE-sheh loh (lOOl-tee-moh) speht-tAH-koh-loh*
I want a seat near the middle (front, rear).	**Desidero un posto al centro (davanti, dietro).** *day-sEE-deh-roh oon pOHs-toh ahl chAYn-troh (dah-vAHn-tee dee-EH-troh)*
Can I check my coat?	**Posso consegnare (lasciare) il mio cappotto?** *pOHs-soh kohn-seh-ny-ee-AH-reh (lah-shee-AH-reh) eel mEE-oh kahp-pOHt-toh*
I need _____ tickets for tonight (tomorrow night).	**Mi occorrono _____ biglietti per stasera (domani sera).** *mee oh-kOHr-roh-noh _____ bee-ly-ee-AYt-tee pehr stah-sAY-rah (doh-mAH-nee sAY-rah)*
■ two orchestra seats	**due poltrone d'orchestra** *doo-eh pohl-trOH-neh dohr-kEHs-trah*
■ two box seats	**due poltrone nei palchi** *doo-eh pohl-trOH-neh nAY-ee pAHl-kee*

■ two mezzanine seats	**due poltrone**	*doo-eh pohl-trOH-neh*
■ two gallery seats	**due posti in galleria**	*doo-eh pOHs-tee een gahl-leh-rEE-ah*

How much are the front-row seats?

Qual è il prezzo dei posti di prima fila? *koo-ah-lEH eel prEH-tsoh dAY-ee pOH-stee dee prEE-mah fEE-lah*

What are the least expensive seats?

Quali sono i posti meno costosi? *koo-AH-lee sOH-noh ee pOH-stee mAY-noh koh-stOH-see*

Are there any seats for tonight's performance?

Ci sono posti per lo spettacolo di stasera? *chee sOH-noh pOH-stee pehr loh speht-tAH-koh-loh dee stah-sAY-rah*

We would like to attend _____.

Vorremmo assistere ad _____. *vohr-rEHm-moh ahs-sEE-steh-reh ahd*

■ a ballet	**un balletto**	*oon bahl-lAYt-toh*
■ a concert	**un concerto**	*oon kohn-chEHr-toh*
■ an opera	**un'opera**	*oo-nOH-peh-rah*

What are they playing (singing)?

Che cosa recitano (cantano)? *kay kOH-sah rEH-chee-tah-noh (kAHn-tah-noh)*

Who is the conductor?

Chi è il direttore d'orchestra? *key-EH eel dee-reht-tOH-reh dohr-kEH-strah*

I prefer _____.

Preferisco _____. *preh-feh-rEE-skoh*

■ classical music	**la musica classica**	*lah mOO-see-kah clAHs-see-kah*
■ popular music	**la musica popolare**	*lah mOO-see-kah poh-poh-lAH-reh*
■ folk dance	**la danza folcloristica**	*lah dAHn-tsah fohl-kloh-rEE-stee-kah*

■ ballet **il balletto** *eel bahl-lAYt-toh*

When does the
season begin
(end)?

**Quando cominicia (finisce) la
stagione (lirica)?** *koo-AHn-doh koh-
mEEn-chee-ah (fee-nEE-sheh) lah
stah-jee-OH-neh (lEE-ree-kah)*

Should I get
the tickets in
advance?

**Debbo comprare i biglietti in
anticipo?** *dAYb-boh kohm-prAH-
reh ee bee-ly-ee-AYt-tee een ahn-tEE-
chee-poh*

Do I have to dress
formally?

È prescritto l'abito da sera?
*EH preh-skrEEt-toh lAH-bee-toh dah
sAY-rah*

May I buy a
program?

**Posso comprare il programma di
sala?** *pOHs-soh kohm-prAH-reh eel
proh-grAHm-mah dee sAH-lah*

What opera
(ballet) are they
performing?

Quale opera (balletto) danno?
*koo-AH-leh OH-peh-rah (bahl-lAYt-
toh) dAHn-noh*

NIGHTCLUBS, DANCING

Let's go to a night-
club.

Andiamo al night club. *ahn-dee-
AH-moh ahl nAH-eet klOOb*

Is a reservation
necessary?

È necessaria la prenotazione?
*EH neh-chehs-sAH-ree-ah lah preh-
noh-tah-tsee-OH-neh*

We haven't got a
reservation.

Non abbiamo la prenotazione.
*nohn ahb-bee-AH-moh lah preh-noh-
tah-tsee-OH-neh*

Is there a good
discotheque here?

C'è una buona discoteca qui?
*chEH OO-nah boo-OH-nah dee-skoh-
tEH-kah koo-EE*

Is there dancing at the hotel?	**Si balla in albergo (all'hotel)?** *see bAHl-lah een ahl-bEHr-goh (ahl-loh-tEHl)*
We'd like a table near the dance floor.	**Vorremmo un tavolo vicino alla pista (di ballo).** *vohr-rEHm-moh oon tAH-voh-loh vee-chEE-noh AHl-lah pEE-stah (dee bAHl-loh)*
Is there a minimum (cover charge)?	**C'è un prezzo minimo (per il tavolo)?** *chEH oon prEH-tsoh mEE-nee-moh (pehr eel tAH-voh-loh)*
Where is the checkroom?	**Dov'è il guardaroba?** *doh-vEH eel goo-ahr-dah-rOH-bah*
At what time does the floor show go on?	**A che ora comincia lo spettacolo (di varietà)?** *ah kay OH-rah koh-mEEn-chee-ah loh speht-tAH-koh-loh (dee vah-ree-eh-tAH)*

SPECTATOR SPORTS

I'd like to watch a soccer game.	**Vorrei vedere una partita di calcio.** *vohr-rEH-ee veh-dAY-reh OO-nah pahr-tEE-tah dee kAHl-chee-oh*
Where's the stadium?	**Dov'è lo stadio?** *doh-vEH loh stAH-dee-oh*
At what time does the match begin?	**A che ora comincia la partita?** *ah kay OH-rah koh-mEEn-chee-ah lah pahr-tEE-tah*
What teams are playing?	**Quali squadre giocano?** *koo-AH-lee skoo-AH-dreh jee-OH-kah-noh*
Is there a racetrack here?	**C'è un ippodromo qui?** *chEH oon eep-pOH-droh-moh koo-EE*

Is there a track and field stadium (sports arena) in this city?	**C'è uno stadio con piste e campo sportivo in questa città?** *chEH OO-noh stAH-dee-oh kohn pEEs-teh ay kAHm-poh spohr-tEE-voh een koo-AY-stah cheet-tAH*
What are the main events today (tomorrow)?	**Quali sono gli spettacoli principali di oggi (domani)?** *koo-AH-lee sOH-noh ly-ee speht-tAH-koh-lee preen-chee-pAH-lee dee OH-jee (doh-mAH-nee)*
Do you think I can get a ticket?	**Pensa che è possibile avere un biglietto?** *pEHn-sah kay-EH pohs-sEE-bee-leh ah-vAY-reh oon bee-ly-ee-AYt-toh*
How much is a ticket?	**Quanto costa un biglietto?** *koo-AHn-toh kOHs-tah oon bee-ly-ee-AYt-toh*

ACTIVE SPORTS

Do you play tennis?	**Gioca a tennis?** *jee-OH-kah ah tEHn-nees*
I (don't) play very well.	**(Non) gioco molto bene.** *(nohn) jee-OH-koh mOHl-toh bEH-neh*
Do you play singles (doubles)?	**Gioca il singolo (in doppio)?** *jee-OH-kah eel sEEn-goh-loh (een dOHp-pee-oh)*
Do you know where there is a court?	**Sa dove c'è un campo da tennis?** *sAH doh-veh-chEH oon kAHm-poh dah tEHn-nees*
Is it a private club? I'm not a member.	**È un club privato? Io non sono socio.** *EH oon clEHb pree-vAH-toh EE-oh nohn sOH-noh sOH-chee-oh*

How much do they charge per hour?	**Quanto si paga all'ora?** *koo-AHn-toh see pAH-gah ahl-lOH-rah*
Can I rent a racquet?	**Posso affittare una racchetta?** *pOHs-soh ahf-feet-tAH-reh OO-nah rahk-kAYt-tah*
Let's rally first to warm up.	**Prima scambiamo qualche battuta per riscaldarci.** *prEE-mah skahm-bee-AH-moh koo-AHl-keh baht-tOO-tah pehr rees-kahl-dAHr-chee*
I serve (you serve) first.	**Io servo (lei serve) per primo.** *EE-oh sEHr-voh (lEH-ee sEHr-veh) pehr prEE-moh*
Let's play another set.	**Giochiamo un altro set.** *jee-oh-key-AH-moh oon AHl-troh seht*
Where is a safe place to run (to jog)?	**Dov'è un posto buono dove si può correre (fare del footing)?** *doh-vEH oon pOHs-toh boo-OH-noh dOH-veh see poo-OH kOHr-reh-reh (fAH-reh dayl fOO-teeng)*
Where is there a health club?	**Dove si può trovare un centro fitness?** *dOH-veh see poo-OH troh-vAH-reh oon chAYn-tro feet-nEHs*
Where can I play bocci?	**Dove posso giocare alle bocce?** *dOH-veh pOHs-soh jee-oh-kAH-reh AHl-leh bOH-cheh*
Where can I rent a _____?	**Dove posso noleggiare _____?** *dOH-veh pOHs-soh noh-lay-jee-AH-reh*
◼ bicycle	**una bicicletta** *OO-nah bee-chee-klAYt-tah*
◼ mountain bike	**un rampichíno (una mountain bike)** *oon rahm-pee-kEE-noh (OO-nah mAH-oon-tahn bAH-eek)*

■ racing bike	**una bicicletta da corsa** *OO-nah bee-chee-klAYt-tah dah kOHr-sah*
■ touring bike	**una bicicletta da passeggio** *OO-nah bee-chee-klAYt-tah dah pahs-sAY-jee-oh*

AT THE BEACH/POOL

Is there a beach nearby?	**C'è una spiaggia qui vicino?** *chEH OO-nah spee-AH-jee-ah koo-ee vee-chEE-noh*
Let's go to the beach (to the pool).	**Andiamo alla spiaggia (in piscina).** *ahn-dee-AH-moh AHl-lah spee-AH-jee-ah (een pee-shEE-nah)*
Which bus will take us to the beach?	**Quale autobus ci porterà alla spiaggia?** *koo-AH-leh AH-oo-toh-boos chee pohr-teh-rAH AHl-lah spee-AH-jee-ah*
Is there an indoor (outdoor) pool in the hotel?	**C'è una piscina coperta (scoperta) nell'hotel?** *chEH OO-nah pee-shEE-nah koh-pEHr-tah (skoh-pEHr-tah) nayl-loh-tEHl*
I (don't) know how to swim well.	**(Non) so nuotare bene.** *(nohn) soh noo-oh-tAH-reh bEH-neh*
Is it safe to swim here?	**Si può nuotare qui senza pericolo?** *see poo-OH noo-oh-tAH-reh koo-EE sEHn-tsah peh-rEE-koh-loh*
Are there sharks?	**Ci sono pescecani?** *chee sOH-noh pay-sheh-kAH-nee*
Is it dangerous for children?	**È pericoloso per i bambini?** *EH peh-ree-koh-lOH-soh pehr ee bahm-bEE-nee*

Is there a lifeguard?	**C'è un bagnino?** *chEH oon bah-ny-EE-noh*
Where can I get _____?	**Dove posso trovare _____?** *dOH-vey pOHs-soh troh-vAH-reh*
■ an air mattress	**un materassino pneumatico** *oon mah-teh-rahs-sEE-noh pneh-oo-mAH-tee-koh*
■ a bathing suit	**un costume da bagno** *oon koh-stOO-meh dah bAH-ny-oh*
■ a beach ball	**un pallone per la spiaggia** *oon pahl-lOH-neh pehr lah spee-AH-jee-ah*
■ a beach chair	**una sedia per la spiaggia** *OO-nah sEH-dee-ah pehr lah spee-AH-jee-ah*
■ a beach towel	**una tovaglia da spiaggia** *OO-nah toh-vAH-ly-ee-ah dah spee-AH-jee-ah*
■ diving equipment	**un equipaggiamento subacqueo** *oon ay-koo-ee-pah-jee-ah-mEHn-toh soob-AH-koo-eh-oh*
■ sunglasses	**degli occhiali da sole** *dAY-ly-ee oh-key-AH-lee dah sOH-leh*
■ suntan lotion	**una lozione per l'abbronzatura** *OO-nah loh-tsee-OH-neh pehr lahb-brohn-tsah-tOO-rah*

ON THE SLOPES

Which ski area do you recommend?	**Quali campi di sci consiglia?** *koo-AH-lee kAHm-pee dee shee kohn-sEE-ly-ee-ah*
I am a novice (intermediate, expert) skier.	**Sono uno sciatore (una sciatrice) (principiante, dilettante, esperto(a)).** *sOH-noh OO-noh shee-ah-tOH-reh (OO-nah shee-ah-trEE-ceh) (preen-chee-pee-AHn-teh dee-leht-tAHn-teh ehs-pEHr-toh(ah))*

What kind of lifts are there?	**Come sono le sciovie?** *kOH-meh sOH-noh leh shee-oh-vEE-eh*
How much does the lift cost?	**Quant'è il biglietto per la sciovia?** *koo-ahn-tEH eel bee-ly-ee-AYt-toh pehr lah shee-oh-vEE-ah*
Do they give lessons?	**Danno lezioni?** *dAHn-noh leh-tsee-OH-nee*
Is there enough snow this time of the year?	**C'è abbastanza neve in questo periodo dell'anno?** *chEH ahb-bah-stAHn-tsah nAY-veh een koo-AYs-toh peh-rEE-oh-doh dayl-lAHn-noh*
Is there any cross-country skiing?	**C'è anche lo sci do fondo?** *chEH AHn-keh loh shee dee fOHn-doh*
How do I get there?	**Come ci si va?** *kOH-meh chee see vAH*
Can I rent _____ there?	**Posso affittare _____ sul posto?** *pOHs-soh ahf-feet-tAH-reh _____ sOOl pOH-stoh*
■ equipment	**l'attrezzatura** *laht-treh-tsah-tOO-rah*
■ poles	**le racchette da sci** *leh rah-kAYt-teh dah shEE*
■ skis	**gli sci** *ly-ee shEE*
■ ski boots	**gli scarponi da sci** *ly-ee skahr-pOH-nee dah shEE*

ON THE LINKS

Is there a golf course here?	**C'è un campo di golf (qui)?** *chEH oon kAHm-poh dee gOHlf (koo-EE)*
Can one rent clubs?	**Si possono affittare le mazze?** *see pOHs-soh-noh ahf-feet-tAH-reh leh mAH-tseh*

CAMPING

Is there a camping area near here?	**C'è un campeggio qui vicino?** *chEH oon kahm-pAY-jee-oh koo-EE vee-chEE-noh*
Do we pick our own site?	**Possiamo scegliere il posto che ci piace?** *pohs-see-AH-moh shay-ly-ee-EH-reh eel pOHs-toh kay chee pee-AH-cheh*
We only have a tent.	**Noi abbiamo solo una tenta.** *nOH-ee ahb-bee-AH-moh sOH-loh OO-nah tEHn-tah*
Where is it on this map?	**Dov'è su questa cartina?** *doh-vEH soo koo-AY-stah kahr-tEE-nah*
Can we park our trailer (caravan)?	**Possiamo posteggiare la nostra roulotte?** *pohs-see-AH-moh poh-steh-jee-AH-reh lah nOH-strah roo-lOH-te*
Can we camp for one night only?	**Possiamo accamparci per una notte solamente?** *pohs-see-AH-moh ahk-kahm-pAHr-chee pehr OO-nah nOHt-teh soh-lah-mEHn-teh*
Is (are) there _____?	**C'è (ci sono) _____?** *cheh (chee sOH-noh)*
■ drinking water	**acqua potabile** *AH-koo-ah poh-tAH-bee-leh*
■ showers	**docce?** *dOH-cheh*
■ grills	**caminetti** *kah-mee-nAYt-tee*
■ picnic tables	**tavoli per il pic-nic** *tAH-voh-lee pehr eel peek-nEEk*
■ electricity	**l'elettricità** *leh-leh-tree-chee-tAH*

■ a grocery store

un negozio di generi alimentari
oon nay-gOH-tsee-oh dee jEH-neh-ree ah-lee-mehn-tAH-ree

■ a children's play-ground

un posto dove far giocare i bambini
oon pOH-stoh dOH-veh fahr jee-oh-kAH-reh ee bahm-bEE-nee

■ flush toilets

gabinetti   *gah-bee-nAYt-tee*

How much do they charge per person (per car)?

Quanto si paga a persona (per macchina)? *koo-AHn-toh see pAH-gah ah pehr-sOH-nah (pehr mAHk-key-nah)*

We intend to stay _____ days (weeks).

Pensiamo di stare _____ giorni (settimane). *pehn-see-AH-moh dee stAH-reh _____ jee-OHr-nee (seht-tee-mAH-neh)*

FOOD AND DRINK

EATING OUT

Do you know a good restaurant?

Scusi, conosce un buon ristorante? *skOO-see koh-nOH-sheh oon boo-OHn ree-stoh-rAHn-teh*

Is it very expensive (dressy)?

È molto costoso (elegante)? *eh mOHl-toh koh-stOH-soh (eh-leh-gAHn-teh)*

Do you know a restaurant that serves typical dishes?

Conosce un ristorante tipico (del luogo)? *koh-nOH-sheh oon res-toh-rAHn-teh tEE-pee-koh (dAYl loo-OH-goh)*

Waiter!

Cameriere!   *kah-meh-ree-EH-reh*

A table for two, please.

Un tavolo per due, per favore. *oon tAH-voh-loh pehr dOO-eh pehr fah-vOH-reh*

- in the corner   **all'angolo**   *ahl-lAHn-goh-loh*
- near the window   **vicino alla finestra**   *vee-chee-noh AHl-lah fee-nEHs-trah*
- on the terrace   **sul terrazzo**   *sOOl tehr-rAH-tsoh*

I'd like to make a reservation ____.   **Vorrei fare una prenotazione ____.**   *vohr-rEH-ee fAH-reh oon-ah preh-noh-tah-tsee-OH-neh*

- for tonight   **per stasera**   *pehr stah-sAY-rah*
- for tomorrow evening   **per domani sera**   *pehr doh-mAH-nee sAY-rah*
- for two (four) persons   **per due (quattro) persone**   *pehr dOO-eh (koo-AHt-troh) pehr-SOH-neh*
- at 8 P.M.   **per le venti**   *pehr leh vAYn-tee*
- at 8:30 P.M.   **per le venti e trenta**   *pehr leh vAYn-tee ay trEHn-tah*

We'd like to have lunch (dinner) now.   **Vorremmo pranzare adesso.**   *vohr-rAYm-moh prahn-tsAH-reh ah-dEHs-soh*

The menu, please.   **Il menù, per piacere.**   *eel may-nOO pehr pee-ah-chAY-reh*

I'd like the set menu.   **Vorrei il menù turistico. (Il menù a prezzo fisso.)**   *vohr-rEH-ee eel meh-nOO too-rEEs-tee-koh (eel meh-nOO ah prEH-tsoh fEEs-soh)*

What's today's special?   **Qual è il piatto del giorno?**   *koo-ah-lEH eel pee-AHt-toh dayl jee-OHr-noh*

What do you recommend?   **Che cosa mi consiglia lei?**   *kay kOH-sah mee kohn-sEE-ly-ee-ah lEH-ee*

What's the house specialty?	**Qual è la specialità della casa?** *koo-ah-lEH lah speh-chee-ah-lee-tAH dAYl-lah kAH-sah*
Do you serve children's portions?	**Si servono porzioni per bambini?** *see sEHr-voh-noh pohr-tsee-OH-nee pehr bahm-bEE-nee*
I'm (not) very hungry.	**(Non) ho molta fame.** *(nohn) oh mOHl-tah fAH-meh*
Are the portions small (large)?	**Le porzioni sono piccole (grandi)?** *leh pohr-tsee-OH-nee sOH-noh pEE-koh-leh (grAHn-dee)*
To begin with, please bring us _____.	**Per cominciare, ci porti _____.** *pehr koh-meen-chee-AH-reh chee pOHr-tee*
■ an aperitif	**un aperitivo** *oon ah-peh-ree-tEE-voh*
■ a cocktail	**un cocktail** *oon kOHk-tayl*
■ some white (red) wine	**del vino bianco (rosso)** *dayl vEE-noh bee-AHn-koh (rOHs-soh)*
■ some water	**dell'acqua** *dayl-LAH-koo-ah*
■ a bottle of mineral water, carbonated (noncarbonated)	**una bottiglia d'acqua minerale gassata (naturale)** *OO-nah boht-tEE-ly-ee-ah dAH-koo-ah mee-neh-rAH-leh gahs-sAH-tah (nah-too-rAH-leh)*
■ a beer	**una birra** *OO-nah bEEr-rah*
I'd like to order now.	**Vorrei ordinare adesso** *vohr-rEH-ee ohr-dee-nAH-reh ah-dEHs-soh*
I'd like _____.	**Vorrei _____.** *vohr-rEH-ee*
Do you have a house wine?	**Hanno il vino della casa?** *AHn-noh eel vEE-noh dAYl-lah kAH-sah*

Is it dry (mellow, sweet)?	**È vino secco (amabile, dolce)?** *EH vEE-noh sAY-koh (ah-mAH-bee-leh dOHl-cheh)*
Please also bring us ____.	**Per piacere ci porti anche ____.** *pehr pee-ah-chAY-reh chee pOHr-tee AHn-keh*

- a roll **un panino** *oon pah-nEE-noh*
- bread **il pane** *eel pAH-neh*
- bread and butter **pane e burro** *pAH-neh ay bOOr-roh*

Waiter, we need ____.	**Cameriere(a), abbiamo bisogno di ____.** *kah-meh-ree-EH-reh(ah) ahb-bee-AH-moh bee-sOH-ny-oh dee*

- a knife **un coltello** *oon kohl-tEHl-loh*
- a fork **una forchetta** *OO-nah fohr-kAYt-tah*
- a spoon **un cucchiaio** *oon koo-key-AH-ee-oh*
- a teaspoon **un cucchiaino** *oon koo-key-ah-EE-noh*
- a soup spoon **un cucchiaio per la minestra (il brodo)** *oon koo-key-AH-ee-oh pehr lah mee-nEHs-trah (eel brOH-doh)*
- a glass **un bicchiere** *oon bee-key-EH-reh*
- a cup **una tazza** *OO-nah tAH-tsah*
- a saucer **un piattino** *oon pee-aht-tEE-noh*
- a plate **un piatto** *oon pee-AHt-toh*
- a napkin **un tovagliolo** *oon toh-vah-ly-ee-ee-OH-loh*

APPETIZERS (STARTERS)

acciughe	*ah-chee-OH-gheh*	anchovies
antipasto misto	*ahn-tee-pAHs-toh mEEs-toh*	assorted appetizers
carciofi	*kahr-chee-OH-fee*	artichoke

mortadella	*mohr-tah-dEHl-lah*	cold sausage, similar to bologna
prosciutto crudo	*proh-shee-OOt-toh krOO-doh*	dry-cured spiced ham
tartufi	*tahr-tOO-fee*	truffles (white)

SOUPS

brodo di manzo	*brOH-doh dee mAHn-tsoh*	broth, generally meat-based
brodo di pollo	*brOH-doh dee pOHl-loh*	chicken broth
brodo magro di vegetali	*brOH-doh mAH-groh dee veh-jeh-tAH-lee*	vegetable broth
crema di _____	*krEH-mah dee*	creamed _____ soup
buridda	*boo-rEEd-dah*	fish stew
cacciucco	*kah-chee-OO-koh*	seafood chowder
minestra in brodo	*mee-nEHs-trah een brOH-doh*	pasta in broth
minestrone	*mee-nehs-trOH-neh*	thick vegetable soup
zuppa di _____	*tsOOp-pah dee*	thick soup of _____

ENTREES (MEAT AND FISH DISHES)

acciughe	*ah-chee-OO-gheh*	anchovies
anguille	*ahn-goo-EEl-leh*	eel
aragosta	*ah-rah-gOHs-tah*	lobster (spiny)
aringa	*ah-rEEn-gah*	herring
■ **affumicata**	*ahf-foo-mee-kAH-tah*	smoked

baccalà	*bah-kah-lAH*	dried salt cod
branzino (nasello)	*brahn-tsEE-noh* (*nah-sEHl-loh*)	bass (hake)
calamari (seppie)	*kah-lah-mAH-ree* (*sAYp-pee-eh*)	squid
cozze	*kOH-tseh*	mussels
gamberetti	*gAHm-beh-rAY-tee*	prawns
granchi	*grAHn-key*	crabs
lumache	*loo-mAH-keh*	snails
merluzzo	*mayr-lOOt-tsoh*	cod
ostriche	*OHs-tree-keh*	oysters
polipo	*pOH-lee-poh*	octopus
salmone	*sahl-mOH-neh*	salmon
sardine	*sahr-dEE-neh*	sardines
scampi	*skAHm-pee*	shrimps
sogliola	*sOH-ly-ee-oh-lah*	flounder (sole)
trota	*trOH-tah*	trout
tonno	*tOHn-noh*	tuna
vongole	*vOHn-goh-leh*	clams
trance di pesce alla griglia	*trAHn-cheh dee pAY-sheh AHl-lah grEE-ly-ee-ah*	grilled fish steaks
fritto misto di pesce	*frEEt-toh mEEs-toh dee pAY-sheh*	mixed fried fish

Meat dishes are often sauced or served with some type of gravy. Here are some basic terms you'll encounter on Italian menus.

agnello (abbacchio)	*ah-ny-EHl-loh* (*ahb-bAH-key-oh*)	lamb

capretto	*kah-prAHy-toh*	goat
maiale	*mah-ee-AH-leh*	pork
manzo	*mAHn-tsoh*	beef
montone	*mohn-tOH-neh*	mutton
vitello	*vee-tEHl-loh*	veal

And some common cuts of meat, plus other terms you'll find on a menu:

affettati	*ahf-fayt-tAH-tee*	cold cuts
costate	*kohs-tAH-teh*	chops
animelle	*ah-nee-mEHl-leh*	sweetbreads
cervello	*chehr-vEHl-loh*	brains
fegato	*fAY-gah-toh*	liver
bistecca	*bees-tAY-kah*	steak
lingua	*lEEn-goo-ah*	tongue
pancetta	*pahn-chAYt-tah*	bacon
polpette	*pohl-pAYt-teh*	meatballs
prosciutto cotto	*proh-shee-OOt-toh kOHt-toh*	ham (cooked)
rognoni	*roh-ny-OH-nee*	kidneys

And some terms for fowl and game:

anitra	*AH-nee-trah*	duck
beccaccia	*bay-kAH-chee-ah*	woodcock
cappone	*kahp-pOH-neh*	capon
carne di cervo	*kAHr-neh dee chEHr-voh*	venison
coniglio	*koh-nEE-ly-ee-oh*	rabbit

fagiano	*fah-jee-AH-noh*	pheasant
faraona	*fah-rah-OH-nah*	guinea fowl
lepre	*lEH-preh*	hare
oca	*OH-kah*	goose
pernice	*pehr-nEE-cheh*	partridge
piccioncino	*pEE-chee-ohn-chEE-noh*	squab (pigeon)
pollo	*pOHl-loh*	chicken
porcellino di latte	*pohr-chehl-lEE-noh dee lAHz-teh*	suckling pig
quaglia	*koo-AH-ly-ee-ah*	quail
tacchino	*tah-kEY-noh*	turkey

I like it _____.	**Mi piace _____.**	*mee pee-AH-cheh*
■ baked	**al forno**	*ahl fOHr-noh*
■ boiled	**bollito**	*bohl-lEE-toh*
■ braised	**brasato al forno**	*brah-sAH-toh ahl fOHr-noh*
■ breaded	**impanato**	*eem-pah-nAH-toh*
■ broiled (grilled)	**alla griglia**	*AHl-lah grEE-ly-ee-ah*
■ browned	**rosolato**	*roh-soh-lAH-toh*
■ chopped	**tritato**	*tree-tAH-toh*
■ fried	**fritto**	*frEEt-toh*
■ in its natural juices	**nei suoi succhi naturali**	*nAY-ee soo-OH-ee sOO-key nah-too-rAH-lee*
■ mashed	**passato (puré)**	*pahs-sAH-toh (poo-rAY)*
■ poached	**bollito**	*bohl-lEE-toh*
■ pureed	**passato (puré)**	*pahs-sAH-toh (poo-rAY)*
■ roasted	**arrosto**	*ahr-rOHs-toh*

■ with sauce	**in salsa**	*een sAHl-sah*
■ sautéed	**soffritto**	*sohf-frEEt-toh*
■ steamed	**al vapore**	*ahl vah-pOH-reh*
■ stewed	**stufato**	*stoo-fAH-toh*
■ wrapped in aluminum foil	**in cartoccio**	*een kahr-tOH-chee-oh*

I prefer my eggs ____.	**Preferisco le uova ____.**	*preh-feh-rEEs-koh leh oo-OH-vah*
■ fried	**al tegame (fritte)**	*ahl teh-gAH-meh (frEEt-teh)*
■ hard-boiled	**sode**	*sOH-deh*
■ medium-boiled	**mollette**	*mohl-lEH-teh*
■ poached	**affogate (in camicia)**	*ahf-foh-gAH-teh (een kah-mEE-chee-ah)*
■ scrambled	**strapazzate**	*strah-pah-tzAH-teh*
■ soft-boiled	**alla coque (al guscio)**	*AHl-lah kOHk (ahl gOO-shee-oh)*

I'd like an omelet.	**Vorrei una frittata.**	*vohr-rEH-ee OO-nah freet-tAH-tah.*

I like the meat ____.	**La carne mi piace ____.**	*lah kAHr-neh mee pee-AH-cheh*
■ well done	**ben cotta**	*bEHn kOHt-tah*
■ medium	**cotta a puntino**	*kOHt-tah ah poon-tEE-noh*
■ rare	**al sangue**	*ahl sAHn-goo-eh*
■ tender	**tenera**	*tEH-neh-rah*

VEGETABLES

asparagi	*ahs-pAH-rah-jee*	asparagus
carciofi	*kahr-chee-OH-fee*	artichoke
carote	*kah-rOH-teh*	carrots

cavoli	*kAH-voh-lee*	cabbage
cavolfiori	*kah-vohl-fee-OH-ree*	cauliflower
ceci	*chay-chee*	chickpeas
cetriolo	*cheh-tree-OO-loh*	cucumber
fagioli	*fah-jee-oh-lEE*	beans (dried)
fagiolini	*fah-jee-oh-lEE-nee*	green beans
fave	*fAH-veh*	broad beans
finocchi	*fee-nOH-key*	fennel
funghi	*fOOn-ghee*	mushrooms
granturco	*grahn-tOO-rkoh*	corn (maize)
lattuga	*laht-tOO-gah*	lettuce
lenticchie	*len-tEE-key-eh*	lentils
melanzana	*meh-lahn-tsAH-nah*	eggplant (aubergine)
patate	*pah-tAH-teh*	potatoes
■ **patatine fritte**	*pah-tah-tEE-neh frEEt-teh*	French fries (chips)
peperoni	*peh-peh-rOH-nee*	pepper
piselli	*pee-sEHl-lee*	peas
pomodoro	*poh-moh-dOH-roh*	tomato
porcini	*pohr-chEE-nee*	wild mushroom, similar to cèpes
sedano	*sAY-dah-noh*	celery
spinaci	*spee-nAH-chee*	spinach
zucchini	*tsoo-KEY-nee*	green squash (courgettes)

SEASONINGS

I'd like _____.	Vorrei _____.	vohr-rEH-ee
■ butter	burro	bOOr-roh
■ horseradish	rafano	rAH-fah-noh
■ ketchup	ketchup	keh-chOHp
■ margarine	margarina	mahr-gah-rEE-nah
■ mayonnaise	maionese	mah-ee-oh-nAY-seh
■ mustard	senape, mostarda	sEH-nah-peh moh-stAHr-dah
■ olive oil	olio d'oliva	OH-lee-oh doh-lEE-vah
■ pepper (black)	pepe (nero)	pAY-peh (nAY-roh)
■ pepper (red)	pepe (rosso)	pAY-peh (rOHs-soh)
■ salt	sale	sAH-leh
■ sugar	zucchero	tsOO-keh-roh
■ saccharin	saccarina, dolcificante	sah-kah-rEE-nah dohl-chee-fee-kAHn-teh
■ vinegar	aceto	ah-chAY-toh

CHEESE

Is the cheese _____?	È il formaggio _____?	eh eel fohr-mAH-jee-oh
■ mild	dolce	dOHl-cheh
■ sharp	piccante	pee-kAHn-teh
■ hard	duro	dOO-roh
■ soft	molle	mOHl-leh

FRUITS AND NUTS

What kind of fruit do you have?	**Che frutta c'è?**	*kay frOOt-tah chEH*
albicocca	*ahl-bee-kOH-kah*	apricot
ananasso	*ah-nah-nAHs-soh*	pineapple
anguria	*ahn-gOO-ree-ah*	watermelon
arancia	*ah-rAHn-chee-ah*	orange
castagne	*kahs-tAH-ny-eh*	chestnuts
cedro	*chAY-droh*	lime
ciliege	*chee-lee-EH-jee-eh*	cherries
datteri	*dAHt-teh-ree*	dates
fichi	*fEE-key*	figs
fragole	*frAH-goh-leh*	strawberries
lampone	*lahm-pOH-neh*	raspberry
limone	*lee-mOH-neh*	lemon
mandarini	*mahn-dah-rEE-nee*	tangerines
mandorle	*mAHn-dohr-leh*	almonds
mela	*mAY-lah*	apple
more	*mOH-reh*	mulberries
noci	*nOH-chee*	nuts
nocciole	*noh-chee-OH-leh*	hazelnuts (filberts)
melone	*meh-lOH-neh*	melon
pera	*pAY-rah*	pear
pesca	*pAYs-kah*	peach
pompelmo	*pohm-pEHl-moh*	grapefruit

prugne	*prOO-ny-eh*	plum
uva	*OO-vah*	grape

DESSERT—SWEETS

torta	*tOHr-tah*	cake
dolci	*dOHl-chee*	sweets
macedonia di frutta	*mah-cheh-dOH-nee-ah dee frOOt-tah*	fresh fruit salad
mousse al cioccolato	*mOOs ahl chee-oh-koh-lAH-toh*	chocolate mousse
crema inglese	*krEH-mah een-glAY-seh*	custard
crostata	*kroh-stAH-tah*	pie
budino	*boo-dEE-noh*	pudding
■ **di pane**	*dee pAH-neh*	bread
■ **di crema**	*dee krEH-mah*	cream
■ **di riso**	*dee rEE-soh*	rice
crema di cara-mello	*crEH-mah dee kah-rah-mEHl-loh*	caramel custard
gelato	*jeh-lAH-toh*	ice cream
■ **al cioccolato**	*ahl chee-oh-koh-lAH-toh*	chocolate
■ **alla vaniglia**	*AHl-lah vah-nEE-ly-ee-ah*	vanilla
■ **alla fragola**	*AHl-lah frAH-goh-lah*	strawberry
■ **di caffè (con panna)**	*dee kahf-fEH (kOHn pAHn-nah)*	coffee (with whipped cream)

SPECIAL CIRCUMSTANCES

I am on a diet.	**Sono a dieta.**	*sOH-noh ah dee-EH-tah*
I'm a vegetarian.	**Sono vegetariano(a).**	*SOH-noh veh-jeh-tah-ree-AH-noh(nah)*
I can't eat anything made with _____.	**Non posso mangiare niente con _____.**	*nohn pOHs-soh mahn-jee-AH-reh nee-EHn-teh kohn*
I can't have any _____.	**Non posso avere _____.**	*Nohn pOHs-soh ah-vAY-reh*
■ alcohol	**sostanze alcoliche**	*soh-stAHn-tzeh ahl-kOH-lee-keh*
■ dairy products	**latticini**	*laht-tee-chEE-nee*
■ saturated fats	**grassi animali**	*grAHs-see ah-nee-mAH-lee*
■ seafood	**frutti di mare**	*frOOt-tee dee mAH-reh*
I'm on a _____ diet.	**Faccio una dieta _____.**	*fAH-chee-oh OO-nah dee-EH-tah*
■ diabetic	**per diabetici**	*pehr dee-ah-bEH-tee-chee*
■ low-fat	**a basso contenuto di grassi**	*ah bAHs-soh kohn-teh-nOO-toh dee grAHs-see*
■ low-sodium	**a basso contenuto di sale**	*ah bAHs-soh kohn-teh-nOO-toh dee sAH-leh*
■ restricted	**stretta**	*strAYt-tah*
■ simple	**semplice**	*sAYm-plee-cheh*
I'm looking for a dish _____.	**Cerco un piatto _____.**	*chAYr-koh oon pee-AHt-toh*
■ high in fiber	**ricco di fibra**	*rEEk-koh dee fEE-brah*

■ low in cholesterol **a basso contenuto di colesterolo** *ah bAHs-soh kohn-teh-nOO-toh dee koh-leh-steh-rOH-loh*

■ low in fat **a basso contenuto di grassi** *ah bAHs-soh kohn-teh-nOO-toh dee grAHs-see*

■ low in sodium **a basso contenuto di sale** *ah bAHs-soh kohn-teh-nOO-toh dee sAH-leh*

■ nondairy **senza prodotti lattici** *sEHn-tsah proh-dOHt-tee lAHt-tee-chee*

■ salt-free **senza sale** *sEHn-tsah sAH-leh*

■ sugar-free **senza zucchero** *sEHn-tsah tsOO-keh-roh*

■ without artificial coloring **senza coloranti artificiali** *sEHn-tsah koh-loh-rAHn-tee ahr-tee-fee-chee-AHl-ee*

■ without preservatives **senza preservativi** *sEHn-tsah pray-sayr-vah-tEE-vee*

I don't want anything fried (salted). **Non posso mangiare cose fritte (salate).** *nohn pOHs-soh mahn-jee-AH-reh kOH-seh frEEt-teh (sah-lAH-teh)*

Is this very spicy? **Questo è molto piccante?** *koo-AY-stoh eh mOHl-toh pee-kAHn-teh*

Do you have any dishes without meat? **Hanno piatti (cibi) senza carne?** *AHn-noh pee-AHt-tee (chEE-bee) sEHn-tsah kAHr-neh*

CULINARY PROBLEMS

It's _____. **È _____.** *EH*

■ bitter **acre** *AH-kreh*

■ burned **bruciato(a)** *broo-chee-AH-toh(ah)*

■ cold **freddo(a)** *frAYd-doh(ah)*

◼ overcooked	**troppo cotto(a)**	*trOHp-poh kOHt-toh(ah)*
◼ spoiled	**guasto(a)**	*goo-AHs-toh(ah)*
◼ too rare	**non è cotto(a) abbastanza**	*nohn eh kOHt-toh(ah) ahb-bah-stAHn-tzah*
◼ too salty	**troppo salato(a)**	*trOHp-poh sah-lAH-toh(ah)*
◼ too spicy	**troppo piccante**	*trOHp-poh pee-kAHn-teh*
◼ too sweet	**troppo dolce**	*trOHp-poh dOHl-che*
◼ tough	**duro(a)**	*dOO-roh(ah)*

BEVERAGES

Waiter, please bring me _____.	**Cameriere(a), per piacere mi porti _____.**	*kah-meh-ree-EH-reh(ah) pehr pee-ah-chAY-reh mee pOHr-tee*
coffee (regular or American)	**caffè**	*kahf-fEH*
◼ with milk	**caffelatte**	*kahf-fEH-lAHt-teh*
◼ with sugar	**con zucchero**	*kohn tsOO-keh-roh*
◼ without sugar	**senza zucchero**	*sEHn-tsah tsOO-keh-roh*
◼ with saccharin	**con saccarina**	*kohn sah-kah-rEE-nah*
◼ with cream	**con panna**	*kohn pAHn-nah*
Italian coffee	**espresso**	*ehs-prEHs-soh*
◼ with anisette	**corretto all' anisetta**	*kohr-rEHt-toh ahl-lah-nee-sAYt-tah*
iced (coffee)	**freddo**	*frAYd-doh*
tea	**tè**	*tEH*
◼ with milk	**con latte**	*kohn lAHt-teh*

■ with lemon	**con limone**	*kohn lee-mOH-neh*
■ with sugar	**con zucchero**	*kohn tsOO-keh-roh*
■ iced	**con ghiaccio**	*kohn ghee-AH-chee-oh*
water	**acqua**	*AH-koo-ah*
■ cold	**fredda**	*frAYd-dah*
■ iced	**con ghiaccio**	*kohn ghee-AH-chee-oh*
■ mineral	**minerale**	*mee-neh-rAH-leh*
■ (carbonated)	**gassata**	*gahs-sAH-tah*
■ (non-carbonated)	**naturale**	*nah-too-rAH-leh*
a glass of _____.	**un bicchiere di _____.**	*oon bee-key-EH-reh dee*
■ milk (cold)	**latte (fresco)**	*lAHt-teh (frAY-skoh)*
■ malted milk	**latte con malto**	*lAHt-teh kOHn mAHl-toh*
■ milk shake	**frullato di latte**	*frool-lAH-toh dee lAHt-teh*
■ orangeade	**aranciata**	*ah-rahn-chee-AH-tah*
■ punch	**punch**	*pOHn-ch*
■ soda	**bibita analcolica (soda)**	*bEE-bee-tah ah-nahl-kOH-lee-kah*
■ (fruit) juice	**succo di (frutta)**	*sOO-koh dee (frOOt-tah)*
■ lemonade	**limonata**	*lee-moh-nAH-tah*

SETTLING UP

The check, please.	**Il conto, per favore.**	*eel kOHn-toh pehr fah-vOH-reh*

Separate checks.	**Conti separati.**	*kOHn-tee seh-pah-rAH-tee*
Is the service included?	**È incluso il servizio?**	*EH een-klOO-soh eel sehr-vEE-tsee-oh*
I haven't ordered this.	**Non ho ordinato questo.**	*nohn oh ohr-dee-nAH-toh koo-AY-stoh*
I don't think the bill is right.	**Non penso che il conto sia corretto.**	*nohn pEHn-soh kay eel kOHn-toh sEE-ah kor-rEHt-toh*
We're in a hurry.	**Abbiamo fretta.**	*ahb-bee-AH-moh frAYt-tah*
This is for you.	**Questo è per lei.**	*koo-AYs-toh EH pehr lEH-ee*

MEETING PEOPLE

SMALL TALK

My name is _____.	**Il mio nome è _____.**	*eel mEE-oh nOH-meh EH*
Do you live here?	**Lei abita qui?**	*lEH-ee AH-bee-tah koo-EE*
Where are you from?	**Lei di dov'è?**	*lEH-ee dee doh-vEH*
I am _____.	**Vengo _____.**	*vEHn-goh*
■ from the United States	**dagli Stati Uniti**	*dAH-ly-ee stAH-tee oo-nEE-tee*
■ from Canada	**dal Canadà**	*dAHl kah-nah-dAH*
■ from England	**dall'Inghilterra**	*dahl-lEEn-gheel-tEHr-rah*

■ from Australia   **dall'Australia**   *dahl-lah-oos-trAH-lee-ah*

I like Italy (Rome) very much.   **L'Italia (Roma) mi piace moltissimo.** *lee-tAH-lee-ah (rOH-mah) mee pee-AH-cheh mohl-tEEs-see-moh*

I would like to go there.   **Mi piacerebbe andarci.**   *mee pee-ah-cheh-rAYb-beh ahn-dAHr-chee*

How long will you be staying?   **Quanto tempo resterà qui?** *koo-AHn-toh tEHm-poh reh-steh-rAH koo-EE*

I'll stay for a few days (a week).   **Resterò alcuni giorni (una settimana).**   *reh-steh-rOH ahl-kOO-nee jee-OHr-nee (OO-nah seht-tee-mAH-nah)*

What hotel are you staying at?   **In quale hotel (albergo) sta?** *een koo-AH-leh oh-tEHl (ahl-bEHr-goh) stAH*

What do you think of it?   **Che ne pensa?**   *kay nay pEHn-sah*

I (don't) like it very much.   **(Non) mi piace tanto.**   *(nohn) mee pee-AH-cheh tAHn-toh*

I think it's _____.   **Penso che sia _____.** *pEHn-soh kay sEE-ah*

■ beautiful   **bello**   *bEHl-loh*

■ interesting   **interessante**   *een-teh-rehs-sAHn-teh*

■ magnificent   **splendido (magnifico)**   *splEHn-dee-doh (mah-ny-EE-fee-koh)*

■ wonderful   **stupendo**   *stoo-pEHn-doh*

May I introduce _____?   **Posso presentarle _____?** *pOHs-soh preh-sehn-tAHr-leh*

■ my brother
(sister)

mio fratello (mia sorella)
mEE-oh frah-tEHl-loh (mEE-ah soh-rEHl-lah)

■ my father
(mother)

mio padre (mia madre) *mEE-oh pAH-dreh (mEE-ah mAH-dreh)*

■ my friend

il mio amico *eel mEE-oh ah-mEE-koh*

■ my husband (wife)

mio marito (mia moglie) *mEE-oh mah-rEE-toh (mEE-ah mOH-ly-ee-eh)*

■ my sweetheart

il mio ragazzo (la mia ragazza) *eel mEE-oh rah-gAH-tsoh (lah mEE-ah rah-gAH-tsah)*

■ my son (daughter)

mio figlio (mia figlia) *mEE-oh fEE-ly-ee-oh (mEE-ah fEE-ly-ee-ah)*

Glad to meet you.

Piacere. Lieto(a) di conoscerla. *pee-ah-chAY-reh lee-EH-toh(ah) dee koh-nOH-shehr-lah*

How do you do?

Come sta? *kOH-meh stah*

I am a(n) _____.

Sono _____. *sOH-noh*

■ accountant

ragioniere *rah-jee-oh-nee-EH-reh*

■ artist

artista *ahr-tEEs-tah*

■ businessperson

persona d'affari *pehr-sOH-nah dahf-fAH-ree*

■ construction
worker

operaio edile *oh-peh-rAH-ee-oh eh-dEE-leh*

■ cook

cuoco *koo-OH-koh*

■ dentist

dentista *dehn-tEE-stah*

■ doctor

dottore (dottoressa) *doht-tOH-reh (doht-toh-rAYs-sah)*

■ firefighter

vigile del fuoco *vEE-jee-leh dayl foo-OH-koh*

■ hairdresser   **parrucchiere(a)**   *pahr-roo-key-AY-reh(ah)*

■ lawyer   **avvocato (avvocatessa)**   *ahv-voh-kAH-toh (ahv-voh-kah-tAYs-sah)*

■ manager   **dirigente (manager)**   *dee-ree-jEHn-teh (manager)*

■ nurse   **infermiere(a)**   *een-fehr-mee-EH-reh(ah)*

■ police officer   **poliziotto(a)**   *poh-lee-tzee-OHt-toh(ah)*

■ salesperson   **commesso(a)**   *kohm-mAYs-soh(ah)*

■ secretary   **segretario(a)**   *seh-greh-tAH-ree-oh(ah)*

■ student   **studente (studentessa)**   *stoo-dEHn-teh (stoo-dehn-tAYs-sah)*

■ teacher   **maestro(a)**   *mah-AYs-troh(ah)*

■ waiter (waittress)   **cameriere(a)**   *kah-meh-ree-EH-reh(ah)*

Would you like a picture (snapshot)?   **Vuole che le scatti una foto (un'instantanea)?**   *voo-OH-leh kay leh skAHt-tee OO-nah fOH-toh (oon-een-stahn-tAH-neh-ah)*

Stand here (there).   **Si metta qui (lì).**   *see mAYt-tah koo-EE (lEE)*

Don't move.   **Non si muova.**   *nohn see moo-OH-vah*

Smile. That's it.   **Sorrida. Ecco fatto.**   *sohr-rEE-dah EH-koh fAHt-toh*

Will you take a picture of me (us)?   **Può farmi (farci) una foto?**   *poo-OH fAHr-mee (fAHr-chee) OO-nah fOH-toh*

DATING AND SOCIALIZING

May I have this dance?	**Le piacerebbe ballare con me?** *leh pee-ah-cheh-rAYb-beh bahl-lAH-reh kohn mAY*
With pleasure.	**Con piacere.** *kohn pee-ah-chAY-reh*
Would you like a drink (a cigarette)?	**Potrei offrirle da bere (una sigaretta)?** *poh-trEH-ee ohf-frEEr-leh dah bAY-reh (OO-nah see-gah-rAYt-tah)*
Do you have a light (matches)?	**Ha un accendino (un fiammifero)?** *ah oon ah-chayn-dEE-noh (oon fee-ahm-mEE-feh-roh)*
Do you mind if I smoke?	**Le dispiace se fumo?** *leh dee-spee-AH-cheh say fOO-moh*
May I call you?	**Posso telefonarle?** *pOHs-soh teh-leh-foh-nAHr-leh*
May I take you home?	**L'accompagno a casa?** *lahk-kohm-pAH-ny-oh ah kAH-sah*
Are you doing anything tomorrow?	**Che fa domani?** *kay fAH doh-mAH-nee*
Are you free this evening?	**È libero(a) stasera?** *EH lEE-beh-roh(ah) stah-sAY-rah*
Would you like to go to ____ together?	**Le piacerebbe andare insieme a ____?** *leh pee-ah-cheh-rEHb-beh ahn-dAH-reh een-see-EH-meh ah*
I'll wait for you in front of the hotel.	**L'aspetterò davanti all'hotel (all'albergo).** *lah-speht-teh-rOH dah-vAHn-tee ahl-loh-tEHl (ahl-lahl-bEHr-goh)*

I'll pick you up at your house (hotel).	**La verrò a prendere a casa sua (all'hotel).** *lah vehr-rOH ah prAYn-day-reh ah kAH-sah sOO-ah (ahl-loh-tEHl)*
What is your telephone number?	**Qual è il suo numero di telefono?** *koo-ahl-EH eel sOO-oh nOO-meh-roh dee teh-lEH-foh-noh*
Here's my telephone number (address).	**Ecco il mio numero di telefono (indirizzo).** *EHk-koh eel mEE-oh nOO-meh-roh dee teh-lEH-foh-noh (een-dee-rEE-tsoh)*
I'm single (married).	**Sono scapolo nubile (sposato[a]).** *sOH-noh scAH-poh-loh nOO-bih-leh (spoh-sAH-toh[ah])*
Is your husband (wife) here?	**Sta qui suo marito (la signora)?** *stAH koo-EE sOO-oh mah-rEE-toh (lah see-ny-OH-rah)*
I'm here with my family.	**Sono qui con la mia famiglia.** *sOH-noh koo-EE kohn lah mEE-ah fah-mEE-ly-ee-ah*
Do you have any children?	**Ha bambini?** *AH bahm-bEE-nee*
How many?	**Quanti?** *koo-AHn-tee*
How old are they?	**Quanti anni hanno?** *koo-AHn-tee AHn-nee AHn-noh*

SAYING GOOD-BYE

Nice to have met you.	**È stato un piacere conoscerla.** *EH stAH-toh oon pee-ah-chAY-reh koh-nOH-shehr-lah*

The pleasure was mine.	**Il piacere è stato mio.** *eel pee-ah-chAY-reh EH stAH-toh mEE-oh*
Regards to ____.	**Saluti a ____.** *sah-lOO-tee ah*
Thanks for the evening.	**Grazie della serata.** *grAH-tsee-eh dAYl-lah say-rAH-tah*
I must go home now.	**Adesso devo andarmene a casa.** *ah-dEHs-soh dAY-voh ahn-dAHr-meh-neh ah kAH-sah*
You must come to visit us.	**Deve venire a farci visita.** *dAY-veh veh-nEE-reh ah fAHr-chee vEE-see-tah*

SHOPPING

GOING SHOPPING

Where can I find ____?	**Dove posso trovare ____?** *dOH-veh pOHs-soh troh-vAH-reh*
▪ a bakery	**un fornaio** *oon fohr-nAH-ee-oh*
▪ a bookstore	**una libreria** *OO-nah lee-bray-rEE-ah*
▪ a butcher	**una macelleria** *OO-nah mah-chehl-leh-rEE-ah*
▪ a camera shop	**un negozio di fotocine** *oon neh-gOH-tsee-oh dee foh-toh-chEE-neh*
▪ a candy store	**un sale e tabacchi** *oon sAH-leh ay tah-bAH-key*
▪ a clothing store	**un negozio di abbigliamento** *oon neh-gOH-tsee-oh dee ahb-bee-ly-ee-ah-mEHn-toh*
▪ for children's clothes	**per bambini** *pehr bahm-bEE-nee*
▪ for men	**per uomini** *pehr oo-OH-mee-nee*

■ for women	**per signore**	*pehr see-ny-OH-reh*
■ a delicatessen	**una salumeria**	*OO-nah sah-loo-meh-rEE-ah*
■ a department store	**i grandi magazzini**	*ee grAHn-dee mah-gah-tsEE-nee*
■ a pharmacy (chemist)	**una farmacia**	*OO-nah fahr-mah-chEE-ah*
■ a florist	**un fioraio**	*oon fee-oh-rAH-ee-oh*
■ a gift (souvenir) shop	**un negozio di regali (souvenir)**	*oon neh-gOH-tsee-oh dee reh-gAH-lee (soo-vay-nEEr)*
■ a grocery store	**un negozio di alimentari**	*oon neh-gOH-tsee-oh dee ah-lee-mehn-tAH-ree*
■ a hardware store (ironmonger)	**un negozio di ferramenta**	*oon neh-gOH-tsee-oh dee fehr-rah-mEHn-tah*
■ a jewelry store	**una gioielleria**	*OO-nah jee-oh-ee-ehl-leh-rEE-ah*
■ a liquor store	**una enoteca**	*OO-nah eh-noh-tEH-kah*
■ a newsstand	**un'edicola (il giornalaio)**	*oo-neh-dEE-koh-lah (eel jee-ohr-nah-lAH-ee-oh)*
■ a record store	**un negozio di dischi**	*oon neh-gOH-tsee-oh dee dEE-skey*
■ a supermarket	**un supermercato**	*oon soo-pehr-mehr-kAH-toh*
■ a tobacco shop	**una tabaccherìa**	*OO-nah tah-bahk-keh-rEE-ah*
■ a toy store	**un negozio di giocattoli**	*oon neh-gOH-tsee-oh dee jee-oh-kAHt-toh-lee*

■ a wine shop	**una mescita, una cantina, una enoteca** *OO-nah mAY-shee-tah OO-nah kahn-tEE-nah OO-nah eh-noh-tEH-kah*
Young man, can you wait on me?	**Giovanotto, può occuparsi di me?** *jee-oh-vah-nOHt-toh poo-OH ohk-koo-pAHr-see dee meh*
Miss, can you help me?	**Signorina, può aiutarmi?** *see-ny-oh-rEE-nah poo-OH ah-ee-oo-tAHr-mee*
Do you take credit cards?	**Accettano carte di credito?** *ah-chEHt-tah-noh kAHr-teh dee krEH-dee-toh*
Can I pay with a traveler's check?	**Posso pagare con un traveler's check?** *pOHs-soh pah-gAH-reh kohn oon trAH-veh-lehs chEH-keh*

BOOKS

Is there a store that carries English-language books?	**C'è un negozio dove si vendono libri in lingua inglese?** *chEH oon neh-gOH-tsee-oh dOH-veh see vAYn-doh-noh lEE-bree een lEEn-goo-ah een-glAY-seh*
What is the best (biggest) bookstore here?	**Dov'è la migliore (la più grande) libreria qui?** *doh-vEH lah mee-ly-ee-OH-reh (lah pee-OO grAHn-deh) lee-breh-rEE-ah koo-EE*
I'm looking for a copy of _____.	**M'interessa una copia di _____.** *meen-teh-rEHs-sah OO-nah kOH-pee-ah dee*
The author of the book is _____.	**L'autore del libro è _____.** *lah-oo-tOH-reh dayl lEE-broh EH*

I'm just looking.	**Sto solo guardando.** *stoh sOH-loh goo-ahr-dAHn-doh*
Do you have books (novels) in English?	**Ha libri (romanzi) in inglese?** *ah lEE-bree (roh-mAHn-tsee) een een-glAY-seh*

I want _____.	**Desidero _____.** *deh-sEE-deh-roh*
■ a guide book	**una guida** *OO-nah goo-EE-dah*
■ a map of this city	**una pianta di questa città** *OO-nah pee-AHn-tah dee koo-AYs-tah cheet-tAH*
■ a pocket dictionary	**un dizionario tascabile** *oon dee-tsee-oh-nAH-ree-oh tah-skAH-bee-leh*
■ an Italian-English dictionary	**un dizionario italiano-inglese** *oon dee-tsee-oh-nAH-ree-oh ee-tah-lee-AH-noh een-glAY-seh*

I'll take these books.	**Prendo questi libri.** *prAYn-doh koo-AYs-tee lEE-bree*
Will you wrap them, please?	**Me l'incarta, per favore?** *meh leen-kAHr-tah pehr fah-vOH-reh*

CLOTHING

Is this the _____ department?	**È questo il reparto (la sezione) di _____?** *EH koo-AYs-toh eel ray-pAHr-toh (lah say-tzee-OH-neh) dee*
Would you please show me _____?	**Per favore, può mostrarmi _____?** *pehr fah-vOH-reh poo-OH moh-strAHr-mee*
■ a bathing suit	**un costume da bagno** *oon koh-stOO-meh dah bAH-ny-ee-oh*
■ a man's (lady's) belt	**una cintura per uomo (per signora)** *OO-nah cheen-tOO-rah pehr oo-OH-moh (pehr see-ny-OH-rah)*

■ a blouse	**una blusa (camicetta)** *OO-nah blOO-sah (kah-mee-chAYt-tah)*
■ boots	**degli stivali** *dAY-ly-ee stee-vAH-lee*
■ a bra	**un reggiseno** *oon reh-jee-sAY-noh*
■ a dress	**una veste** *OO-nah vEH-steh*
■ an evening gown	**un abito da sera** *oon AH-bee-toh dah sAY-rah*
■ leather (suede) gloves	**dei guanti di pelle (scamosciata)** *dAY-ee goo-AHn-tee dee pEHl-leh (skah-moh-shee-AH-tah)*
■ handkerchiefs	**dei fazzoletti** *dAY-ee fah-tsoh-lAYt-tee*
■ a hat	**un cappello** *oon kahp-pEHl-loh*
■ a jacket	**una giacca** *OO-nah jee-AHk-kah*
■ jeans	**dei jeans** *dAY-ee jeans*
■ a jogging suit	**un completo per jogging** *oon kohm-plEH-toh pehr jogging*
■ an overcoat	**un soprabito** *oon soh-prAH-bee-toh*
■ pajamas	**dei pigiama** *dAY-ee pee-jee-AH-mah*
■ panties	**delle mutandine** *dAYl-leh moo-tahn-dEE-neh*
■ pants	**dei pantaloni** *dAY-ee pahn-tah-lOH-nee*
■ panty hose	**un collant** *oon koh-lAHn*
■ a raincoat	**un impermeabile** *oon eem-pehr-meh-AH-bee-leh*
■ a robe (for lady)	**una vestaglia** *OO-nah veh-stAH-ly-ee-ah*
■ a robe (for man)	**una veste da camera** *OO-nah vEH-steh dah kAH-meh-rah*
■ sandals	**dei sandali** *dAY-ee sAHn-dah-lee*
■ sneakers	**delle scarpette** *dAYl-leh skahr-pAYt-teh*

■ a shirt **una camicia** *OO-nah kah-mEE-chee-ah*

■ (a pair of) shoes **un paio di scarpe** *oon pAH-ee-oh dee skAHr-peh*

■ shorts (briefs) **dei pantaloncini (delle mutande)** *dAY-ee pahn-tah-lohn-chEE-nee (dAYl-leh moo-tAHn-deh)*

■ a skirt **una gonna** *OO-nah gOHn-nah*

■ a slip **una sottoveste** *OO-nah soht-toh-vEH-steh*

■ slippers **delle pantofole** *dAYl-leh pahn-tOH-foh-leh*

■ socks **dei calzini** *dAY-ee kahl-tsEE-nee*

■ stockings **delle calze** *dAYl-leh kAHl-tseh*

■ a suit **un vestito** *oon veh-stEE-toh*

■ a sweater **una maglia** *OO-nah mAH-ly-ah*

■ a tee-shirt **una maglietta** *OO-nah mah-ly-ee-AYt-tah*

■ a tie **una cravatta** *OO-nah krah-vAHt-tah*

■ an undershirt **una canottiera** *OO-nah kah-noht-tee-EH-rah*

■ underwear **della biancheria intima** *dAYl-lah bee-ahn-keh-rEE-ah EEn-tee-mah*

■ a wallet **un portafoglio** *oon pohr-tah-fOH-ly-ee-oh*

Is there a special sale today? **Oggi c'è una vendita d'occasione?** *OH-jee chEH OO-nah vAYn-dee-tah dohk-kah-see-OH-neh*

I'd like a shirt with short (long) sleeves. **Vorrei una camicia con le maniche corte (lunghe).** *vohr-rEH-ee OO-nah kah-mEE-chee-ah kohn leh mAH-nee-keh kOHr-teh (lOOn-gheh)*

Do you have anything ____?	**Ha qualche cosa ____?** *AH koo-AHl-keh kOH-sah*
■ else	**d'altro** *dAHl-troh*
■ larger	**più grande** *pee-OO grAHn-deh*
■ less expensive	**meno costoso** *mAY-noh koh-stOH-soh*
■ longer	**più lungo** *pee-OO lOOn-goh*
■ of better quality	**di migliore qualità** *dee mee-ly-ee-OH-reh koo-ah-lee-tAH*
■ shorter	**più corto** *pee-OO kOHr-toh*
■ smaller	**più piccolo** *pee-OO pEE-koh-loh*
I don't like the color.	**Non mi piace il colore.** *nohn mee pee-AH-cheh eel koh-lOH-reh*
Do you have it in ____?	**Lo ha in ____?** *loh AH een*
■ black	**nero** *nAY-roh*
■ blue	**blu** *blOO*
■ brown	**marrone** *mahr-rOH-neh*
■ gray	**grigio** *grEE-jee-oh*
■ green	**verde** *vAYr-deh*
■ pink	**rosa** *rOH-sah*
■ red	**rosso** *rOHs-soh*
■ white	**bianco** *bee-AHn-koh*
■ yellow	**giallo** *jee-AHl-loh*
I want something in ____.	**Voglio qualche cosa ____.** *vOH-ly-ee-oh koo-AHl-keh kOH-sah*
■ chiffon	**di chiffon** *dee sheef-fOHn*
■ corduroy	**di velluto a coste** *dee vehl-lOO-toh ah kOH-steh*

- cotton **di cotone** *dee koh-tOH-neh*
- denim **di denim** *dee dEH-nim*
- felt **di feltro** *dee fAYl-troh*
- flannel **di flanella** *dee flah-nEHl-lah*
- gabardine **di gabardine** *dee gah-bahr-dEE-neh*
- lace **in pizzo** *een pEE-tsoh*
- leather **in pelle** *een pEHl-leh*
- linen **di lino** *dee lEE-noh*
- nylon **di nylon** *dee nAH-ee-lohn*
- permanent press **con piega permanente** *kohn pee-EH-gah pehr-mah-nEHn-teh*
- satin **di raso** *dee rAH-soh*
- silk **di seta** *dee sAY-tah*
- suede **di renna** *dee rAYn-nah*
- synthetic (polyester) **in poliestere** *een poh-lee-EH-steh-reh*
- terrycloth **in tessuto spugnoso** *een tehs-sOO-toh spoo-ny-OH-soh*
- velvet **di velluto** *dee vehl-lOO-toh*
- wool **di lana** *dee lAH-nah*
- wash-and-wear **che non si stira** *kay nohn see stEE-rah*

Show me something _____. **Mi faccia vedere qualche cosa _____.** *mee fAH-chee-ah veh-dAY-reh koo-AHl-kay kOH-sah*

- in a solid color **a tinta unita** *ah tEEn-tah oo-nEE-tah*
- with stripes **a righe** *ah rEE-gheh*
- with polka dots **a pallini** *ah pahl-lEE-nee*
- in plaid **a quadri** *ah koo-AH-dree*

Could you take my measurements? **Può prendermi le misure?** *poo-OH prEHn-dayr-mee leh mee-sOO-reh*

I take size (my size is) _____.	**La mia taglia è _____.** *lah mEE-ah tAH-ly-ee-ah EH*
■ small	**piccola** *pEEk-koh-lah*
■ medium	**media** *mEH-dee-ah*
■ large	**grande** *grAHn-deh*
Can I try it on?	**Posso provarmelo(la)?** *pOHs-soh proh-vAHr-meh-loh(lah)*
Can you alter it?	**Può aggiustarmelo(la)?** *poo-OH ah-jee-oo-stAHr-meh-loh(lah)*
Can I return the article (if I change my mind)?	**(Se non mi va), posso portarlo indietro?** *(say nohn mee vAH) pOHs-soh pohr-tAHr-loh een-dee-EH-troh*
Do you have something handmade?	**Non c'è nulla che sia fatto a mano?** *nohn chEH nOOl-lah kay sEE-ah fAHt-toh ah mAH-noh*
The zipper doesn't work.	**La cerniera non funziona.** *lah chehr-nee-EH-rah nohn fOOn-tsee-OH-nah*
It doesn't fit me.	**Non mi sta bene.** *nohn mee stAH bEH-neh*
It fits very well.	**Mi sta molto bene.** *mee stAH mOHl-toh bEH-neh*
I'll take it.	**Lo(la) prendo.** *loh(lah) prAYn-doh*
Will you wrap it?	**Me lo(la) impacchetta?** *meh loh(lah) eem-pahk-kEHt-tah*
I'd like to see the pair of shoes (boots) in the window.	**Vorrei vedere il paio di scarpe (stivali) in vetrina.** *vohr-rEH-ee veh-dAY-reh eel pAH-ee-oh dee skAHr-peh (stee-vAH-lee) een vay-trEE-nah*
They're too narrow (wide).	**Sono troppo strette (larghe).** *sOH-noh trOHp-poh strAYt-teh (lAHr-gheh)*

They pinch me.	**Mi stanno strette.** *mee stAHn-noh strAYt-teh*
They fit me.	**Mi stanno bene.** *mee stAHn-noh bEH-neh*
I'll take them.	**Le compro.** *leh kOHm-proh*
I also need shoe-laces.	**Ho bisogno anche dei lacci.** *oh bee-sOH-ny-oh AHn-keh dAY-ee lAH-chee*
That's all I want for now.	**Questo è tuttĬo quello che voglio per ora.** *koo-AYs-toh EH tOOt-toh koo-AYl-loh kay vOH-ly-ee-oh pehr OH-rah*

ELECTRICAL APPLIANCES

I want to buy ____.	**Vorrei comprare ____.** *vohr-rEH-ee kohm-prAH-reh*
■ an adapter	**un trasformatore** *oon trahs-fohr-mah-tOH-reh*
■ a battery	**una pila** *OO-nah pEE-lah*
■ a curling iron	**una spazzola riscaldante elettrica per fare la messa in piega** *OO-nah spAH-tzoh-lah ree-skahl-dAHn-teh eh-lEHt-tree-kah pehr FAH-reh lah mAYs-sah een pee-EH-gah*
■ an electric shaver	**un rasoio elettrico** *oon rah-sOH-ee-oh eh-lEHt-tree-koh*
■ an electric water pick	**un idropulsore elettronico per la pulizia dei denti** *oon ee-droh-pool-sOH-reh eh-leht-trOH-nee-koh pehr lah poo-lee-tzEE-ah dAY-ee dEHn-tee*
■ a food processor	**un frullatore** *oon frool-lah-tOH-reh*
■ a hair dryer	**un asciugacapelli** *oon ah-shee-OO-gah-kah-pAYl-lee*

■ a headset   **un casco asciugacapelli**   *oon kAH-skoh ah-shee-OO-gah-kah-pAYl-lee*

■ a manicure set   **un completo per manicure**   *oon kohm-plEH-toh pehr mah-nee-kOO-reh*

■ a plug   **una spina (elettrica)**   *OO-nah spEE-nah eh-lEHt-tree-kah*

■ a microwave   **un forno a micro onde**   *oon fOHr-noh ah mEE-kroh OHn-deh*

■ a toaster   **un tostapane**   *oon toh-stah-pAH-neh*

■ a transformer   **un trasformatore**   *oon trahs-fohr-mah-tOH-reh*

FOOD AND HOUSEHOLD ITEMS

I'd like _____.   **Vorrei _____.**   *vohr-rEH-ee*

Could you give me _____?   **Potrebbe darmi _____?**   *poh-trAYb-beh dAHr-mee*

■ a bar of soap   **una saponetta**   *OO-nah sah-poh-nEHt-tah*

■ a bottle of juice   **un succo di frutta**   *oon sOO-koh dee frOOt-tah*

■ a box of cereal   **una scatola di cereali**   *OO-nah skAH-toh-lah dee cheh-reh-AH-lee*

■ a can (tin) of tomato sauce   **una scatola di conserva di pomodoro**   *OO-nah skAH-toh-lah dee kohn-sEHr-vah dee poh-moh-dOH-roh*

■ a dozen eggs   **una dozzina d'uova**   *OO-nah doh-tsEE-nah doo-OH-vah*

■ a jar of coffee   **un vasetto di caffè**   *oon vah-sAYt-toh dee kahf-fEH*

■ a kilo of potatoes (just over 2 pounds)   **un chilo di patate**   *oon kEE-loh dee pah-tAH-teh*

- a half-kilo of cherries (just over 1 pound)

  mezzo chilo di ciliege *mEH-tsoh kEE-loh dee chee-lee-EH-jeh*

- a liter of milk (about 1 quart)

  un litro di latte *oon LEE-troh dee lAHt-teh*

- a package of candies

  un pacchetto di caramelle *oon pah-kAYt-toh dee kah-rah-mEHl-leh*

- 100 grams of cheese (about $\frac{1}{4}$ pound)

  cento grammi di formaggio (un etto) *chEHn-toh grAHm-mee dee fohr-mAH-jee-oh (oon EHt-toh)*

- a roll of toilet paper

  un rotolo di carta igienica *oon rOH-toh-loh dee kAHr-tah ee-jee-EH-nee-kah*

I'd like a kilo (about 2 pounds) of oranges.

Vorrei un chilo di arance. *vohr-rEY-ee oon kEY-loh dee ah-rAHn-chay*

- a half-kilo of butter

  mezzo chilo di burro *mAY-tsoh kEY-loh dee bOOr-roh*

- 200 grams (about $\frac{1}{2}$ pound) of cookies

  due etti di biscotti *dOO-eh EHt-tee dee bees-kOHt-tee*

- 100 grams (about $\frac{1}{4}$ pound) of bologna

  un etto di mortadella *oon EHt-toh dee mohr-tah-dAYl-lah*

What is this (that)?

Che cosa è questo (quello)? *kay kOH-sah EH koo-AYs-toh (koo-AYl-loh)*

Is it fresh?

È fresco? *EH frAY-skoh*

JEWELRY

I'd like to see _____.

Vorrei vedere _____. *vohr-rEH-ee veh-dAY-reh*

■ a bracelet   **un braccialetto**   *oon brah-chee-ah-lAYt-toh*

■ a brooch   **un fermaglio (una spilla)**   *oon fehr-mAH-ly-ee-oh (OO-nah spEEl lah)*

■ a chain   **una catenina**   *OO-nah kay-teh-nEE-nah*

■ a charm   **un ciondolo**   *oon chee-OHn-doh-loh*

■ some earrings   **degli orecchini**   *dAY-ly-ee oh-rehk-kEE-nee*

■ a necklace   **un monile**   *oon moh-nEE-leh*

■ a pin   **una spilla**   *OO-nah spEEl-lah*

■ a ring   **un anello**   *oon ah-nEHl-loh*

■ a rosary   **una corona del rosario**   *OO-nah koh-rOH-nah dayl roh-sAH-ree-oh*

■ a (wrist) watch   **un orologio da polso**   *oon oh-roh-lOH-jee-oh dah pOHl-soh*

Is this _____?   **Questo è _____?**   *koo-AYs-toh EH*

■ gold   **d'oro**   *dOH-roh*

■ platinum   **di platino**   *dee plAH-tee-noh*

■ silver   **d'argento**   *dahr-jEHn-toh*

■ stainless steel   **d'acciaio inossidabile**   *dah-chee-AH-ee-oh ee-nohs-see-dAH-bee-leh*

Is it solid gold or gold plated?   **È oro massiccio oppure oro placcato?**   *EH OH-roh mahs-sEE-chee-oh ohp-pOO-reh OH-roh plahk-kAH-toh*

How many carats is it?   **Di quanti carati è?**   *dee koo-AHn-tee kah-rAH-tee EH*

What is that (precious) stone?   **Che pietra (preziosa) è?**   *kay pee-EH-trah (preh-tsee-OH-sah) EH*

I want _____.   **Vorrei (voglio) _____.**   *vohr-rEH-ee (vOH-ly-ee-oh)*

■ an amethyst	**un'ametista**	*oo-nah-meh-tEE-stah*
■ an aqua-marine	**un'acquamarina**	*oo-nah-koo-ah-mah-rEE-nah*
■ a coral	**un corallo**	*oon koh-rAHl-loh*
■ a diamond	**un diamante**	*oon dee-ah-mAHn-teh*
■ an emerald	**uno smeraldo**	*OO-noh smeh-rAHl-doh*
■ ivory	**una cosa d'avorio**	*OO-nah kOH-sah dah-vOH-ree-oh*
■ jade	**una giada**	*OO-nah jee-AH-dah*
■ onyx	**un'onice**	*oon-OH-nee-cheh*
■ pearls	**delle perle**	*dAYl-leh pEHr-leh*
■ a ruby	**un rubino**	*oon roo-bEE-noh*
■ a sapphire	**uno zaffiro**	*OO-noh tsahf-fEE-roh*
■ a topaz	**un topazio**	*oon toh-pAH-tsee-oh*
■ a turquoise	**un turchese**	*oon toor-kAY-seh*
How much is it?	**Quanto costa?**	*koo-AHn-toh kOH-stah*
I'll take it.	**Lo(a) prendo.**	*loh(ah) prAYn-doh*

AUDIOVISUAL EQUIPMENT

Where is the _____ section?	**Dov'è la sezione _____?**	*doh-vEH lah seh-tsee-OH-neh*
■ classical music	**di musica classica**	*dee mOO-see-kah clAHs-see-kah*
■ popular music	**di musica popolare**	*dee mOO-see-kah poh-poh-lAH-reh*
■ latest hits	**degli ultimi successi**	*dAY-ly-ee OOl-tee-mee soo-chEHs-see*

■ Italian music **della musica italiana** *dAYl-lah mOO-see-kah ee-tah-lee-AH-nah*

■ opera **di musica d'opera** *dee mOO-see-kah dOH-peh-rah*

Do you have any songs of _____? **Avete la canzone di _____?** *ah-vay-teh lah kahn-tzOH-neh dee*

Is it recorded digitally? **È una registrazione digitale?** *EH OO-nah reh-jee-strah-tzee-OH-neh dee-jee-tAH-leh*

Is there an audio/video store in the neighborhood? **C'è qui vicino un negozio di articoli audio/video?** *chEH koo-ee vee-chEE-noh oon neh-gOH-tsee-oh dee ahr-tEE-koh-lee AH-oo-dee-oh/VEE-deh-oh*

I would like to buy _____. **Vorrei comprare _____.** *vohr-rEH-ee kohm-prAH-reh*

■ an analog cassette **una cassetta analogica** *OO-nah kahs-sAYt-tah ah-nah-lOH-jee-kah*

■ a portable CD player **un lettore CD portatile** *oon leht-tOH-reh see-dEE pohr-tAH-tee-leh*

■ CDs **dei CD** *dAY-ee see-dEE*

■ minidisks **dei minidischetti** (or **minidisks**) *dAY-ee mee-nee-dee-skAYt-tee*

■ recordable CDs **dei compact disks vuoti (registrabili, vergini)** *dAY-ee compact disks voo-OH-tee (reh-jee-strAH-bee-lee vAYr-jee-nee)*

■ a small cassette player **un piccolo stereo** *oon pEEk-koh-loh st-EH-reh-oh*

■ a small cassette recorder **un piccolo registratore a cassetta** *oon pEEk-koh-loh reh-jee-strah-tOH-reh ah kahs-sAYt-tah*

I need _____. **Ho bisogno di _____.** *oh bee-sOH-ny-oh dee*

■ a (digital) camcorder | **una videocamera (digitale)** *OO-nah vEE-deh-oh-kAH-meh-rah (dee-jee-tAH-leh)*

■ digital videofilm | **un videofilm digitale** *oon vee-deh-oh-fEElm dee-jee-tAH-leh*

■ DVD movies | **dei film DVD** *dAY-ee fEElm dee-vee-dee*

■ videofilm | **un film registrato su nastro video** *oon fEElm reh-jee-strAH-toh soo nAH-stroh vEE-deh-oh*

■ a VCR tape | **una videocassette** *OO-nah vee-deh-oh-kahs-sEHt-teh*

Do you have VCR or DVD movies with subtitles in English? | **Avete film con sottotitolo in inglese per videoregistratore o per DVD?** *ah-vAY-teh fEElm kohn soht-toh-tEE-toh-loh een-glAY-seh pehr vee-deh-oh-reh-jee-strah-tOH-reh oh pehr dee-vee-dee*

Will the warranty be honored in the U.S.? | **La garanzia sarà valida (accettata) negli Stati Uniti?** *lah gah-rahn-tsEE-ah sah-rAH vAH-lee-dah (ah-cheht-tAH-tah) nAYly-ee stAH-tee oo-nEE-tee*

Whom shall I contact if this malfunctions? | **Chi dovrò contattare se non funziona bene?** *key doh-vrOH kohn-taht-tAH-reh say nohn foon-tsee-OH-nah bEH-neh*

PHOTOGRAPHIC EQUIPMENT

Where is there a camera shop? | **Dov'è un negozio di fotocine (machine fotografiche)?** *doh-vEH oon neh-GOH-tsee-oh dee foh-toh-chEE-neh (mAHk-kee-neh foh-toh-grAH-fee-keh)*

I want a roll of color (black and white) film.	**Voglio un rullino a colori (in bianco e nero).** *vOH-ly-ee-oh oon rool-lEE-noh ah koh-lOH-ree (een bee-AHn-koh ay nAY-roh)*
I want a roll of 20 (36) exposures (for slides).	**Vorrei un rullino (per diapositive) di venti (trentasei) pose.** *vohr-rEH-ee oon rool-lEE-noh (pehr dee-ah-poh-see-tEE-veh) dee vAYn-tee (trehn-tah-sEH-ee) pOH-seh*
I want a Polaroid filmpack.	**Vorrei (voglio) un rullino per istantanee (polaroid).** *vohr-rEH-ee (vOH-ly-ee-oh) oon rool-lEE-noh pehr ee-stahn-tAH-neh-eh (polaroid)*
I need _____.	**Ho bisogno di _____.** *oh bee-sOH-ny-oh dee*
■ black and white film	**un film in bianco e nero** *oon fEElm een bee-AHn-koh ay nAY-roh*
■ a camera bag	**una custodia della macchina fotografica** *OO-nah koo-stOH-dee-ah dAYl-lah mAH-key-nah foh-toh-grAH-fee-kah*
■ camera batteries	**pile per la macchina fotografica** *pEE-leh pehr lah mAH-key-nah foh-toh-grAH-fee-kah*
■ digital camera disks	**dischetti digitali per la macchina fotografica** *dee-skAYt-tee dee-jee-tAH-lee pehr lah mAH-key-nah foh-toh-grAH-fee-kah*
■ a disposable camera	**una macchina fotografica usa e getta** *OO-nah mAII-key-nah foh-toh-grAH-fee-kah OO-sah ay jEHt-tah*
■ an expensive (inexpensive) camera	**una buona macchina fotografica (a buon mercato).** *OO-nah boo-OH-nah mAHk-kee-nah foh-toh-grAH-fee-kah (ah boo-OHn mayr-kAH-toh)*

■ film   **un rullino**   *oon rool-lEE-noh*

■ a flash   **il flash**   *eel flash*

■ a lens   **una lente**   *OO-nah lEHn-teh*

■ a point-and-shoot camera   **una macchina fotografica "vai e clicca"**   *OO-nah mAHk-kee-nah foh-toh-grAH-fee-kah vAH-ee ay klEEk-kah*

■ slide film   **un rullino per diapositive**   *oon rool-lEE-noh pehr dee-ah-poh-see-tEE-veh*

■ an SLR camera   **una macchina fotografica SLR**   *OO-nah mAHk-kee-nah foh-toh-grAH-fee-kah EHs-seh Ehl-leh Ehr-reh*

■ a tripod   **un treppiede**   *oon trehp-pee-EH-deh*

■ a zoom lens   **un obiettivo con zoom**   *oon oh-bee-ayt-tEE-voh kohn zoom*

Do they develop film?   **Sviluppano i rullini?**   *svee-lOOp-pah-noh ee rool-lEE-nee*

How much does it cost to develop a roll?   **Quanto costa far sviluppare un rullino?**   *koo-AHn-toh kOH-stah fahr svee-loop-pAH-reh oon rool-lEE-noh*

I want one print of each.   **Voglio una copia per ogni fotografia.**   *vOH-ly-ee-oh OO-nah kOH-pee-ah pehr OH-ny-ee foh-toh-grah-fEE-ah*

I want _____.   **Vorrei (voglio) _____.**   *vohr-rEH-ee (vOH-ly-ee-oh)*

■ an enlargement   **un ingrandimento**   *oon een-grahn-dee-mEHn-toh*

with a glossy (matte) finish   **su carta lucida (opaca, matta)**   *soo kAHr-tah lOO-chee-dah (oh-pAH-kah mAHt-tah)*

When can I pick up the pictures?   **Quando vengo a ritirarle?**   *koo-AHn-doh vEHn-goh ah ree-tee-rAHr-leh*

NEWSPAPERS AND MAGAZINES

Do you carry English newspapers (magazines)? | **Ha giornali (riviste) in inglese?** *a jee-ohr-nAH-lee (ree-vEE-steh) een een-glAY-seh*

I'd like to buy some (picture) postcards. | **Vorrei comprare delle cartoline (illustrate).** *vohr-rEH-ee kohm-prAH-reh dAYl-leh kahr-toh-lEE-neh (eel-loo-strAH-teh)*

SOUVENIRS, HANDICRAFTS

I'd like _____. | **Vorrei _____.** *vohr-rEH-ee*

■ a pretty gift | **un bel regalo** *oon bEHl reh-gAH-loh*

■ a small gift | **un regalino** *oon reh-gah-lEE-noh*

■ a souvenir | **un souvenir** *oon soo-veh-nEEr*

It's for _____. | **È per _____.** *EH pehr*

I don't want to spend more than 20 (30) dollars. | **Non voglio spendere più di venti (trenta) dollari.** *nohn vOH-ly-ee-oh spEHn-deh-reh pee-OO dee vAYn-tee (trEHn-tah) dOHl-lah-ree*

Could you suggest something? | **Potrebbe suggerirmi qualche cosa?** *poh-trAYb-beh soo-jeh-rEEr-mee koo-AHl-keh kOH-sah*

Would you show me your selection of _____? | **Che cosa potrebbe mostrarmi di _____?** *kay kOH-sah poh-trAYb-beh moh-strAHr-mee dee*

■ blown glass | **vetro soffiato** *vAY-troh sohf-fee-AH-toh*

■ carved objects | **legno intagliato** *lAY-ny-oh een-tah-ly-ee-AH-toh*

■ crystal | **cristallo** *kree-stAHl-loh*

■ earthenware (pottery)	**ceramiche**	*cheh-rAH-mee-keh*
■ fans	**ventagli**	*vehn-tAH-ly-ee*
■ jewelry	**oggetti preziosi**	*oh-jEHt-tee preh-tsee-OH-see*
■ lace	**pizzi**	*pEE-tsee*
■ leather goods	**articoli in pelle**	*ahr-tEE-koh-lee een pEHl-leh*
■ liqueurs	**liquori**	*lee-koo-OH-ree*
■ local handicrafts	**prodotti dell'artigianato locale?**	*proh-dOHt-tee dayl-lahr-tee-jee-ah-nAH-toh loh-kAH-leh*
■ musical instruments	**strumenti musicali**	*stroo-mEHn-tee moo-see-kAH-lee*
■ perfumes	**profumi**	*proh-fOO-mee*
■ (miniature) pictures	**quadretti (in miniatura)**	*koo-ah-drAYt-tee (een mee-nee-ah-tOO-rah)*
■ posters	**affissi, manifesti, poster**	*ahf-fEEs-see mah-nee-fEH-stee pOH-stehr*
■ religious articles	**articoli religiosi**	*ahr-tEE-koh-lee reh-lee-jee-OH-see*

STATIONERY ITEMS

I want to buy _____.	**Voglio comprare _____.**	*vOH-ly-ee-oh kohm-prAH-reh*
■ a ballpoint pen	**una penna a sfera**	*OO-nah pAYn-nah ah sfEH-rah*
■ a deck of cards	**un mazzo di carte**	*oon mAH-tsoh dee kAHr-teh*
■ envelopes	**delle buste**	*dAYl-leh bOO-steh*

■ an eraser **una gomma per cancellare** *OO-nah gOHm-mah pehr kahn-chehl-lAH-reh*

■ glue **della colla** *dAYl-lah kOHl-lah*

■ a notebook **un taccuino** *oon tahk-koo-EE-noh*

■ pencils **delle matite** *dAYl-leh mah-tEE-teh*

■ a pencil sharpener **un temperamatite** *oon tehm-peh-rah-mah-tEE-teh*

■ a ruler **una riga** *OO-nah rEE-gah*

■ Scotch tape **un nastro adesivo (uno scotch)** *oon nAH-stroh ah-deh-sEE-voh (OO-noh skO-ch)*

■ some string **del filo** *dayl fEE-loh*

■ typing paper **della carta per battere a macchina** *dAYl-lah kAHr-tah pehr bAHt-teh-reh ah mAH-kee-nah*

■ wrapping paper **della carta da imballaggio** *dAYl-lah kAHr-tah dah eem-bahl-lAH-jee-oh*

■ a writing pad **un blocchetto di carta** *oon blohk-kAYt-toh dee kAHr-tah*

■ writing paper **della carta da scrivere** *dAYl-lah kAHr-tah dah scrEE-veh-reh*

TOBACCO

A pack (carton) of cigarettes, please. **Un pacchetto (una stecca) di sigarette, per piacere.** *oon pah-kAYt-toh (OO-nah stAYk-kah) dee see-gah-rAYt-teh pehr pee-ah-chAY-reh*

■ filtered **con filtro** *kohn fEEl-troh*

■ unfiltered **senza filtro** *sEHn-tsah fEEl-troh*

■ menthol **alla menta** *ahl-lah mEHn-tah*

■ king-size **lunghe** *lOOn-gheh*

Are these cigarettes (very) strong (mild)?	**Sono (molto) forti (leggere) queste sigarette?** *sOH-noh (mOHl-toh) fOHr-tee (leh-jEH-reh) koo-AYs-teh see-gah-rAYt-teh*
Do you have American cigarettes?	**Ha sigarette americane?** *AH see-gah-rAYt-teh ah-meh-ree-kAH-neh*
What brand?	**Di che marca?** *dee kay mAHr-kah*
Please give me a pack of matches also.	**Mi dia anche una scatola di fiammiferi, per piacere.** *mee dEE-ah AHn-kay OO-nah skAH-toh-lah dee fee-ahm-mEE-fay-ree pehr pee-ah-chAY-reh*

TOILETRIES

Do you have _____?	**Ha _____?** *ah*
■ bobby pins	**delle forcine** *dAYl-leh fohr-chEE-neh*
■ a brush	**una spazzola** *OO-nah spAH-tsoh-lah*
■ cleansing cream	**della crema detergente** *dAYl-lah crEH-mah day-tehr-jEHn-teh*
■ a comb	**un pettine** *oon pEHt-tee-neh*
■ a deodorant	**un deodorante** *oon deh-oh-doh-rAHn-teh*
■ (disposable) diapers	**dei pannolini usa e getta** *dAY-ee pahn-noh-lEE-nee OO-sah ay jEHt-tah*
■ emery boards	**delle limette per le unghie** *dAYl-leh lee-mEHt-teh pehr leh OOn-ghee-eh*
■ eyeliner	**un eye liner** *oon eye liner*

■ eye shadow   **l'ombretto**   *lohm-brAYt-toh*

■ eyebrow pencil   **una matita per le sopracciglia**
OO-nah mah-tEE-tah pehr leh soh-prah-chEE-ly-ee-ah

■ hair spray   **della lacca per capelli**   *dAYl-la lAHk-kah pehr kah-pAYl-lee*

■ lipstick   **il lipstick (rossetto per le labbra)**
eel lipstick (rohs-sEHt-toh pehr leh lAHb-brah)

■ make-up   **il make-up (trucco)**   *eel make up (trOOk-koh)*

■ mascara   **del mascara**   *dAYl mah-skAH-rah*

■ a mirror   **uno specchio**   *OO-noh spEHk-key-oh*

■ mouthwash   **del disinfettante per la bocca**
dayl dee-seen-feht-tAHn-teh pehr lah bOHk-kah

■ nail clippers   **dei tagliaunghie**   *dAY-ee tah-ly-ee-ah-OOn-ghee-eh*

■ a nail file   **una limetta per le unghie**   *OO-nah lee-mAYt-tah pehr leh OOn-ghee-eh*

■ nail polish   **dello smalto per le unghie**   *dAYl-loh smAHl-toh pehr leh OOn-ghee-eh*

■ nail polish remover   **dell'acetone**   *dayl-lah-cheh-tOH-neh*

■ a razor   **un rasoio di sicurezza**   *oon rah-sOH-ee-oh dee see-koo-rAY-tsah*

■ razor blades   **delle lamette**   *dAYl-leh lah-mAYt-teh*

■ rouge   **il rossetto (belletto)**   *eel rohs-sEHt-toh (behl-lEHt-toh)*

■ sanitary napkins   **degli assorbenti (igienici)**   *dAY-ly-ee ahs-sohr-bEHn-tee (ee-jee-EH-nee-chee)*

■ (cuticle) scissors	**delle forbicine**	*dAYl-leh fohr-bee-chEE-neh*
■ shampoo	**dello shampoo**	*dAYl-loh ShAHm-poh*
■ shaving lotion	**un dopobarba**	*oon doh-poh-bAHr-bah*
■ soap	**del sapone**	*dayl sah-pOH-neh*
■ a sponge	**una spugna**	*OO-nah spOO-ny-ah*
■ tampons	**dei tamponi**	*dAY-ee tahm-pOH-nee*
■ tissues	**dei fazzolettini di carta**	*dAY-ee fah-tsoh-leht-tEE-nee dee kAHr-tah*
■ toilet paper	**della carta igienica**	*dAYl-lah kAHr-tah ee-jee-EH-nee-kah*
■ a toothbrush	**uno spazzolino per i denti**	*OO-noh spah-tsoh-lEE-noh pehr ee dEHn-tee*
■ toothpaste	**un dentifricio**	*oon dEHn-tee-frEE-chee-oh*
■ tweezers	**delle pinzette**	*dAYl-leh peen-tsEHt-teh*

PERSONAL CARE AND SERVICES

AT THE BARBER

Where is there a good barbershop?	**Dove potrei trovare (una buona barberia) un buon parrucchiere?** *dOH-veh poh-trEH-ee troh-vAH-reh (OO-nah boo-OH-nah bahr-beh-rEE-ah) oon boo-OHn pahr-rook-key-EH-reh*
Do I have to wait long?	**C'è da aspettare molto?** *chEH dah-speht-tAH-reh mOHl-toh*

Am I next?	**È arrivato il mio turno?** *EH ahr-ree-vAH-toh eel mEE-oh tOOr-noh*
I want a shave.	**Voglio farmi la barba.** *vOH-ly-ee-oh fAHr-mee lah bAHr-bah*
I want a haircut.	**Voglio un taglio di capelli.** *vOH-ly-ee-oh oon tAH-ly-ee-oh dee kah-pAYl-lee*
Short in back, long in front.	**Corti dietro, lunghi davanti.** *kOHr-tee dee-EH-troh lOOn-ghee dah-vAHn-tee*
Leave it long.	**Me li lasci lunghi.** *meh-lee lAH-shee lOOn-ghee*
I want it (very) short.	**Li voglio (molto) corti.** *lee vOH-ly-ee-oh (mOHl-toh) kOHr-tee*
You can cut a little _____.	**Me li può tagliare un po' _____.** *meh lee poo-OH tah-ly-ee-AH-reh oon pOH*
■ in back	**di dietro** *dee dee-EH-troh*
■ in front	**sul davanti** *sool dah-vAHn-tee*
■ off the top	**sopra** *sOH-prah*
I part my hair _____.	**Porto la riga _____.** *pOHr-toh lah rEE-gah*
■ on the left	**a sinistra** *ah see-nEE-strah*
■ on the right	**a destra** *ah dEH-strah*
■ in the middle	**al centro** *ahl chEHn-troh*
I comb my hair straight back.	**Porto i capelli pettinati all'indietro.** *pOHr-toh ee kah-pAYl-lee peht-tee-nAH-tee ahl-leen-dee-EH-troh*
Cut a little bit more here.	**Tagli un po'di più qui (per favore).** *tAH-ly-ee oon pOH dee pee-OO koo-EE (pehr fah-vOH-reh)*

That's enough.	**Basta così.** *bAH-stah koh-sEE*
It's fine that way.	**Così è magnifico.** *Koh-sEE EH mah-ny-EE-fee-koh*
Please trim _____.	**Può spuntarmi _____.** *poo-OH spoon-tAHr-mee*
■ my beard	**il pizzo (la barba)** *eel pEE-tsoh (lah bAHr-bah)*
■ my moustache	**i baffi** *ee bAHf-fee*
■ my sideburns	**le basette** *leh bah-sAYt-teh*
Where's the mirror?	**Dov'è lo specchio?** *doh-vEH loh spEHK-key-oh*
How much do I owe you?	**Quanto le devo?** *koo-AHn-toh leh dAY-voh*
Is service included?	**È incluso il servizio?** *EH een-klOO-soh eel sehr-vEE-tsee-oh*

AT THE BEAUTY PARLOR

Is there a beauty parlor (hairdresser) near the hotel?	**C'è una parrucchiera vicino all'albergo?** *chEH OO-nah pahr-rook-key-EH-rah vee-chEE-noh ahl-lahl-bEHr-goh*
I'd like an appointment for this afternoon (tomorrow).	**Vorrei un appuntamento per questo pomeriggio (per domani).** *vohr-rEH-ee oon ahp-poon-tah-mEHn-toh pehr koo-AYs-toh poh-meh-rEE-jee-oh (pehr doh-mAH-nee)*
Can you give me _____?	**Può farmi _____?** *poo-OH fAHr-mee*
■ a color rinse	**un cachet** *oon kah-shEH*

■ a facial massage   **un massaggio facciale**   *oon mahs-sAH-jee-oh fah-chee-AH-leh*

■ a haircut ·   **un taglio di capelli**   *oon tAH-ly-oh dee kah-pAYl-lee*

■ a blunt haircut   **una spuntatina**   *OO-nah spoon-tah-tEE-nah*

■ a layered haircut   **un taglio scalato**   *oon tAH-ly-oh skah-lAH-toh*

■ a manicure   **la manicure**   *lah mah-nee-kOO-reh*

■ a pedicure   **il pedicure**   *eel peh-dee-kOO-reh*

■ a permanent   **una permanente**   *OO-nah pehr-mah-nAYn-teh*

■ a shampoo   **lo shampoo**   *loh shAHm-poh*

■ a shave   **una depilazione**   *OO-nah deh-pee-lah-tzee-OH-neh*

■ a tint   **una tintura**   *OO-nah teen-tOO-rah*

■ a touch-up   **una ritoccatina**   *OO-nah ree-tohk-kah-tEE-nah*

■ a trim   **una spuntatina**   *OO-nah spoon-tah-tEE-nah*

■ a wash and set   **shampoo e messa in piega**   *shAHm-poh ay mAYs-sah een pee-AY-gah*

■ a waxing   **una depilazione mediante ceretta**   *OO-nah deh-pee-lah-tzee-OH-neh meh-dee-AHn-teh cheh-rAYt-tah*

I'd like to see a color chart.   **Vorrei vedere il cartellino dei colori.** *vohr-rEH-ee veh-dAY-reh eel kahr-tehl-lEE-noh dAY-ee koh-lOH-ree*

I want _____.   **Voglio _____.**   *vOH-ly-ee-oh*

■ auburn   **un color rame**   *oon koh-lOHr rAH-meh*

■ (light) blond   **un biondo (chiaro)**   *oon bee-OHn-doh (key-AH-roh)*

■ brunette   **un bruno**   *oon brOO-noh*

■ a darker color   **un colore più scuro**   *oon koh-lOH-reh pee-OO skOO-roh*

■ a lighter color   **un colore più chiaro**   *oon koh-lOH-reh pee-OO key-AH-roh*

■ the same color   **lo stesso colore**   *loh stAYs-soh koh-lOH-reh*

■ highlights   **i colpi di sole**   *ee kOHl-pee dee sOH-leh*

Don't apply any hair spray.   **Non mi metta nessuna lacca.** *nohn mee mEHt-tah nays-sOO-nah lAHk-kah*

Not too much hair spray.   **Non troppa lacca.**   *nohn trOHp-pah lAHk-kah*

I want my hair _____.   **Vorrei (voglio) i capelli _____.** *vohr-rEH-ee (vOH-ly-ee-oh) ee kah-pEHl-lee*

■ with bangs   **con la frangia**   *kohn lah frAHn-jee-ah*

■ in a bun   **a nodo (a crocchia)**   *ah nOH-doh (ah krOHk-key-ah)*

■ in curls   **a boccoli**   *ah bOHk-koh-lee*

■ with waves   **ondulati**   *ohn-doo-lAH-tee*

Where's the mirror?   **Dov'è lo specchio?**   *doh-vEH loh spEHk-key-oh*

How much do I owe you?   **Quanto le devo?**   *koo-AHn-toh leh dAY-voh*

Is service included?   **È incluso il servizio?**   *EH een-klOO-soh eel sehr-vEE-tsee-oh*

LAUNDRY AND DRY CLEANING

Where is the nearest laundry (dry cleaner's)?	**Dov'è la lavanderia (la tintoria) più vicina?** *doh-vEH lah lah-vahn-deh-rEE-ah (lah teen-toh-rEE-ah) pee-OO vee-chEE-nah*
I have a lot of (dirty) clothes to be _____.	**Ho molta biancheria (sporca) da _____.** *oh mOHl-tah bee-ahn-keh-rEE-ah (spOHr-kah) dah*

- dry-cleaned   **lavare a secco** *lah-vAH-reh ah sAYk-koh*
- washed   **lavare** *lah-vAH-reh*
- mended   **rammendare** *rahm-mehn-dAH-reh*
- ironed   **stirare** *stee-rAH-reh*

Here's the list:	**Ecco l'elenco:** *EHk-koh leh-lEHn-koh*

- 3 shirts (men's)   **tre camicie (da uomo)** *tray kah-mEE-chee-eh (dah oo-OH-moh)*
- 12 handkerchiefs   **dodici fazzoletti** *dOH-dee-chee fah-tsoh-lAYt-tee*
- 6 pairs of socks   **sei paia di calzini** *sAY-ee pAH-ee-ah dee kahl-tsEE-nee*
- 1 blouse (nylon)   **una blusa (di nylon)** *oo-nah blOO-sah (dee nAH-ee-lohn)*
- 4 shorts   **quattro mutande** *koo-AHt-tro moo-tAHn-deh*
- 2 pajamas   **due pigiama** *dOO-eh pee-jee-AH-mah*
- 2 suits   **due vestiti** *dOO-eh veh-stEE-tee*
- 3 ties   **tre cravatte** *tray krah-vAHt-teh*
- 2 dresses (cotton)   **due vesti (di cotone)** *dOO-eh vEH-stee (dee koh-tOH-neh)*
- 2 skirts   **due gonne** *dOO-eh gOHn-neh*
- 1 sweater (wool)   **una maglia (di lana)** *OO-nah mAH-ly-ah (dee lAH-nah)*

I need them (for) _____.	**Mi occorrono (per) _____.** *mee ohk-kOHr-roh-noh (pehr)*
■ as soon as possible	**al più presto possibile** *ahl pee-OO prEH-stoh pohs-sEE-bee-leh*
■ tonight	**stasera** *stah-sAY-rah*
■ tomorrow	**domani** *doh-mAH-nee*
■ next week	**la settimana prossima** *lah seht-tee-mAH-nah prOHs-see-mah*
■ the day after tomorrow	**dopodomani** *doh-poh-doh-mAH-nee*
When will you bring it (them) back?	**Quando lo (li) riporterà?** *koo-AHn-doh loh (lee) ree-pohr-teh-rAH*
When will it be ready?	**Quando sarà pronto?** *koo-AHn-doh sah-rAH prOHn-toh*
There's a button missing.	**Manca un bottone.** *mAHn-kah oon boht-tOH-neh*
Can you sew it on?	**Può riattaccarlo?** *poo-OH ree-aht-tahk-kAHr-loh*
This isn't my laundry.	**Questa non è la mia biancheria.** *koo-AYs-tah nohn EH lah mEE-ah bee-ahn-keh-rEE-ah*

SHOE REPAIRS

Can you fix these shoes (boots)?	**Può ripararmi queste scarpe (questi stivali)?** *poo-OH ree-pah-rAHr-mee koo-AYs-teh skAHr-peh (koo-AYs-tee stee-vAH-lee)*
Put on (half) soles and rubber heels.	**Ci metta le (mezze) suole e i tacchi di gomma.** *chee mEHt-tah leh (mEH-tseh) soo-OH-leh ay ee tAH-key dee gOHm-mah*

I'd like to have my shoes shined too.	**Vorrei anche che mi lucidasse le scarpe.** *vohr-rEH-ee AHn-keh kay mee loo-chee-dAHs-seh leh skAHr-peh*
When will they be ready?	**Quando saranno pronte?** *koo-AHn-doh sah-rAHn-noh prOHn-teh*
I need them by Saturday (without fail).	**Mi occorrono per sabato (assolutamente).** *mee ohk-kOHr-roh-noh pehr sAH-bah-toh (ahs-soh-loo-tah-mEHn-teh)*

WATCH REPAIRS

Can you fix this watch (alarm clock) (for me)?	**(Mi) può aggiustare quest'orologio (questa sveglia)?** *(mee) poo-OH ah-jee-oo-stAH-reh koo-ay-stoh-roh-lOH-jee-oh (koo-AYs-tah svAY-ly-ee-ah)*
Can you clean it?	**Può pulirlo(la)?** *poo-OH poo-lEEr-loh(lah)*
I dropped it.	**L'ho lasciato(a) cadere.** *lOH lah-shee-AH-toh(tah) kah-dAY-reh*
It's running slow (fast).	**Va piano (in anticipo).** *vAH pee-AH-noh (een ahn-tEE-chee-poh)*
It's stopped.	**S'è fermato(a).** *sEH fehr-mAH-toh(tah)*
I need _____.	**Ho bisogno di _____.** *oh bee-sOH-ny-oh dee*
■ a crystal, glass	**un vetro** *oon vAY-troh*
■ an hour hand	**una lancetta delle ore** *OO-nah lahn-chAYt-tah dAYl-leh OH-reh*
■ a minute hand	**una lancetta dei minuti** *OO-nah lahn-chAYt-tah dAY-ee mee-nOO-tee*
■ a second hand	**una lancetta dei secondi** *OO-nah lahn-chAYt-tah dAY-ee seh-kOHn-dee*

■ a stem   **una vite**   *oo-nah vEE-teh*

■ a battery   **una pila**   *oo-nah pEE-lah*

When will it be
ready?

Quando sarà pronto?   *koo-AHn-doh
sah-rAH prOHn-toh*

May I have a
receipt?

Posso avere la ricevuta?   *pOHs-
soh ah-vAY-reh lah ree-cheh-vOO-tah*

CAMERA REPAIRS

Can you fix this
camera (movie
camera)?

**Può aggiustare questa macchina
fotografica (questa cinepresa)?**
*poo-OH ah-jee-oo-stAH-reh koo-
AYs-tah mAH-kee-nah foh-toh-grAH-
fee-kah (koo-AYs-tah chee-neh-prAY-
sah)*

The film doesn't
advance.

Si è bloccato il rullino.   *see EH
bloh-kAH-toh eel rool-lEE-noh*

I think I need new
batteries.

**Penso di aver bisogno delle pile
nuove.**   *pEHn-soh dee ah-vAYr bee-
sOH-ny-oh dAYl-leh pEE-leh noo-OH-
veh*

How much will
the repair cost?

Quanto mi costerà farla aggiustare?
*koo-AHn-toh mee koh-steh-rAH fAHr-
lah ah-jee-oo-stAH-reh*

When can I come
and get it?

Quando posso venire a ritirarla?
*koo-AHn-doh pOHs-soh veh-nEE-reh
ah ree-tee-rAHr-lah*

I need it as soon as
possible.

Ne ho bisogno al più presto possibile.
*nay oh bee-sOH-ny-oh ahl pee-OO
prEH-stoh pohs-sEE-bee-leh*

MEDICAL CARE

THE PHARMACY (CHEMIST)

Where is the nearest (all-night) pharmacy (chemist)?	**Dov'è la farmacia (notturna) più vicina?** *doh-vEH lah fahr-mah-chEE-ah (noht-tOOr-nah) pee-OO vee-chEE-nah*
At what time does the pharmacy open (close)?	**A che ora apre (chiude) la farmacia?** *ah kay OH-rah AH-preh (key-OO-deh) lah fahr-mah-chEE-ah*
I need something for _____.	**Ho bisogno di qualche cosa per _____.** *oh bee-sOH-ny-oh dee koo-AHl-keh kOH-sah pehr*

- a cold   **il raffreddore** *eel rahf-frehd-dOH-reh*
- constipation   **la stitichezza** *lah stee-tee-kAY-tsah*
- a cough   **la tosse** *lah tOHs-seh*
- diarrhea   **la diarrea** *lah dee-ahr-rEH-ah*
- a fever   **la febbre** *lah fEHb-breh*
- hay fever   **una rinite da fieno** *OO-nah ree-nEE-teh dah fee-EH-noh*
- a headache   **il mal di testa** *eel mAHl dee tEHs-tah*
- insomnia   **l'insonnia** *leen-sOHn-nee-ah*
- motion sickness (seasickness)   **il mal d'auto (di mare)** *eel mAHl dAH-oo-toh (dee mAH-reh)*
- sunburn   **la scottatura solare** *lah skoht-tah-tOO-rah soh-lAH-reh*
- a toothache   **il mal di denti** *eel mAHl dee dEHn-tee*
- an upset stomach   **il mal di stomaco** *eel mAHl dee stOH-mah-koh*

I do not have a prescription.	**Non ho la ricetta medica.** *nohn OH lah ree-chEHt-tah mEH-dee-kah*
May I have it right away?	**Posso averla subito?** *pOHs-soh ah-vAYr-lah sOO-bee-toh*
It's an emergency.	**È un'emergenza.** *eh oo-neh-mehr-jEHn-tsah*
How long will it take?	**Quanto tempo ci vorrà?** *koo-AHn-toh tEHm-poh chee vohr-rAH*
When can I come for it?	**Quando potrò venire a prenderla?** *koo-AHn-doh poh-trOH veh-nEE-reh ah prAYn-dehr-lah*
I would like _____.	**Vorrei _____.** *vohr-rEH-ee*
■ adhesive tape	**un nastro adesivo** *oon nAH-stroh ah-deh-sEE-voh*
■ alcohol	**dell'alcool** *dayl-lAHl-koh-ohl*
■ an antacid	**un antiacido** *oon ahn-tee-AH-chee-doh*
■ an antiseptic	**un antisettico** *oon ahn-tee-sEHt-tee-koh*
■ aspirins	**delle aspirine** *dAYl-leh ah-spee-rEE-neh*
■ Band-Aids	**dei cerotti** *dAY-ee cheh-rOHt-tee*
■ contraceptives	**dei contraccettivi** *dAY-ee kohn-trah-cheht-tEE-vee*
■ corn plasters	**dei callifughi** *dAY-ee kahl-lEE-foo-ghee*
■ cotton balls	**del cotone idrofilo** *dayl koh-tOH-neh ee-drOH-fee-loh*
■ cough drops (syrup)	**delle pasticche (dello sciroppo) per la tosse** *dAYl-leh pahs-tEEk-keh (dAHl-loh shee-rOHp-poh) pehr lah tOHs-seh*
■ eardrops	**delle gocce per gli orecchi** *dAYl-leh gOH-cheh pehr ly-ee oh-rAYk-key*

■ eyedrops	**del collirio**	*dayl kohl-lEE-ree-oh*
■ iodine	**della tintura di iodio**	*dAYl-lah teen-tOO-rah dee ee-OH-dee-oh*
■ a (mild) laxative	**un lassativo (leggero)**	*oon lahs-sah-tEE-voh (lay-jEH-roh)*
■ milk of magnesia	**della magnesia**	*dAYl-lah mah-ny-ee-EH-see-ah*
■ prophylactics	**dei profilattici**	*dAY-ee proh-fee-lAHt-tee-chee*
■ sanitary napkins	**degli assorbenti (igienici)**	*dAY-ly-ee ahs-sohr-bEHn-tee (ee-jee-EH-nee-chee)*
■ suppositories	**delle supposte**	*dAYl-leh soop-pOH-steh*
■ talcum powder	**del borotalco**	*dayl boh-roh-tAHl-koh*
■ tampons	**dei tamponi**	*dAY-ee tahm-pOH-nee*
■ a thermometer	**un termometro**	*oon tehr-mOH-meh-troh*
■ vitamins	**delle vitamine**	*dAYl-leh vee-tah-mEE-neh*

WITH THE DOCTOR

I don't feel well.	**Non mi sento bene.**	*nohn mee sEHn-toh bEH-neh*
I feel sick.	**Mi sento male.**	*mee sEHn-toh mAH-leh*
I need a doctor right away.	**Ho bisogno urgente del medico.**	*oh bee-sOH-ny-oh oor-jEHn-teh dayl mEH-dee-koh*
Do you know a doctor who speaks English?	**Conosce un dottore che parla inglese?**	*koh-nOH-sheh oon doht-tOH-reh kay pAHr-lah een-glAY-seh*

Where is his office (surgery)?	**Dov'è il suo ambulatorio?** *doh-vEH eel sOO-oh ahm-boo-lah-tOH-ree-oh*
Will the doctor come to the hotel?	**Il dottore potrà venire all'hotel?** *eel doht-tOH-reh poh-trAH veh-NEE-reh ahl-loh-tEHl*
I feel dizzy.	**Mi gira la testa (ho le vertigini).** *mee jEE-rah lah tEHs-tah (oh leh vehr-tEE-jee-nee)*
I feel weak.	**Mi sento debole.** *mee sEHn-toh dAY-boh-leh*
I (think I) have _____.	**(Credo che) ho _____.** *(kreh-doh kay) oh*
▪ an abscess	**un ascesso** *oon ah-shEHs-soh*
▪ a broken bone	**una frattura** *OO-nah frat-tOO-rah*
▪ a bruise	**una contusione** *OO-nah kohn-too-see-OH-neh*
▪ a burn	**un'ustione** *oo-noo-stee-oH-neh*
▪ the chills	**i brividi** *ee brEE-vee-dee*
▪ a cold	**un raffreddore** *oon rahf-frehd-dOH-reh*
▪ constipation	**stitichezza** *stee-tee-kAY-tsah*
▪ a cut	**una ferita (un taglio)** *OO-nah feh-rEE-tah (oon tAH-ly-ee-oh)*
▪ diarrhea	**la diarrea** *lah dee-ahr-rEH-ah*
▪ a fever	**la febbre** *la fEHb-breh*
▪ a headache	**un mal di testa** *oon mAHl dee tEHs-tah*
▪ an infection	**un'infezione** *oo-neen-feh-tsee-OH-neh*
▪ a lump	**un gonfiore** *oon gohn-fee-OH-reh*
▪ rheumatism	**i reumatismi** *ee reh-oo-mah-tEE-smee*
▪ something in my eye	**qualche cosa nell'occhio** *koo-AHl-keh kOH-sah nayl-lOHk-key-oh*

■ a sore throat	**un mal di gola**	*oon mAHl dee gOH-lah*
■ stomach cramps	**crampi allo stomaco**	*krAHm-pee AHl-loh stOH-mah-koh*
■ a stomachache	**un mal di stomaco**	*oon mAHl dee stOH-mah-koh*

TELLING THE DOCTOR

It hurts me here.	**Mi fa male qui.** *mee fah mAH-leh koo-EE*
My whole body hurts.	**Mi fa male dappertutto.** *Mee fah mAH-leh dahp-pehr-tOOt-toh*
I'm presently taking antibiotics.	**Sto prendendo degli antibiotici.** *stoh prayn-dEHn-doh dAY-ly-ee ahn-tee-bee-OH-tee-chee*
I'm constipated.	**Soffro di stitichezza.** *sOHf-froh dee stee-tee-kAY-tsah*
I'm flatulent.	**Ho gas intestinali.** *oh gAHs een-teh-stee-nAH-lee*
I need a laxative.	**Ho bisogno di un lassativo.** *oh bee-sOH-ny-oh dee oon lahs-sah-tEE-voh*
I have (hay) fever.	**Ho la febbre (da fieno).** *oh lah fEHb-breh (dah fee-EH-noh)*
My _____ hurts.	**Mi fa male _____.** *mee fah mAH-leh*
■ appendix	**l'appendicite** *lahp-pehn-dee-chEE-teh*
■ ankle	**la caviglia** *lah kah-vEE-ly-ah*
■ arm	**il braccio** *eel brAH-chee-oh*
■ back	**la schiena** *lah skey-EH-nah*
■ breast	**il petto** *eel pEHt-toh*
■ cheek	**la guancia** *lah goo-AHn-chee-ah*
■ ear	**l'orecchio** *loh-rAY-key-oh*
■ elbow	**il gomito** *eel gOH-mee-toh*

■ eye	**l'occhio**	*lOH-key-oh*
■ face	**la faccia**	*lah fAH-chee-ah*
■ finger	**il dito**	*eel dEE-doh*
■ foot	**il piede**	*eel pee-EH-deh*
■ hand	**la mano**	*lah mAH-noh*
■ head	**la testa**	*lah tEHs-tah*
■ heart	**il cuore**	*eel koo-OH-reh*
■ hip	**l'anca**	*lAHn-kah*
■ knee	**il ginocchio**	*eel jee-nOH-key-oh*
■ leg	**la gamba**	*lah gAHm-bah*
■ lip	**il labbro**	*eel lAHb-broh*
■ mouth	**la bocca**	*lah bOH-kah*
■ neck	**il collo**	*eel kOHl-loh*
■ nose	**il naso**	*eel nAH-soh*
■ shoulder	**la spalla**	*lah spAHl-lah*
■ throat	**la gola**	*lah gOH-lah*
■ thumb	**il pollice**	*eel pOHl-lee-cheh*
■ toe	**l'alluce**	*lAHl-loo-cheh*
■ tooth	**il dente**	*eel dEHn-teh*
■ wrist	**il polso**	*eel pOHl-soh*

I've had this pain since yesterday.

Ho questo dolore da ieri. *oh koo-AYs-toh doh-lOH-reh dah ee-EH-ree*

There's a (no) history of asthma (diabetes, heart problems) in my family.

(Non) c'è anamnesi di asma (diabete, problemi cardiaci) nella mia famiglia. *(nohn) chEH ah-nahm-nEH-see dee AH-smah (dee-ah-bEH-teh proh-blEH-mee kahr-dEE-ah-chee) nAYl-lah mEE-ah fah-mEE-ly-ee-ah*

I'm (not) allergic to antibiotics (penicillin).	**(Non) sono allergico agli antibiotici (alla penicillina).** *(nohn)* sOH-noh ahl-lEHr-jee-koh AH-ly-ee ahn-tee-bee-OH-tee-chee (AHl-lah peh-nee-cheel-lEE-nah)
I have chest pains.	**Ho dolori al petto.** oh doh-lOH-ree ahl pEHt-toh
I had a heart attack _____.	**Ho avuto un attacco cardiaco _____.** oh ah-vOO-toh oon aht-tAHk-koh kahr-dEE-ah-koh
■ last year	**l'anno scorso** lAHn-noh skOHr-soh
■ (three) years ago	**(tre) anni fa** trEH AHn-nee fah
I'm taking this medicine (insulin).	**Sto prendendo questa medicina (insulina).** stOH prehn-dEHn-doh koo-AYs-tah meh-dee-chEE-nah (een-soo-lEE-nah)
I'm pregnant.	**Sono incinta.** sOH-noh een-chEEn-tah
I feel faint.	**Mi sento svenire.** mee sEHn-toh sveh-nEE-reh
I feel all right now.	**Mi sento bene adesso.** mee sEHn-toh bEH-neh ah-dEHs-soh
I feel better (worse).	**Mi sento meglio (peggio).** mee sEHn-toh mEH-ly-ee-oh (pEH-jee-oh)
Is it serious (contagious)?	**È serio (contagioso)?** EH sEH-ree-oh (kohn-tah-jee-OH-soh)
Do I have to go to the hospital?	**Devo andare in ospedale?** dAY-voh ahn-dAH-reh een oh-speh-dAH-leh
When can I continue my trip?	**Quando potrò continuare la mia gita?** koo-AHn-doh poh-trOH kohn-tee-noo-AH-reh lah mEE-ah jEE-tah

QUESTIONS

Are you giving me a prescription?

Mi darà una ricetta? *mee dah-rAH OO-nah ree-chEHt-tah*

How often must I take this medicine (these pills)?

Quante volte devo prendere questa medicina (queste pillole)? *koo-AHn-teh vOHl-teh dAY-voh prAYn-deh-reh koo-AYs-tah meh-dee-chEE-nah (koo-AYs-teh pEEl-loh-leh)*

(How long) do I have to stay in bed?

(Quanto) devo rimanere a letto? *(koo-AHn-toh) dAY-voh ree-mah-nAY-reh ah lEHt-toh*

Thank you (for everything) doctor.

Grazie (di tutto), dottore. *grAH-tsee-eh (dee tOOt-toh) doht-tOH-reh*

How much do I owe you for your services?

Quanto le devo per la visita? *koo-AHn-toh leh dAY-voh pehr lah vEE-see-tah*

May I have a receipt?

Può darmi la ricevuta? *poo-OH dAHr-mee lah ree-chay-vOO-tah*

I have medical insurance.

Ho l'assicurazione (l'assistenza) medica. *oh lahs-see-koo-rah-tsee-OH-neh (lahs-sees-stEHn-tsah) mEH-dee-kah*

Will you accept my medical insurance?

Accetta la mia assicurazione (assistenza) medica? *ah-chEHt-tah lah mEE-ah ahs-see-koo-rah-tsee-OH-neh (ahs-see-stEHn-tsah) mEH-dee-kah*

Is there a co-payment?

C'è qualche pagamento a carica del paziente? *chEH koo-AHl-kay pah-gah-mEHn-toh ah kaH-ree-kah dayl pah-tsee-EHn-teh*

IN THE HOSPITAL (ACCIDENTS)

Help!	**Aiuto!** *ah-ee-OO-toh*
Get a doctor, quick!	**Chiamate un medico, subito!** *key-ah-mAH-teh oon mEH-dee-koh sOO-bee-toh*
Call an ambulance!	**Chiamate un'ambulanza!** *key-ah-mAH-teh oo-nahm-boo-lAHn-tsah*
Take him to the hospital.	**Portatelo in ospedale.** *pohr-tAH-teh-loh een oh-speh-dAH-leh*
I've fallen.	**Sono caduto(a).** *sOH-noh kah-dOO-toh(ah)*
I was knocked down.	**Mi hanno buttato(a) a terra.** *mee AHn-noh boot-tAH-toh(ah) ah tEHr-rah*
She was run over.	**È stata investita.** *EH stAH-tah een-veh-stEE-tah*
I think I've had a heart attack.	**Credo che ho avuto un collasso cardiaco.** *krEH-do kay oh ah-vOO-toh oon kohl-lAHs-soh kahr-dEE-ah-koh*
I burned myself.	**Mi sono ustionato(a).** *mee sOH-noh oo-stee-oh-nAH-toh(ah)*
I cut myself.	**Mi sono tagliato(a).** *mee sOH-noh tah-ly-ee-AH-toh(ah)*
I'm bleeding.	**Sto sanguinando.** *stOH sahn-goo-ee-nAHn-doh*
He's lost a lot of blood.	**Ha perduto molto sangue.** *ah pehr-dOO-toh mOHl-toh sAHn-goo-eh*
I think the bone is broken (dislocated).	**Penso che mi si sia fratturato (lussato) l'osso.** *pEHn-soh kay mee see sEE-ah fraht-too-rAH-toh (loos-sAH-toh) lOHs-soh*

The leg is swollen.	**La gamba è gonfia.** *lah gAHm-bah EH gOHn-fee-ah*
The ankle is sprained (twisted).	**Mi si è slogata (storta) la caviglia.** *mee see-EH sloh-gAH-tah (stOHr-tah) lah kah-vEE-ly-ee-ah*
I can't move my elbow (knee).	**Non posso muovere il gomito (il ginocchio).** *nohn pOHs-soh moo-OH-veh-reh eel gOH-mee-toh (eel jee-nOHk-key-oh)*

AT THE DENTIST

I have to go to the dentist.	**Devo andare dal dentista.** *dAY-voh ahn-dAH-reh dAHl dehn-tEEs-tah*
Can you recommend a dentist?	**Può raccomandarmi un dentista?** *poo-OH rahk-koh-mahn-dAHr-mee oon dehn-tEEs-tah*
I have a toothache that's driving me crazy.	**Ho un mal di denti che mi fa impazzire.** *oh oon mAHl dee dEHn-tee kay mee fah eem-pah-tsEE-reh*
I've lost a filling.	**Ho perduto l'otturazione.** *oh payr-dOO-toh loht-too-rah-tsee-OH-neh*
I've a broken tooth.	**Mi son rotto un dente.** *mee sOHn rOHt-toh oon dEHn-teh*
My gums hurt me.	**Mi fanno male le gengive.** *mee fAHn-noh mAH-leh leh jehn-jEE-veh*
Is there an infection?	**C'è un'infezione?** *chEH oo-neen-feh-tsee-OH-neh*
Will you have to extract the tooth?	**Deve estrarre il dente?** *dAY-veh ehs-trAHr-reh eel dEHn-teh*

I'd prefer you filled it _____.	**Preferisco farlo otturare _____.** *preh-feh-rIH-skoh fAHr-loh oht-too-rAH-reh*
■ with amalgam	**con l'algama** *kohn lAHl-gah-mah*
■ with gold	**con oro** *kohn OH-roh*
■ with silver	**con argento** *kohn ahr-jEHn-toh*
■ for now (temporarily)	**provvisoriamente** *prohv-vee-soh-ree-ah-mEHn-teh*
Can you fix _____?	**Può riparare _____?** *poo-OH ree-pah-rAH-reh*
■ this bridge	**questo ponte** *koo-AYs-toh pOHn-teh*
■ this crown	**questa corona** *koo-AYs-tah koh-rOH-nah*
■ these dentures	**questi denti finti** *koo-AYs-tee dEHn-tee fEEn-tee*
When should I come back?	**Quando dovrei ritornare?** *koo-AHn-doh doh-vrEH-ee ree-tohr-nAH-reh*
How much do I owe you for your services?	**Quanto le devo per la visita?** *koo-AHn-toh leh dAY-voh pehr lah vEE-see-tah*

WITH THE OPTICIAN

Can you repair these glasses (for me)?	**Può aggiustar(mi) questi occhiali?** *poo-OH ah-jee-oo-stAHr (mee) koo-AYs-tee oh-key-AH-lee*
I've broken a lens (the frame).	**Mi si è rotta una lente (la montatura).** *mee see-EH rOHt-tah OO-nah lEHn-teh (lah mohn-tah-tOO-rah)*

Can you put in a new lens?	**Può metterci una lente nuova?** *poo-OH mAYt-tehr-chee OO-nah lEHn-teh noo-OH-vah*
I do not have a prescription.	**Non ho la ricetta medica.** *nohn oh lah ree-chEHt-tah mEH-dee-kah*
I need the glasses as soon as possible.	**Ho bisogno degli occhiali al più presto possibile.** *oh bee-sOH-ny-oh dAY-ly-ee oh-key-AH-lee ahl pee-OO prEH-stoh pohs-sEE-bee-leh*

COMMUNICATIONS

POST OFFICE

I want to mail a letter.	**Voglio spedire una lettera.** *vOH-ly-ee-oh speh-dEE-reh OO-nah lAYt-teh-rah*
Where's the post office?	**Dov'è l'ufficio postale?** *doh-vEH loof-fEE-chee-oh poh-stAH-leh*
Where's a letter box?	**Dov'è una cassetta postale?** *doh-vEH OO-nah kas-sAYt-tah poh-stAH-leh*
What is the postage on _____ to the United States (Canada, England, Australia)?	**Qual è l'affrancatura per _____ per gli Stati Uniti (Canadà, Inghilterra, Australia)?** *koo-ah-lEH lahf-frahn-kah-tOO-rah pehr _____ pehr ly-ee stAH-tee oo-nEE-tee (kah-nah-dAH een-gheel-tEHr-rah ahoo-strAH-lee-ah)*
■ a letter	**una lettera** *OO-nah lAYt-teh-rah*
■ an airmail letter	**una lettera via aerea** *OO-nah lAYt-teh-rah vEE-ah ah-EH-reh-ah*

■ an insured letter **una lettera assicurata** *OO-nah lAYt-teh-rah ahs-see-koo-rAH-tah*

■ a registered letter **una lettera raccomandata** *OO-nah lAYt-teh-rah rahk-koh-mahn-dAH-tah*

■ a special delivery letter **una lettera espresso** *OO-nah lAYt-teh-rah ehs-prEHs-soh*

■ a package **un pacco** *oon pAHk-koh*

■ a postcard **una cartolina postale** *OO-nah kahr-toh-lEE-nah poh-stAH-leh*

When will it arrive? **Quando arriverà?** *koo-AHn-doh ahr-ree-veh-rAH*

Which is the _____ window? **Qual è lo sportello per _____?** *koo-ah-lEH loh spohr-tEHl-loh pehr*

■ general delivery **il fermo posta** *eel fAYr-moh pOH-stah*

■ money order **i vaglia postali** *ee vAH-ly-ee-ah poh-stAH-lee*

■ stamp **i francobolli** *ee frahn-koh-bOHl-lee*

Are there any letters for me? My name is _____. **Ci sono lettere per me? Il mio nome è _____.** *chee sOH-noh lAYt-teh-reh pehr mAY eel mEE-oh nOH-meh EH*

I'd like _____. **Vorrei _____.** *vohr-rEH-ee*

■ 10 postcards **dieci cartoline postali** *dee-EH-chee kahr-toh-lEE-neh poh-stAH-lee*

■ 5 (airmail) stamps **cinque francobolli (via aerea)** *chEEn-koo-eh frahn-koh-bOHl-lee (vEE-ah ah-EH-reh-ah)*

Do I fill out a customs receipt? **Devo compilare una ricevuta?** *dAY-voh kohm-pee-lAH-reh OO-nah ree-cheh-vOO-tah*

TELEPHONES

Where is _____?	**Dov'è _____?** *doh-vEH*
■ a public telephone	**un telefono pubblico** *oon teh-lEH-foh-noh-pOOb-blee-koh*
■ a telephone booth	**una cabina telefonica** *OO-nah kah-bEE-nah teh-leh-fOH-nee-kah*
■ a telephone directory	**un elenco telefonico** *oon eh-lEHn-koh teh-leh-fOH-nee-koh*
May I use your phone?	**Posso usare il suo telefono?** *pOHs-soh oo-sAH-reh eel sOO-oh teh-lEH-foh-noh*
Can I call direct?	**Posso telefonare direttamente?** *pOHs-soh teh-leh-foh-nAH-reh dee-reht-tah-mEHn-teh*
I want to reverse the charges.	**Desidero fare una riversibile.** *deh-sEE-deh-roh fAH-reh OO-nah ree-vehr-sEE-bee-leh*
I'd like a three-way call.	**Vorrei un collegamento in simultanea a tre.** *vohr-rEH-ee oon kohl-lay-gah-mEHn-toh een see-mool-tAH-neh-ah ah trAY*
Do I need a magnetic phone card?	**Occorre una scheda magnetica?** *ohk-kOHr-reh oo-nah skEH-dah mah-nyEH-tee-kah*
Can you give me a phone card, please?	**Può darmi una scheda telefonica?** *poo-OH dAHr-mee OO-nah skEH-dah teh-leh-fOH-nee-kah*
I want to make a _____ to _____.	**Vorrei fare una _____ a _____.** *vohr-rEH-ee fAH-reh OO-nah_____ ah _____*
■ local call	**telefonata urbana** *teh-leh-foh-nAH-tah oor-bAH-nah*

■ long-distance call	**una telefonata in teleselezione (interurbana, internazionale)** *OO-nah teh-leh-foh-nAH-tah een teh-leh-seh-leh-tsee-OH-neh (een-tehr-oor-bAH-nah een-tehr-nah-tsee-oh-nAH-leh)*
■ person-to-person call	**una telefonata diretta con preavviso** *OO-nah teh-leh-foh-nAH-tah dee-rEHt-tah kohn preh-ahv-vEE-soh*
How do I get the operator?	**Come si ottiene il centralino?** *kOH-meh see oht-tee-EH-neh eel chehn-trah-lEE-noh*
Operator, can you give me ____?	**Signorina (signore, centralino), può darmi ____?** *see-ny-oh-rEE-nah (see-ny-OH-reh chehn-trah-lEE-noh) poo-OH dAHr-mee*
■ number 23 345	**il ventitrè trecentoquarantacinque** *eel vayn-tee-trEH treh-chEHn-toh-koo-ah-rahn-tah-chEEn-koo-eh*
■ extension 19	**interno diciannove** *een-tEHr-noh dee-chee-ahn-nOH-veh*
■ area code ____	**prefisso numero ____** *preh-fEEs-soh nOO-meh-roh*
■ country code ____	**prefisso internazionale ____** *preh-fEEs-soh een-tehr-nah-tzee-oh-nAH-leh*
■ city code ____	**prefisso interurbano ____** *preh-fEEs-soh een-tehr-oor-bAH-noh*
My number is ____.	**Il mio numero è ____.** *eel mEE-oh nOO-meh-roh EH*
May I speak to ____?	**Potrei parlare con ____?** *poh-trEH-ee pahr-lAH-reh kohn*
Is ____ in?	**C'è ____?** *chEH*
■ Mr. ____	**il signor ____** *EEl sy-nee-Ohr*

■ Mrs. ___	**la signora** ___	*lah sy-nee-OH-rah*
■ Miss ___	**la signorina** ___	*lah sy-nee-oh-rEE-nah*
Speaking.	**Sono io.**	*sOH-noh EE-oh*
Hello.	**Pronto.**	*prOHn-toh*
Who is it?	**Chi è?**	*key EH*

PROBLEMS ON THE LINE

I can't hear.	**Non si sente bene.** *nohn see sEHn-teh bEH-neh*
Speak louder (please).	**Parli più forte (per favore).** *pAHr-lee pee-OO fOHr-teh (pehr fah-vOH-reh)*
Don't hang up.	**Non appenda il ricevitore.** *nohn ahp-pEHn-dah eel ree-cheh-vee-tOH-reh*
This is ___.	**Parla** ___. *pAHr-lah*
Do you have an answering machine?	**Ha una segreteria telefonica?** *ah OO-nah seh-greh-teh-rEE-ah teh-leh-fOH-nee-kah*
The line is busy.	**La linea è occupata.** *lah lEE-neh-ah EH ohk-koo-pAH-tah*
You gave me (that was) a wrong number.	**Mi ha dato (era) un numero sbagliato.** *mee ah dAH-toh (EH-rah) oon nOO-meh-roh sbah-ly-ee-AH-toh*
I was cut off.	**È caduta la linea.** *EH kah-dOO-tah lah lEE-neh-ah*
Please dial it again.	**Per favore, rifaccia il numero.** *pehr fah-vOH-reh ree-fAH-chee-ah eel nOO-meh-roh*
I want to leave a message.	**Voglio lasciare un (messaggio) appunto.** *vOH-ly-ee-oh lah-shee-AH-reh oon (mehs-sAH-jee-oh) ahp-pOOn-toh*

FAXES

Do you have a fax machine?	**Ha un fax?** *ah oon fahcs*
What is your fax number?	**Qual è il numero del fax?** *koo-ahl-EH eel nOO-meh-roh dayl fahcs*
I'd like to fax ____.	**Vorrei faxare ____.** *vohr-rEH-ee fahc-sAH-reh*
▪ a document	**un documento** *oon doh-koo-mEHn-toh*
▪ an invoice	**una fattura** *OO-nah faht-tOO-rah*
▪ a letter	**una lettera** *OO-nah lAYt-teh-rah*
▪ a receipt	**una ricetta** *OO-nah ree-chEHt-tah*
May I fax it to you?	**Glielo posso faxare?** *ly-ay-loh pOHs-soh fahc-sAH-reh*
Fax it to me.	**Me lo faxi.** *may-loh fAHc-see*
I didn't get your fax.	**Non ho ricevuto il suo fax.** *nohn oh ree-cheh-vOO-toh eel sOO-oh fahcs*
Did you receive my fax?	**Ha ricevuto il mio fax?** *ah ree-cheh-vOO-toh eel mEE-oh fahcs*
Your fax is illegible.	**Il suo fax è illegibile.** *eel sOO-oh fahcs EH eel-leh-jEE-bee-leh*
Please, send it again.	**Per favore, me lo(la) faxi di nuovo.** *pAYr fah-vOH-reh may-loh(lah) fahc-see dee noo-OH-voh*

PHOTOCOPIES

Do you have a photocopier?	**C'è una fotocopiatrice?** *chEH OO-nah foh-toh-koh-pee-ah-trEE-ceh*

I would like to make a photocopy of this ____.	**Vorrei fare una fotocopia di ____.** *vohr-rEH-ee fAH-reh OO-nah foh-toh-kOH-pee-ah dee*
■ page	**questa pagina** *koo-AYs-tah pAH-jee-nah*
■ document	**questo documento** *koo-AYs-toh doh-koo-mEH-ntoh*
What is the cost per page?	**Quanto costa per pagina?** *koo-AHn-toh kOH-stah pehr pAH-jee-nah*
Can you enlarge it (by 25%)?	**Può ingrandirlo (del 25%)?** *poo-OH een-grahn-dEEr-loh (dayl vayn-tee-chEEn-koo-eh pehr chEHn-toh)*
Can you reduce it (by 50%)?	**Può ridurlo (del 50%)?** *poo-OH ree-dOOr-loh (dayl cheen-koo-AHn-tah pehr chEHn-toh)*
Can you make a color copy?	**Può fare una copia a colori?** *poo-OH fAH-reh OO-nah kOH-pee-ah ah koh-lOH-ree*

TELEGRAMS

Where is the telegraph window?	**Dov'è il finestrino per i telegrammi?** *doh-vEH eel fee-neh-strEE-noh pehr ee teh-leh-grAHm-mee*
How late is the telegraph window open (till what time)?	**L'ufficio Poste e Telegrafi sta aperto fino a tardi (fino a che ora)?** *loof-fEE-chee-oh pOHs-teh ay teh-lEH-grah-fee stah ah-pEHr-toh fEE-noh ah tAHr-dee (fEE-noh ah kay OH-rah)*
I'd like to send a telegram to ____.	**Vorrei spedire un telegramma a ____.** *vohr-rEH-ee speh-dEE-reh oon teh-leh-grAHm-mah ah*

| How much is it per word? | **Quanto costa per parola?** *koo-AHn-toh kOH-stah pehr pah-rOH-lah* |
| Where are the forms? | **Dove sono i moduli (le schede)?** *dOH-veh sOH-noh ee mOH-doo-lee (leh skEH-deh)* |

GENERAL INFORMATION

TELLING TIME

What time is it?   **Che ora è?**   *kay OH-rah EH*

When telling time in Italian, *it is* is expressed by **è** for 1:00, noon, and midnight; **sono** is used for all other numbers.

It's 1:00.	**È l'una.** *EH lOO-nah*
It's 12 o'clock (noon).	**È mezzogiorno.** *EH meh-tsoh-jee-OHr-noh*
It's midnight.	**È mezzanotte.** *EH meh-tsah-nOHt-teh*
It's early (late).	**È presto (tardi).** *EH prEH-stoh (tAHr-dee)*
It's 2:00.	**Sono le due.** *sOH-noh leh dOO-eh*
It's 3:00, etc.	**Sono le tre.** *sOH-noh leh trAY*

The number of minutes after the hour is expressed by adding **e** ("and"), followed by the number of minutes.

| It's 4:10. | **Sono le quattro e dieci.** *sOH-noh leh koo-AHt-roh ay dee-EH-chee* |
| It's 5:20. | **Sono le cinque e venti.** *sOH-noh leh chEEn-koo-eh ay vAYn-tee* |

Fifteen minutes after the hour and half past the hour are expressed by placing **e un quarto** and **e mezzo** after the hour.

It's 6:15.	**Sono le sei e un quarto.** *sOH-noh leh sEH-ee ay oon koo-AHr-toh*
It's 7:30.	**Sono le sette e mezzo.** *sOH-noh leh sEHt-teh ay mEH-tsoh*

After passing the half-hour point on the clock, time is expressed in Italian by *subtracting* the number of minutes to the *next* hour.

It's 7:40.	**Sono le otto meno venti.** *sOH-noh leh OHt-toh mEH-noh vAYn-tee*
It's 8:50.	**Sono le nove meno dieci.** *sOH-noh leh nOH-veh mAY-noh dee-EH-chee*
At what time?	**A che ora?** *ah kay OH-rah*
At 1:00.	**All'una.** *ahl-lOO-nah*
At 2:00 (3:00, etc.).	**Alle due (tre, . . .).** *AHl-leh dOO-eh (trAY)*
A.M. (in the morning)	**del mattino** *dayl maht-tEE-noh*
P.M. (in the afternoon)	**del pomeriggio** *dayl poh-meh-rEE-jee-oh*
At night.	**della notte.** *dAYl-lah nOHt-teh*

Official time is based on the 24-hour clock. You will find train schedules and other such times expressed in terms of a point within a 24-hour sequence.

The train leaves at 15.30.	**Il treno parte alle quindici a trenta.** *eel trEH-noh pAHr-teh AHl-leh koo-EEn-dee-chee ay treHn-tah*
The time is now 21.15.	**Ora sono le ventuno e quindici.** *OH-rah sOH-noh leh vayn-tOO-noh ay koo-EEn-dee-chee.*

DAYS OF THE WEEK

What day is it?	**Che giorno è oggi?**	*kAY jee-OHr-noh EH OH-jee*
Today is ____.	**Oggi è ____.**	*OH-jee EH*
■ Monday	**lunedì**	*loo-neh-dEE*
■ Tuesday	**martedì**	*mahr-teh-dEE*
■ Wednesday	**mercoledì**	*mehr-koh-leh-dEE*
■ Thursday	**giovedì**	*jee-oh-veh-dEE*
■ Friday	**venerdì**	*veh-nehr-dEE*
■ Saturday	**sabato**	*sAH-bah-toh*
■ Sunday	**domenica**	*doh-mAY-nee-kah*
Yesterday	**Ieri**	*ee-EH-ree*
Tomorrow	**Domani**	*doh-mAH-nee*
The day after tomorrow	**Dopodomani**	*doh-poh-doh-mAH-nee*
Last week	**La settimana passata**	*lah seht-tee-mAH-nah pahs-sAH-tah*
Next week	**La settimana prossima**	*lah seht-tee-mAH-nah prOHs-see-mah*
Tonight	**Questa notte (stanotte)**	*koo-AYs-tah nOHt-teh (stah-nOHt-teh)*
Last night	**La notte passata**	*lah nOHt-teh pahs-sAH-tah*

MONTHS OF THE YEAR

January	**gennaio**	*jehn-nAH-ee-oh*
February	**febbraio**	*fehb-brAH-ee-oh*

March	**marzo**	*mAHr-tsoh*
April	**aprile**	*ah-prEE-leh*
May	**maggio**	*mAH-jee-oh*
June	**giugno**	*jee-OO-ny-ee-oh*
July	**luglio**	*lOO-ly-ee-oh*
August	**agosto**	*ah-gOH-stoh*
September	**settembre**	*seht-tEHm-breh*
October	**ottobre**	*oht-tOH-breh*
November	**novembre**	*noh-vEHm-breh*
December	**dicembre**	*dee-chEHm-breh*
What's today's date?	**Che data è oggi?**	*kay dAH-ta EH OH-jee*

The first of the month is *il primo* (an ordinal number). All other dates are expressed with *cardinal* numbers.

Today is August *first*.	**Oggi è *il primo* di agosto.**	*OH-jee EH eel prEE-moh dee ah-gOH-stoh*
■ second	**il due** *eel dOO-eh*	
■ fourth	**il quattro** *eel koo-AHt-troh*	
■ 25th	**il venticinque** *eel vayn-tee-chEEn-koo-eh*	
This month	**Questo mese** *koo-AYs-toh mAY-seh*	
Last month	**Il mese scorso** *eel mAY-seh skOHr-soh*	
Next month	**Il mese prossimo** *eel mAY-seh prOHs-see-moh*	
Last year	**L'anno scorso** *lAHn-noh skOHr-soh*	
Next year	**L'anno prossimo** *lAHn-noh prOHs-see-moh*	

May 1, 1876	**Il primo maggio, mille ottocento settanta sei** *eel prEE-moh mAH-jee-oh mEEl-leh oht-toh-chEHn-toh seht-tAHn-tah sEH-ee*	
July 4, 1984	**Il quattro luglio, mille novecento ottanta quattro** *eel koo-AHt-troh lOO-ly-ee-oh mEEl-leh noh-veh-chEHn-toh oht-tAHn-tah koo-AHt-troh*	

THE FOUR SEASONS

Spring	**la primavera**	*lah pree-mah-vEH-rah*
Summer	**l'estate**	*leh-stAH-teh*
Fall	**l'autunno**	*lah-oo-tOOn-noh*
Winter	**l'inverno**	*leen-vEHr-noh*

THE WEATHER

How is the weather today?	**Che tempo fa oggi?**	*kay tEHm-poh fAH OH-jee*
It's good (bad) weather.	**Fa bel (cattivo) tempo.**	*fah behl (kaht-tEE-voh) tEHm-poh*
It's hot.	**Fa caldo.**	*fah kAHl-doh*
■ cold	**freddo**	*frAYd-doh*
■ cool	**fresco**	*frAY-skoh*
It's windy.	**Tira vento.**	*tEE-rah vEHn-toh*
It's sunny.	**C'è il sole.**	*chEH eel sOH-leh*
It's raining.	**Piove.**	*pee-OH-veh*
It's snowing.	**Nevica.**	*nAY-vee-kah*
It's drizzling.	**Pioviggina.**	*pee-oh-vEE-jee-nah*

IMPORTANT SIGNS

Acqua (non) potabile	(Not) drinking water
Alt	Stop
Aperto	Open
Ascensore	Elevator (Lift)
Attenzione	Caution, watch out
Avanti	Enter (come in, go, walk [at the lights])
Caldo or "C"	Hot
Cassa	Cashier
Chiuso	Closed
Divieto di sosta	No parking
Divieto di transito	No entrance, keep out
Freddo or "F"	Cold
Gabinetti (WC)	Toilets
Ingresso	Entrance
Libero	Vacant
Non calpestare le aiuole	Keep off the grass
Non ostruire l'ingresso	Don't block entrance
Non toccare	Hands off, don't touch
Occupato	Occupied
Pericolo	Danger
Riservato	Reserved
Si affitta (si loca)	For rent
Si vende	For sale
Donne	Women's room
Uomini	Men's room

Spingere		Push
Strada privata		Private road
Tirare		Pull
Uscita		Exit
Vietato fumare		No smoking
Vietato nuotare		No bathing
Vietato sputare		No spitting

COMMON ABBREVIATIONS

AA	**Azienda Autonoma di Soggiorno e Turismo**	Local Tourist Information Center
ACI	**Automobile Club d'Italia**	Automobile Club of Italy
Cap.	**Capoluogo**	Province
C.P.	**Casella Postale**	Post Office Box
CAP	**Codice Postale**	Zip Code
ENIT	**Ente Nazionale per il Turismo**	Italian State Tourist Office
EPT	**Ente Provinciale per il Turismo**	Provincial Tourist Information Center
F.lli	**Brothers**	Inc.
FS	**Ferrovie dello Stato**	Italian State Railways
IVA	**Imposte sul Valore Aggiunto**	Italian State Tax
L.	**Lire**	Italian currency
N., n°	**Numero**	Number
Pro Loco	**Ente Locale per il Turismo**	Local Tourist Information Office

Prov.	**Provincia**	Province
P.za	**Piazza**	(City) Square
S.	**San, Santo(a)**	Saint
S.A.	**Società Anonima**	Inc.
Sig.	**Signor**	Mr.
Sig.na	**Signorina**	Miss
Sig.ra	**Signora**	Mrs.
TCI	**Touring Club Italiano**	Italian Touring Club
v.	**Via**	Street
v.le	**Viale**	Boulevard

SPANISH

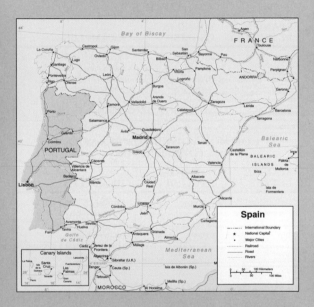

QUICK PRONUNCIATION GUIDE

VOWELS

SPANISH LETTER(S)	SOUND IN ENGLISH	EXAMPLES
a	ah (y<u>a</u>cht)	taco *(TAH-koh)*
e	ay (d<u>ay</u>)	mesa *(MAY-sah)*
	eh (p<u>e</u>t)	perro *(PEH-roh)*
i	ee (m<u>ee</u>t)	libro *(LEE-broh)*
o	oh (<u>o</u>pen)	foto *(FOH-toh)*
u	oo (t<u>oo</u>th)	mucho *(MOO-choh)*

COMMON VOWEL COMBINATIONS (DIPHTHONGS)

SPANISH LETTER(S)	SOUND IN ENGLISH	EXAMPLES
au	ow (c<u>ow</u>)	causa *(COW-sah)*
		auto *(OW-toh)*
ei	ay (d<u>ay</u>)	aceite *(ah-SAY-tay)*
ai	y (t<u>y</u>pe)	baile *(BY-lay)*
ie	yeh (y<u>e</u>t)	abierto *(ah-BYEHR-toh)*
ue	weh (w<u>e</u>t)	bueno *(BWEH-noh)*

CONSONANTS

SPANISH LETTER(S)	SOUND IN ENGLISH	EXAMPLES
c (before *a, o, u*)	hard k sound (<u>c</u>at)	campo *(KAHM-poh)*
		cosa *(KOH-sah)*
		Cuba *(KOO-bah)*
c (before *e, i*)	soft s sound (<u>c</u>ent)	central *(sehn-TRAHL)*
		cinco *(SEEN-koh)*
cc	hard and soft cc (ks sound) (a<u>cc</u>ept)	acción *(ahk-see-OHN)*

SPANISH LETTER(S)	SOUND IN ENGLISH	EXAMPLES
ch	hard ch sound (chair)	muchacho (moo-CHAH-choh)
g (before a, o, u)	hard g (go)	gafas (GAH-fahs) goma (GOH-mah)
g (before e, i)	breathy h (hot)	general (hehn-eh-RAHL)
h	always silent	hasta (AHS-tah)
j	breathy as in h sound (hot)	José (ho-SAY)
l	English l sound (lamp)	lámpara (LAHM-pahr-ah)
ll	as in English y (yes)	pollo (POH-yoh)
n	English n (no)	naranja (nah-RAHN-ha)
ñ	English ny (canyon)	señorita (seh-nyoh-REE-tah)
qu	English k (keep)	que (kay)
r	trilled once	caro (KAH-roh)
rr (or r at beginning of word)	trilled strongly (operator, three)	rico (RREE-koh) perro (PEH-rroh)
s	English s (see)	rosa (ROH-sah)
v	Approximately as in English b (book)	primavera (pree-mah-BEHR-ah)
x	English s, ks (sign, socks)	extra (ES-trah) examinar (ek-sah-mee-NAHR)
y	English y (yes) (by itself y = i)	yo (yoh) y (ee)
z	English s	zapato (sah-PAH-toh)

The above pronunciations apply to the Spanish that is spoken in Central and South America, and that is also spoken in parts of southern Spain. The remaining areas of Spain use the Castilian pronunciation, which differs mostly in the sound of the letters *ll* and of the *z* and the *c* before *e* and *i*. For example, the Castilian pronunciations are as follows:

SPANISH LETTER(S)	SOUND IN ENGLISH	EXAMPLES
ll	ly sound as in million	llamo *(LYAH-moh)*
c (before *e* or *i*) z	a <u>th</u> sound instead of an s sound	gracias *(GRAH-thee-ahs)* lápiz *(LAH-peeth)*

THE BASICS FOR GETTING BY

MOST FREQUENTLY USED EXPRESSIONS

Hello!	**¡Hola!** *OH-lah*
Yes	**Sí** *see*
No	**No** *noh*
Maybe	**Quizás** *kee-SAHS*
Please	**Por favor** *pohr-fah-BOHR*
Thank you (very much).	**(Muchas) gracias.** *(MOO-chahs) GRAH-see-ahs*
You're welcome.	**De nada.** *day NAH-dah*

Excuse me

- (having disturbed or bumped into someone) — **Perdón** *pehr-DOHN*
- (leaving a group or walking in front of a person) — **Con permiso** *kohn pehr-MEE-soh*
- (getting one's attention) — **Por favor** *pohr fah-BOHR*

I'm sorry.	**Lo siento.** *loh see-EHN-toh*
Just a second.	**Un momento.** *oon moh-MEN-toh*
That's all right, okay.	**Está bien.** *eh-STAH bee-ehn*
It doesn't matter.	**No importa.** *noh eem-PORT-ah*
Good morning.	**Buenos días.** *bway-nohs DEE-ahs*
Good afternoon.	**Buenas tardes.** *bway-nahs TAHR-dehs*
Good evening (night).	**Buenas noches.** *bway-nahs NOH-chehs*
Sir	**Señor** *seh-NYOHR*
Madame	**Señora** *seh-NYOHR-ah*
Miss	**Señorita** *seh-nyohr-EE-tah*
Good-bye.	**Adiós.** *ah-DYOHS*
See you later (so long).	**Hasta la vista (Hasta luego).** *AH-stah lah BEE-stah (AH-stah loo-AY-goh)*
See you tomorrow.	**Hasta mañana.** *AH-stah mah-NYAH-nah*
Do you speak English?	**¿Habla usted inglés?** *ah-blah oos-TEHD een-GLAYS*
I speak (a little) Spanish.	**Hablo español (un poco).** *AH-bloh ehs-pah-NYOHL (oon POH-koh)*
I don't speak Spanish.	**No hablo español.** *noh AH-bloh ehs-pah-NYOHL*

Is there anyone here who speaks English?	**¿Hay alguien aquí que hable inglés?** *AH-ee AHL-ghee-ehn ah-KEE kay AH-blay een-GLAYS*
Do you understand?	**¿Comprende usted?** *kohm-PREHN-day oos-tehd*
I understand.	**Yo comprendo.** *yoh kohm-PREHN-doh*
I don't understand.	**No comprendo.** *noh kohm-PREHN-doh*
What? What did you say?	**¿Cómo?** *KOH-moh*
How do you say ____ in Spanish?	**¿Cómo se dice ____ en español?** *KOH-moh say DEE-say ____ ehn ehs-pah-NYOHL*
What do you call this (that) in Spanish?	**¿Cómo se llama esto (eso) en español?** *KOH-moh say YAH-mah EHS-toh (EHS-oh) ehn ehs-pahn-YOHL*
Please speak slowly.	**Hable despacio, por favor.** *AH-blay dehs-PAH-see-oh pohr fah-BOHR*
Please repeat.	**Repita, por favor.** *ray-PEE-tah pohr fah-BOHR*

INTRODUCTIONS

I'm American (English) (Australian) (Canadian).	**Soy norteamericano(a), (inglés, inglesa), (australiano, australiana), (canadiense).** *soy nohr-tay-ah-mehr-ee-KAH-noh (nah) (een-GLAYS een-GLAY-sah) (ow-strahl-YAH-noh nah) (kah-nah-DYEHN-say)*
My name is ____.	**Me llamo ____.** *may YAH-moh*

What's your name?	**¿Cómo se llama usted?** *KOH-moh say YAH-mah oos-TEHD*
How are you?	**¿Cómo está usted?** *KOH-moh ehs-TAH oos-TEHD*
How's everything?	**¿Qué tal?** *kay tahl*
Very well, thanks. And you?	**Muy bien, gracias. ¿Y usted?** *mwee bee-EHN GRAH-see-ahs ee oos-TEHD*

GETTING AROUND

Where is ____?	**¿Dónde está ____?** *DOHN-day ehs-TAH*
■ the bathroom	**el baño** *ehl BAH-nyoh*
■ the bus stop	**la parada de autobuses** *lah pahr-AH-dah day ow-tow-BOOS-ehs*
■ the dining room	**el comedor** *ehl koh-meh-DOHR*
■ the entrance	**la entrada** *lah ehn-TRAH-dah*
■ the exit	**la salida** *lah sahl-EE-dah*
■ the subway	**el metro** *ehl MEH-troh*
■ the taxi stand	**la parada de taxis** *lah pah-RAH-dah day TAHK-sees*
■ the telephone	**el teléfono** *ehl tehl-EHF-oh-noh*
■ the train station	**la estación de trenes** *lah esh-tah-SYOHN day TREH-nehs*
I'm lost.	**Me he perdido.** *may heh pehr-DEE-doh*
We're lost.	**Nos hemos perdido.** *nohs HEH-mohs pehr-DEE-doh*
Where are ____?	**¿Dónde están ____?** *dohn-day ehs-TAHN*

I am looking ____.	**Busco ____.** *BOOS-koh*
■ to the left	**a la izquierda** *ah lah ees-kee-EHR-dah*
■ to the right	**a la derecha** *ah lah dehr-EH-chah*
■ straight ahead	**derecho** *deh-REH-choh*

QUESTIONS

Where is (are) ____?	**¿Dónde está (están) ____?** *DOHN-day eh-STAH (STAHN)*
When?	**¿Cuándo?** *KWAHN-doh*
How?	**¿Cómo?** *KOH-moh*
How much?	**¿Cuánto?** *KWAHN-toh*
Who?	**¿Quién?** *key-EN*
Why?	**¿Por qué?** *pohr KAY*
Which?	**¿Cuál?** *kwal*
What?	**¿Qué?** *kay*

PROBLEMS, PROBLEMS, PROBLEMS (EMERGENCIES)

Watch out!	**¡Cuidado!** *kwee-DAH-doh*
Hurry up!	**¡Dése prisa!** *day-say PREE-sah*
Look!	**¡Mire!** *MEE-reh*
Listen!	**¡Escuche!** *ehs-KOO-cheh*

Wait!	**¡Espere!** *ehs-PEHR-eh*
Fire!	**¡Fuego!** *FWAY-goh*
Leave me alone!	**¡Déjeme en paz!** *DAY-heh-meh ehn PAHS*
Help, police!	**¡Socorro, policía!** *soh-KOH-roh poh-lee-SEE-yah*
That guy is a thief!	**¡Ese tipo es un ladrón!** *ehs-eh tee-poh ehs oon lah-DROHN*
He has stolen ____.	**Me ha robado ____.** *may ah roh-BAH-doh*
▨ my car	**el coche** *ehl KOH-chay*
▨ my passport	**el pasaporte** *ehl pah-sah-POHR-tay*
▨ my purse	**la bolsa** *lah BOHL-sah*
▨ my suitcase	**la maleta** *lah mahl-EH-tah*
▨ my wallet	**la cartera** *lah kahr-TEHR-ah*
▨ my watch	**el reloj** *ehl ray-LOH*
I want to go ____.	**Quiero ir ____.** *kee-YEHR-oh eer*
▨ to the American (British) (Australian) (Canadian) Consulate	**al consulado norteamericano (inglés), (australiano), (canadiense)** *ahl kohn-soo-LAH-doh nohr-tay-ah-mehr-ee-KAH-noh (een-GLAYS) (ow-strahl-YAH-noh) (kah-nah-DYEHN-say)*
▨ to the police station	**al cuartel de policía** *ahl kwahr-TEHL day poh-lee-SEE-ah*
I need help, quick.	**Necesito ayuda, pronto.** *nehs-ehs-EE-toh ah-YOO-dah PROHN-toh*
Can you help me, please?	**¿Puede usted ayudarme, por favor?** *pweh-day oos-TEHD ah-yoo-DAHR-may pohr fah-BOHR*

I have lost ___.	**He perdido ___.** *ay pehr-DEE-doh*
Does anyone here speak English?	**¿Hay alguien aquí que hable inglés?** *AHl-ee AHL-ghee-yehn ah-KEE kay AH-blay een-GLEHS*
I need an interpreter.	**Necesito un intérprete.** *neh-seh-SEE-toh oon een-TEHR-preh-tay*

NUMBERS

CARDINAL NUMBERS

0	**cero** *SEHR-oh*
1	**uno** *OO-noh*
2	**dos** *dohs*
3	**tres** *trehs*
4	**cuatro** *KWAH-troh*
5	**cinco** *SEEN-koh*
6	**seis** *sayss*
7	**siete** *SYEH-tay*
8	**ocho** *OH-choh*
9	**nueve** *NWEH-bay*
10	**diez** *dyehs*
11	**once** *OHN-say*
12	**doce** *DOH-say*
13	**trece** *TREH-say*
14	**catorce** *kah-TOHR-say*

15	**quince** *KEEN-say*
16	**diez y seis (dieciséis)** *dyeh-see-SAYSS*
17	**diez y siete (diecisiete)** *dyeh-see-SYEH-tay*
18	**diez y ocho (dieciocho)** *dyeh-see-OH-choh*
19	**diez y nueve (diecinueve)** *dyeh-see-NWEH-bay*
20	**veinte** *BAYN-tay*
21	**veintiuno** *bayn-tee-OO-noh*
22	**veintidós** *bayn-tee-DOHS*
23	**veintitrés** *bayn-tee-TREHS*
24	**veinticuatro** *bayn-tee-KWAH-troh*
25	**veinticinco** *bayn-tee-SEEN-koh*
26	**veintiséis** *bayn-tee-SAYSS*
27	**veintisiete** *bayn-tee-SYEH-tay*
28	**veintiocho** *bayn-tee-OH-choh*
29	**veintinueve** *bayn-tee-NWEH-bay*
30	**treinta** *TRAYN-tah*
40	**cuarenta** *kwahr-EHN-tah*
50	**cincuenta** *seen-KWEHN-tah*
60	**sesenta** *seh-SEHN-tah*
70	**setenta** *seh-TEHN-tah*
80	**ochenta** *oh-CHEHN-tah*

90	**noventa**	*noh-BEHN-tah*
100	**cien(to)**	*syehn(toh)*
■ 101	**ciento uno**	*SYEHN-toh OO-noh*
■ 102	**ciento dos**	*SYEHN-toh DOHS*
200	**doscientos (as)**	*dohs-SYEHN-tohs (tahs)*
300	**trescientos (as)**	*trehs-SYEHN-tohs (tahs)*
400	**cuatrocientos (as)**	*kwah-troh-SYEHN-tohs (tahs)*
500	**quinientos (as)**	*kee-NYEHN-tohs (tahs)*
600	**seiscientos (as)**	*sayss-SYEHN-tohs (tahs)*
700	**setecientos (as)**	*seh-teh-SYEHN-tohs (tahs)*
800	**ochocientos (as)**	*oh-choh-SYEHN-tohs (tahs)*
900	**novecientos (as)**	*noh-beh-SYEHN-tohs (tahs)*
1.000	**mil**	*meel*
2.000	**dos mil**	*dohs meel*
1.000.000	**un millón**	*oon mee-YOHN*
2.000.000	**dos millones**	*dohs mee-YOHN-ays*

Note: In Spanish, thousands are separated by periods, not commas.

ORDINAL NUMBERS

first	**primero (primer, -a)** *pree-MEH-roh (rah)*
second	**segundo (a)** *seh-GOON-doh (dah)*
third	**tercero (tercer,-a)** *tehr-SEH-roh (rah)*
fourth	**cuarto (a)** *KWAHR-toh (tah)*
fifth	**quinto (a)** *KEEN-toh (tah)*
sixth	**sexto (a)** *SEHS-toh (tah)*
seventh	**séptimo (a)** *SEHT-tee-moh (mah)*
eighth	**octavo (a)** *ohk-TAH-boh (bah)*
ninth	**noveno (a)** *noh-BAY-noh (nah)*
tenth	**décimo (a)** *DEH-see-moh (mah)*
last	**último (a)** *OOL-tee-moh (mah)*
once	**una vez** *OO-nah behs*
twice	**dos veces** *dohs BEH-sehs*
three times	**tres veces** *trehs BEH-sehs*

FRACTIONS

half of ____.	**la mitad de ____.** *lah mee-TAHD day*
▪ half (of) the money	**la mitad del dinero** *lah mee-TAHD del dee-NEH-row*
half a ____.	**medio ____.** *MEH-dyoh*
▪ half a kilo	**medio kilo** *MEH-dyoh KEE-loh*
a fourth (quarter)	**un cuarto** *oon KWAHR-toh*

WHEN YOU ARRIVE

PASSPORT AND CUSTOMS

My name is ____.	**Me llamo ____.** *may YAH-moh*
I'm American (British) (Australian) (Canadian).	**Soy norteamericano(a), (inglés, a), (australiano, a), (canadiense).** *soy nohr-tay-ah-mehr-ee-KAH-noh(nah) (een-GLAYS ah) (ow-strahl-YAH-noh nah) (kah-nah-DYEHN-say)*
My address is ____.	**Mi dirección es ____.** *mee dee-rehk-SYOHN ehs*
I'm staying at ____.	**Estoy en el hotel ____.** *ehs-TOY ehn ehl oh-TEHL*
Here is (are) ____.	**Aquí tiene ____.** *ah-KEE TYEHN-ay*

■ my documents — **mis documentos** *mees doh-koo-MEHN-tohs*

■ my passport — **mi pasaporte** *mee pah-sah-POHR-tay*

■ my tourist card — **mi tarjeta de turista** *mee tahr-HAY-tah day toor-EES-tah*

I'm ____.	**Estoy ____.** *ehs-TOY*

■ on a business trip — **en un viaje de negocios** *ehn oon bee-AH-hay day neh-GOH-see-ohs*

■ on vacation — **de vacaciones** *day bah-kah-SYOHN-ays*

■ visiting relatives — **visitando a mis familiares** *bee-see-TAHN-doh ah mees fah-meel-YAHR-ays*

| just passing through | **solamente de paso** *soh-lah-MEHN-tay day PAH-soh* |

I'll be staying here ____. | **Me quedaré aquí ____.** *may kay-dahr-AY ah-KEE* |

a few days	**unos días** *OON-ohs DEE-ahs*
a few weeks	**unas semanas** *OON-ahs seh-MAH-nahs*
a week	**una semana** *OON-ah seh-MAH-nah*
a month	**un mes** *oon mehs*

I'm traveling ____. | **Viajo ____.** *bee-AH-hoh* |

alone	**solo(a)** *SOH-loh(lah)*
with my husband	**con mi marido** *kohn mee mah-REE-doh*
with my wife	**con mi mujer** *kohn mee moo-HAIR*
with my family	**con mi familia** *kohn mee fah-MEEL-yah*
with my friend	**con mi amigo(a)** *kohn mee ah-MEE-go(ah)*

These are my bags. | **Estas son mis maletas.** *EHS-tahs sohn mees mah-LAY-tahs* |

I have nothing to declare. | **No tengo nada que declarar.** *noh tehn-goh NAH-dah kay day-klahr-AHR* |

I only have ____. | **Sólo tengo ____.** *SOH-loh tehn-goh* |

| a carton of cigarettes | **un cartón de cigarrillos** *oon kahr-TOHN day see-gahr-EE-yohs* |
| a bottle of whisky | **una botella de whisky** *OON-nah boh-TEH-yah day WEE-skee* |

What's the problem? | **¿Hay algún problema?** *AH-ee ahl-GOON proh-BLAY-mah* |

They're gifts (for my personal use).	**Son regalos (para mi uso personal).** *sohn ray-GAH-lohs (pah-rah mee OO-soh pehr-sohn-AHL)*
Do I have to pay duty?	**¿Tengo que pagar impuestos?** *ten-goh kay pah-GAHR eem-PWEHS-tohs*

BAGGAGE AND PORTERS

Where can I find a baggage cart?	**¿Dónde está un carrito para-maletas?** *DOHN-day eh-STAH oon kahr-REE-toh pah-rah mah-LEH-tahs*
I need a porter!	**¡Necesito un maletero!** *neh-seh-SEE-toh oon mah-leh-TEH-roh*
These are our (my) bags.	**Estas son nuestras (mis) maletas.** *EHS-tahs sohn NWEHS-trahs (mees) mah-LEH-tahs*
■ that big (little) one	**esa grande (pequeña)** *EH-sah GRAHN-day (peh-KAYN-yah)*
■ these two black (green) ones	**estas dos negras (verdes)** *EHS-tahs dos NEH-grahs (BEHR-days)*
Put them here (there).	**Póngalas aquí (allí).** *POHN-gah-lahs ah-KEE (ah-YEE)*
Be careful with that one!	**¡Cuidado con ésa!** *kwee-DAH-doh kohn EH-sah*
I'm missing a suitcase.	**Me falta una maleta.** *may FAHL-tah oo-nah mah-LEH-tah*
How much do I owe you?	**¿Cuánto le debo?** *KWAHN-toh lay DEHB-oh*

Thank you (very much). This is for you.	**(Muchas) gracias. Esto es para usted.** *(moo-chahs) GRAHS-yahs EHS-toh ehs pah-rah oos-TEHD*
Where can I get a taxi?	**¿Dónde puedo tomar un taxi?** *DOHN-deh PWEH-doh toh-MAHR oon TAHK-see*
How much is the taxi ride into the city?	**¿Cuánto cuesta el viaje en taxi a la ciudad?** *KWAHN-toh KWEHS-tah ehl BYAH-heh ehn TAHK-see ah lah see-yoo-DAHD*
What buses go into the city?	**¿Qué autobuses van a la ciudad?** *KAY ow-toh-BOOS-ehs bahn ah lah see-you-DAHD*
Where is the bus stop?	**¿Dónde está la parada del autobús?** *DOHN-deh ehs-TAH lah pah-RAH-dah del ow-toh-BOOS*
How much is the fare?	**¿Cuánto cuesta el viaje?** *KWAHN-toh KWEHS-tah ehl BYAH-heh*
Where can I rent a car?	**¿Donde puedo arrendar un coche?** *DOHN-deh PWEH-doh ah-ren-DAHR oon KOH-cheh*

BANKING AND MONEY MATTERS

EXCHANGING MONEY

Where can I find an ATM machine?	**¿Dónde hay un cajero automático?** *DOHN-day AH-ee oon kah-HEHR-oh ow-toh-MAH-tee-koh*

Where is the currency exchange (bank)?	**¿Dónde hay un banco para cambiar moneda extranjera?** *DOHN-day AH-ee oon BAHN-koh pah-rah kahm-bee-AHR moh-NAY-dah ehs-trahn-HEHR-ah*
I wish to change ____.	**Quiero cambiar ____.** *kee-YEHR-oh kahm-bee-YAHR*
■ money	**dinero** *dee-NEHR-oh*
■ dollars	**dólares** *DOH-lahr-ays*
travelers checks ■	**cheques de viajero** *CHEH-kays day bee-ah-HAIR-oh*
Can I cash a personal check?	**¿Puedo cambiar un cheque personal?** *PWEH-doh kahm-bee-YAHR oon CHEH-kay pehr-sohn-AHL*
At what time do they open (close)?	**¿A qué hora abren (cierran)?** *ah kay ohra AH-brehn (SYEHR-ahn)*
Where is the cashier's window?	**¿Dónde está la caja, por favor?** *DOHN-day eh-STAH lah KAH-hah pohr fah-BOHR*
What's the current exchange rate for dollars?	**¿A cómo está el cambio hoy del dólar?** *ah KOH-moh ehs-TAH ehl KAHM-bee-oh oy del DOH-lahr*
What commission do you charge?	**¿Cuál es el interés que ustedes cobran?** *kwahl ehs ehl een-tehr-AYS kay oos-TEHD-ays KOH-brahn*
I'd like to cash this check.	**Quisiera cobrar este cheque.** *kee-SYEHR-ah koh-BRAHR EHS-teh CHEH-kay*
Where do I sign?	**¿Dónde debo firmar?** *DOHN-day DEH-boh feer-MAHR*

I'd like the money ____.	**Quisiera el dinero ____.** *kee-SYEHR-ah ehl dee-NEHR -oh*
■ in (large) bills	**en billetes (grandes)** *ehn bee-YEH-tehs (GRAHN-days)*
■ in small change	**en suelto** *ehn SWEHL-toh*
Give me two twenty-peso bills.	**Déme dos billetes de a veinte pesos.** *DEH-may dohs bee-YEH-tays day ah BAYN-tay PAY-sohs*
■ fifty-peso bills	**cincuenta** *seen-KWEHN-tah*
■ one hundred-euro bills	**cien** *see-YEHN*
Do you accept credit cards?	**¿Acepta usted tarjetas de crédito?** *a-SEHP-tah oo-STEHD tahr-HAY-tahs day KREHD-ee-toh*

AT THE HOTEL

CHECKING IN

I'd like a single (double) room for tonight.	**Quisiera una habitación con una sola cama (con dos camas) para esta noche.** *kee-SYEHR-ah OO-nah ah-bee-tah-SYOHN kohn OO-nah SOH-lah KAH-mah (kohn dohs KAH-mahs) pah-rah EHS-tah NOH-chay*
How much is the room ____?	**¿Cuánto cuesta el cuarto ____?** *KWAHN-toh KWEHS-tah ehl KWAHR-toh*
■ with a shower	**con ducha** *kohn DOO-chah*
■ with a private bath	**con baño privado** *kohn BAHN-yoh pree-BAH-doh*
■ with a balcony	**con balcón** *kohn bahl-KOHN*
■ facing the ocean	**con vista al mar** *kohn bees-tah ahl mahr*

■ facing the street	**que dé a la calle** *kay day ah lah KAH-yeh*
Does it have ___?	**¿Tiene ___?** *tee-YEH-neh*
■ air-conditioning	**aire acondicionado** *AH-ee-ray ah-kohn-dee-syohn-AH-doh*
■ television	**televisión** *teh-lay-bee-SYOHN*
Is there ___ at the hotel?	**¿Hay ___ en el hotel?** *AH-ee ehn ehl oh-TEL*
■ a fitness center	**un gimnasio** *oon heem-NAH-see-yoh*
■ a restaurant	**un restaurante** *oon rest-ow-RAHN-teh*
■ a swimming pool	**una piscina** *oo-nah pee-SEE-nah*
■ a gift shop	**una tienda de regalos** *oo-nah TYEHN-dah day reh-GAH-lohs*
■ valet parking	**personal de estacionamiento** *pehr-sohn-AHL day es-tah-syohn-ah-MYEHN-toh*
■ a laundry	**una lavandería** *oo-nah lah-bahn-dehr-EE-ah*
■ dry cleaning service	**servicio de limpiado en seco** *sehr-BEE-syoh day leem-PYAH-doh en SEH-koh*
I (don't) have a reservation.	**(No) tengo reserva.** *(noh) ten-goh reh-SEHR-bah*
May I see the room?	**¿Podría ver la habitación?** *poh-DREE-ah behr lah ah-bee-tah-SYOHN*
I (don't) like it.	**(No) me gusta.** *(noh) may GOOS-tah*
Do you have something ___?	**¿Hay algo ___?** *AH-ee ahl-goh*
■ better	**mejor** *may-HOHR*

larger	**más grande** *mahs GRAHN-day*
smaller	**más pequeño** *mahs peh-KAYN-yo*
cheaper	**más barato** *mahs bah-RAH-toh*
quieter	**donde no se oigan ruidos** *DOHN-day noh say OY-gahn RWEE-dohs*

| What floor is it on? | **¿En qué piso está?** *ehn kay PEE-soh ehs-TAH* |

| Is there an elevator? | **¿Hay ascensor?** *AH-ee ah-sen-SOHR* |

| Is everything included? | **¿Está todo incluído?** *eh-STAH toh-doh een-kloo-EE-doh* |

| How much is the room with ____? | **¿Cuánto cobra usted por la habitación ____?** *KWAHN-toh KOH-brah oos-TEHD pohr lah ah-bee-tah-SYOHN* |

the American plan (2 meals a day)	**con media pensión** *kohn MEH-dee-yah pen-SYOHN*
bed and breakfast	**con desayuno** *kohn dehs-ah-YOO-noh*
no meals	**sin la comida** *seen lah koh-MEE-dah*

| The room is very nice. I'll take it. | **La habitación es muy bonita. Me quedo con ella.** *lah ah-bee-tah-SYOHN ehs mwee boh-NEE-tah may KAY-doh kohn EH-ya* |

We'll be staying ____.	**Nos quedamos ____.** *nohs kay-DAH-mohs*
one night	**una noche** *oo-nah NOH-chay*
a few nights	**unas noches** *oo-nahs NOH-chays*
one week	**una semana** *oo-nah seh-MAH-nah*

How much do you charge for children?	**¿Cuanto cobra por los niños?** *kwahn-toh KOH-brah pohr lohs NEEN-yohs*
Could you put another bed in the room?	**¿Podría poner otra cama en la habitación?** *poh-DREE-ah poh-NEHR oh-trah KAH-mah ehn lah ah-bee-tah-SYOHN*
Is there a charge? How much?	**¿Hay que pagar más? ¿Cuánto?** *AH-ee kay pah-GAHR mahs? KWAHN-toh*
Do you have a crib for the baby?	**¿Tiene una cuna para el nene (la nena)?** *TYEHN-eh oo-nah COO-nah pah-rah el NEH-neh (lah NEH-nah)*
Do you know someone who baby-sits? (a sitter)	**¿Conoce a alguien que pueda cuidar a los niños? (un síter)** *coh-NOH-say AHL-ghee-ehn kay PWEH-day kwee-DAHR ah lohs NEE-nyohs (oon SEE-tehr)*
Does the room have T.V.?	**¿Hay televisión en la habitación?** *AH-ee tel-eh-bee-SYOHN en lah ah-bee-tah-SYOHN*
Do you receive satellite programs (cable, CNN, programs in English)?	**¿Recibe programas de satélite (cable, CNN, en inglés)?** *reh-SEE-beh pro-GRAH-mahs deh sah-TEL-ee-tay (KAH-blay seh ehn-eh ehn-eh ehn een-GLEHS)*

TRAVELERS WITH SPECIAL NEEDS

Do you have facilities for the disabled?	**¿Tienen facilidades para los incapacitados?** *tee-EH-nen fah-see-lee-DAH-dehs PAH-rah lohs een-kah-pah-see-TAH-dohs*

Do you have a toilet equipped for the handicapped?	**¿Tienen baños equipados para gente incapacitada?** *tee-YEN-en BAHN-yohs eh-kee-PAH-dos par-rah HEN-teh een-kah-pah-see-TAH-dah*
Can you provide a wheelchair?	**¿Podría facilitar una silla de ruedas?** *po-DREE-ah fah-see-lee-TAHR oo-nah SEE-yah day RWAY-dahs*
Is there room in the elevator for a wheelchair?	**¿Tiene espacio el ascensor para una silla de ruedas?** *tee-YEN-eh es-PAH-see-oh el ah-sen-SOHR pah-rah oo-nah SEE-yah day RWAY-dahs*
I cannot climb stairs/walk by myself.	**No puedo subir las escaleras/caminar por mí mismo.** *noh PWAY-doh soo-BEER lahs es-cah-LEHR-ahs/kah-mee-NAHR por mee MEES-moh*
Is there an ambulance (ambulette, taxi, private car) service available?	**¿Hay un servicio de ambulancia (transporte médico especializado, taxi, coche privado) disponible?** *AH-ee oon sehr-BEE-see-yoh day ahm-boo-LAHN-syah (trahns-POHR-teh MEH-dee-koh ehs-peh-see-ah-lee-SAH-doh TAHK-see COH-chay pree-BAH-doh) dees-pohn-EE-blay*
Is there a doctor in the hotel?	**¿Hay un médico en el hotel?** *AH-ee oon MED-ee-ko en ehl oh-TEL*
How can we get a doctor in an emergency?	**¿Cómo podemos conseguir un médico en caso de emergencia?** *KOH-moh poh-day-mohs kohn-say-GEER oon MED-ee-koh en KAH-soh day ehm-ehr-HEN-syah.*
Do you allow seeing-eye dogs?	**¿Se permiten perros de guía?** *say pehr-MEE-ten PEH-rohs day GHEE-ah*

I have asthma/heart problems.	**Padezco de asma/de problemas del corazón.** *pah-DES-coh deh AHS-mah/dey pro-BLAY-mahs dehl cohr-ah-SOHN*
We need a crutch (crutches, a walker, a cane).	**Necesitamos una muleta (muletas, un caminante, un bastón).** *neh-ses-ee-TAH-mohs oo-nah moo-LET-ah (moo-LET-ahs, oon cah-mee-NAHN-tay, oon bah-STOHN)*
Are there access ramps for wheelchairs?	**¿Hay rampas de acceso para sillas de ruedas?** *AH-ee RAHM-pahs day ahk-SES-oh pah-rah SEE-yahs day RWAY-das*

ORDERING BREAKFAST

We'll have breakfast in the room.	**Queremos desayunar en nuestra habitación.** *keh-RAY-mohs dehs-ah-yoo-NAHR ehn NWEHS-trah ah-bee-tah-SYOHN*
We'd like _____.	**Quisiéramos _____.** *kee-SYEHR-ah-mohs*
Please send up _____.	**Haga el favor de mandarnos.** *AH-gah ehl fah-BOHR day mahn-DAHR-nohs*
◼ one (two) coffee(s)	**una taza (dos tazas) de café** *oo-nah TAH-sah (dohs TAH-sahs) day kah-FAY*
◼ butter	**mantequilla** *mahn-teh-KEE-yah*
◼ cold cuts	**fiambres** *fee-AHM-brehs*
◼ cereal	**cereal** *sehr-eh-AHL*

■ grapefruit	**toronja (pomelo)**	*tohr-OHN-ha (poh-MEH-loh)*
■ white bread	**pan blanco**	*pahn BLAHN-koh*
■ black bread	**pan moreno (pan negro)**	*pahn morh-EH-noh (pan NEH-groh)*
■ rye bread	**pan de centeno**	*pahn day sehn-TEH-noh*
■ margarine	**margarina**	*mahr-gahr-EE-nah*
■ tea	**una taza de té**	*oo-nah TAH-sah day teh*
■ hot chocolate	**una taza de chocolate**	*oo-nah TAH-sah day cho-koh-LAH-tay*
■ a sweet roll	**un pan dulce**	*oon pahn DOOL-say*
■ fruit (juice)	**un jugo (de fruta)**	*oon HOO-goh day FROO-tah*
■ bacon and eggs	**huevos con tocino**	*WEH-bohs kohn toh-SEE-noh*
■ scrambled (fried, boiled) eggs	**huevos revueltos (fritos, pasados por agua)**	*WEH-bohs ray-BWEHL-tohs (FREE-tohs pah-SAH-dohs pohr AH-gwah)*
■ toast	**pan tostado**	*pahn tohs-TAH-doh*
■ jam (marmalade)	**mermelada**	*mehr-may-LAH-dah*
Please don't make it too spicy.	**No lo haga muy picante.**	*noh loh AH-gah mwee pee-KAHN-tay*

HOTEL SERVICES

Where is ____?	**¿Dónde esta ____?**	*dohn-day ehs-TAH*
■ the dining room	**el comedor**	*ehl koh-meh-DOHR*
■ the bathroom	**el baño**	*ehl BAHN-yo*

■ the elevator (lift)	**el ascensor** *ehl ah-sen-SOHR*
■ the phone	**el teléfono** *ehl tel-EF-oh-no*
What is my room number?	**¿Cuál es el número de mi cuarto?** *kwahl ehs ehl NOO-mehr-oh day mee KWAR-toh*
May I please have my key?	**Mi llave, por favor.** *mee YAH-bay pohr fah-BOHR*
I've lost my key.	**He perdido mi llave.** *eh pehr-DEE-doh mee YAH-bay*
I need ____.	**Necesito ____.** *neh-seh-SEE-toh*
■ a bellhop	**un botones** *oon boh-TOH-nays*
■ a chambermaid	**una camarera** *oo-nah kah-mah-REHR-ah*
Please send ____ to my room.	**Haga el favor de mandar ____ a mi habitación.** *AH-gah ehl fah-BOHR day mahn-DAHR ah mee ah-bee-tah-SYOHN*
■ a towel	**una toalla** *oo-nah toh-AH-yah*
■ a bar of soap	**una pastilla de jabón** *oo-nah pahs-TEE-yah day hah-BOHN*
■ some hangers	**unas perchas** *oo-nahs PEHR-chahs*
■ a pillow	**una almohada** *oo-nah ahl-moh-AH-dah*
■ a blanket	**una manta** *oo-nah MAHN-tah*
■ some ice cubes	**cubitos de hielo** *koo-BEE-tohs day YEH-loh*
■ some ice water	**agua helada** *ah-guah eh-LAH-dah*
■ a bottle of mineral water	**una botella de agua mineral** *oo-nah boh-TEH-yah day AH-guah mee-nehr-AHL*
■ an ashtray	**un cenicero** *oon sen-ee-SEHR-oh*

▨ toilet paper	**papel higiénico** *pah-PEHL ee-HYEHN-ee-koh*
▨ an electric adapter	**un adaptador eléctrico** *oon ah-dahp-tah-DOHR eh-LEK-tree-koh*
Who is it?	**¿Quién es?** *kee-EHN ehs*
Just a minute.	**Un momento.** *oon moh-MEN-toh*
Come in.	**Adelante.** *ah-del-AHN-tay*
Put it on the table.	**Póngalo en la mesa.** *POHN-gah-loh ehn lah MAY-sah*
Please wake me tomorrow at ____.	**¿Puede despertarme mañana a ____?** *PWEH-day dehs-pehr-TAHR-may mahn-YAH-nah ah*

COMPLAINTS

There is no ____.	**No hay ____.** *noh AH-ee*
▨ running water	**agua corriente** *AH-gwah kohr-YEN-tay*
▨ hot water	**agua caliente** *AH-gwah kahl-YEN-tay*
▨ electricity	**electricidad** *eh-lek-tree-see-DAHD*
The ____ doesn't work.	**No funciona ____.** *noh foon-SYOHN-ah*
▨ air-conditioning	**el aire acondicionado** *ehl AH-ee-ray ah-kohn-dees-yohn-AH-doh*
▨ fan	**el ventilador** *ehl ben-tee-lah-DOHR*
▨ faucet	**el grifo** *ehl GREE-foh*
▨ lamp	**la lámpara** *lah LAHM-pah-rah*
▨ light	**la luz** *lah loos*
▨ radio	**la radio** *lah RAH-dee-oh*
▨ electric socket	**el enchufe** *ehl ehn-CHOO-fay*

■ light switch	**el interruptor**	*ehl een-tehr-oop-TOHR*
■ television	**el televisor**	*ehl tel-eh-bee-SOHR*
Can you fix it ____?	**¿Puede arreglarlo ____?**	*PWEH-day ah-ray-GLAHR-loh*
■ now	**ahora**	*ah-OH-rah*
■ as soon as possible	**lo más pronto posible**	*loh mahs PROHN-toh poh-SEE-blay*

AT THE DESK

Are there any ____ for me?	**¿Hay ____ para mí?**	*AH-ee pah-rah MEE*
■ letters	**cartas**	*KAHR-tahs*
■ messages	**recados**	*ray-KAH-dohs*
■ packages	**paquetes**	*pah-KEH-tays*
■ postcards	**postales**	*pohs-TAH-lays*
Did anyone call for me?	**¿Preguntó alguien por mí?**	*preh-goon-TOH AHL-ghee-ehn pohr MEE*

CHECKING OUT

I'd like the bill, please.

Quisiera la cuenta, por favor.
kee-SYEHR-ah lah KWEHN-tah pohr fah-BOHR

I'll be checking out today (tomorrow).

Pienso marcharme hoy (mañana).
PYEHN-soh mahr-CHAR-may oy (mahn-YA-nah)

Please send some-one up for our baggage.

Haga el favor de mandar a alguien para recoger nuestro equipaje.
AH-gah ehl fah-BOHR day mahn-DAHR ah AHL-ghy-ehn pah-rah ray-koh-HEHR NWEHS-troh AY-kee-PAH-hay

GETTING AROUND TOWN

THE BUS

Where is the bus stop (terminal)?	**¿Dónde esta la parada (la terminal) de autobús?** *DOHN-day ehs-TAH lah pah-RAH-dah (lah tehr-mee-NAHL) day AH-oo-toh-BOOS*
Which bus do I take to get to ____?	**¿Qué autobús hay que tomar para ir a ____?** *kay AH-oo-toh-BOOS AH-ee kay toh-MAHR PAH-rah eer ah*
Do I need exact change?	**¿Necesito tener cambio exacto?** *neh-seh-SEE-toh ten-EHR KAHM-bee-oh ehk-SAHK-toh*
In which direction do I have to go?	**¿Qué rumbo tengo que tomar?** *kay ROOM-boh TEN-goh kay toh-MAHR*
How often do the buses run?	**¿Con qué frecuencia salen los autobuses?** *kohn kay freh-KWEHN-see-ah SAH-lehn lohs AH-oo-toh-BOOS-ehs*
Do you go to ____?	**¿Va usted a ____?** *bah oos-TEHD ah*
Is it far from here?	**¿Está lejos de aquí?** *eh-STAH LAY-hos day ah-KEE*
How many stops are there?	**¿Cuántas paradas hay?** *KWAHN-tahs pah-RAH-dahs AH-ee*
Do I have to change?	**¿Tengo que cambiar?** *TEN-goh kay kahm-bee-AHR*

How much is the fare?	**¿Cuánto es el billete?** *KWAHN-toh ehs ehl bee-YEH-tay*
Where do I have to get off?	**¿Dónde tengo que bajarme?** *DOHN-day ten-goh kay bah-HAHR-may*
Please tell me where to get off.	**Dígame, por favor, dónde debo bajarme.** *DEE-gah-may pohr fa-BOHR DOHN-day deh-boh bah-HAHR-may*

THE SUBWAY (UNDERGROUND)

Is there a subway (underground) in this city?	**¿Hay un metro en esta ciudad?** *AH-ee oon MEHT-roh ehn EHS-tah syoo-DAHD*
Where is the closest subway (underground) station?	**¿Dónde está la estación más cercana?** *DOHN-day eh-STAH lah ehs-tah-SYOHN mahs sehr-KAH-nah*
How much is the fare?	**¿Cuánto es la tarifa?** *KWAHN-toh ehs lah tah-REE-fah*
Where can I buy a token (a ticket)?	**¿Dónde puedo comprar una ficha (un billete)?** *DOHN-day PWEH-doh kohm-PRAHR oo-nah FEE-chah (oon bee-YEH-teh)*
Which is the line that goes to _____?	**¿Cuál es la línea que va a _____?** *kwahl ehs lah LEEN-eh-ah kay bah ah*
Does this train go to _____?	**¿Va este tren a _____?** *bah ehs-teh trehn ah*
Do you have a map showing the stops?	**¿Tiene un mapa que indique las paradas?** *TYEH-nay oon MAH-pah kay een-DEE-kay lahs pahr-AH-dahs*

How many more stops?	**¿Cuántas paradas más?** *KWAHN-tahs pah-RAH-dahs mahs?*
What's the next station?	**¿Cuál es la próxima estación?** *kwahl ehs lah PROHK-see-mah ehs-tah-SYOHN*
Where should I get off?	**¿Dónde debo bajarme?** *DOHN-day deh-boh bah-HAHR-may*
Do I have to change?	**¿Tengo que hacer trasbordo?** *ten-goh kay ah-SEHR trahs-BOHRD-oh*
Please tell me when we get there.	**Haga el favor de avisarme cuando lleguemos.** *AH-gah ehl fah-BOHR day ah-bee-SAHR-may kwahn-doh yeh-GAY-mohs*

TAXIS

Is there a taxi stand near here?	**¿Hay una parada de taxis por aquí?** *AH-ee oo-nah pah-RAH-dah day TAHK-sees pohr ah-KEE*
Please get me a taxi.	**¿Puede usted conseguirme un taxi, por favor?** *PWEH-day oos-TEHD kohn-say-GHEER-may oon TAHK-see pohr fah-BOHR*
Where can I get a taxi?	**¿Dónde puedo tomar un taxi?** *DOHN-day PWEH-doh toh-MAHR oon TAHK-see*
Taxi! Are you free (available)?	**¡Taxi! ¿Está libre?** *TAHK-see ehs-TAH LEE-bray*
Take me (I want to go) _____.	**Lléveme (Quiero ir) _____.** *YEHV-eh-may (kee-EHR-oh eer)*

■ to the airport	**al aeropuerto** *ahl ah-ehr-oh-PWEHR-toh*
■ to this address	**a esta dirección** *ah ehs-tah dee-rehk-SYOHN*
■ to the hotel	**al hotel** *ahl o-TEL*
■ to the station	**a la estación** *ah lah ehs-tah-SYOHN*
■ to ____ street	**a la calle ____** *ah lah KAH-yeh*

Do you know where it is? **¿Sabe dónde está?** *sah-bay DOHN-day ehs-TAH*

How much is it to ____? **¿Cuánto cuesta hasta ____?** *KWAHN-toh KWEHS-tah AHS-tah*

Faster! I'm in a hurry. **¡Más rápido, tengo prisa!** *mahs RAH-pee-doh ten-goh PREE-sah*

Please drive slower. **Por favor, conduzca más despacio.** *pohr fah-BOHR kohn-DOOS-kah mahs dehs-PAH-see-oh*

Stop here ____. **Pare aquí ____.** *PAH-ray ah-KEE*

■ at the corner	**en la esquina** *ehn lah ehs-KEE-nah*
■ at the next block	**en la otra calle** *ehn lah OH-trah KAH-yeh*

How much do I owe you? **¿Cuánto le debo?** *KWAHN-toh lay DEHB-oh*

This is for you. **Esto es para usted.** *ehs-toh ehs PAH-rah oos-TEHD*

SIGHTSEEING AND TOURS

Where is the Tourist Information Office? **¿Dónde está la oficina de turismo?** *DOHN-day ehs-TAH lah of-fee-SEEN-ah day toor-EES-moh*

I need a(n) (English-speaking) guide.	**Necesito un guía (de habla inglesa).** *neh-seh-SEE-toh oon GHEE-ah (day AH-blah een-GLAY-sah)*
How much does he charge ____?	**¿Cuánto cobra ____?** *KWAHN-toh KOH-brah*
▪ per hour	**por hora** *pohr OHR-ah*
▪ per day	**por día** *pohr DEE-ah*
There are two (four, six) of us.	**Somos dos (cuatro, seis).** *soh-mohs dohs (KWAHT-roh sayss)*
Where can I buy a guidebook (map)?	**¿Dónde puedo comprar una guía (un mapa)?** *DOHN-day PWEH-doh kohm-PRAHR oo-nah GHEE-ah (oon MAH-pah)*
What are the things of interest here?	**¿Qué cosas interesantes hay aquí?** *kay KOH-sahs een-tehr-ehs-AHN-tays AH-ee ah-KEE*
Are there trips through the city?	**¿Hay excursiones por la ciudad?** *AH-ee ehs-koor-SYOHN-ehs pohr lah see-oo-DAHD*
When does the tour begin?	**¿Cuando empieza la excursión?** *KWAHN-doh ehm-PYEH-sah lah ehs-koor-SOYHN*
How long is the tour?	**¿Cuánto tiempo dura?** *KWAHN-toh TYEHM-poh DOOR-ah*
Where do they leave from?	**¿De dónde salen?** *day DOHN-day SAHL-ehn*
We want to see ____.	**Queremos ver ____.** *kehr-EHM-ohs behr*
▪ the botanical garden	**el jardín botánico** *ehl har-DEEN boh-TAHN-ee-koh*
▪ the bullring	**la plaza de toros** *lah plah-sah day TOHR-ohs*

the business center	**el centro comercial** *ehl SEN-troh koh-mehr-SYAHL*
the castle	**el castillo** *ehl kahs-TEE-yoh*
the cathedral	**la catedral** *lah kah-tay-DRAHL*
the church	**la iglesia** *lah eeg-LEHS-ee-ah*
the concert hall	**la sala de conciertos** *lah SAH-lah day kohn-see-EHR-tohs*
the downtown area	**el centro de la ciudad** *ehl SEN-troh day lah see-oo-DAHD*
the fountains	**las fuentes** *lahs FWEHN-tays*
the library	**la biblioteca** *lah beeb-lee-oh-TAY-kah*
the main park	**el parque central** *ehl pahr-kay sen-TRAHL*
the main square	**la plaza mayor** *lah plah-sah my-YOR*
the market	**el mercado** *ehl mehr-KAH-doh*
the mosque	**la mezquita** *lah mehs-KEE-tah*
the museum (of fine arts)	**el museo (de bellas artes)** *ehl moo-SAY-oh (day bel-yahs AHR-tays)*
a nightclub	**un club nocturno** *oon kloob nohk-TOOR-noh*
the old part of town	**la ciudad vieja** *lah see-oo-DAHD BYEH-ha*
the opera	**la ópera** *lah OH-pehr-ah*
the palace	**el palacio** *ehl pah-LAH-see-oh*
the stadium	**el estadio** *ehl ehs-TAHD-ee-oh*
the synagogue	**la sinagoga** *lah seen-ah-GOH-gah*
the university	**la universidad** *lah oon-ee-behr-see-DAHD*
the zoo	**el parque zoológico** *ehl PAHR-kay soh-oh-LOH-hee-koh*
Is it all right to go in now?	**¿Se puede entrar ahora?** *say PWEH-day ehn-TRAHR ah-OHR-ah*

Is it open (closed)?	**¿Está abierto (cerrado)?** *ehs-TAH ah-bee-YEHR-toh (sehr-AH-doh)*
At what time does it open (close)?	**¿A qué hora se abre (cierra)?** *ah kay OHR-ah say AH-bray (see-YEHR-ah)*
What's the admission price?	**¿Cuánto es la entrada?** *KWAHN-toh ehs lah ehn-TRAH-dah*
How much do children pay?	**¿Cuánto pagan los niños?** *KWAHN-toh pah-GAHN lohs NEEN-yohs*
Is it all right to take pictures?	**¿Se puede sacar fotos?** *say PWEH-deh sah-KAHR FOH-tohs*

PLANNING A TRIP

AIR SERVICES

When is there a flight to ____?	**¿Cuándo hay un vuelo a ____?** *KWAHN-doh AH-ee oon BWEHL-oh ah*
I would like a ____ ticket.	**Quisiera un billete ____.** *kee-see-YEHR-ah oon bee-YEH-tay*
■ round-trip	**de ida y vuelta** *day EE-dah ee BWEHL-tah*
■ one-way	**de ida** *day EE-dah*
■ tourist class	**en clase turista** *ehn KLAH-say toor-EES-tah*
■ first class	**en primera clase** *ehn pree-MEHR-ah KLAH-say*
I would like a seat ____.	**Quisiera un asiento ____.** *kee-see-YEHR-ah oon ah-SYEHN-toh*
■ in the smoking section	**en la sección de fumadores** *ehn lah sehk-SYOHN day foo-mah-DOHR-ehs*

■ in the nonsmoking section **en la sección de no fumadores** *ehn lah sehk-SYOHN day noh foo-mah-DOHR-ehs*

■ next to the window **de ventanilla** *day behn-tah-NEE-yah*

■ on the aisle **de pasillo** *day pah-SEE-yoh*

What is the fare? **¿Cuál es la tarifa?** *kwahl ehs lah tah-REE-fah*

Are meals served? **¿Se sirven comidas?** *say seer-behn koh-MEE-dahs*

When does the plane leave (arrive)? **¿A qué hora sale (llega) el avión?** *ah kay oh-ra SAH-lay (YEH-gah) ehl ah-BYOHN*

When must I be at the airport? **¿Cuándo debo estar en el aeropuerto?** *KWAHN-doh deh-boh ehs-TAHR en ehl ah-ehr-oh-PWEHR-toh*

What is my flight number? **¿Cuál es el número del vuelo?** *kwahl ehs ehl NOO-mehr-oh dehl BWEH-loh*

What gate do we leave from? **¿De qué puerta se sale?** *day kay PWEHR-tah say sah-lay*

I want to confirm (cancel) my reservation for flight ____. **Quiero confirmar (cancelar) mi reservación para el vuelo ____.** *kee-YEHR-oh kohn-feer-MAHR (kahn-say-LAHR) mee reh-sehr-bah-SYOHN pah-rah ehl BWEH-loh*

I'd like to check my bags. **Quisiera facturar mis maletas.** *kee-SYEHR-ah fahk-too-RAHR mees mah-LEH-tahs*

I have only carry-on baggage. **Tengo solo equipaje de mano.** *TEN-goh so-loh ay-kee-PAH-hay day MAH-noh*

Can you pass my film (camera) through by hand?	**¿Podría inspeccionar el film (la cámara) a mano?** *poh-DREE-ah een-spek-syohn-AHR ehl feelm (lah KAH-mahr-ah) ah MAHN-oh*

TRAIN SERVICE

A first- (second-) class ticket to ____ please.	**Un billete de primera (segunda) clase a ____ por favor.** *oon bee-YEH-teh day pree-MEHR-ah (say-GOON-dah) KLAH-say ah pohr fah-BOHR*
Give me a half price ticket	**Deme un medio billete** *DEH-meh oon MEH-dee-oh bee-YEH-teh*
Give me a round-trip ticket	**Deme un billete de ida y vuelta** *DEH-meh oon bee-YEH-teh day EE-dah ee BWEHL-tah*
Give me a one-way ticket	**Deme un billete de ida** *DEH-meh oon bee-YEH-teh day EE-dah*
I'd like a (no) smoking compartment.	**Quisiera Ïun departamento para (no) fumadores.** *kee-SYEHR-ah oon day-pahr-tah-MEHN-toh pah-rah (noh) foo-mah-DOHR-ays*
When does the train arrive (leave)?	**¿Cuándo llega (sale) el tren?** *kwahn-doh YEH-gah (SAH-lay) ehl trehn*
From (at) what platform does it leave (arrive)?	**¿De (A) qué andén sale (ilega)?** *day (ah) kay ahn-DEHN SAH-lay (YEH-gah)*
Does this train stop at ____?	**¿Para este tren en ____?** *PAH-rah ehs-tay trehn ehn*

Is the train late?	**¿Tiene retraso el tren?** *tee-YEH-nay ray-TRAH-soh ehl trehn*
How long does it stop?	**¿Cuánto tiempo para?** *kwahn-toh tee-EHM-poh PAH-rah*
Are there discounts for students (seniors, groups, the handicapped)?	**¿Hay descuentos para estudiantes (ancianos, grupos, los invalidos)?** *AH-ee des-KWEHN-tohs pah-rah ehs-too-dee-YAHN-tehs (ahn-see-YAH-nohs GROO-pohs lohs een-BAH-lee-dohs)*
How can I obtain a refund?	**¿Cómo puedo obtener un reembolso?** *KOH-moh PWAY-doh ob-ten-EHR oon ray-ehm-BOHL-so*
Are there special (weekly, monthly, group, tourist) passes?	**¿Hay pases especiales (para una semana, para un mes, para turistas)?** *AH-ee PAH-sehs ehs-pehs-YAHL-ehs (pah-rah oo-nah seh-MAH-nah oon mehs pah-rah toor-EES-tahs)*
Is there a dining car (sleeping car)?	**¿Hay coche-comedor (cochecama)?** *ahy KOH-chay koh-may-DOHR (KOH-chay KAH-mah)*
Is it ____?	**¿Es ____?** *ehs*
▧ a through train	**un tren directo** *oon trehn dee-REHK-toh*
▧ a local	**un tren local (ómnibus, ordinario)** *oon trehn loh-KAHL (OHM-nee-boos ohr-dee-NAH-ree-oh)*
▧ an express	**un expreso (rápido)** *oon eks-PREHS-oh (RAH-pee-doh)*
Do I have to change trains?	**¿Tengo que trasbordar?** *TEHN-goh kay trahs-bohr-DAHR*

Is this seat taken?	**¿Está ocupado este asiento?** *ehs-TAH oh-koo-PAH-doh EHS-tay ah-SYEHN-toh*
Where are we now?	**¿Dónde estamos ahora?** *DOHN-day ehs-TAH-mohs ah-OHR-ah*
Will we arrive on time (late)?	**¿Llegaremos a tiempo (tarde)?** *yeh-gahr-EH-mohs ah tee-EHM-poh (tahr-day)*
Can I check my bag through to ____?	**¿Puedo facturar mi maleta hasta ____?** *PWEH-doh fahk-toor-AHR mee mah-LEH-tah AHS-tah*
Excuse me, but you are in my seat.	**Perdón, creo que está ocupando mi asiento.** *pehr-DOHN KRAY-oh key ehs-TAH oh-koo-PAHN-doh mee ah-SYEHN-toh*

SHIPBOARD TRAVEL

Where is the dock?	**¿Dónde está el muelle?** *DOHN-day ehs-TAH ehl MWEH-yeh*
When does the next boat leave for ____?	**¿Cuándo sale el próximo barco para ____?** *KWAHN-doh SAH-lay ehl PROHKS-ee-moh BAHR-koh PAH-rah*
How long does the crossing take?	**¿Cuánto dura la travesía?** *KWAHN-toh DOO-rah lah trah-beh-SEE-ah*
Do we stop at any other ports?	**¿Hacemos escala en algunos puertos?** *ah-SAY-mohs ehs-KAH-lah ehn ahl-GOO-nohs PWEHR-tohs*

How long will we remain in the port?	**¿Cuánto tiempo permaneceremos en el puerto?** *KWAHN-toh tee-EHM-poh pehr-mah-neh-sehr-EH-mohs ehn ehl PWEHR-toh*
When do we land?	**¿Cuándo desembarcamos?** *KWAHN-doh dehs-ehm-bahr-KAH-mohs*
At what time do we have to be back on board?	**¿A qué hora debemos volver a bordo?** *ah kay OHR-ah deh-BAY-mohs bohl-BEHR ah BOHR-doh*
I'd like a _____ ticket.	**Quisiera un pasaje _____.** *kee-SYEHR-ah oon pah-SAH-hay*
▨ first-class	**de primera clase** *day pree-MEHR-ah KLAH-say*
▨ tourist-class	**de clase turista** *day KLAH-say toor-EES-tah*
▨ cabin	**para un camarote** *PAH-rah oon kah-mah-ROH-tay*
I don't feel well.	**No me siento bien.** *noh may SYEHN-toh byehn*
Can you give me something for sea-sickness?	**¿Puede usted darme algo contra el mareo?** *PWEH-day oos-TEHD DAHR-may AHL-goh KOHN-trah ehl mah-RAY-oh*

DRIVING A CAR

CAR RENTALS

Where can I rent _____?	**¿Dónde puedo alquilar _____?** *dohn-day PWEH-doh ahl-kee-LAHR*
▨ a car	**un coche** *oon KOH-chay*

■ a four-wheel-drive vehicle	**un vehículo con tracción en las cuatro ruedas** *oon-beh-EE-koo-loh kohn trahk-SYOHN en lahs KWAH-troh roo-WAY-dahs*
■ a minivan	**un mínivan** *oon MEE-nee-bahn*
I want a ____.	**Quiero ____.** *kee-EH-roh*
■ small car	**un coche pequeño** *oon KOH-chay peh-KAYN-yoh*
■ large car	**un coche grande** *oon KOH-chay GRAHN-day*
■ sports car	**un coche deportivo** *oon KOH-chay day-pohr-TEE-boh*
I prefer automatic transmission (power steering, power windows, power mirrors).	**Prefiero el cambio automático (dirección asistida, ventanillas eléctricas, espejos eléctricos).** *preh-fee-EHR-oh ehl KAHM-bee-oh AH-oo-toh-MAH-tee-koh dee-rehk-SYOHN ah-sees-TEE-dah ben-tah-NEE-yahs eh-LEK-tree-kahs ehs-PEH-hohs eh-LEK-tree-kohs*
How much does it cost ____?	**¿Cuánto cuesta ____?** *KWAHN-toh KWEHS-tah*
■ per day	**por día** *pohr DEE-ah*
■ per week	**por semana** *pohr seh-MAHN-ah*
■ per kilometer	**por kilómetro** *pohr kee-LOH-meht-roh*
■ with unlimited mileage	**con kilometraje ilimitado** *kohn kee-loh-may-TRAH-hay ee-lee-mee-TAH-doh*
How much is the insurance?	**¿Cuánto es el seguro?** *KWAHN-toh ehs ehl seh-GOOR-oh*

Is the gas included?	**¿Está incluída la gasolina?** *ehs-TAH een-kloo-EE-dah lah gahs-oh LEEN-ah*
Do you accept credit cards?	**¿Acepta usted tarjetas de crédito?** *ah-sehp-tah oos-TEHD tahr-HAY-tahs day KREH-dee-toh*
Here's my driver's license.	**Aquí tiene mi licencia de conducir.** *ah-KEE tee-EH-nay mee lee-SEN-see-ah day kohn-doo-SEER*
Do I have to leave a deposit?	**¿Tengo que dejar un depósito?** *ten-goh kay day-hahr oon day-POHS-ee-toh*
I want to rent the car here and leave it in ____.	**Quiero alquilar el coche aquí y dejarlo en ____.** *kee-YEHR-oh ahl-kee-LAHR ehl KOH-chay ah-KEE ee day-HAHR-loh ehn*
What kind of gasoline does it take?	**¿Qué tipo de gasolina necesita?** *kay TEE-poh day gah-so-LEE-nah neh-seh-SEE-tah*

ON THE ROAD

Excuse me, can you tell me ____?	**Por favor, ¿puede usted decirme ____?** *pohr fah-BOHR pweh-day oos-TEHD day-SEER-may*
I think we're lost.	**Creo que estamos perdidos.** *KRAY-oh kay ehs-TAH-mohs pehr-DEE-dohs*
Is this the way to ____?	**¿Es éste el camino a ____?** *ehs EHS-tay ehl kah-MEE-noh ah*

Are there any detours?	**¿Hay desviaciones?** *AH-ee des-bee-ah-SYOHN-ays*
Do I go straight?	**¿Sigo derecho?** *see-goh deh-RAY-choh*
Do I turn to the right (to the left)?	**¿Doblo a la derecha (a la izquierda)?** *DOH-bloh ah lah deh-RAY-chah (ah lah ees-kee-YEHR-dah)*
How far is it from here to the next town?	**¿Cuánta distancia hay de aquí al primer pueblo?** *KWAHN-tah dees-TAHN-see-ah ah-ee day ah-KEE ahl pree-MEHR PWEH-bloh*
How far away is ____?	**¿A qué distancia está ____?** *ah kay dees-TAHN-see-ah ehs-tah*
Do you have a road map?	**¿Tiene usted un mapa de carreteras?** *tee-yehn-ay oos-TEHD oon MAH-pah day kahr-ray-TEHR-ahs*

AT THE SERVICE STATION

Where is there a gas (petrol) station?	**¿Dónde hay una estación de gasolina?** *DOHN-day AH-ee oo-nah ehs-tah-SYOHN day gahs-oh-LEE-nah*
Fill it up with ____.	**Llénelo con ____.** *YAY-nay-loh kohn*
■ diesel	**diesel** *dee-EH-sel*
■ regular (90 octane)	**normal** *nohr-MAHL*
■ super (96 octane)	**super** *SOO-pehr*
■ extra (98 octane)	**extra** *EHS-trah*
Give me ____ liters.	**Déme ____ litros.** *DAY-may LEE-trohs*
Please check ____.	**¿Quiere inspeccionar ____?** *kee-YEHR-ay eens-pehk-syohn-ahr*

■ the battery	**la batería**	*lah bah-tehr-EE-ah*
■ the caburetor	**el carburador**	*ehl kahr-boor-ah-DOHR*
■ the oil	**el aceite**	*ehl ah-SAY-tay*
■ the spark plugs	**las bujías**	*lahs boo-HEE-ahs*
■ the tires	**las llantas, los neumáticos**	*lahs YAHN-tahs lohs new-MAH-tee-kohs*
■ the tire pressure	**la presión de las llantas**	*lah preh-SYOHN day lahs YAHN-tahs*
■ the antifreeze	**el agua del radiador**	*ehl AH-gwah dehl rah-dee-ah-DOHR*
Change the oil.	**Cambie el aceite.**	*KAHM-bee-ay ehl ah-SAY-tay*
Charge the battery.	**Cargue la batería.**	*KAHR-gay lah bah-tehr-EE-ah*
Change the tire.	**Cambie esta llanta.**	*KAHM-bee-ay ehs-tah YAHN-tah*

ACCIDENTS AND REPAIRS

My car has broken down.	**Mi coche se ha averiado.**	*mee KOH-chay say ah ah-behr-ee-AH-doh*
It overheats.	**Se calienta demasiado.**	*say kahl-YEN-tah day-mahs-ee-AH-doh*
It doesn't start.	**No arranca.**	*noh ah-RAHN-kah*
I have a flat tire.	**Se me ha pinchado una rueda.**	*say may ah peen-CHAH-doh oon-ah RWEH-dah*
Is there a garage (repair shop) near here?	**¿Hay un garage (taller) por aquí?**	*AH-ee oon gah-RAH-hay (tah-YEHR) pohr ah-KEE*

I need a mechanic (tow truck).	**Necesito on mecánico (remolcador).** *neh-seh-SEE-toh oon meh-KAHN-ee-koh (ray-mohl-kah-DOHR)*
Can you _____?	**¿Puede usted _____?** *PWEH-day oos-TEHD*
■ give me a push	**empujarme** *ehm-poo-HAHR-may*
■ help me	**ayudarme** *ah-yoo-DAHR may*
Can you fix the car?	**¿Puede usted arreglar el coche?** *PWEH-day oos-TEHD ah-ray-GLAHR ehl KOH-chay*
Can you repair it temporarily?	**¿Puede repararlo temporalmente?** *PWEH-day ray-pahr-AHR-loh tem-pohr-AHL-men-tay*
I think there's something wrong with _____.	**Creo que pasa algo con _____.** *KRAY-oh kay PAH-sah AHL-goh kohn*
■ the directional signal	**el indicador de dirección** *ehl een-dee-kah-DOHR day dee-rek-SYOHN*
■ the electrical system	**el sistema eléctrico** *ehl sees-TAY-mah eh-LEK-tree-koh*
■ the fan	**el ventilador** *ehl ben-tee-lah-DOHR*
■ the fan belt	**la correa de ventilador** *lah koh-ray-ah day ben-tee-lah-DOHR*
■ the fuel pump	**la bomba de gasolina** *lah BOHM-bah day gahs-oh-LEE-nah*
■ the gearshift	**el cambio de velocidad** *ehl KAHM-bee-oh day beh-loh-see-DAHD*
■ the headlight	**el faro delantero** *ehl fah-ROH deh-lahn-TEHR-oh*
■ the horn	**la bocina** *lah boh-SEEN-ah*
■ the ignition	**el encendido** *ehl ehn-sehn-DEE-doh*
■ the radio	**la radio** *lah RAH-dee-oh*

Guarded railroad crossing

Yield

Stop

Right of way

Dangerous intersection ahead

Gasoline (petrol) ahead

Parking

No vehicles allowed

Dangerous curve

Pedestrian crossing

Oncoming traffic has right of way

No bicycles allowed

No parking allowed

No entry

No left turn

No U-turn

No passing

Border crossing

Traffic signal ahead

Speed limit (kilometers)

Traffic circle (roundabout) ahead

Minimum speed limit (kilometers)

All traffic turns left

End of no passing zone

One-way street

Detour

Danger ahead

Entrance to expressway

Expressway ends

the starter	**el arranque** *ehl ah-RAHN-kay*
the steering wheel	**el volante** *ehl boh-LAHN-tay*
the taillight	**el faro trasero** *ehl fah-ROH trah-SEHR-oh*
the transmission	**la transmisión** *lah trahns-mee-SYOHN*
the water pump	**la bomba de agua** *lah BOHM-bah day AH-gwah*
the windshield (windscreen) wiper	**el limpiaparabrisas** *ehl LEEM-pee-ah-pah-rah-BREE-sahs*

ENTERTAINMENT AND DIVERSIONS

MOVIES, THEATER, CONCERTS, OPERA, BALLET

Let's go to the ____.	**Vamos al ____.** *BAH-mohs ahl*
movies (cinema)	**cine** *SEE-nay*
theater	**teatro** *tay-AH-troh*
What are they showing today?	**¿Qué ponen hoy?** *kay POH-nehn oy*
Is it a ____?	**¿Es ____?** *ehs*
mystery	**un misterio** *oon mee-STEHR-ee-oh*
comedy	**una comedia** *oo-nah koh-MEH-dee-ah*
drama	**un drama** *oon DRAH-mah*
musical	**una obra musical** *oo-nah OH-brah moo-see-KAHL*

▨ romance	**una obra romántica**	*oo-nah OH-brah roh-MAHN-tee-kah*
▨ Western	**una película del Oeste**	*oo-nah pehl-EE-koo-lah del OWEST-ay*
▨ war film	**una película de guerra**	*oo-nah pehl-EE-koo-lah day GHEHR-ah*
▨ science fiction film	**una película de ciencia ficción**	*oo-nah pehl-EE-koo-lah day see-EHN-see-ah feek-SYOHN*

Is it in English? **¿Es hablada en inglés?** *ehs ah-BLAH-dah ehn een-GLAYSS*

Has it been dubbed? **¿Ha sido doblada?** *ah SEE-doh doh-BLAH-dah*

Where is the box office? **¿Dónde está la taquilla?** *DOHN-day ehs-TAH lah tah-KEE-yah*

What time does the (first) show begin? **¿A qué hora empieza la (primera) función?** *ah kay OHR-ah ehm-PYEH-sah lah (pree-MEHR-ah) foon-SYOHN*

What time does the (last) show end? **¿A qué hora termina la (última) función?** *ah kay OHR-ah tehr-MEEN-ah lah (OOL-tee-mah) foon-SYOHN*

I want a seat near the middle (front, rear). **Quisiera un asiento en el centro (al frente, atrás).** *kee-SYEHR-ah oon ah-SYEHN-toh ehn ehl SEHN-troh (ahl FREHN-tay ah-TRAHS)*

I need two ____ tickets for tonight. **Necesito dos entradas ____ para esta noche.** *neh-seh-SEE-toh dohs ehn-TRAH-dahs pah-rah ehs-tah NOH-chay*

▨ orchestra	**de platea**	*day plah-TAY-ah*
▨ balcony	**de galería**	*day gahl-ehr-EE-ah*
▨ mezzanine	**de anfiteatro**	*day ahn-fee-tay-AH-troh*

We would like to attend _____.	**Quisiéramos asistir a _____.** *kee-SYEHR-ah-mohs ah-sees-TEER ah*
■ a ballet	**un ballet** *oon bah-LEH*
■ a concert	**un concierto** *oon kohn-SYEHR-toh*
■ an opera	**una ópera** *oo-nah OH-pehr-ah*
What are they playing (singing)?	**¿Qué están interpretando?** *kay ehs-TAHN een-tehr-pray-TAHN-doh*
I prefer _____.	**Prefiero _____.** *preh-fee-YEHR-oh*
■ classical music	**la música clásica** *lah MOO-see-kah KLAH-see-kah*
■ popular music	**la música popular** *lah MOO-see-kah poh-poo-LAHR*
■ folk dance	**el ballet folklórico** *ehl bah-LEH fohl-KLOHR-ee-koh*
■ ballet	**el ballet** *ehl bah-LEH*
Are there any seats for tonight's performance?	**¿Hay localidades para la representación de esta noche?** *AH-ee loh-kahl-ee-DAHD-ays pah-rah lah rep-reh-sen-tah-SYOHN day ehs-tah NOH-chay*
When does the season begin (end)?	**¿Cuándo empieza (termina la temporada?** *KWAHN-doh ehm-PYEH-sah (tehr-MEEN-ah) lah tem-pohr-AH-dah*
Should I get the tickets in advance?	**¿Debo sacar las entradas de antemano?** *deh-boh sah-KAHR lahs ehn-TRAH-dahs day ahn-tay-MAH-noh*
Do I have to dress formally?	**¿Tengo que ir de etiqueta?** *TEN-goh kay eer day eh-tee-KEH-tah*

How much are the front row seats?	**¿Cuánto vaten los asientos delanteros?** *KWAHN-toh bah-lehn lohs ahs-YEHN-tohs day-lahn-TEHR-ohs*
What are the least expensive seats?	**¿Cuáles son los asientos más baratos?** *KWAHL-ays sohn lohs ahs-YEHN-tohs mahs bah-RAH-tohs*
May I buy a program?	**¿Puedo comprar un programa?** *PWEH-doh kohm-PRAHR oon pro-GRAHM-ah*
What opera (ballet) are they performing?	**¿Qué ópera (ballet) ponen?** *kay OH-pehr-ah (bah-LEH) POH-nen*

NIGHTCLUBS, DANCING

Let's go to a nightclub.	**Vamos a un cabaret.** *BAH-mohs ah oon kah-bah-REH*
Is a reservation necessary?	**¿Hace falta una reserva?** *ah-say FAHL-tah oo-nah reh-SEHR-bah*
Is it customary to dine there as well?	**¿Se puede comer allá también?** *say PWEH-day koh-MEHR ah-YAH tahm-BYEHN*
Is there a good discotheque here?	**¿Hay aquí una buena discoteca?** *AH-ee ah-KEE oo-nah BWEH-nah dees-koh-TAY-kah*
Is there dancing at the hotel?	**¿Hay un baile en el hotel?** *AH-ee oon BAH-ee-lay ehn ehl oh-TEL*
We'd like a table near the dance floor.	**Quisiéramos una mesa cerca de la pista.** *kee-SYEHR-ah-mohs oo-nah MAY-sah SEHR-kah day lah PEES-tah*

Is there a minimum (cover charge)?	**¿Hay un mínimo?** *AH-ee oon MEE-nee-moh*
Where is the check-room?	**¿Dónde está el guardarropa?** *DOHN-day eh-STAH ehl gwahr-dah-ROH-pah*
At what time does the floor show go on?	**¿A qué hora empieza el espectáculo?** *ah kay OH-rah ehm-pee-EH-sah ehl ehs-peh-TAH-kool-oh*

SPECTATOR SPORTS

THE BULLFIGHT

el matador	kills the bull with his **espada** (sword)
el banderillero	thrusts three sets of long darts (**banderillas**) into the bull's neck to enfuriate him
el picador	bullfighter mounted on a horse who weakens the bull with his lance (**pica**)
la cuadrilla	a team of helpers for the torero, who confuse and tire the bull with their capes (**capas**)
el monosabio	assistant who does various jobs in the **redondel** (bullring)
Is there a bullfight this afternoon? (every Sunday)?	**¿Hay una corrida de toros esta tarde (todos los domingos)?** *AH-ee oo-nah koh-REE-dah day TOH-rohs ehs-tah TAHR-day (toh-dohs lohs doh-MEEN-gohs)*
Take me to the bullring.	**Lléveme a la Plaza de Toros.** *YEH-bay-may ah lah PLAH-sah day TOHR-ohs*

| I'd like a seat in the shade (in the sun). | **Quisiera un sitio a la sombra (al sol).** *kees-YEH-rah oon SEE-tee-oh ah lah SOHM-brah (ahl sohl)* |

| When does the parade of the bullfighters begin? | **¿Cuándo empieza el desfile de la cuadrilla?** *KWAHN-doh ehm-PYEH-sah ehl dehs-FEEL-ay day lah kwahd-REE-yah* |

| When does the first bull appear? | **¿Cuándo sale el primer toro?** *KWAHN-doh sah-lay ehl pree-MEHR TOH-roh* |

| Bravo! | **¡Ole!** *oh-LAY* |

SOCCER

| I'd like to watch a soccer match. | **Quisiera ver un partido de fútbol.** *kee-SYEHR-ah behr oon pahr-TEE-doh day FOOT-bohl* |

| Where's the stadium? | **¿Dónde está el estadio?** *DOHN-day ehs-TAH ehl ehs-TAH-dee-oh* |

| When does the first half begin? | **¿Cuándo empieza el primer tiempo?** *KWAHN-doh ehm-pee-EH-sah ehl pree-MEHR tee-EM-poh* |

| What teams are going to play? | **¿Qué equipos van a jugar?** *kay eh-KEE-pohs bahn ah hoo-GAHR* |

| What is the score? | **¿Cuál es la anotación?** *kwahl ehs lah ah-noh-tah-SYOHN* |

JAI ALAI

| I'd like to see a jai alai match. | **Me gustaría ver un partido de pelota.** *may goos-tahr-EE-ah behr oon par-TEE-doh day pel-OH-tah* |

| Where can I get tickets? | **¿Dónde puedo conseguir billetes?** *DOHN-day pweh-doh kohn-seh-GEER bee-YEH-tays* |

Where is the jai alai court?	**¿Dónde está el frontón?** *DOHN-day ehs-TAH ehl frohn-TOHN*
Who are the players?	**¿Quiénes son los jugadores?** *kee-YEHN-ehs sohn lohs hoo-gah-DOHR-ays*
Where do I place my bet?	**¿Dónde hago la apuesta?** *DOHN-day ah-goh lah ah-PWEH-stah*

PLAYING FIELDS

Shall we go to the ____?	**¿Vamos ____?** *BAH-mohs*
▪ beach	**a la playa** *ah lah-PLAH-yah*
▪ court	**al patio** *ahl PAH-tee-yoh*
▪ field	**a la cancha** *ah lah KAHN-chah*
▪ golf course	**al campo de golf** *ahl KAHM-poh day gohlf*
▪ gymnasium	**al gimnasio** *ahl heem-NAH-see-yoh*
▪ jai alai court	**a la cancha de jai alai** *ah lah KAHN-chah day HA-ee ah-LAH-ee*
▪ mountain	**a la montaña** *ah lah mohn-TAHN-yah*
▪ ocean	**al océano** *ahl oh-SAY-ah-no*
▪ park	**al parque** *ahl PAHR-keh*
▪ path	**al camino** *ahl kah-MEE-no*
▪ pool	**a la piscina** *ah lah pee-SEE-nah*
▪ rink	**a la pista de patinaje** *ah lah PEES-tah day pah-tee-NAH-hay*
▪ sea	**al mar** *ahl MAHR*
▪ stadium	**al estadio** *ahl es-TAH-dee-yo*
▪ track	**a la pista** *ah lah PEES-tah*

TENNIS

Do you play tennis?	**¿Sabe usted jugar al tenis?** *SAH-bay oos-TEHD hoo-GAHR ahl TEN-ees*
I (don't) play very well.	**(No) juego muy bien.** *(noh) hoo-AY-goh mwee bee-EHN*
Do you play singles (doubles)?	**¿Juega usted solo (en pareja)?** *HWAY-gah oos-TEHD SOH-loh (ehn pahr-AY-hah)*
Do you know where there is a court?	**¿Sabe usted dónde hay una cancha?** *SAH-bay oos-TEHD DOHN-day AH-ee oo-nah KAHN-chah*
Is it a private club? I'm not a member.	**¿Es un club privado? No soy socio.** *ehs oon kloob pree-BAH-do noh soy SOH-see-oh*
Can I rent a racquet?	**¿Se puede alquilar una raqueta?** *say PWEH-day ahl-kee-LAHR oo-nah rah-KAY-tah*
How much do they charge per hour (per day)?	**¿Cuánto cobran por hora (por día)?** *KWAHN-toh KOH-brahn pohr OH-rah (pohr DEE-ah)?*

AT THE BEACH/POOL

Let's go to the beach (to the pool).	**Vamos a la playa (piscina).** *BAH-mohs ah lah PLAH-ee-ah (pee-SEEN-ah)*
Which bus will take us to the beach?	**¿Qué autobús nos lleva a la playa?** *kay AH-oo-toh-BOOS nohs yeh-bah oh lah PLAH-ee-ah*
Is there an indoor (outdoor) pool in the hotel?	**¿Hay una piscina cubierta (al aire libre) en el hotel?** *AH-ee oo-nah pee-SEE-nah ehn ehl oh-TEL*

I (don't) know how to swim well.	**(No) sé nadar bien.** *(noh) say nah-DAHR bee-EHN*
Is it safe to swim here?	**¿Se puede nadar aquí sin peligro?** *say PWEH-day nah-DAHR ah-KEE seen peh-LEE-groh*
Is it dangerous for children?	**¿Hay peligro para los niños?** *AH-ee pel-EE-groh pah-rah lohs NEEN-yohs*
Is there a lifeguard?	**¿Hay salvavidas?** *AH-ee sahl-bah-BEE-dahs*
Help! I'm drowning!	**¡Auxilio! ¡Socorro! ¡Me ahogo!** *owk-SEEL-yo so-COHR-oh may ah-OH-go*
Where can I get ____?	**¿Dónde puedo conseguir ____?** *DOHN-day PWEH-doh kohn-seh-GHEER*
◼ an air mattress	**un colchón flotante** *oon kohl-CHOHN floh-tahn-tay*
◼ a bathing suit	**un traje de baño** *oon trah-hay day BAHN-yoh*
◼ a beach ball	**una pelota de playa** *oo-nah pel-OH-tah day PLAH-ee-ah*
◼ a beach chair	**un sillón de playa** *oon see-YOHN day PLAH-ee-ah*
◼ a beach towel	**una toalla de playa** *oo-nah toh-AH-yah day PLAH-ee-yah*
◼ a beach umbrella	**una sombrilla playera** *oo-nah sohm-BREE-yah plah-YEHR-ah*
◼ diving equipment	**equipo de buceo** *eh-KEE-poh day boo-SAY-oh*
◼ sunglasses	**gafas de sol** *GAH-fahs day sohl*
◼ suntan lotion	**loción para broncear** *loh-SYOHN pah-rah brohn-SAY-ahr*

ON THE SLOPES

Which ski area do you recommend?	**¿Qué sitio de esquiar recomienda usted?** *kay SEE-tee-oh day ehs-kee-AHR ray-koh-MYEHN-dah oos-TEHD*
I am a novice (intermediate, expert) skier.	**Soy principiante (intermedio, experto).** *soy preen-seep-YAHN-tay (een-tehr-MEHD-ee-oh ehs-PEHR-toh)*
Is there enough snow at this time of year?	**¿Hay bastante nieve durante esta temporada?** *AH-ee bahs-TAHN-tay nee-EHB-ay door-ahn-tay ehs-tah temp-ohr-AH-dah*
How would I get to that place?	**¿Por dónde se va a ese sitio?** *pohr DOHN-day say bah ah eh-say SEE-tee-oh*
Can I rent ____ there?	**¿Puedo alquilar ____?** *PWEH-doh ahl-kee-lahr*
■ equipment	**equipo** *eh-KEEP-oh*
■ poles	**palos** *PAH-lohs*
■ skis	**esquís** *ehs-KEES*
■ ski boots	**botas de esquiar** *BOH-tahs day ehs-kee-AHR*
Do they have ski lifts?	**¿Tienen funicular?** *TYEHN-eh foo-nee-koo-LAHR*
How much does the lift cost?	**¿Cuánto cobran?** *KWAHN-toh KOH-brahn*
Do they give lessons?	**¿Dan lecciones?** *dahn lek-SYOHN-ays*
Where can I stay?	**¿Dónde puedo alojarme?** *DOHN-day PWEH-doh ah-loh-HAHR-may*

ON THE LINKS

Is there a golf course?	**¿Hay un campo de golf?** *AH-ee oon KAHM-poh day gohlf*
Can one rent clubs?	**¿Se puede alquilar los palos?** *say PWEH-day ahl-kee-LAHR lohs PAH-lohs*

CAMPING

Is there a camping area near here?	**¿Hay un camping cerca de aquí?** *AH-ee oon KAHM-peeng sehr-kah day ah-KEE*
Do we pick our own site?	**¿Escogemos nuestro propio sitio?** *ehs-koh-HAY-mohs NWEHS-troh PROH-pee-oh SEE-tee-oh*
We only have a tent.	**Tenemos solo una tienda.** *ten-AY-mohs SOH-loh oo-nah TYEHN-dah*
Can we camp for one night only?	**¿Se puede acampar por una noche sola?** *say PWEH-day ah-kahm-pahr pohr oo-nah noh-chay SOH-lah*
Can we park our trailer (our caravan)?	**¿Podemos estacionar nuestro coche-vivienda (nuestra caravana)?** *poh-DAY-mos eh-stah-syohn-AHR nwehs-troh KOH-chay bee-bee-EHN-dah (NWEHS-trah kahr-ah-BAHN-ah)*
Is (are) there ____?	**¿Hay ____?** *AH-ee*
■ camp guards	**guardias de campamento** *GWAHR-dee-yahs day kahm-pah-MEN-toh*

■ a children's play-
ground

un parque infantil *oon PAHR-kay
een-fahn-TEEL*

■ cooking facilites

instalaciones para cocinar *een-
stah-lah-SYOHN-ays pah-rah koh-
see-NAHR*

■ drinking water

agua potable *AH-gwah poh-TAH-
blay*

■ electricity

electricidad *eh-lek-tree-see-DAHD*

■ fireplaces

hogueras *oh-GEHR-ahs*

■ flush toilets

servicios *sehr-BEE-see-ohs*

■ a grocery store

una tienda de comestibles *oo-nah
tee-EHN-dah day koh-mes-TEE-blays*

■ picnic tables

mesas de camping *may-sahs day
KAHM-peeng*

■ showers

duchas *DOO-chahs*

How much do they
charge per person
(per car)?

**¿Cuánto cobran por persona (por
coche)?** *KWAHN-toh KOH-brahn
pohr pehr-SOHN-ah (pohr koh-chay)*

We intend staying
____ days (weeks).

**Pensamos quedamos ____ días
(semanas).** *pen-SAH-mohs kay-
DAHR-nohs DEE-ahs (seh-MAHN-ahs)*

FOOD AND DRINK

EATING OUT

Do you know a good
restaurant?

**¿Conoce usted un buen restau-
rante?** *koh-NOH-say oos-TEHD oon
bwehn rehs-tah-oo-RAHN-tay*

Is it very expensive?

¿Es muy caro? *ehs mwee KAH-roh*

Do you know a
restaurant that
serves native dishes?

**¿Conoce usted un restaurante
típico?** *koh-NOH-say oos-TEHD oon
rehs-tah-oo-RAHN-tay TEE-pee-koh*

Waiter!	**¡Camarero!** *kah-mah-REHR-oh*
Miss!	**¡Señorita!** *sen-yohr-EE-tah*
A table for two, _____ please.	**Una mesa para dos, por favor.** *oo-nah MAY-sah pah-rah dohs pohr fa-BOHR*
▦ in the corner	**en el rincón** *ehn ehl reen-KOHN*
▦ near the window	**cerca de la ventana** *sehr-kah day lah ben-TAHN-ah*
▦ on the terrace	**en la terraza** *ehn lah teh-RAH-sah*
I would like to make a reservation _____.	**Quisiera hacer una reserva _____.** *kee-see-EHR-ah ah-SEHR oo-nah ray-SEHR-bah*
▦ for tonight	**para esta noche** *pah-rah ehs-tah NOH-chay*
▦ for tomorrow evening	**para mañana por la noche** *pah-rah mahn-YAH-nah pohr lah NOH-chay*
▦ for two (four) persons	**para dos (cuatro) personas** *pah-rah dohs (KWAH-troh) pehr-SOHN-ahs*
▦ for 9 P.M.	**para las nueve** *pah-rah las NWEH-bay*
▦ for 9:30	**para las nueve y media** *pah-rah lahs NWEH-bay ee MEHD-yah*
We'd like to have lunch now.	**Queremos almorzar ahora.** *kehr-AY-mohs ahl-mohr-SAHR oh-OHR-ah*
The menu, please.	**La carta, por favor.** *lah KAHR-tah pohr fa-BOHR*
What's today's special?	**¿Cuál es el plato del día de hoy?** *KWAHL ehs ehl PLAH-toh del DEE-ah day oy*

What do you recommend?	**¿Qué recomienda usted?** *KAY reh-koh-mee-EHN-dah oos-TEHD*
Do you serve children's portions?	**¿Hay platos especiales para niños?** *AH-ee PLAH-tohs ehs-peh-see-AHL-ays pah-rah NEEN-yohs*
Are the portions small (large?)	**¿Son pequeñas (grandes) las porciones?** *sohn peh-KAYN-yahs (GRAHN-days) lahs pohr-SYOHN-ays*
To begin with, please bring us ___.	**Para empezar, tráiganos ___ por favor.** *pahr-rah ehm-peh-SAHR TRAH-ee-gah-nohs pohr fa-BOHR*
▪ an aperitif	**un aperitivo** *oon ah-pehr-ee-TEE-boh*
▪ a cocktail	**un coctel** *oon cohk-TEHL*
▪ some white (red) wine	**un vino blanco (tinto)** *oon BEE-noh BLAHN-koh (TEEN-toh)*
▪ some ice water	**agua helada** *AH-gwah eh-LAH-dah*
▪ a bottle of mineral water, with (without) gas	**una botella de agua mineral, con (sin) gas** *oo-nah boh-TEH-yah day AH-gwah mee-nehr-AHL kohn (seen) gahs*
▪ a beer	**una cerveza** *oo-nah sehr-BEH-sah*
I'd like (to order now).	**Me gustaría (ordenar ahora).** *may goos-tahr-EE-ah (ohr-den-AHR-ah ah-OHR-ah)*
Do you have a house wine?	**¿Tiene un vino de la casa?** *tee-YEHN-ay oon BEE-noh day lah KAH-SAH*
Please also bring us ___.	**Tráiganos también ___.** *TRAH-ee-gah-nohs tahm-BYEHN*
▪ a roll	**un panecillo** *oon pah-neh-SEE-yoh*
▪ bread	**pan** *pahn*

■ bread and butter	**pan y mantequilla** *pahn ee mahn-tay-KEE-yah*
■ tortillas (Mexico)	**tortillas** *tahr-TEE-yahs*
Waiter, we need ____.	**Camarero, necesitamos ____.** *kah-mah-REH-roh neh-seh-see-TAH-mohs*
■ a knife	**un cuchillo** *oon koo-CHEE-yoh*
■ a fork	**un tenedor** *oon ten-eh-DOHR*
■ a spoon	**una cuchara** *oo-nah koo-CHAHR-ah*
■ a teaspoon	**una cucharita** *oo-nah koo-chahr-EE-tah*
■ a soup spoon	**una cuchara de sopa** *oo-nah koo-CHAH-rah day SOH-pah*
■ a glass	**un vaso** *oon BAH-soh*
■ a cup	**una taza** *oo-nah TAH-sah*
■ a saucer	**un platillo** *oon plah-TEE-yoh*
■ a plate	**un plato** *oon PLAH-toh*
■ a napkin	**una servilleta** *oo-nah sehr-bee-YEH-tah*

APPETIZERS (STARTERS)

alcachofas	artichokes
almejas	clams
anguilas ahumadas	smoked eels
calamares	squid
caracoles	snails
champiñones	mushrooms
chorizo	spicy sausage, usually pork
cigalás	crayfish
gambas (Spain only)	shrimp
huevos	eggs

jamón serrano (Spain only)	cured ham
melón	melon
moluscos	mussels
ostras (ostiones)	oysters
quisquillas (Spain only)	small shrimp
sardinas	sardines

And in Latin America, there would be some of the following:

camarones	shrimp
guacamole	puréed avocado spread
tostadas	tortilla chips with various pepper and cheese toppings

SOUPS

gazpacho	a highly variable purée of fresh, uncooked vegetables, including cucumbers, peppers, onions, and tomatoes; served cold
potaje madrileño	a thick soup of puréed chick peas, cod, and spinach
sopa de ajo	garlic soup
sopa de cebolla	onion soup
sopa de fideos	noodle soup
sopa de mariscos	seafood soup
sopa de gambas	shrimp soup
sopa de albóndigas	soup with meatballs
sopa de pescado	fish soup
sopa de verduras	soup made from puréed greens and vegetables

In Latin America, particularly Mexico, you are also likely to find:

cazuela	a spicy soup-stew, simmered for a long time in an earthenware pot; can be fish, vegetables, or meat
pozole	a hearty pork and hominy stew
sopa de aguacate	creamed avocado soup
sopa de huitlacoche	black corn soup made from the fungus that grows on corn cobs

ENTREES (MEAT AND FISH DISHES)

carne de	*KAHR-nay day*	meat of
▪ **buey**	*bway*	beef
▪ **cabrito**	*kah-BREE-toh*	goat (kid)
▪ **carnero**	*kahr-NEHR-oh*	mutton
▪ **cerdo**	*SEHR-doh*	pork
▪ **cordero**	*kohr-DEHR-oh*	lamb
▪ **ternera**	*tehr-NEHR-ah*	veal
▪ **vaca, res**	*BAH-kah rehs*	beef

Here is a list of some fish and shellfish.

almejas	*ahl-MAY-has*	clams
anchoas	*ahn-CHOH-ahs*	anchovies
anguilas	*ahn-GHEE-lahs*	eels
arenque, ahumado	*ah-REHN-kay ah-oo-MAH-doh*	smoked herring
atún	*ah-TOON*	tuna
bacalao	*bah kah-LAH-oh*	codfish
besugo	*beh-SOO-goh*	sea bream

boquerones	*boh-keh-ROH-nehs*	whitebait
caballa	*kah-BAH-yah*	mackerel
calamares	*kahl-ah-MAHR-ayss*	squid
camarones	*kah-mah-ROH-nayss*	shrimp
cangrejos	*kahn-GRAY-hohs*	crabs
caracoles	*kahr-ah-KOH-layss*	snails
cigalas	*see-GAH-lahs*	large crayfish
congrio	*KOHN-gree-oh*	conger eel
gambas	*GAHM-bahs*	large shrimp
lampreas	*lahm-PRAY-ahs*	lamprey
langosta	*lahn-GOH-stah*	spiny lobster
langostino	*lahn-gohs-TEE-noh*	small crayfish
lenguado	*len-GWAH-doh*	flounder, sole
mejillones	*meh-hee-YOH-nayss*	mussels
mújol	*MOO-hohl*	mullet
merluza	*mehr-LOOS-ah*	bass, hake
pescadilla	*pehs-kah-DEE-yah*	whiting
pulpo	*POOL-poh*	octopus
quesquillas	*kehs-KEE-yahs*	shrimp
rape	*RAH-pay*	monkfish, anglerfish
salmón	*sahl-MOHN*	salmon

sardinas	*sahr-DEE-nahs*	sardines
trucha	*TROO-chah*	trout

And some terms for fowl and game:

capón	*kah-POHN*	capon
codorniz	*koh-dohr-NEES*	quail
conejo	*kohn-AY-hoh*	rabbit
faisán	*fah-ee-SAHN*	pheasant
ganso	*GAHN-soh*	goose
pato	*PAH-toh*	duck
pavo	*PAH-boh*	turkey
perdiz	*pehr-DEES*	partridge
pichón	*pee-CHOHN*	squab
pollo	*POH-yoh*	chicken
venado	*beh-NAH-doh*	venison

Is the meat ____? **¿Es carne ____?** *ehs KAHR-nay*

- baked **al horno** *ahl OHR-noh*
- boiled **guisada** *ghee-SAH-dah*
- braised (stewed) **estofada** *ehs-toh-FAH-dah*
- broiled **a la parrilla** *ah lah pahr-EE-yah*
- roasted **asada** *ah-SAH-dah*
- poached **escalfada** *ehs KAHL-fah-dah*

I like the meat ____. **Me gustaría la carne ____.** *may goos-tah-REE-ah lah KAHR-nay*

■ well done   **bien hecha**   *bee-EHN EH-chah*

■ medium   **término medio**   *TEHR-mee-noh MED-yoh*

■ rare   **poco hecha**   *POH-koh EH-chah*

■ tender   **tierna**   *tee-EHR-nah*

RICE DISHES

a la campesina	with ham, chicken, sausage, and small game birds
a la catalana	with sausages, pork, squid, chilies, and peas, or with chicken, snails, beans, and artichokes
alicantina	with rabbit, mussels, and shrimp
bruta	with pork, chicken, and whitefish
de mariscos	with crayfish, anglerfish, and other seafood
valenciana	with chicken, seafood, peas, and tomatoes—the most well-known version

TORTILLA-BASED DISHES

chalupas	tortillas that have been curled at the edges and filled with cheese or a ground pork filling, served with a green chili sauce
chilaquiles	layers of tortillas, alternated with beans, meat, chicken, and cheese, then baked
enchiladas	soft corn tortillas rolled around meat and topped with sauce and melted cheese

flautas		sort of a tortilla sandwich that is then rolled and deep-fried
quesadillas		tortillas that are stuffed with cheese and deep-fried
tacos		crisp toasted tortillas stuffed with a variety of fillings (chopped beef, refried beans, turkey, chicken) topped with shredded lettuce, cheese, and sauce

VEGETABLES

alcachofas	*ahl-kah-CHOH-fahs*	artichokes
apio	*AH-pee-oh*	celery
berenjena	*behr-ehn-HAY-nah*	eggplant (aubergine)
calabacín	*kah-lah-bah-SEEN*	zucchini
cebollas	*seh-BOH-yahs*	onions
col	*kohl*	cabbage
coliflor	*kohl-ee-FLOHR*	cauliflower
espinacas	*eh-spee-NAH-kahs*	spinach
espárragos	*ehs-PAHR-ah-gohs*	asparagus
champiñones	*chahm-peen-YOH-nays*	mushrooms
garbanzos	*gahr-BAHN-sohs*	chickpeas
guisantes	*ghee-SAHN-tays*	peas
judías	*hoo-DEE-ahs*	green beans
papas, patatas	*PAH-pahs pah-TAH-tahs*	potatoes
▪ **papas fritas**	*PAH-pahs FREE-tahs*	french fries

pimiento	*pee-MYEHN-toh*	pepper
puerros	*PWEHR-ohs*	leeks
maíz	*mah-EES*	corn
tomate	*toh-MAH-tay*	tomato
zanahorias	*sah-nah-OHR-ee-ahs*	carrots

In parts of Latin America you are likely also to see the following on a menu:

chile	*CHEE-lay*	chili peppers, of any variety (see pages 141–142)
frijoles	*free-HOH-lays*	beans, usually kidney or pinto
huitlacoche	*WEET-lah-koh-chay*	corn fungus
nopalito	*noh-pah-LEE-toh*	prickly pear cactus
yuca	*YOO-kah*	root vegetable, from yucca plant

DESSERTS—SWEETS

arroz con leche	*ah ROHS kohn LEH-chay*	rice pudding
crema catalana or **flan**	*krem-ah kah-tah-LAN-nah* or *flahn*	caramel custard
galletas	*gah-YEH-tahs*	cookies (biscuits)
helado	*ay-LAH-doh*	ice cream
■ **de chocolate**	*day cho-koh-LAH-tay*	chocolate
■ **de pistacho**	*day pees-TAH-choh*	pistachio

■ **de vainilla**	*day bah-ee-NEE-yah*	vanilla
■ **de nueces**	*day NWEH-says*	walnut
■ **de fresa**	*day FRAY-sah*	strawberry
mazapán	*mah-sah-PAHN*	marzipan
merengue	*meh-REHN-gay*	meringue
natilla	*nah-TEE-yah*	cream pudding
pastel	*pahs-TEHL*	pastry
tarta	*TAHR-tah*	tart, usually fruit

FRUITS AND NUTS

What kind of fruit do you have?	**¿Qué frutas tiene?**	*kay FROO-tahs tee-YEHN-ay*
albaricoque	*ahl-bahr-ee-KOH-kay*	apricot
banana, plátano	*bah-NAH-nah PLAH-ta-noh*	banana, plantain (green banana)
cereza	*sehr-AY-sah*	cherry
ciruela	*seer-WEH-lah*	plum
coco	*KOH-koh*	coconut
dátil	*DAH-teel*	date
frambuesa	*frahm-BWEH-sah*	raspberry
fresa	*FRAY-sah*	strawberry
guayaba	*gwah-ee-AH-bah*	guava
higo	*EE-goh*	fig
jicama	*hee-KAH-mah*	jicama

lima	*LEE-mah*	lime
limón	*lee-MOHN*	lemon
mandarina	*mahn-dahr-EE-nah*	tangerine
mango	*MAHN-goh*	mango
manzana	*mahn-SAH-nah*	apple
melocotón	*mel-oh-koh-TOHN*	peach
melón	*meh-LOHN*	melon
naranja	*nah-RAHN-hah*	orange
pera	*PEH-rah*	pear
piña	*PEEN-yah*	pineapple
pomelo	*poh-MEH-loh*	grapefruit
sandía	*sahn-DEE-ah*	watermelon
tuna	*TOO-nah*	prickly pear
uva	*OO-bah*	grape

SPECIAL CIRCUMSTANCES

I am on a diet.	**Estoy en dieta.** *es-TOY en DYEH-tah*
I am a vegetarian.	**Soy vegetariano(a).** *soy beh-heh-tahr-ee-YAH-no(nah)*
I want a dish ____.	**Quiero un plato ____.** *KYEHR-oh oon PLAH-toh*
■ high in fiber	**con mucha fibra** *kohn MOO-chah FEE-brah*
■ low in cholesterol	**con poco colesterol** *kohn POH-koh koh-les-tehr-OHL*

■ low in fat	**con poca grasa** *kohn POH-kah GRAH-sah*
■ low in sodium	**con poco contenido de sodio** *kohn POH-koh kohn-ten-EE-doh day SO-dee-oh*
■ nondairy	**sin productos lácteos** *seen pro-DOOK-tohs LAHK-tay-ohs*
■ salt-free	**sin sal** *seen sahl*
■ sugar-free	**sin azúcar** *seen ah-SOO-kahr*
■ without artificial coloring	**sin colorantes artificiales** *seen koh-lohr-AHN-tays ahr-tee-fee-SYAHL-ays*
■ without preservatives	**sin preservativos** *seen pray-sehr-bah-TEE-bohs*
■ without garlic	**sin ajo** *seen AH-ho*
I don't want anything fried (salted).	**No quiero nada frito (salado).** *noh kee-YEHR-oh nah-dah FREE-toh (sah LAH-doh)*
Do you have anything that is not spicy?	**¿Tiene algo que no sea picante?** *tee-YEHN-ay AHL-goh kay noh SAY-ah pee-KAHN-tay*
Do you have any dishes without meat?	**¿Tiene platos sin carne?** *tee-YEHN-ay PLAH-tohs seen KAHR-nay*

BEVERAGES

Waiter, please bring me _____.	**Camarero, tráiganos por favor** _____. *kah-mah-REHR-oh, TRAH-ee-gah-nohs pohr fah-BOHR*
coffee	**café** *kah-FAY*
■ black coffee	**café solo** *kah-FAY SOH-loh*
■ with cream	**café con crema** *kah-FAY kohn KRAY-mah*
■ with milk	**un cortado** *oon kohr-TAH-doh*

■ espresso	**un exprés (un expreso)** *oon ehs-PRESS (oon ehs-PRESS-oh)*
■ half coffee/half milk (drunk in morning)	**café con leche** *kah-FAY kohn LEH-chay*
■ iced coffee	**café helado** *kah FAY eh-LAH-doh*
tea	**té** *tay*
■ with milk	**con leche** *kohn LEH-chay*
■ with lemon	**con limón** *kohn lee-MOHN*
■ with sugar	**con azúcar** *kohn ah-SOO-kahr*
■ iced tea	**té helado** *tay eh-LAH-doh*
chocolate (hot)	**chocolate** *choh-koh-LAH-tay*
water	**agua** *AH-gwah*
■ cold	**agua fría** *AH-gwah FREE-ah*
■ ice	**agua helada** *AH-gwah ay-LAH-dah*
■ mineral, with gas (without gas)	**agua mineral, con gas (sin gas)** *AH-gwah mee-nehr-AHL kohn gahs (seen gahs)*
cider	**una sidra** *oo-nah SEE-drah*
juice	**un jugo** *oon HOO-goh*
lemonade	**una limonada** *oo-nah lee-moh-NAH-dah*
milk	**leche** *LEH-chay*
■ malted milk	**una leche malteada** *oo-nah LEH-chay mahl-tay-AH-dah*
■ milk shake	**un batido de leche** *oon bah-TEE-doh day LEH-chay*
orangeade	**una naranjada** *oo-nah nahr-ahn-HAH-dah*

punch	**un ponche** *oon POHN-chay*
soda	**una gaseosa** *oo-nah gah-say-OH-sah*
tonic water	**un agua tónica** *oon AH-gwah TOH-nee-kah*
The check, please.	**La cuenta, par favor.** *lah KWEHN-tah pohr fah-BOHR*
Separate checks.	**Cuentas saparadas.** *KWEHN-tahs sep-ahr-AH-dahs*
Is the service (tip) included?	**¿Está incluida la propina?** *ehs-TAH een-kloo-EE-dah lah proh-PEE-nah*
I haven't ordered this.	**No he pedido ésto.** *noh ay ped-EE-doh EHS-toh*
I don't think the bill is right.	**Me parece que hay un error en la cuenta.** *may pah-RAY-say kay AH-ee oon ehr-OHR ehn lah KWEHN-tah*
This is for you.	**Esto es para usted.** *EHS-toh ehs pah-rah oos-TEHD*
We're in a hurry.	**Tenemos prisa.** *ten-EH-mohs PREE-sah*

DRINKS AND SNACKS

TAPAS (BAR SNACKS)

aceitunas	olives
alcachofas a la vinagreta	artichokes with vinaigrette dressing
almejas en salsa de ajo	clams in a garlic sauce

anguilas	fried baby eels
calamares a la romana	batter-fried squid strips
caracoles en salsa	snails in a tomato sauce
chorizo al diablo	sausage, especially spicy
entremeses variados	platter of assorted snacks
gambas a la plancha	grilled shrimp
huevos rellenos	stuffed hard-boiled eggs
palitos de queso	cheese straws
pan con jamón	toast slices with ham
pinchitos	kebabs
salchichón	salami

WINES

I would like ____.	**Quisiera ____.** *kee-SYEHR-ah*
▪ a glass of wine	**un vaso de vino** *oon BAH-soh day BEE-noh*
▪ a bottle of wine	**una botella de vino** *oo-nah boh-TEH-yah day BEE-noh*
Is it ____?	**¿Es ____?** *ehs*
▪ red	**tinto** *TEEN-toh*
▪ white	**blanco** *BLAHN-koh*
▪ rosé	**rosado** *oh-SAH-doh*
light	**ligero** *lee-GEH-roh*

sparkling	**espumoso**	*ehs-poo-MOH-soh*
dry	**seco**	*SAY-koh*
sweet	**dulce**	*DOOL-say*

LATIN AMERICAN DRINKS

cuba libre rum, lime juice, and Coca Cola

margarita tequila, lime juice, and salt

piña colada coconut cream, pineapple juice, and rum

ponche fruit juice and rum or tequila

pulque the fermented juice of the agave (maguey) plant, often with flavorings added such as herbs, pineapple, celery; available in special pulque bars

tequila sunrise orange juice, grenadine, tequila

FOOD SPECIALTIES OF SPAIN

bacalao a la vizcaína salt cod stewed with olive oil, peppers, tomatoes and onions

calmares en su tinta baby squid cooked in its own ink

callos a la andaluza tripe stew, with sausages, vegetables and seasonings

camarones en salsa verde shrimps in a green sauce

capón relleno a la catalana roasted capon stuffed with meat and nuts

carnero verde	stewed lamb with herbs and pignolis
cocido madrileño	mixed meat stew with chickpeas and vegetables
criadillas fritas	fried prairie oysters
empanadas	deep-fried pies filled with meat and vegetables
fabada asturiana	spicy mixture of white beans, pork, and sausages
gallina en pepitoria	chicken (fish with nuts, rice, garlic, and herbs)
huevos a la flamenca	baked eggs with green vegetables, pimento, tomato, chorizo and ham (a popular first course or light supper)
langosta a la barcelonesa	spiny lobster sauteed with chicken and tomatoes, garnished with almonds
lenguado a la andaluza	stuffed flounder or sole with a vegetable sauce
liebre estofada	hare and green beans, cooked in a tart liquid
marmitako	Basque tuna stew
pato a la sevillana	duck with olives
pescado a la sal	a white fish, packed in salt and roasted
pisto manchego	vegetable stew of tomatoes, peppers, onions, eggplant, and zucchini
rabo de toro	oxtail stewed in wine sauce
riñones al jerez	kidneys in sherry wine

sesos en caldereta	calves brains, simmered in wine
zarzuela	fish stew; varies greatly depending on region but usually similar to a bouillabaisse

SOME MEXICAN SPECIALTIES

amarillito	chicken or pork stew with green tomatoes, pumpkin, and chilies
carne asada	marinated pieces of beef that have been grilled
ceviche acapulqueño	raw fish or shellfish marinated in lime juice
chile relleno	stuffed chile (usually with cheese), that is coated with a light batter and fried
cochinita pibil	a suckling pig stuffed with fruits, chilies, and spices, then wrapped and baked in a pit
coloradito	chicken stew made with ancho chilies, tomatoes, and red peppers
frijoles refritos	kidney or pinto beans that have been cooked then mashed and reheated, often with chilies
guajolote relleno	turkey stuffed with fruit, nuts, and chilies and braised in wine
gorditas	bits of meat and cheese, fried and served with guacamole

guacamole	a purée of avocado, onion, garlic, and chilies, used as a condiment and a sauce for a variety of dishes
huachinango a la veracruzana	red snapper marinated in lime juice and baked with tomatoes, olives, capers, and chilies
jaibas en chilpachole	crabs cooked in a tomato sauce, flavored with the Mexican spice epazote
mancha manteles	a stew of chicken or pork, with a mixture of vegetables and in a sauce of nuts, green tomatoes, and chilies
muk-bil pollo	chicken pie with a cornmeal topping
papazul	rolled tortillas in a pumpkin sauce
panuchos	chicken dish baked with black beans and eggs
puchero	a stew made from a variety of meats, vegetables, fruits; served as a soup, then a main course
sopa de lima	a chicken soup laced with lime

SOUTH AND CENTRAL AMERICAN FOODS

anticuchos	skewered chunks of marinated beef heart, served with a hot sauce
caldillo de congrio	conger eel in a stew
humitas	cornmeal bits flavored with onion, peppers, and spices
llapingachos	potato-cheese croquettes

papas a la huancaína	potatoes in a spicy cheese sauce
pupusas (El Salvador)	cornmeal tortillas, stuffed with mashed kidney beans and crumbled fried bacon, cheese or pork

FOODS OF THE CARIBBEAN

asopao	a chicken and rice soup-stew with ham, peas, and peppers
chicharrones	deep-fried pork cracklings
frituras de bacalao (bacalaítos)	fish cakes that are fried in hot oil
mondongo	thick stew of beef tripe, potatoes, tomatoes, pumpkin, chickpeas and tropical vegetables
moros y cristianos	black beans and rice
pasteles	a mixture of plantain and seasonings, steamed in a banana leaf
picadillo	mixture of chopped pork and beef with peppers, olives, raisins, and tomatoes
plátanos fritos	sliced, fried green bananas (plantains)
relleno de papa	potato dough stuffed with a mixture of meat, olives, and tomatoes
ropa vieja	literally "old clothes," this is shredded beef cooked with tomatoes and peppers

sancocho	a hearty Dominican stew with beef, pork, chicken, potatoes, tomatoes, and tropical vegetables (plantains, yams, pumpkin, yucca, yautía)
sandwich cubano	a half-loaf of crisp Italian or French bread filled with fresh pork, ham, cheese, and pickle, served oven-warmed
tostones	fried green plantain slices
yuca con mojo	stewed yucca root (cassava), in a garlic sauce

MEETING PEOPLE

SMALL TALK

My name is ____.	**Me llamo ____.**	*may YAH-mo*
Do you live here?	**¿Vive usted aquí?**	*BEE-bay oos-TEHD ah-KEE*
Where are you from?	**¿De dónde es usted?**	*day DOHN-day ehs oos-TEHD*
I am ____.	**Soy ____.**	*soy*
■ from the United States	**de Estados Unidos**	*day ehs-TAH-dohs oo-NEE-dohs*
■ from Canada	**del Canadá**	*del cah-nah-DAH*
■ from England	**de Inglaterra**	*day een-glah-TEHR-ah*
■ from Australia	**de Australia**	*day ow-STRAHL-yah*
I like Spain (South America) very much.	**Me gusta mucho España (Sud América).**	*may GOOS-tah MOO-choh ehs-PAHN-yah (sood ah-MEHR-ee-kah)*

How long will you be staying?	**¿Cuánto tiempo va a quedarse?** *KWAHN-toh tee-EHM-poh bah ah kay-DAHR-say*
I'll stay for a few days (a week).	**Me quedaré unos días (una semana).** *may kay-dahr-AY oo-nohs DEE-ahs (oo-nah sehm-AHN-ah)*
What hotel are you at?	**¿En qué hotel está?** *ehn kay oh-TEL ehs-TAH*
I think it's ____.	**Creo que es ____.** *KREH-oh kay ehs*
■ (very) beautiful	**(muy) bonito(a)** *(mwee) bohn-EE-toh(ah)*
■ interesting	**interesante** *een-tehr-ehs-AHN-tay*
■ magnificent	**magnífico(a)** *mahg-NEEF-ee-koh(kah)*
■ wonderful	**maravilloso(a)** *mahr-ah-bee-YOH-soh(sah)*
■ boring	**aburrido(a)** *ah-boo-REE-doh(ah)*
■ ugly	**feo(a)** *FEH-oh(ah)*
■ too expensive	**demasiado caro(a)** *day-mah-SYAH-doh KAR-oh(ah)*
■ inexpensive	**barato(a)** *bah-RAH-toh(ah)*

INTRODUCTIONS

May I introduce my ____?	**Le presento a mi ____.** *lay pray-SENT-oh ah mee*
■ brother (sister)	**hermano(a)** *ehr-MAH-noh(nah)*
■ father (dad) [mother (mom)]	**padre (papá) [madre (mamá)]** *PAH-dray (pah-PAH) MAH-dray (mah-MAH)*
■ friend	**amigo(a)** *ah-MEE-goh(gah)*
■ husband (wife)	**marido (esposa)** *mahr-EE-doh (ehs-POH-sah)*

■ sweetheart	**novio(a)** *NOH-bee-oh(ah)*
■ son (daughter)	**hijo(a)** *EE-hoh(hah)*

How do you do? (Glad to meet you.)	**Mucho gusto (en conocerle).** *MOO-choh GOOS-toh (ehn koh-noh-SEHR-lay)*

How do you do? (The pleasure is mine.)	**El gusto es mío.** *ehl GOOS-toh ehs MEE-oh*

I am a ____.	**Soy ____.** *soy*
■ teacher	**maestro(a)** *mah-EHS-troh(trah)*
■ doctor	**médico** *MED-ee-koh*
■ lawyer	**abogado** *ah-boh-GAH-doh*
■ businessperson	**persona de negocios** *pehr-SOHN-ah day neh-GOH-see-ohs*
■ student	**estudiante** *ehs-too-DYAHN-tay*
■ accountant	**contador** *kohn-tah-DOHR*
■ dentist	**dentista** *den-TEES-tah*
■ jeweler	**joyero** *hoy-EHR-oh*
■ merchant	**comerciante** *koh-mehr-SYAHN-teh*
■ nurse	**enfermera** *en-fehr-MEHR-ah*
■ manager	**gerente** *hehr-EN-teh*
■ salesman	**vendedor** *ben-deh-DOHR*
■ I'm retired	**estoy jubilado(a)** *es-toy hoo-bee-LAH-doh(ah)*

Would you like a picture (snapshot)?	**¿Quiere una foto?** *kee-YEHR-ay oo-nah FOH-toh*

Will you take a picture of me (us)?	**¿(Nos)Me quiere sacar una foto?** *(nos)may kee-YEHR-ay sah-KAHR oo-nah FOH-toh*

DATING AND SOCIALIZING

May I have this dance?	**¿Quiere usted bailar?** *kee-YEHR-ay oos-TEHD bah-ee-LAHR*
Yes, of course.	**Sí, con mucho gusto.** *see kohn MOO-choh GOOS-toh*
Would you like a cigarette (drink)?	**¿Quiere fumar (tomar algo)?** *kee-YEHR-ay fo-MAHR (toh-MAHR AHL-goh)*
Do you have a light (a match)?	**¿Tiene fuego (un fósforo)?** *tee-YEH-nay FWAY-goh (oon FOHS-fohr-oh)*
Do you mind if I smoke?	**¿Le molesta que fume?** *lay moh-LEHS-tah kay FOO-may*
Would you like us to go together to ____?	**¿Quiere acompañarme a ____?** *kee-YEHR-ay ah-kohm-pahn-YAHR-may ah*
What is your telephone number?	**¿Cuál es su número de teléfono?** *kwahl ehs soo NOO-mehr-oh day tel-EH-foh-noh*
Here's my telephone number (address).	**Aquí tiene mi número de teléfono (mi dirección).** *ah-KEE tee-EH-nay mee NOO-mehr-oh day tel-EH-foh-noh (mee dee-rehk-SYOHN)*
Will you write to me?	**¿Me escribirá?** *may ehs-kree-beer-AH*
I'm single (married).	**Soy soltero(a) casado(a).** *soy sohl-TEHR-oh(ah) kah-SAH-doh(ah)*

Is your husband (wife) here?	**¿Está aquí so esposo (esposa)?** *eh-STAH ah-KEE soo ehs-POH-soh (ehs-POH-sah)*
I'm here with my family.	**Estoy aquí con mi familia.** *ehs-TOY ah-KEE kohn mee fah-MEEL-yah*
Do you have any children?	**¿Tiene usted hijos?** *tee-EH-nay oos-TEHD EE-hohs*
How many?	**¿Cuántos?** *KWAHN-tohs*

SAYING GOOD-BYE

Nice to have met you.	**Ha sido un verdadero gusto.** *ah SEED-oh oon behr-dah-DEHR-oh GOOS-toh*
The pleasure was mine.	**El gusto ha sido mío.** *ehl GOOS-toh ah SEE-doh MEE-oh*
Regards to ____.	**Saludos a ____ de mi parte.** *sah-LOO-dohs ah day mee PAHR-tay*
Thanks for a wonderful evening.	**Gracias por su invitación. Ha sido una noche extraordinaria.** *GRAH-see-ahs pohr soo een-bee-tah-SYOHN. Ah see-doh oo-nah NOH-chay ehs-trah-ohr-dee-NAHR-ee-ah*
I must go home now.	**Tengo que marcharme ahora.** *TEN-goh kay mahr-CHAR-may ah-OH rah*
You must come to visit us.	**Debe venir a visitarnos.** *DEH-bay ben-EER ah bee-see-TAHR-nohs*

SHOPPING

GOING SHOPPING

Where can I find ____?	**¿Dónde se puede encontrar ____?** *DOHN-day say pweh-day ehn-kohn-TRAHR*
■ a bakery	**una panadería** *oo-nah pah-nah-dehr-EE-ah*
■ a bookstore	**una librería** *oo-nah leeb-rehr-EE-ah*
■ a butcher shop	**una carnicería** *oo-nah kahr-nee-sehr-EE-ah*
■ a camera shop	**una tienda de fotografía** *oo-nah tee-EHN-dah day foh-toh-grah-FEE-ah*
■ a candy store	**una confitería** *oo-nah kohn-fee-tehr-EE-ah*
■ a clothing store	**una tienda de ropa** *oo-nah tee-YEHN-dah day ROH-pah*
■ a delicatessen	**una tienda de ultramarinos** *oo-nah tee-YEHN-dah day ool-trah-mah-REE-nohs*
■ a department store	**un almacén** *oon ahl-mah-SEHN*
■ a pharmacy (chemist)	**una farmacia** *oo-nah fahr-MAH-see-ah*
■ a florist	**una florería** *oo-nah flohr-ehr-EE-ah*
■ a gift (souvenir) shop	**una tienda de regalos (recuerdos)** *oo-nah tee-YEHN-dah day ray-GAHL-ohs (ray-kwehr-dohs)*
■ a grocery store	**una tienda de comestibles** *oo-nah tee-YEHN-dah day koh-mehs-TEE-blays*
■ a hardware store (ironmonger)	**una ferretería** *oo-nah feh-reh-teh-REE-ah*

▨ a jewelry store	**una joyería** *oo-nah hoy-ehr-EE-ah*
▨ a liquor store	**una licorería** *oo-nah lee-kohr-ehr-EE-ah*
▨ a newsstand	**un puesto de periódicos** *oon PWEHS-toh day peh-ree-OH-dee-kohs*
▨ a record store	**una tienda de discos** *oo-nah tee-yehn-dah day DEES-kohs*
▨ a shoe store	**una zapatería** *oo-nah sah-pah-tehr-EE-ah*
▨ a supermarket	**un supermercado** *oon SOO-pehr-mehr-KAH-doh*
▨ a tobacco shop	**un estanco** *oon ehs-TAHN-koh*
▨ a toy store	**una juguetería** *oo-nah hoo-get-ehr-EE-ah*
Do you take credit cards?	**¿Acepta tarjetas de crédito?** *ah-SEP-tah tahr-HAY-tahs day KRED-ee-toh*
Can I pay with a traveler's check?	**¿Puedo pagar con un cheque de viajero?** *PWEH-doh pah-GAHR kohn oon CHEH-kay day bee-ah-HEHR-oh*

BOOKS

Is there a store that carries English-language books?	**¿Hay una tienda que lleve libros en inglés?** *AH-ee oo-nah TYEHN-dah kay YEH-bay LEE-brohs ehn een-GLAYS*
What is the best (biggest) bookstore here?	**¿Cuál es la mejor librería (la librería más grande) de aquí?** *kwahl ehs lah meh-HOHR lee-brehr-EE-ah (lah lee-brehr-EE-ah mahs grahn-day) day ah-KEE*

I'm looking for a copy of ____.	**Busco un ejemplar de ____.** *boos-koh oon eh-hem-PLAHR day*
I don't know the title (author).	**No sé el título (autor).** *noh say ehl TEE-too-loh (AH-oo-TOHR)*
I'm just looking.	**Estoy sólo mirando.** *ehs-TOY SOH-loh meer-AHN-doh*
Do you have books (novels) in English?	**¿Tiene usted libros (novelas) en inglés?** *tee-EHN-eh oos-TEHD LEE-brohs (noh-BEL-ahs) ehn een-GLAYSS*
I want a ____.	**Quiero ____.** *kee-EHR-oh*
◼ guidebook	**una guía** *oon-ah GHEE-ah*
◼ map of this city	**un plano de esta ciudad** *oon PLAH-noh day ehs-tah see-oo-DAHD*
◼ pocket dictionary	**un diccionario de bolsillo** *oon deek-syohn-AHR-ee-oh day bohl-SEE-yoh*
◼ Spanish-English dictionary	**un diccionario español-inglés** *oon deek-syohn-AHR-ee-oh ehs-pahn-YOHL-een-GLAYSS*
I'll take these books.	**Me quedo con estos libros.** *may kay-doh kohn EHS-tohs LEE-brohs*
Will you wrap them, please?	**¿Quiere envolverlos, por favor?** *kee-YEHR-ay ehn-bohl-BEHR-lohs pohr fah-BOHR*

CLOTHING

Would you please show me ____?	**¿Quiere enseñarme ____, por favor?** *kee-YEHR-ay ehn-sehn-YAHR-may pohr fah-BOHR*
◼ a bathing suit	**un traje de baño** *oon TRAH-hay day BAHN-yo*

a belt	**un cinturón**	*oon seen-toor-OHN*
a blouse	**una blusa**	*oon-ah BLOO-sah*
boots	**botas**	*BOH-tahs*
a bra	**un sostén**	*oon soh-STEHN*
a dress	**un vestido**	*oon bes-tee-doh*
an evening gown	**un traje de noche**	*oon TRAH-hay day NOH-chay*
leather (suede) gloves	**guantes de cuero (de gamuza)**	*GWAHN-tays day KWEHR-oh (day gah-MOOS-ah)*
handkerchiefs	**pañuelos**	*pahn-yoo-EH-lohs*
a hat	**un sombrero**	*oon sohm-BREHR-oh*
a jacket	**una chaqueta**	*oon-nah chah-KAY-tah*
a pair of jeans	**un par de vaqueros, un par de jeans**	*oon pahr day bah-KEHR-ohs oon pahr day jeens*
a jogging suit	**un traje de footing**	*oon trah-hay day FOO-teen*
an overcoat	**un abrigo**	*oon ah-BREE-goh*
pajamas	**piyamas**	*pee-YAH-mahs*
panties	**bragas**	*BRAH-gahs*
pants	**pantalones**	*pahn-tah-LOHN-ays*
pantyhose	**pantimedias**	*pahn-tee-MEHD-ee-ahs*
a raincoat	**un impermeable**	*oon eem-pehr-may-AH-blay*
a robe	**una bata**	*oon-nah BAH-tah*
sandals	**sandalias**	*sahn-DAHL-ee-ahs*
a scarf	**una bufanda**	*oo-nah boo-FAHN-dah*
a shirt	**una camisa**	*oo-nah kah-MEES-ah*
(a pair of) shoes	**(un par de) zapatos**	*(oon pahr day) sah-PAH-tohs*
shorts (briefs)	**calzoncillos**	*kahl-sohn-SEE-yohs*

■ stockings	**medias** *MED-ee-ahs*
■ a t-shirt	**una camiseta** *oo-nah kah-mee-SEH-tah*
Do you have something ____?	**¿Tiene algo ____?** *tee-EH-nay AHL-goh*
■ else	**más** *mahs*
■ larger	**más grande** *mahs grahn-day*
■ less expensive	**menos caro** *may-nohs KAHR-oh*
■ longer	**más largo** *mahs LAHR-goh*
■ of better quality	**de más alta calidad** *day mahs AHL-tah kahl-ee-DAHD*
■ shorter	**más corto** *mahs KOHR-toh*
■ smaller	**más pequeño** *mahs peh-KAYN-yoh*
I (don't) like the color.	**(No) me gusta este color.** *(noh) may GOOS-tah ehs-tay koh-LOHR*
Do you have it in ____?	**¿Tiene algo en ____?** *tee-EHN-ay ahl-goh ehn*
■ black	**negro** *NEH-groh*
■ blue	**azul** *ah-SOOL*
■ brown	**marrón, pardo** *mah-ROHN PAHR-doh*
■ gray	**gris** *grees*
■ green	**verde** *BEHR-day*
■ orange	**anaranjado** *ah-nah-rahn-HAH-do*
■ pink	**rosado** *roh-SAH-doh*
■ red	**rojo** *ROH-hoh*
■ white	**blanco** *BLAHN-koh*
■ yellow	**amarillo** *ah-mah-REE-yoh*
I want something in ____.	**Quiero algo en ____.** *kee-YEHR-oh AHL-goh ehn*
■ chiffon	**gasa** *GAH-sah*

▣ corduroy	**pana**	*PAH-nah*
▣ cotton	**algodón**	*ahl-goh-DOHN*
▣ denim	**dril de algodón, tela tejana**	*dreel day ahl-goh-DOHN TEH-la tay-HAH-nah*
▣ felt	**fieltro**	*fee-EHL-troh*
▣ flannel	**franela**	*frah-NEHL-ah*
▣ gabardine	**gabardina**	*gah-bahr-DEEN-ah*
▣ lace	**encaje**	*ehn-KAH-hay*
▣ leather	**cuero**	*KWEHR-oh*
▣ linen	**hilo**	*EE-loh*
▣ nylon	**nilón**	*nee-LOHN*
▣ satin	**raso**	*RAH-soh*
▣ silk	**seda**	*SAY-dah*
▣ suede	**gamuza**	*gah-MOO-sah*
▣ taffeta	**tafetán**	*tah-fay-TAHN*
▣ terrycloth	**tela de toalla**	*TEHL-ah day toh-AH-yah*
▣ velvet	**terciopelo**	*tehr-see-oh-PEHL-oh*
▣ wool	**lana**	*LAH-nah*
▣ worsted	**estambre**	*ehs-TAHM-bray*
▣ synthetic (polyester)	**sintético**	*seen-TET-ee-koh*

I prefer ____.	**Prefiero ____.**	*preh-FYEHR-oh*
▣ permanent press	**algo inarrugable**	*AHL-goh een-ah-roo-GAH-blay*
▣ wash and wear	**algo que no se necesita planchar**	*AHL-goh kay noh seh neh-seh-SEE-tah plahn-CHAHR*

Show me something ____.	**Muéstreme algo ____.**	*MWEHS-ray-may AHL-goh*
▣ in a solid color	**de color liso**	*day koh-LOHR LEE-soh*
▣ with stripes	**de rayas**	*day RAH-ee-ahs*

■ with polka dots	**de lunares** *day loo-NAHR-ays*
■ in plaid	**de cuadros** *day KWAH-drohs*
Please take my measurements,	**¿Quiere tomarme la medida?** *kee-YEHR-ay toh-MAHR-may lah meh-DEE-dah*
I take size (My size is) ____.	**Llevo el tamaño (Mi talla es)** *YEH-boh ehl tah-MAHN-yoh (mee TAH-yah ehs)*
■ small	**pequeño(a)** *peh-KAYN-yoh(yah)*
■ medium	**mediano(a)** *meh-dee-AH-noh(yah)*
■ large	**grande** *GRAHN-day*
Can I try it on?	**¿Puedo probármelo?** *PWEHD-oh proh-BAHR-may-loh*
Can you alter it?	**¿Puede arreglarlo?** *PWEH-day ah-ray-GLAHR-loh*
Can I return the article?	**¿Puedo devolver el artículo?** *PWEH-doh day-bohl-BEHR ehl ahr-TEE-koo-loh*
It doesn't fit me.	**No me queda bien.** *noh may KAY-dah BYEHN*
It fits very well.	**Me queda muy bien.** *may KAY-dah mwee BYEHN*
I'll take it.	**Me lo llevo.** *may loh YEH-boh*
Will you wrap it?	**¿Quiere envolverlo?** *kee-YEHR-ay ehn-bohl-BEHR-loh*
I'd like to see the pair of shoes (boots) in the window.	**Quisiera ver el par de zapatos (botas) de la vitrina.** *kee-see-YEH-rah behr ehl pahr day sah-PAH-tohs (BOH-tahs) day lah bee-TREE-nah*

They're too narrow (wide).	**Son demasiado estrechos (anchos).** *sohn day-mahs-ee-AH-doh ehs-TRAY-chohs (AHN-chohs)*
I'll take them.	**Me los llevo.** *may lohs YEH-boh*
I also need shoe-laces.	**También necesito cordones de zapato.** *tahm-BYEHN neh-say-SEE-toh kohr-DOHN-ays day sah-PAH-toh*
That's all I want for now.	**Eso es todo por ahora.** *eh-soh ehs TOH-doh pohr ah-OHR-ah*

FOOD AND HOUSEHOLD ITEMS

I'd like ____.	**Quisiera ____.** *kee-SYEHR-ah*
▪ a bar of soap	**una pastilla de jabón** *oo-nah pahs-TEE-yah day hah-BOHN*
▪ a bottle of juice	**una botella de jugo** *oo-nah boh-TEH-yah day HOO-goh*
▪ a box of cereal	**una caja de cereal** *oo-nah KAH-hah day sehr-ay-AHL*
▪ a can (tin) of tomato sauce	**una lata de salsa de tomate** *oo-nah LAH-tah day SAHL-sah day toh-MAH-tay*
▪ a dozen eggs	**una docena de huevos** *oo-nah doh-SAY-nah day WAY-bohs*
▪ a jar of coffee	**un pomo de café** *oon POH-moh day kah-FAY*
▪ a kilo of potatoes (2.2 lbs)	**un kilo de papas (patatas)** *oon KEE-loh day PAH-pahs (pah-TAH-tahs)*
▪ a half-kilo of cherries	**medio kilo de cerezas** *MED-ee-oh KEE-loh day sehr-AY-sahs*

■ a liter of milk **un litro de leche** *oon LEE-troh day LEH-chay*

■ a package of candies **un paquete de dulces** *oon pah-KEH-tay day dool-sayss*

■ 100 grams of cheese **cien gramos de queso** *see-EHN GRAH-mohs day KAY-soh*

■ a roll of toilet paper **un rollo de papel higiénico** *oon ROH- yoh day pah-pel ee-hee-EHN-ee-koh*

What is this (that)? **¿Qué es esto (eso)?** *kay ehs EHS-toh (EHS-oh)*

Is it fresh? **¿Está fresco?** *ehs-TAH FRES-koh*

I'd like a kilo (about 2 pounds) of oranges. **Quisiera un kilo de naranjas.** *kee-SYEHR-ah oon KEE-loh day nah-RAHN-hahs*

■ a half-kilo of butter **medio kilo de mantequilla** *MED-ee-oh KEE-loh day mahn-tay-KEE-yah*

■ 200 grams (about ¹/₂ pound) of cookies (cakes) **doscientos gramos de galletas (pasteles)** *dohs-SYEHN-tohs GRAH-mohs day gah-YEH-tahs (pahs-TEH-lehs)*

■ 100 grams (about ¹/₄ pound) of ham **cien gramos de jamón** *SYEHN GRAH-mohs day hah-MOHN*

JEWELRY

I'd like to see _____. **Quisiera ver _____.** *kee-SYEHR-ah behr*

■ a bracelet **un brazalete** *oon brah-sah-LAY-tay*

■ a brooch **un broche** *oon BROH-chay*

■ a chain **una cadena** *oon-nah kah-DAY-nah*

▨ a charm	**un dije** *oon DEE-hay*
▨ some earrings	**unos aretes** (in Spain, **pendientes**) *oo-nohs ah-REH-tays (pen-DYEHN-tays)*
▨ a necklace	**un collar** *oon koh-YAHR*
▨ a pin	**un alfiler** *oon ahl-fee-LEHR*
▨ a ring	**un anillo (una sortija)** *oon ahn-EE-yoh (oo-nah sohr-TEE-hah)*
▨ a rosary	**un rosario** *oon roh-SAHR-ee-oh*
▨ a (wrist) watch	**un reloj (de pulsera)** *oon ray-LOH (day pool-SEHR-ah)*
Is this ____?	**¿Es esto ____?** *ehs EHS-toh*
▨ gold	**oro** *OH-roh*
▨ platinum	**platino** *plah-TEE-noh*
▨ silver	**plata** *PLAH-tah*
▨ stainless steel	**acero inoxidable** *ah-SEHR-oh een-ohks-ee-DAH-blay*
Is it solid or gold-plated?	**¿Es macizo o dorado?** *ehs mah-SEE-soh oh dohr-AH-doh*
How many carats is it?	**¿De cuántos quilates es?** *day KWAHN-tohs kee-LAH-tays ehs*
What is that stone?	**¿Qué es esa piedra?** *kay ehs EHS-ah pee-YEHD-drah*
I want ____.	**Quiero ____.** *kee-YEHR-oh*
▨ an amethyst	**una amatista** *oo-nah ah-mah-TEES-tah*
▨ an aquamarine	**una aguamarina** *oo-nah ah-gwah-mah-REE-nah*
▨ a diamond	**un diamante** *oon dee-ah-MAHN-tay*
▨ an emerald	**una esmeralda** *oon-nah ehs-mehr-AHL-dah*

■ ivory	**marfil**	*mahr-FEEL*
■ jade	**jade**	*HAH-day*
■ onyx	**ónix**	*OH-neeks*
■ pearls	**perlas**	*PEHR-lahs*
■ a ruby	**un rubí**	*oon roo-BEE*
■ a sapphire	**un zafiro**	*oon sah-FEER-oh*
■ a topaz	**un topacio**	*oon toh-PAH-see-oh*
■ turquoise	**turquesa**	*toor-KAY-sah*

How much is it?   **¿Cuánto vale?**   *KWAHN-toh BAH-lay*

NEWSPAPERS AND MAGAZINES

Do you carry
English newspapers
(magazines)?

**¿Tiene usted periódicos (revistas)
en inglés?** *tee-YEHN-ay oos-TEHD
peh-ree-OH-dee-kohs (ray-BEES-tahs)
en een-GLAYSS*

I'd like to buy some
postcards.

Quisiera comprar postales.
*kee-SYEHR-ah kohm-PRAHR pohs-
TAHL-ays*

Do you have
stamps?

¿Tiene sellos? *tee-YEHN-ay SEH-
yohs*

How much is that?   **¿Cuánto es?**   *KWAHN-toh ehs*

PHOTOGRAPHY AND VIDEO EQUIPMENT

Where is there a
camera shop?

**¿Dónde hay una tienda de artícu-
los fotográficos?** *DOHN-day AH-ee
oo-nah tee-YEHN-dah day ahr-TEEK-
oo-lohs foh-toh-GRAHF-ee-kohs*

Do you develop film here?	**¿Aquí revelan películas?** *ah-KEE ray-BEHL-ahn pel-EE-koo-lahs*
How much does it cost to develop a roll?	**¿Cuánto cuesta revelar un carrete?** *KWAHN-toh KWEHS-tah ray-behl-AHR oon kahr-REH-tay*
I want ____.	**Quiero ____.** *kee-YEHR-oh*
▩ one print of each	**una copia de cada uno** *oo-nah KOH-pee-ah day kah-dah oo-noh*
▩ an enlargement	**una ampliación** *oo-nah ahm-plee-ah-SYOHN*
▩ with a glossy (matte) finish	**con acabado brillante (mate)** *kohn ah-kah-bah-doh bree-YAHN-tay (MAH-tay)*
I want a roll of color (black and white) film.	**Quiero un rollo de películas en colores (en blanco y negro).** *kee-YEHR-oh oon roh-yoh day pehl-EE-koo-lahs ehn koh-lohr-ays (ehn BLAHN-koh ee NEH-groh)*
When can I pick up the pictures?	**¿Cuándo puedo recoger las fotos?** *KWAHN-doh PWEH-doh ray-koh-HEHR lahs FOH-tohs*
Do you sell cameras?	**¿Vende usted cámaras?** *ben-day oos-TEHD KAH-mah-rahs*
I want an inexpensive camera.	**Quiero una cámara barata.** *kee-YEHR-oh oo-nah KAH-mah-rah bah-RAH-tah*
▩ a disposable camera	**una cámara desechable** *oo-nah KAH-mah-rah des-eh-CHAH-blay*
▩ a digital camera	**una cámara digital** *oo-nah KAH-mah-rah dee-hee-TAHL*
▩ a point-and-shoot camera	**una cámara automática** *oo-nah KAH-mah-rah ow-toh-MAH-tee-kah*

■ an SLR camera	**una cámara réflex** *oo-nah KAH-mah-rah RAY-fleks*
■ a flash	**un flash** *oon flahsh*
■ a roll of slide film	**un rollo para diapositivas** *oon ro-yoh pah-rah dee-ah-poh-see-TEE-bahs*
Do you have ____?	**¿Tiéne usted ____?** *tee-YEHN-ay oos-TEHD*
■ a camcorder	**una filmadora** *oo-nah feel-mah-DOHR-ah*
■ digital videofilm	**película digital de vídeo** *pel-EE-koo-lah dee-hee-TAHL day VEE-day-oh*
■ DVD movies	**películas en DVD** *pel-EE-koo-lahs en day-bay-day*
■ VCR tape	**cinta de vídeo** *oo-nah seen-tah day BEE-day-oh*
Do you have VCR or DVD movies with English subtitles?	**¿Tiene películas de vídeo o DVD con subtítulos en inglés?** *TYEHN-ay pel-EE-koo-lahs day BEE-day-oh o day-bay-day kohn soob-TEE-too-lohs en een-GLAYS*
Will the warranty be honored in the US?	**¿Sera válida la garantía en los Estados Unidos?** *sehr-AH BAH-lee-dah lah gahr-ahn-TEE-ah en lohs es-TAH-dohs oo-NEE-dohs*
Who should I contact if this malfunctions?	**¿A quién debo contactar si ésto deja de funcionar?** *ah KYEHN deh-boh kohn-tahk-TAHR see ES-toh DEH-hah day foon-syohn-AHR*

AUDIO EQUIPMENT

Is there a record shop around here?	**¿Hay una tienda de discos por aquí?** *AH-ee oo-nah tee-yehn-dah day DEES-kohs pohr ah-KEE*

Do you sell ____?	**¿Vende usted ____?** *BEN-day oos-TEHD*
■ analog cassettes	**casetes analógicos** *kah-SEH-tehs ah-nah-LO-hee-kohs*
■ cassette players	**caseteros** *kah-seh-TEHR-ohs*
■ cassette recorders	**grabadoras** *grah-bah-DORH-ahs*
■ CD players	**tocadiscos** *toh-kah-DEES-kohs*
■ CD recorders	**grabadiscos** *grah-bah-DEES-kohs*
■ CDs	**discos** *DEES-kohs*
■ digital cassettes	**casetes digitales** *kah-SEH-tehs dee-hee-TAH-lays*
■ metal cassettes	**casetes metálicos** *kah-SEH-tays meh-TAHL-ee-kohs*
■ minidisk players	**tocadoras de minidiscos** *toh-kah-DOHR-ahs day mee-nee-DEES-kohs*
■ minidisk recorders	**grabadoras de minidiscos** *grah-bah-DOHR-ahs day mee-nee-DEES-kohs*
■ minidisks	**minidiscos** *mee-nee-DEES-kohs*
■ recordable CDs	**discos grabables** *DEES-kohs grah-BAH-blays*
Do you have an album of ____?	**¿Tiene un álbum de ____?** *tee-EHN-ay oon AHL-boom day*
Where is the ____ section?	**¿Dónde está la sección de ____?** *DOHN-day ehs-TAH lah sek-SYOHN day*
■ classical music	**la música clásica** *lah MOO-see-kah KLAHS-ee-kah*
■ folk music	**la música folklórica** *lah MOO-see-kah fohl-KLOHR-ee-kah*
■ latest hits	**los últimos éxitos** *lahs OOL-tee-mohs EHK-see-tohs*
■ rock 'n roll	**el rocanrol** *ehl rohk-ahn-ROHL*

▨ opera	**la ópera** *lah OH-pehr-ah*
▨ popular music	**la música popular** *lah MOO-see-kah poh-poo-LAHR*
▨ Spanish music	**la música española** *lah MOO-see-kah ehs-pahn-YOH-lah*
▨ Latin music	**la música latina** *lah MOO-see-kah lah-TEEN-ah*

SOUVENIRS, HANDICRAFTS

I'd like ____.	**Quisiera ____.** *kee-SYEHR-ah*
▨ a pretty gift	**un regalo bonito** *oon ray-GAH-loh boh-NEE-toh*
▨ a small gift	**un regalito** *oon ray-gah-LEE-toh*
▨ a souvenir	**un recuerdo** *oon ray-KWEHR-doh*
It's for ____.	**Es para ____.** *ehs pah-rah*
I don't want to spend more than ____ dollars.	**No quiero gastar más de ____ dólares.** *noh kee-YEHR-oh gahs-TAHR mahs day ___ DOH-lahr-ays*
Could you suggest something?	**¿Podría usted sugerir algo?** *poh-DREE-ah oos-TEHD soo-hehr-EER AHL-goh*
Would you show me your selection of ____?	**¿Quiere enseñarme su surtido de ____?** *kee-YEHR-ay ehn-sen-YAHR-may soo soor-TEE-doh day*
▨ blown glass	**vidrio soplado** *BEE-dree-oh soh-PLAH-doh*
▨ carved objects	**objetos de madera tallada** *ohb-HET-ohs day mah-DEHR-ah tah-YAH-dah*

▓ cut crystal	**vidrio tallado** *BEE-dree-oh tah-YAH-doh*
▓ dolls	**muñecas** *moon-YEH-kahs*
▓ earthenware (pottery)	**loza** *LOH-sah*
▓ fans	**abanicos** *ah-bah-NEE-kohs*
▓ jewelry	**joyas** *HOY-ahs*
▓ lace	**encaje** *ehn-KAH-hay*
▓ leather goods	**objetos de cuero** *ohb-HET-ohs day KWEHR-oh*
▓ liqueurs	**licores** *lee-KOHR-ays*
▓ musical instruments	**instrumentos musicales** *een-stroo-MEN-tohs moo-see-KAHL-ays*
▓ perfumes	**perfumes** *pehr-FOO-mays*
▓ pictures	**dibujos** *dee-BOO-hohs*
▓ posters	**carteles** *kahr-TEHL-ays*
▓ religious articles	**artículos religiosos** *ahr-TEE-koo-lohs ray-lee-hee-OH-sohs*

BARGAINING

Please, madam, how much is this?	**Por favor, señora, ¿cuánto vale ésto?** *pohr fah-BOHR sehn-YOHR-ah KWAHN-toh BAH-lay EHS-toh*
Oh, no, that is more than I can spend.	**Ay, no, eso es más de lo que puedo gastar.** *AH-ee noh EHS-oh ehs MAHS day loh kay PWEH-doh gahs-TAHR*
How about ___?	**¿Y si le doy ___?** *EE see lay doy*
No, that is too high. Would you take ___?	**No, eso es demasiado. ¿Aceptaría ___?** *noh EHS-oh ehs day-mahs-ee-AH-doh ah-sep-tahr-ER-ah*

Yes, that's fine. I'll take it.	**Así está bien. Me lo llevo.** *ah-SEE ehs-TAH byehn may loh YEH-boh*
Thank you. Have a nice day.	**Gracias. Que lo pase bien.** *GRAH-see-ahs kay loh PAH-say byehn*

STATIONERY ITEMS

I want to buy ____.	**Quiero comprar ____.** *kee-YEHR-oh kohm-PRAHR*
▪ a ball-point pen	**un bolígrafo** *oon boh-LEE-grah-foh*
▪ a deck of cards	**una baraja** *oo-nah bahr-AH-hah*
▪ envelopes	**sobres** *SOH-brays*
▪ an eraser	**una goma de borrar** *oo-nah GOH-mah day bohr-AHR*
▪ glue	**cola de pegar** *koh-lah day peh-GAHR*
▪ a notebook	**un cuaderno** *oon kwah-DEHR-noh*
▪ pencils	**lápices** *LAH-pee-sayss*
▪ a pencil sharpener	**un sacapuntas** *oon sah-kah-POON-tahs*
▪ printing paper	**papel para impresora** *pah-PEL PAH-rah eem-preh-SOH-rah*
▪ a ruler	**una regla** *oo-nah REHG-lah*
▪ Scotch tape	**cinta adhesiva** *SEEN-tah ahd-ehs-EE-bah*
▪ some string	**cuerda** *KWEHR-dah*
▪ typing paper	**papel de máquina** *pah-PEL day MAH-kee-nah*
▪ wrapping paper	**papel de envolver** *pah-PEL day ehn-bohl-BEHR*
▪ a writing pad	**un bloc de papel** *oon blohk day pah-PEL*

TOBACCO

A pack (carton) of cigarettes, please.	**Un paquete (cartón) de cigarrillos, por favor.** *oon pah-KAY-tay (kahr-TOHN) day see-gahr-EE-yohs pohr fah-BOHR*
■ filtered	**con filtro** *kohn FEEL-troh*
■ unfiltered	**sin filtro** *seen FEEL-troh*
■ menthol	**de mentol** *day mehn-TOHL*
■ king-size	**extra largos** *EHS-trah LAHR-gohs*
Are these cigarettes (very) strong (mild)?	**¿Son (muy) fuertes (suaves) estos cigarrillos?** *sohn (mwee) FWEHR-tays (SWAH-bays) ehs-tohs see-gahr-EE-yohs*
Do you have American cigarettes?	**¿Tiene usted cigarrillos norteamericanos?** *tee-YEHN-ay oos-TEHD see-gahr-EE-yohs nohr-tay-ah-mehr-ee-KAH-nohs*
What brands?	**¿De qué marcas?** *day kay MAHR-kahs*
Please give me a pack of matches also.	**Déme una caja de fósforos también.** *DAY-may oo-nah KAH-hah day FOHS-for-ohs tahm-bee-EHN*

TOILETRIES

Do you have ____?	**¿Tiene usted ____?** *tee-YEHN-ay oo-STEHD*
■ bobby pins	**horquillas** *ohr-KEE-yahs*
■ a brush	**un cepillo** *oon sep-EE-yoh*
■ cleansing cream	**crema limpiadora** *KRAY-mah leem-pee-ah-DOHR-ah*

■ a comb	**un peine** *oon PAY-nay*
■ deodorant	**un desodorante** *oon dehs-oh-dohr-AHN-tay*
■ (disposable) diapers	**pañales (desechables)** *pahn-YAH-lays (dehs-ay-CHAH-blays)*
■ emery boards	**limas de cartón** *LEE-mahs day kahr-TOHN*
■ eyeliner	**un lápiz de ojos** *oon LAH-pees day OH-hohs*
■ hairspray	**laca** *LAH-kah*
■ lipstick	**lápiz de labios** *LAH-pees day LAH-bee-ohs*
■ makeup	**maquillaje** *mah-kee-YAH-hay*
■ mascara	**rimel** *ree-MEHL*
■ a mirror	**un espejo** *oon ehs-PAY-ho*
■ mouthwash	**un lavado bucal** *oon lah-bah-doh boo-kahl*
■ nail clippers	**un cortauñas** *oon kohr-tah-oon-yahs*
■ a nail file	**una lima de uñas** *oo-nah lee-mah day OON-yahs*
■ nail polish	**esmalte de uñas** *ehs-MAHL-tay day OON-yahs*
■ nail polish remover	**un quita-esmalte** *oon kee-tah ehs-MAHL-tay*
■ a razor	**una navaja** *oo-nah nah-BAH-hah*
■ razor blades	**hojas de afeitar** *OH-hahs day ah-fay-TAHR*
■ sanitary napkins	**servilletas higiénicas** *sehr-bee-YEH-tahs ee-HYEHN-ee-kahs*
■ (cuticle) scissors	**tijeras (de cutículas)** *tee-HAIR-ahs (day koo-TEE-kool-ahs)*
■ shampoo	**champú** *chahm-POO*

■ shaving lotion	**loción de afeitar** *loh-SYOHN day ah-fay-TAHR*
■ soap	**jabón** *hah-BOHN*
■ a sponge	**una esponja** *oo-nah ehs-POHN-hah*
■ tampons	**tapones** *tah-POHN-ays*
■ tissues	**pañuelos de papel** *pahn-yoo-EH-lohs day pah-PEL*
■ toilet paper	**papel higiénico** *pah-PEL ee-hy-EHN-ee-koh*
■ a toothbrush	**un cepillo de dientes** *oon sep-EE-yoh day dee-YEHN-tays*
■ toothpaste	**pasta de dientes** *pah-stah day dee-YEHN-tays*
■ tweezers	**pinzas** *PEEN-sahs*

PERSONAL CARE AND SERVICES

AT THE BARBER

Where is there a good barber shop?	**¿Dónde hay una buena barbería?** *DOHN-day AH-ee oo-nah BWEH-nah bahr-behr-EE-ah*
Do I have to wait long?	**¿Tengo que esperar mucho?** *ten-goh kay ehs-pehr-AHR MOO-choh*
Am I next?	**¿Me toca a mí?** *may TOH-kay ah mee*
I want a shave.	**Quiero que me afeiten.** *kee-YEHR-oh kay may ah-FAY-tehn*
I want a haircut (razorcut).	**Quiero un corte de pelo (a navaja)** *kee-YEHR-oh oon KOHR-tay day PEH-loh (ah nah-BAH-hah)*

Short in back, long in front.	**Corto por detrás, largo por delante.** *KOHR-toh pohr day-TRAHS lahr-goh pohr day-LAHN-tay*
Leave it long.	**Déjelo largo.** *DAY-hay-loh LAHR-goh*
I want it (very) short.	**Lo quiero (muy) corto.** *loh kee-YEHR-oh (mwee) KOHR-toh*
You can cut a little ____.	**Puede cortar on poquito ____.** *PWEH-day kohr-TAHR oon poh-KEE toh*
▪ in back	**por detrás** *pohr day-TRAHS*
▪ in front	**por delante** *pohr day-LAHN-tay*
▪ off the top	**de arriba** *day ah-REE-bah*
▪ on the sides	**a los lados** *ah lohs LAH-dohs*
Cut a little bit more here.	**Córteme on poco más aquí.** *KOHR-tay-may oon POH-koh mahs ah-KEE*
That's enough.	**Eso es bastante.** *EH-soh ehs bah-STAHN-tay*
I (don't) want ____.	**(No) quiero ____.** *(noh) kee-YEHR-oh*
▪ shampoo	**champú** *chahm-POO*
▪ tonic	**tónico** *TOHN-ee-koh*
Use the scissors only.	**Use sólo las tijeras.** *oo-say soh-loh lahs tee-HAIR-ahs*
Trim my ____.	**Recórteme ____.** *ray-KOHR-tay-may*
▪ beard	**la barba** *lah bahr-bah*
▪ moustache	**el bigote** *ehl bee-GOH-tay*
▪ sideburns	**las patillas** *lahs pah-TEE-yahs*

I'd like to look at myself in the mirror.	**Quisiera mirarme al espejo.** *kee-SYEHR-ah meer-AHR-may ahl ehs-PAY-hoh*
How much do I owe you?	**¿Cuánto le debo?** *KWAHN-toh lay DEH-boh*
Is tipping included?	**¿Está incluída la propina?** *eh-STAH een-kloo-EE-dah lah proh-PEE-nah*

AT THE BEAUTY PARLOR

Is there a beauty parlor (hairdresser) near the hotel?	**¿Hay un salón de belleza (una peluquería) cerca del hotel?** *AH-ee oon sah-LOHN day beh-YEH-sah (oo-nah pel-oo-kehr-EE-ah) SEHR-kah del oh-TEL*
I'd like an appointment for this afternoon (tomorrow).	**Quisiera hacer una cita para esta tarde (mañana).** *kee-SYEHR-ah ah-SEHR oo-nah SEE-tah pah-rah EHS-tah TAHR-day (mahn-YA-nah)*
Can you give me ____?	**¿Puede darme ____?** *PWEH-day DAHR-may*
■ a color rinse	**un enjuague de color** *oon ehn-hoo-AH-gay day koh-LOHR*
■ a facial massage	**un masaje facial** *oon mah-SAH-hay fah-see-AHL*
■ a haircut	**un corte de pelo** *oon KOHR-tay day PEH-loh*
■ a manicure	**una manicura** *oon-nah mah-nee-KOOR-ah*
■ a pedicure	**una pedicura** *oo-nah ped-ee-KOOR-ah*
■ a permanent	**una permanente** *oon-nah pehr-mah-NEN-tay*

▧ a shampoo	**un champú**	*oon-chahm-POO*
▧ a tint	**un tinte**	*oon TEEN-tay*
▧ a touch-up	**un retoque**	*oon ray-TOH-kay*
▧ a wash and set	**un lavado y peinado**	*oon lah-bah-doh ee pay-NAH-doh*
▧ just a trim	**sólo las puntas**	*soh-loh lahs POON-tahs*

I'd like to see a color chart.

Quisiera ver un muestrario. *kee-SYEHR-ah behr oon mwehs-TRAHR-ee-oh*

I want a ____ color.

Quiero un color ____. *kee YEHR-oh oon koh-LOHR*

▧ auburn	**rojizo**	*roh-HEE-soh*
▧ (light) blond	**un rubio (claro)**	*oon ROO-bee-oh (KLAHR-oh)*
▧ brunette	**castaño**	*kas-TAHN-yo*
▧ a darker color	**un color más oscuro**	*oon koh-LOHR mahs oh-SKOOR-oh*
▧ a lighter color	**un color más claro**	*oon koh-LOHR mahs KLAH-roh*
▧ the same color	**el mismo color**	*ehl MEES-moh koh-LOHR*

Don't apply any hair-spray.

No me ponga laca. *noh may POHN-gah LAH-kah*

Not too much hair-spray.

Sólo un poco de laca. *SOH-loh oon POH-koh day LAH-kah*

I want my hair ____.

Quiero el pelo ____. *kee-YEHR-oh ehl peh-loh*

▧ with bangs	**con flequillo**	*kohn fleh-KEE-yoh*
▧ in a bun	**con un moño**	*kohn oon MOHN-yoh*
▧ in curls	**con bucles**	*kohn boo-KLAYS*

■ with waves	**con ondas** *kohn OHN-dahs*	

I'd like to look at myself in the mirror.	**Quiero mirarme al espejo.** *kee-YEHR-oh meer-AHR-may ahl ehs-PAY-hoh*
How much do I owe you?	**¿Cuánto le debo?** *KWAHN-toh lay DEH-boh*
Is tipping included?	**¿Está incluída la propina?** *es-TAH een-kloo-EE-dah lah proh-PEE-nah*

LAUNDRY AND DRY CLEANING

Where is the nearest laundry (dry cleaners)?	**¿Dónde está la lavandería (la tintorería) más cercana?** *DOHN-day ehs-TAH lah lah-bahn-deh-REE-ah (lah teen-TOHR-ehr-EE-ah) mahs sehr-KAH-nah*
I have a lot of (dirty) clothes to be ____.	**Tengo mucha ropa (sucia) que ____.** *TEN-goh MOO-chah ROH-pah (SOO-see-ah) kay*
■ (dry) cleaned	**limpiar (en seco)** *leem-pee-AHR (ehn SEH-koh)*
■ washed	**lavar** *lah-BAHR*
■ mended	**arreglar** *ah-ray-GLAHR*
■ ironed	**planchar** *plahn-CHAHR*
I need them for ____.	**Las necesito para ____.** *lahs neh-seh-SEE-toh PAH-rah*
■ tonight	**esta noche** *EHS-tah NOH-chay*
■ tomorrow	**mañana** *mahn-YAH-nah*
■ next week	**la semana próxima** *lah seh-MAH-nah PROHK-see-mah*
■ the day after tomorrow	**pasado mañana** *pah-SAH-doh mahn-YAH-nah*

When will you bring it back?	**¿Cuándo la traerá?** *KWAHN-doh lah trah-ehr-AH*
When will it be ready?	**¿Cuándo estará lista?** *KWAHN-doh ehs-tah-RAH LEES-tah*
Can you sew it on?	**¿Puede usted coserlo?** *PWEH-deh oos-TEHD koh-SEHR-loh*
This isn't my laundry.	**Esta no es mi ropa.** *EHS-tah noh ehs mee ROH-pah*

SHOE REPAIRS

Can you fix these shoes (boots)?	**¿Puede arreglar estos zapatos (estas botas)?** *PWEH-day ah-ray-GLAHR ehs-tohs sah-PAH-tohs (ehs-tahs BOH-tahs)*
Put on (half) soles and rubber heels.	**Póngales (medias) suelas y tacones de goma.** *POHN-gah-lays (MED-ee-ahs) SWAY-lahs ee tah-KOHN-ays day GOH-mah*
When will they be ready?	**¿Para cuándo los tendrá?** *pah-rah KWAHN-doh los ten-DRAH*
I need them by Saturday (without fail).	**Los necesito para el sábado (sin falta).** *lohs nes-ehs-see-toh pah-rah ehl SAH-bah-doh (seen FAHL-tah)*

WATCH REPAIRS

Can you fix this watch (alarm clock) (for me)?	**¿(Me) puede arreglar este reloj (despertador)?** *(may) PWEH-day ah-ray-GLAHR EHS-tay ray-LOH (dehs-pehr-tah-dohr)*

Can you clean it?	**¿Puede usted limpiarlo?** *PWEH-day oos-TEHD leem-pee-AHR-loh*
I dropped it.	**Se me cayó.** *say may kah-YOH*
It's running slow (fast).	**Se atrasa (se adelanta).** *say ah-TRAH-sah (say ah-deh-LAHN-tah)*
It's stopped.	**Está parado.** *ehs-TAH pah-RAH-doh*
When will it be ready?	**¿Cuándo estará listo?** *KWAHN-doh ehs-tah-RAH LEES-toh*
May I have a receipt?	**¿Me puede dar un recibo?** *may PWEH-day dahr oon ray-SEE-boh*

CAMERA REPAIRS

Can you fix this camera?	**¿Puede usted arreglar esta cámara?** *PWEH-deh oos-TEHD ah-ray-GLAHR ehs-tah KAH-mah-rah*
The film doesn't advance.	**El carrete no se mueve.** *ehl kah-REH-tay noh say MWEH-bay*
I think I need new batteries.	**Creo que necesito una nueva pila.** *KRAY-oh kay neh-seh-SEE-toh oo-nah NWEH-bah PEE-lah*
How much will the repair cost?	**¿Cuánto costará el arreglo?** *KWAHN-toh kohs-tah-RAH ehl ah-REG-loh*
When can I come and get it?	**¿Cuándo puedo venir a buscarla?** *KWAHN-doh PWEH-doh ben-EER ah boos-KAHR-lah*

I need it as soon as possible.	**La necesito lo más pronto posible.** *lah neh-say-SEE-toh loh mahs PROHN-toh poh-SEE-blay*

MEDICAL CARE

THE PHARMACY (CHEMIST)

Where is the nearest (all-night) pharmacy (chemist)?	**¿Dónde está la farmacia (de guardia) más cercana?** *DOHN-day ehs-TAH lah fahr-MAH-see-ah (day GWAHR-dee-ah) mahs sehr-KAH-nah*
At what time does the pharmacy open (close)?	**¿A qué hora se abre (se cierra) la farmacia?** *ah kay OH-rah say AH-bray (say SYEHR-ah) lah fahr-MAH-see-ah*
I need something for ____.	**Necesito algo para ____.** *neh-seh-SEE-toh AHL-goh pah-rah*
▪ a cold	**on catarro** *oon kah-TAH-roh*
▪ constipation	**el estreñimiento (constipación estomacal)** *ehl ehs-trayn-yee-MYEHN-toh*
▪ a cough	**la tos** *lah tohs*
▪ diarrhea	**la diarrea** *lah dee-ahr-RAY-ah*
▪ a fever	**la fiebre** *lah fee-YEHB-ray*
▪ flatulence	**flatulencia** *flah-too-LEN-see-ah*
▪ hay fever	**la fiebre del heno** *lah fee-YEHB-ray del AY-noh*
▪ a headache	**un dolor de cabeza** *oon doh-LOHR day kah-BAY-sah*
▪ insomnia	**el insomnio** *ehl een-SOHM-nee-oh*
▪ nausea	**náuseas** *NAH-oo-say-ahs*

◾ sunburn	**la quemadura del sol**	*lah kay-mah-DOOR-ah del SOHL*
◾ a toothache	**un dolor de muelas**	*oon doh-LOHR day MWEH-lahs*
◾ an upset stomach	**la indigestión**	*la een-dee-hes-TYOHN*
I do not have a prescription.	**No tengo la receta.**	*noh TEN-goh lah reh-SAY-tah*
May I have it right away?	**¿Me la puede dar en seguida?**	*May lah PWEH-day DAHR ehn seh-GHEE-dah*
It's an emergency!	**¡Es urgente!**	*ehs oor-HEN-tay*
How long will it take?	**¿Cuánto tiempo tardará?**	*KWAHN-toh tee-YEHM-poh tahr-dahr-AH*
When can I come for it?	**¿Cuándo puedo venir a recogerla?**	*KWAHN-doh PWEH-doh ben-EER ah ray-koh-HAIR-lah*
I would like ____.	**Quisiera ____.**	*kee-see-YEHR-ah*
◾ adhesive tape	**esparadrapo**	*ehs-pah-rah-DRAH-poh*
◾ alcohol	**alcohol**	*ahl-koh-OHL*
◾ an antacid	**un antiácido**	*oon ahn-tee-AH-see-doh*
◾ an antihistamine	**un antihistamínico**	*oon ahn-tee-ees-tah-MEEN-ee-koh*
◾ an antiseptic	**un antiséptico**	*oon ahn-tee-SEP-tee-koh*
◾ aspirins	**aspirinas**	*ahs-peer-EE-nahs*
◾ Band-Aids	**curitas**	*koor-EE-tahs*
◾ contraceptives	**contraceptivos**	*kohn-trah-sep-TEE-bohs*
◾ corn plasters	**callicidas**	*kah-yee-SEE-dahs*

▨ cotton	**algodón** *ahl-goh-DOHN*
▨ cough drops	**pastillas para la tos** *PAHS-TEE-yahs pah-rah lah TOHS*
▨ cough syrup	**jarabe para la tos** *hah-RAH-bay PAH-rah lah TOHS*
▨ ear drops	**gotas para los oídos** *GOH-tahs PAH-rah lohs oh-EE-dohs*
▨ eye drops	**gotas para los ojos** *GOH-tahs PAH-rah lohs OH-hohs*
▨ iodine	**yodo** *YOH-doh*
▨ a (mild) laxative	**un laxante (ligero)** *oon lahk-SAHN-tay (lee-HEHR-oh)*
▨ milk of magnesia	**una leche de magnesia** *oo-nah leh-chay day mahg-NAY-see-ah*
▨ prophylactics	**profilácticos** *pro-fee-LAHK-tee-kohs*
▨ sanitary napkins	**servilletas higiénicas** *sehr-bee-YEH-tahs ee-HYEHN-ee-kahs*
▨ suppositories	**supositorios** *soo-pohs-ee-TOHR-ee-ohs*
▨ talcum powder	**polvos de talco** *POHL-bohs day TAHL-koh*
▨ tampons	**tapones** *tah-POHN-ays*
▨ a thermometer	**un termómetro** *oon tehr-MOH-met-roh*
▨ tranquilizers	**un tranquilizante** *oon trahn-kee-lee-SAHN-tay*
▨ vitamins	**vitaminas** *bee-tah-MEE-nahs*

WITH THE DOCTOR

I don't feel well.	**No me siento bien.** *noh may SYEHN-toh BYEHN*

I need a doctor (right now).	**Necesito un médico (ahora mismo).** *neh-seh-SEE-toh oon MEH-dee-koh (ah-OHR-ah MEES-moh)*
Do you know a doctor (chiropractor) who speaks English?	**¿Conoce un médico (quiropráctico) que hable inglés?** *koh-NOH-say oon MEH-dee-koh (kee-rho-PRAHK-tee-koh) kay ah-blay een-GLAYSS*
Where is his office (surgery)?	**¿Dónde está su consultorio?** *DOHN-day ehs-TAH soo kohn-sool-TOHR-ee-oh*
Will the doctor come to the hotel?	**¿Vendrá el medico al hotel?** *ben-DRAH ehl MED-ee-koh ahl oh-TEL*
I feel dizzy.	**Estoy mareado.** *ehs-TOY mahr-ay-AH-doh*
I feel weak.	**Me siento débil.** *may SYEHN-toh DAY-beel*
My temperature is normal (37°C).	**Tengo la temperatura normal (treinta y siete grados).** *TEN-goh lah tem-pehr-ah-TOOR-ah nohr-MAHL (TRAYN-tah ee see-EH-tay GRAH-dohs)*
I (think I) have ____.	**(Creo que) tengo ____.** *KRAY-oh kay TEN-goh*
▪ an abscess	**un absceso** *oon ahb-SEHS-oh*
▪ a broken bone	**un hueso roto** *oon WAY-soh ROH-toh*
▪ a bruise	**una contusión** *oo-nah kohn-too-SYOHN*
▪ a burn	**una quemadura** *oo-nah kay-mah-DOOR-ah*
▪ something in my eye	**algo en el ojo** *AHL-goh ehn ehl OH-hoh*

◼ the chills	**escalofríos** *ehs-kah-loh-FREE-ohs*
◼ a chest (head) cold	**un catarro (resfriado)** *oon kah-TAHR-oh (res-free-AH-doh)*
◼ constipation	**estreñimiento** *ehs-trayn-yee-mee-YENT-oh*
◼ stomach cramps	**calambres** *kahl-AHM-brays*
◼ a cut	**una cortadura** *oo-nah kohr-tah-DOOR-ah*
◼ diarrhea	**diarrea** *dee-ah-RAY-ah*
◼ a fever	**fiebre** *fee-YEHB-bray*
◼ a fracture	**una fractura** *oo-nah frahk-TOOR-ah*
◼ a backache	**un dolor de espalda** *oon doh-LOHR day es-PAHL-dah*
◼ an earache	**un dolor de oído** *oon doh-LOHR day oh-EE-doh*
◼ a headache	**un dolor de cabeza** *oon doh-LOHR day kah-BAY-sah*
◼ an infection	**una infección** *oo-nah een-fek-SYOHN*
◼ a lump	**un bulto** *oon BOOL-toh*
◼ a sore throat	**un dolor de garganta** *oon doh-LOHR day gahr-GAHN-tah*
◼ a stomachache	**un dolor de estómago** *oon doh-lohr day ehs-TOH-mah-goh*
It hurts me here.	**Me duele aquí.** *may DWEH-lay ah-KEE*
My whole body hurts.	**Me duele todo el cuerpo.** *may DWEH-lay toh-doh ehl KWEHR-poh*

TELLING THE DOCTOR

I've had this pain since yesterday.	**Tengo este dolor desde ayer.** *TEN-goh EHS-tay doh-LOHR des-day ah-YEHR*

There's a (no) history of asthma (diabetes) in my family.	**(No) hay incidencia de asma (diabetes) en mi familia.** *(noh) AH-ee een-see-DEN-see-ah day AHS-mah (dee-ah-BEH-tays) ehn mee fah-MEEL-yah*
I'm (not) allergic to antibiotics (penicillin).	**(No) soy alérgico(a) a los antibióticos (penicilina).** *(noh) soy ah-LEHR-hee-koh(kah) ah lohs ahn-tee-bee-OH-tee-kohs (pen-ee-see-LEE-nah).*
I have a pain in my chest.	**Tengo dolor en el pecho.** *TEN-goh doh-LOHR ehn ehl PAY-choh*
I have heart trouble.	**Tengo problemas cardíacos** *TEN-goh pro-BLAY-mahs kahr-DEE-ah-kohs*
I had a heart attack ____ year(s) ago.	**Tuve on ataque al corazón hace ____ año(s).** *TOO-bay oon ah-TAH-kay ahl kohr-ah-SOHN ah-say ahn-yoh(s)*
I'm taking this medicine (insulin).	**Tomo esta medicina (insulina).** *TOH-moh EHS-tah med-ee-SEE-nah (een-soo-LEE-nah)*
I'm pregnant.	**Estoy embarazada.** *EHS-toy ehm-bahr-ah-SAH-dah*
I feel better (worse).	**Me siento mejor (peor).** *may see-YEN-toh may-HOHR (pay-OHR)*
Is it serious (contagious)?	**¿Es grave (contagioso)?** *ehs GRAH-bay (kohn-tah-hee-OH-soh)*
Do I have to go to the hospital?	**¿Tengo que ir al hospital?** *TEN-goh kay eer ahl ohs-pee-TAHL*
When can I continue my trip?	**¿Cuándo puedo continuar mi viaje?** *KWAHN-doh PWEH-doh kon-teen-oo-AHR mee bee-AH-hay*

FOLLOWING UP

Are you giving me a prescription? **¿Va a darme una receta?** *bah ah DAHR-may oo-nah ray-SAY-tah*

How often must I take this medicine (these pills)? **¿Cuántas veces al día tengo que tomar esta medicina (estas píldoras)?** *KWAHN-tahs BEH-says ahl DEE-ah TEN-goh kay toh-MAHR EHS-tah med-ee-SEE-nah (EHS-tahs PEEL-dohr-ahs)*

(How long) do I have to stay in bed? **¿(Cuánto tiempo) tengo que quedarme en cama?** *(KWAHN-toh tee-YEHM-poh) TEN-goh kay kay-DAHR-may ehn KAH-mah*

Thank you (for everything), doctor. **Muchas gracias (por todo), doctor.** *MOO-chahs GRAH-see-ahs (pohr TOH-doh) dohk-TOHR*

How much do I owe you for your services? **¿Cuánto le debo?** *KWAHN-toh lay DEHB-oh*

Will you accept my medical insurance? **¿Acepta mi seguro médico?** *ah-SEP-tah mee seh-GOOR-oh MED-ee-koh*

IN THE HOSPITAL (ACCIDENTS)

Help! **¡Socorro!** *soh-KOH-roh*

Get a doctor, quick! **¡Busque un médico, rápido!** *BOO-skay oon MED-ee-koh RAH-pee-doh*

Call an ambulance! **¡Llame una ambulancia!** *YAH-may oo-nah ahm-boo-LAHN-see-ah*

Take me to the hospital!	**¡Lléveme al hospital!** *YEV-eh-may ahl ohs-pee-TAHL*
I've fallen.	**Me he caído.** *may ay kah-EE-doh*
I was knocked down (run over).	**Fui atropellado(a).** *fwee ah-troh-peh-YAH-doh*
I think I've had a heart attack.	**Creo que he tenido un ataque al corazón.** *KRAY-oh kay ay ten-EE-doh oon ah-TAH-kay ahl kohr-ah-SOHN*

AT THE DENTIST

Can you recommend a dentist?	**¿Puede recomendar un dentista?** *PWEH-day reh-koh-men-DAHR oon den-TEES-tah*
I have a toothache that's driving me crazy.	**Tengo un dolor de muela que me vuelve loco.** *ten-goh oon doh-LOHR day MWEH-lah kay may BWEHL-bay loh-koh*
I've lost a filling.	**Se me ha caído un empaste.** *say may ah kah-EE-doh oon ehm-PAHS-tay*
I've broken a tooth.	**Me rompí un diente.** *may rohm-PEE oon dee-EHN-tay*
My gums hurt.	**Me duelen las encías.** *may DWEH-len lahs ehn-SEE-ahs*
Is there an infection?	**¿Hay una infección?** *AH-ee oo-nah een-fehk-SYOHN*
Will you have to extract the tooth?	**¿Tendrá que sacar la muela (el diente)?** *ten-DRAH kay sah-kahr lah MWEH-lah (ehl dee-EHN-tay)*

Can you fill it ____?	**¿Podría empastarlo ____?** *poh-DREE-ah ehm-pahs-TAHR-loh*
Can you fix ____?	**¿Puede usted reparar ____?** *PWEH-day oo-STEHD ray-pah-RAHR*
▪ this bridge	**este puente** *EHS-tay PWEHN-tay*
▪ this crown	**esta corona** *EHS-tah kohr-OH-nah*
▪ these dentures	**estos dientes postizos** *EHS-tohs dee-EHN-tays pohs-TEE-sohs*
When should I come back?	**¿Cuándo debo volver?** *KWAHN-doh DEH-boh bohl-BEHR*
How much do I owe you for your services?	**¿Cuánto le debo?** *KWAHN-toh lay DEH-boh*

WITH THE OPTICIAN

Can you repair these glasses (for me)?	**¿Puede usted arreglar(me) estas gafas? (estos lentes)** *PWEH-day oos-TEHD ah-ray-GLAHR (may) EHS-tahs GAH-fahs (EHS-tohs LEN-tehs)*
I've broken a lens (the frame).	**Se me ha roto un cristal (la armadura).** *say may oh ROH-toh oon krees-TAHL (lah ahr-mah-DOOR-ah)*
Can you put in a new lens?	**¿Puede usted ponerme un cristal nuevo?** *PWEH-day oos-TEHD poh-NEHR-may oos krees-TAHL NWEH-boh*
I (do not) have a prescription.	**(No) tengo receta.** *noh TEN-goh ray-SAY-tah*

I need the glasses as soon as possible.	**Necesito las gafas urgentemente.** *neh-seh-SEE-toh lahs GAH-fahs oor-hen-tay-MEN-tay*
I've lost a contact lens.	**Se me ha perdido un lente de contacto.** *say may ah pehr-DEE-doh oon LEN-tay day kohn-TAHK-toh*
Can you replace it quickly?	**¿Puede reemplazarlo rápidamente?** *PWEH-day ray-ehm-plah-SAHR-loh rah-pee-dah-MEN-tay*

COMMUNICATIONS

POST OFFICE

I want to mail a letter.	**Quiero echar una carta al correo.** *kee-YEHR-oh ay-CHAHR oo-nah KAHR-tah ahl kohr-AY-oh*
Where's the post office?	**¿Dónde está correos?** *DOHN-day ehs-TAH kohr-AY-ohs*
Where's a letterbox?	**¿Dónde hay un buzón?** *DOHN-day AH-ee oon boo-SOHN*
What is the postage on ____ to the United States (Canada, England, Australia)?	**¿Cuánto es el franqueo de ____ a los Estados Unidos (al Canadá, a Inglaterra, a Australia)?** *KWAHN-toh ehs ehl frahn-KAY-oh day ah lohs ehs-TAH-dohs oo-NEE-dohs (ahl kahn-ah-DAH ah eeng-lah-TEHR-ah ah ow-STRAHL-yah)*
■ a letter	**una carta** *oo-nah KAHR-tah*
■ an insured letter	**una carta asegurada** *oo-nah KAHR-tah ah-say-goor-AH-dah*

▪ a registered letter	**una carta certificada** *oo-nah KAHR-tah sehr-teef-ee-KAH-dah*
▪ a special delivery letter	**una carta urgente** *oo-nah KAHR-tah oor-HEN-tay*
▪ a package	**un paquete postal** *oon pah-kay-tay pohs-TAHL*
▪ a postcard	**una postal** *oo-nah pohs-TAHL*
When will it arrive?	**¿Cuándo llegará?** *KWAHN-doh yeh-gahr-AH*
Which is the ____ window?	**¿Cuál es la ventanilla de ____?** *kwahl ehs lah ben-tah-NEE-yah day*
▪ general delivery	**la lista de correos** *lah LEES-tah day kohr-AY-ohs*
▪ money order	**los giros postales** *lohs HEER-ohs pohs-TAHL-ays*
▪ stamp	**los sellos** *lohs SEH-yohs*
Are there any letters for me? My name is ____.	**¿Hay cartas para mí? Me llamo ____.** *AH-ee KAHR-tahs pah-rah mee may YAH-moh*
I'd like ____.	**Quisiera ____.** *kee-see-YEHR-ah*
▪ 10 envelopes	**diez sobres** *dee-EHS SOH-brays*
▪ 6 postcards	**seis postales** *sayss pohs-TAHL-ays*
▪ 5 (airmail) stamps	**cinco sellos (aéreos)** *SEEN-koh SEH-yohs (ah-EHR-ay-ohs)*
Do I fill out a customs receipt?	**¿Hay un recibo de aduana?** *AH-ee oon ray-SEE-boh day ah-DWAHN-ah*

TELEPHONES

Where is ____?	**¿Donde hay ____?** *DOHN-day AH-ee*
▣ a public telephone	**un teléfono público** *oon tel-EHF-oh-noh POO-blee-koh*
▣ a telephone booth	**una cabina telefónica** *oo-nah kah-BEE-nah tel-eh-FOHN-ee-kah*
▣ a telephone directory	**una guía telefónica** *oo-nah GHEE-ah tel-eh-FOHN-ee-kah*
May I use your phone?	**¿Me permite usar su teléfono?** *may pehr-MEE-tay oo-sahr soo tel-EHF-oh-noh*
I want to make a ____ call.	**Quiero hacer una llamada ____.** *kee-YEHR-oh ah-SEHR oo-nah yah-MAH-dah*
▣ local	**local** *loh-kahl*
▣ long-distance	**a larga distancia** *ah LAHR-gah dees-TAHN-see-ah*
▣ person-to-person	**personal** *pehr-SOHN-ahl*
▣ collect	**a cobro revertido** *ah KOH-broh ray-behr-TEE-doh*
Can I call direct?	**¿Puedo marcar directamente?** *PWEH-doh mahr-KAHR dee-rehk-tah-MEN-tay*
Do I need tokens for the phone? (a phone card)	**¿Necesito fichas para el teléfono? (una tarjeta telefónica)** *neh-seh-SEE-toh FEE-chahs pah-rah ehl tel-EHF-oh-no (oo-nah tahr-HEH-ta tel-eh-FOHN-ee-kah)*

How do I get the operator?	**¿Cómo puedo conseguir la central?** *KOH-moh PWEH-doh kon-seh-GHEER lah sehn-TRAHL*
Operator, can you get me number ____?	**Señorita, quiere comunicarme con ____?** *sehn-yohr-EE-tah, kee-YEHR-ay koh-moo-nee-KAHR-may kohn*
My number is ____.	**Mi número es ____.** *mee NOO-mehr-oh ehs*
May I speak to ____?	**¿Puedo hablar con ____?** *PWEH-doh ah-BLAHR kohn*
This is ____.	**Habla ____.** *AH-blah*
Operator, there's no answer (they don't answer).	**Señorita, no contestan.** *sen-yohr-EE-tah noh kohn-TEST-ahn*
The line is busy.	**La línea está ocupada.** *lah LEE-nay-ah ehs-TAH oh koo-PAH-dah*
You gave me (that was) a wrong number	**Me ha dado (fue) un número equivocado.** *may ah DAH-doh (fway) oon NOO-mehr-oh ay-kee-boh-KAH-doh*
I was cut off.	**Me han cortado.** *may ahn kohr-TAH-doh*
Please dial it again.	**Llame otra vez, por favor.** *YAH-may OH-trah bes pohr fah-BOHR*
I want to leave a message.	**Quiero dejar un recado.** *kee-YEHR-oh day-HAHR oon ray-KAH-doh*
How much do I have to pay?	**¿Cuánto tengo que pagar?** *KWAHN-toh TEN-goh kay pah-GAHR?*

FAX

Do you have a fax machine?	**¿Tiene usted una máquina de fax?** *TYEHN-eh oos-TED oo-nah MAH-kee-nah day-FAHKS*
What is your fax number?	**¿Cuál es su número de fax?** *KWAHL ehs soo NOO-mehr-oh day FAHKS*
I want to send a fax.	**Quiero mandar un fax.** *KYEHR-oh mahn-DAHR oon FAHKS*
Can I send a fax from here?	**¿Puedo enviar un fax desde aquí?** *PWEH-do en-bee-YAHR oon FAHKS DES-day ah-KEE*
Fax it to me.	**Mándemelo por fax.** *MAHN-day-may-loh pohr FAHKS*
I didn't get your fax.	**No recibí su fax.** *No reh-see-BEE soo fahks*
Did you receive my fax?	**¿Recibió usted mi fax?** *reh-see-BYOH oos-TED mee fahks*
Your fax is illegible.	**Su fax está ilegible.** *soo fahks ehs-TAH ee-leh-HEE-blay*
Please send it again.	**Por favor, mándelo de nuevo.** *Por fah-BOHR MAHN-day-lo day NWEH-boh*

TELEGRAMS

Where's the telegraph office?	**¿Dónde está Correos y Telégrafos?** *DOHN-day ehs-TAH kohr-AY-ohs ee tel-AY-grah fohs*

How late is it open?	**¿Hasta cuándo está abierto?** *AH-stah KWAHN-doh ehs-TAH ah bee-YEHR-toh*
I'd like to send a telegram (night letter) to ____.	**Quisiera mandar un telegrama (un cable nocturno) a ____.** *kee-see-YEHR-ah mahn-DAHR oon teh-lay-GRAH-mah (oon KAH-blay nohk-TOOR-noh) ah*
May I please have a form?	**¿Puede darme un formulario, por favor?** *PWEH-deh DAHR-may oon fohr-moo-LAHR-ee-oh pohr fah-BOHR*
How much it is per word?	**¿Cuánto cuesta por palabra?** *KWAHN-toh KWEHS-tah pohr pah-LAH-brah*
I need to send a telex.	**Tengo que enviar un télex.** *TEN-goh kay ehm-bee-AHR oon TEL-eks*
I want to send it collect.	**Quiero mandarlo con cobro revertido.** *kee-YEHR-oh mahn-DAHR-loh kohn KOH-broh reh-behr-TEE-doh*

GENERAL INFORMATION

TELLING TIME

What time is it?	**¿Qué hora es?** *kay OH-rah ehs*

When telling time in Spanish, *It is* is expressed by **Es la** for 1:00 and **Son las** for all other numbers.

It's 1:00.	**Es la una.** *ehs lah oo-nah*

It's 2:00.	**Son las dos.** *sohn lahs dohs*

It's 3:00, etc.	**Son las tres, etc.** *sohn lahs trehs*

The number of minutes after the hour is expressed by adding **y** (and) followed by the number of minutes.

It's 4:10.	**Son las cuatro y diez.** *sohn lahs KWAH-troh ee dyehs*

It's 5:20.	**Son las cinco y veinte.** *sohn lahs SEEN-koh ee BAYN-tay.*

A quarter after and half past are expressed by placing **y cuarto** and **y media** after the hour.

It's 6:15.	**Son las seis y cuarto.** *sohn lahs sayss ee KWAHR-toh*

It's 7:30.	**Son las siete y media.** *sohn lahs SYEH-tay ee MEH-dyah*

After passing the half-hour point on the clock, time is expressed in Spanish by *subtracting* the number of minutes from the next hour.

It's 7:35.	**Son las ocho menos veinticinco.** *sohn lahs OH-choh MEH-nohs bayn-tee-SEEN-koh*

It's 8:50.	**Son las nueve menos diez.** *sohn lahs NWEH-bay meh-nohs dyehs*

At what time?	**¿A qué hora?** *ah kay OH-rah*

At 1:00.	**A la una.** *ah lah OO-nah*

At 2:00 (3:00, etc.)	**A las dos (tres, etc.)** *ah lahs dohs (trehs)*

| A.M. | **de la mañana (in the morning)** *day lah man-YAH-nah* |

| P.M. | **de la tarde (in the afternoon)** *day lah TAHR -day* |
| | **de la noche (at night)** *day lah NOH-chay* |

| It's noon. | **Es mediodía.** *ehs meh-dee-ohd-EE-oh* |

| It's midnight. | **Es medianoche.** *ehs MEH-dee-ah-NOH-chay* |

| It's early (late). | **Es temprano (tarde).** *ehs temp-RAH-noh (TAHR-day)* |

Official time is based on the 24-hour clock. You will find train schedules and other such times expressed in terms of a point within a 24-hour sequence.

| The train leaves at 15:30. | **El tren sale a las quince y media.** *ehl trehn SAH-lay ah lahs KEEN-say ee MEH-dee-ah* |

| The time is now 21:15. | **Son las veintiuna y cuarto.** *sohn lahs bayn-tee-OO-nah ee KWAHR-toh* |

DAYS OF THE WEEK

| What day is today? | **¿Qué día es hoy?** *kay DEE-ah ehs oy* |

Today is ____.	**Hoy es ____.** *oy ehs*
▦ Monday	**lunes** *LOO-nehs*
▦ Tuesday	**martes** *MAHR-tays*
▦ Wednesday	**miércoles** *MYEHR-kohl-ays*
▦ Thursday	**jueves** *HWEB-ays*
▦ Friday	**viernes** *bee-EHR-nays*

Saturday	**sábado**	*SAH-bah-doh*
Sunday	**domingo**	*doh-MEEN-goh*
yesterday	**ayer**	*ah-YEHR*
the day before yesterday	**anteayer**	*ant-ay-ah-YEHR*
tomorrow	**mañana**	*mahn-YAH-nah*
the day after tomorrow	**pasado mañana**	*pah-SAH-doh mahn-YAH-nah*
last week	**la semana pasada**	*ah seh-MAH-nah pah-SAH-dah*
next week	**la semana próxima**	*lah seh-MAH-nah PROHK-see-mah*
tonight	**esta noche**	*EHS-tah NOH-chay*
last night	**anoche**	*ahn-OH-chay*

MONTHS OF THE YEAR

January	**enero**	*ay-NEHR-oh*
February	**febrero**	*fay-BREH-roh*
March	**marzo**	*MAHR-soh*
April	**abril**	*ah-BREEL*
May	**mayo**	*MAH-yoh*
June	**junio**	*HOO-nee-oh*
July	**julio**	*HOO-lee-oh*

August	**agosto** *ah-GOHS-toh*
September	**septiembre** *sep-tee-EHMB-ray*
October	**octubre** *ohk-TOO-bray*
November	**noviembre** *noh-bee-EHMB-ray*
December	**diciembre** *dee-SYEHM-bray*
What's today's date?	**¿Cuál es la fecha de hoy?** *kwahl ehs lah FAY-chah day oy*

The first of the month is *el primero* (an ordinal number). All other dates are expressed with *cardinal* numbers.

Today is August ____.	**Hoy es ____ de agosto.** *oy ehs ____ day ah-GOHS-tah*
▨ first	**el primero** *ehl pree-MEHR-oh*
▨ second	**el dos** *ehl dos*
▨ fourth	**el cuatro** *ehl KWAH-troh*
▨ 25th	**el veinticinco** *ehl bayn-tee-SEENK-oh*
this month	**este mes** *EHS-tay mehs*
last month	**el mes pasado** *ehl mehs pah-SAH-doh*
next month	**el mes próximo** *ehl mehs PROHK-see-moh*
last year	**el año pasado** *ehl AHN-yoh pah-SAH-doh*
next year	**el año que viene** *ehl AHN-yoh kay bee-EN-ay*

THE FOUR SEASONS

spring	**la primavera** *lah pree-mah-BEHR-ah*
summer	**el verano** *ehl behr-AH-noh*
fall	**el otoño** *ehl oh-TOHN-yoh*
winter	**el invierno** *ehl eem-BYEHR-noh*

THE WEATHER

How is the weather today?	**¿Qué tiempo hace hoy?** *kay TYEHM-poh ah-say oy*
It's nice (bad) weather.	**Hace buen (mal) tiempo.** *ah-say bwehn (mahl) TYEHM-poh*
It's raining.	**Llueve.** *YWEHB-ay*
It's snowing.	**Nieva.** *NYEHB-ah*
It's ____.	**Hace ____.** *AH-say*
▪ hot	**calor** *kah-LOHR*
▪ cold	**frío** *FREE-oh*
▪ cool	**fresco** *FREHS-koh*
▪ windy	**viento** *BYEHN-toh*
▪ sunny	**sol** *sohl*

IMPORTANT SIGNS

Abajo	Down
Abierto	Open

Alto	Stop
Arriba	Up
Ascensor	Elevator
Caballeros	Men's room
Caja	Cashier
Caliente or "C"	Hot
Carretera particular	Private road
Cerrado	Closed
Completo	Filled up
Cuidado	Watch out, caution
Damas	Ladies room
Empuje	Push
Entrada	Entrance
Frío or "F"	Cold
Libre	Vacant
No obstruya la entrada	Don't block entrance
No pisar el césped	Keep off the grass
No tocar	Hands off, don't touch
Ocupado	Busy, occupied

¡Pase!	Walk, cross
Peligro	Danger
Prohibido	Forbidden, No _____
■ _____ **el paso**	No entrance, Keep out
■ _____ **escupir**	No spitting
■ _____ **fumar**	No smoking
■ _____ **estacionarse**	No parking
■ _____ **bañarse**	No bathing
Reservado	Reserved
Sala de espera	Waiting room
Salida	Exit
Se alquila	For rent
Señoras	Ladies room
Servicios	Toilets
Se vende	For sale
Tire	Pull
¡Veneno!	Poison!
Venta	Sale

COMMON ABBREVIATIONS

apdo.	**apartado de correos**	post office box
Av., Avda.	**avenida**	avenue

C., Cía	**compañía**	company
c.	**calle**	street
D.	**don**	title of respect used before a masculine first name: don Pedro
Da., Dª	**doña**	title of respect used before a feminine first name: doña María
EE.UU	**los Estados Unidos**	United States (U.S.)
F.C.	**ferrocarril**	railroad
Hnos.	**hermanos**	brothers
N°, num.	**número**	number
1°	**primero**	first
pta.	**peseta**	peseta (Spanish monetary unit)
RENFE	**Red Nacional de Ferrocarriles**	Spanish National Railroad System
2°	**segundo**	second
S., Sta.	**San, Santa**	Saint
S.A.	**Sociedad Anónima**	Inc.
Sr.	**Señor**	Mr.
Sra.	**Señora**	Mrs.

Sres., Srs.	**Señores**	Gentlemen
Srta.	**Señorita**	Miss
Ud., Vd.	**Usted**	You (polite sing.)
Uds., Vds.	**Ustedes**	You (polite & familiar)